P9-EFG-060

[redacted]

[redacted]

DATE DUE

NOV 24 1975		
DEC 27 1982		
APR 8 1980		
MAY 21 1981		

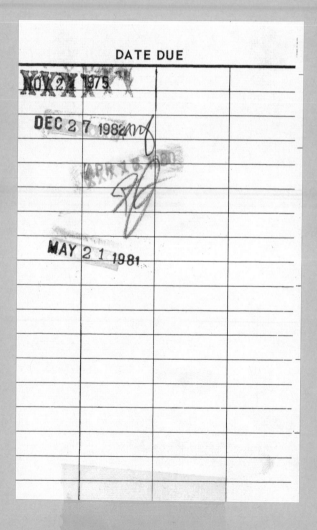

ZOOLOGICAL MYTHOLOGY.

ZOOLOGICAL MYTHOLOGY

OR

THE LEGENDS OF ANIMALS

BY

ANGELO DE GUBERNATIS

PROFESSOR OF SANSKRIT AND COMPARATIVE LITERATURE IN THE ISTITUTO DI STUDII SUPERIORI E DI PERFEZIONAMENTO, AT FLORENCE

FOREIGN MEMBER OF THE ROYAL INSTITUTE OF PHILOLOGY AND ETHNOGRAPHY OF THE DUTCH INDIES

IN TWO VOLUMES

VOL. I.

LONDON

TRÜBNER & CO., 60 PATERNOSTER ROW

1872

Detroit: Reissued by Singing Tree Press, Book Tower, 1968

291.212
G921z
1968
v.1

Library of Congress Catalog Card Number 68–58904

TO

MICHELE AMARI AND MICHELE COPPINO

This Work

IS DEDICATED

AS A TRIBUTE OF LIVELY GRATITUDE AND

PROFOUND ESTEEM

BY

THE AUTHOR.

PREFACE.

It is not without some little anxiety and trepidation that I, for the first time in my career as a student, venture to address myself to a foreign public, and clothe my ideas in a foreign tongue ; nor is it without considerable diffidence in my own powers that I have chosen to do so on a subject which, however interesting it is on account of its novelty and its historical significance, has brought me face to face with difficulties, and a range of scholarship and speculation, which, as in the presence of a foolhardy enterprise, have more than once given me pause. If, however, notwithstanding these incessant fears of mine, and the caution they so naturally inspire, I have, from other considerations, suffered myself to be hurried away into statements which may appear crude or inconclusive, I cast myself at the outset on the kindness of my readers, and respectfully bespeak their indulgent regards. The essential defect of this book will, without doubt, lie in its incompleteness. Of this I am myself all too sensibly conscious ; but I trust that the reader will be kind enough to attribute this defect to the impatience of the author, and not to anything inherent in the work itself, which, if owing to its modest proportions and imperfect construction, it offers little in itself, does, if I do not deceive myself, nevertheless supply a secure enough framework upon which others may hereafter weave a stronger, more compact, and more comprehensive history of comparative mythology. I am well aware that mythical and legendary lore could offer me ten or twenty times as much material as I have here elaborated, which I might, with more leisure-time and more exemplary patience, have collected, examined, sifted, and sorted, so that when I had come to the end—which, however, is perhaps infinite—of my work, my humble octavo volume would have probably assumed the respectable proportions of a colossal folio ; and that I might, in many instances, have improved the arrangement, filled up gaps, demonstrated better the validity of certain hypotheses, which, as it is, may seem to be built upon air, and have perhaps even modified some secondary hypotheses by new materials of conjecture. But the fear, which is always present to the student, that his life may come to an end before he can complete his last and naturally most cherished design, obliged me, at whatever hazard to myself, to hasten the progress of my work, like the son of the fabled hero, who grew, not year by year, but day by day and hour by hour.

And this slender product of the talent and researches of an Italian, which a well-deserving English publisher has been good enough to honour with his confidence, while it may possibly throw a ray of light here and there upon a field which is almost unexplored, will too often seem like the essay of a precocious youth, and betray too obviously an insufficient maturity. It was, however, almost impossible, from the novelty of the undertaking, to escape being seduced into unknown bypaths, and being tempted at times to make an over-hasty observation ; yet I am sustained by a lively confidence that the book may help its reader to understand the great historical principle which presides over and regulates the development of zoological mythology, from its primary formation up to its more recent traditional forms, and may also demonstrate, beyond the possibility of a doubt, the necessity of henceforward connecting in one study that which is properly called mythology, with all the immense popular traditional lore, edited and inedited, which is contained in poems, legends, songs, popular tales, proverbs, and superstitious beliefs.

It is by no means true that the ancient systems of mythology have ceased to exist; they have only been diffused and transformed. The *nomen* is changed, the *numen* remains. Its splendour is diminished because it has lost its celestial reference and significance, because it has become more earthly; but its vitality is still enormous. One can almost say of the gods, as of the relics of saints in the Roman Catholic Church, that the more they are divided, the more they multiply. They still feast upon the ambrosia which has made them immortal, but not in heaven alone; for as they minister to us, so we give them day by day the bread of life; and this earthly ambrosia, this immortal nourishment of the gods, is the mystery with which the fancy delights to envelop them, invested with which, they seem solemn and terrible to the unscientific minds of the people. Nothing clings more to the earth, nothing is more vegetative, than a superstition. A scientific truth requires years and sometimes centuries of demonstration before it can obtain for itself general acceptance, and, rather than suffer martyrdom, its defender will generally prefer to succumb to the infamous papal motto of "Laudabiliter se subjecit;" but an error that is founded upon a sense of the supernatural does not need the electric wires to flash it from heart to heart and awaken a response in the credulous world; while the ponderous dialectics of an entire army of rationalists will not thereafter suffice to dislodge it.

Since, then, the ancient myths still exist, although only in a fragmentary shape, in the popular traditions of Europe, these fragments, connected together, offer a precious material for comparison with the ancient forms, which the genius of poets and artists has coloured, but which could not be easily interpreted without the aid of the remaining traditions. The ancient myth often gives us the germ of many existing traditions, and, in the same manner, existing legends resolve the enigma of more than one ancient celestial personification. Their relation to each other is almost immediate, and the demonstration of this is the precise object of the science in the interest of which I now offer my first modest contribution.

As, in the history of the Indo-European languages, Sanskṛit serves as the starting-point, having more than any other language preserved its primitive elementary characters, so, in the complex history of mythology, it is the ancient Vedic texts, and especially the *Ṛigvedas,* to which we must before all refer as the main pivot or axis of a comparative study. The undoubted antiquity of these literary documents; the spontaneous character of their lyrical poetry; its precedence to all epic and dramatic literature, in which the gods present themselves in their second form, that is, in the company of earthly heroes and nearer to earth than heaven; the possibility that these texts afford us of making an easy transition from celestial phenomena to the divine image; the contemporaneousness, in a word, of song and of mythical creation, force us to search in these pages of natural poesy for the first notions of Âryan mythology. But as it would be unwarrantable to say that Sanskṛit contains in itself all the Indo-European forms of language, it would be equally rash to assert that the Vedic hymns contain all our mythology. In them we only look for ancient and authentic proofs to demonstrate how, before the dispersion of the Âryans, certain essential myths were formed; and the norm or law of development of these being proved, it will then be possible to reconstruct even the history of those that remain by analogy, and by employing the corresponding materials of the various popular literatures, including the Hindoo literature itself which followed immediately after the Vedic, where we find legends and mythical notions which sometimes enable us to clear up and complete several obscure Vedic passages, as well as sometimes offer us new myths of which none of the Vedic hymns that have come down to us preserve any trace. For, bearing in mind the duration of the Vedic period, and the extension of the territory which, during two thousand years, from the foot of the Western Himâlayas to the banks of the Ganges, was successively occupied by the nations who sang the Vedic hymns, the hymns which still remain—although in the *Ṛigvedas* alone they number more than a thousand—cannot be called many, and leave us to suppose that, in the darkness of ages and in the disorder of migrations, many others must have been lost for ever. Nor was every myth set to song; many were only noted and collected as domestic traditions; hence that secret science which partly reveals itself to us in the exorcisms and the invocations of the *Atharvavedas;* hence those mythical beliefs which tell of household usages in the *Gṛihyâsûtraṇi;* hence the abundance of supplementary legends contained in every *Brâḥmaṇam* of the Vedâs, and the infinite mass of legends collected together in the epic poems, in the Pâuranic tales, and by the novelists.

All this abundance of mythical tradition having passed into the Hindoo literature, gives it an especial importance as a means of comparison; but as, notwithstanding this exuberance of legendary literature, many myths have disappeared entirely from the Hindoo tradition, we must acknowledge that if India, in the history of mythology, as well as the Âryan form of speech, represents the field richest in elements, and therefore the most precious term of comparison, it cannot serve as the sole concentric type for all comparison.

In some respects, the Hellenic mythology, and in others the Slavonian, Scandinavian, and German traditions, offer far clearer evidences, and display far more extensively the mythic motive (or original principle), which they possess in common with India; in some cases (as already remarked with respect to languages), the Indian element is absolutely wanting in the myth, whilst the European manifests extraordinary vitality and expansion. It is sufficient here to cite the complete epos which formed itself in Europe concerning the fox, to which the Indian traditions, which prefer to dilate upon the cunning of the serpent, assign quite a secondary place. It is true that here zoological geography comes in to explain the apparent interruption in the series of comparisons, showing how it was impossible that in the Hindoo legends the fox, an animal far less familiar to those regions, should become the highest type of feminine malice; while, for the same reason, the elephant, the giant ape, the gigantic turtle, which occupy such an important position in the Brâhmanic mythology, could scarcely find a place in the mythical legends of Europe, where these animals are much less known, and were therefore less adapted to retain the ancient mythical image, or to modify it. But although the various forms of animals are now and then, for geographical reasons, exchanged with each other, the mythical motive upon which they are based is the same always and everywhere. Thus the different characters, the different necessities and tendencies of the peoples of which our race is composed, requiring them to adopt different homes and climates, led to this result, among others, that what was loved and desired in one place should be feared and dreaded in another, and *vice versa;* that an object should assume a divine aspect in one place, which would in another be considered demoniacal; but the common basis belonging to this variety of mythical forms is the observation of the same celestial phenomena. Besides this, a myth which among one people was almost forgotten, was by another and kindred one retained in lively recollection, and often developed into greater and greater fulness of meaning and finish of form. This difference was due partly to the greater or less impression produced on the mind by the contemplation of celestial phenomena, partly to the different conditions (physical, social, and otherwise) to which, from their diverse geographical situations, they were severally subject; still, in the midst of the immense variety of forms which any particular myth underwent, we can always, without much difficulty, trace out the unity of its origin.

In attempting to describe, in three books, the history of the animals of mythology, I do not think it necessary to indicate particularly the primitive domain of the myth; for although the first book bears the title of Animals of the Earth, the second Animals of the Air, and the third Animals of the Water, there is but one general domain in which all the animals of mythology are produced, and made to enact their respective parts. This domain is always the heavens; whilst the time during which the mythical action lasts is subject to many variations, being now the day of twelve hours, now that of twenty-four, now the three watches of the night; at one time the lunar month of twenty-seven days, at another the solar month of thirty; sometimes the year of twelve solar, and sometimes that of thirteen lunar months. The drama of mythology has its origin in the sky; but the sky may be either clear or gloomy; it may be illumined by the sun or by the moon; it may be obscured by the darkness of night, or the condensation of its vapours into clouds. Again, the clear heavens assume at times the appearance of a milky sea; this milky appearance gives rise to the idea of a cow, and hence the most splendid aspects of the sky are often represented as herds or flocks. The god who causes rain to fall, who, from the highest heaven, fertilises the earth, takes the form now of a ram, now of a bull; the lightning that flies like a winged arrow is represented now as a bird, now as a winged horse; and thus, one after another, all the shifting phenomena of the heavens take the forms of animals, becoming, at length, now the hero himself, now the animal that waits upon the hero, and without which he would possess no supernatural power whatever. In one of the Buddhist legends there is a stanza which says—"Even the beasts remember the services once rendered them; and when we implore them, they do not desert us, for they know what has happened."[1] On the other hand, the cloudy or the dark sky assumed in the myths the aspect now of a grotto or den, now of a stable, now of a tree, a forest, a rock, a mountain, an ocean; and linguistic analysis shows how natural such equivocal meanings are; and these having once taken root, it was still more natural to people

[1] *Rasavâhinî*, 4th ed., Spiegel, Leipzig, 1845.

the grotto with wolves, the stable with sheep, cows, and horses, the tree with birds, the forest with deer and wild boars, the rock with dragons who keep guard over fountains and treasures, the mountain with serpents, the ocean with fish and aquatic monsters. In a stanza of a Vedic hymn to the gods Indras and Agnis, composed with the greatest artistic elegance, the poet sings how the two gods fought side by side for a common conquest, which takes the different names of cows, waters, regions, light, and ravished dawns.[1] The Vedic poet gives us, in that single stanza, a whole mythical drama, explains it, and moreover introduces the mythical personage by name in the form of a common noun.

And the popular tradition of India, even the most recent, has preserved the understanding of the latent sense of the myth, which learned Hindoos would perhaps have been unable to comprehend. In the last book of the *Râmâyaṇam*, in which are collected together many popular legends relating to the god Vishṇus, incarnate under the form of Râmas, the monster Râvaṇas assumes the same variety of forms as the dark sky of the Vedâs, except that of the tiger, which the Vedic texts do not as yet explicitly mention, but which is probably implied in the epithet they frequently employ of wild beast (mṛigaḥ), to denote the demoniacal monster. The *Râmâyaṇam* says[2] that the monster with ten faces was seen in the shapes of a tiger, a wild boar, a cloud, a mountain, a sea, a tree, and in his proper form of a demon. In another song,[3]

[1] Tâ yodhishṭam abhi gâ indra nûnam apaḥ svar ushaso agna ûḷhâḥ diçaḥ svar ushasa indra ćitrâ apo gâ agne yuvase niyutvân; *Ṛigv.* vi. 60, 2.

[2] Vyâghro varâho ǵîmûtaḥ parvataḥ sâgaro drumaḥ yakshâir dâittyasvarûpî ća so 'driçyata daçânanaḥ; *Râm.* vii. 15.

[3] *Râm.* vii. 18.

we are told how, at the appearance of Râvaṇas, the alarmed gods transformed themselves into animals—Indras becoming a peacock, Yamas a crow, Kuveras a chameleon, Varuṇas a swan—and thus escaped the ire of the enemy. We shall see that each of these transfortions, far from being capricious, was natural and almost necessary to the several gods, so that in this great mythical scene we have in reality only an imaginary picture of a grand sunset spectacle. The animal is the shadow that follows the hero; it is his form, his shield. When Râmas sets out on his way to heaven, the bears, the monkeys, and all the other animals of his dominions follow him;[1] when Râmas, in the sacred waves of the Sarayû, recovers his divine form of Vishṇus, even the bodies of the animals assume glorious and divine shapes in those blessed waters.[2] In several Slavonic popular tales—the Russian in particular—no sooner is the hero separated from the animals who chase the beasts of prey, from his chase (ahóta), than the charm is broken, and he falls an easy prey to the monster. The animal is so identified with the hero, that it may often be said to be the hero himself; and the popular tales of the Slaves, which more than any others have retained the character of primitive simplicity, might, instead of a heroic poem, in this way supply materials for quite an epos of animals.

No wonder, then, that, next to the Indian, I should assign the chief place to the Slavonic traditions: the language, imagery, belief, and mode of life of the Slavonic peasant are still primitive and patriarchal; one could almost swear to his having undergone no change for

---

1 *Râm.* vii. 114.

2 Tiryagyonigatânâṁ ća sarveshâṁ Sarayûǵale divyaṁ vapuḥ samabhavat; *Râm.* vii. 115.

three thousand years. I know not whether he will always remain so, in the face and in spite of the invasion of Western civilisation on Slavonic soil, but the race is certainly one of the most tenacious existing, preserving, as it does to this hour, all its primitive rudeness and early poetic nature, and that too while it goes on assimilating extraneous elements. The communication which, from sheer necessity, the Slaves had with the Tataric tribes, by no means disturbed the monotony of their original habits, nor altered their ancient beliefs. At the most, as the Slavonic peasant is greedy of tales, and as battles between black monsters and heroes occupy an important position in popular legends, he gave the names of Tatars, or Turks, to the black monsters; just as the Turks were the impersonations of the fiends in the epic poems of Persia, and the Saracens or Turks (often confounded with one another) took the place of the black demons in the poems of mediæval France, and the popular tales of Greece, Naples, and Spain. Under the same jealous animus of race, the popular Turkish and Tatar literature often transformed the gods and heroes of the Âryans into malignant spirits and horrid fiends; in the same way as, through the hatred of caste, the black ones (kṛishṇâs), the enemies of Indras (the war-god of the Vedic period), were elevated to the dignity and invested with the attributes of deities during the Brâhmanic period, during which one of them, their type Kṛishṇas, became a highly-venerated god, in opposition to Indras, who was now proscribed and persecuted as a demon. There are black devils and red devils even in the beliefs which are called Christian; the black, in contrast with the red, sometimes bearing the name and enjoying the honours of deity. But, more generally, the red devil was represented as a god, and the black one as a demon;

and the black man, the Turk, the Tatar, or the gipsy of the Russian popular tales, the coal-seller, the Romagnuolo (that is, he who goes into the forest to cut wood), and the Saracen of the Italian legends, are all variations of the kṛishṇas or the black monster of remote Vedic antiquity.

It can therefore be affirmed as an indisputable fact, that the incursions of the Tatars into Central Europe towards the end of the Middle Ages, not only did not alter the Slavonic tradition, but rather revived it; and the Tatar, who was himself a great teller of stories, only increased the taste of the Slavonic peasant for tales, and did not change his legends, nor, consequently, change the character of the people to whom those legends belonged. Besides, the popular tales of the Tatars do not differ enough from those of the Âryans to infuse into them anything like new blood, or affect in any degree their radical nature; on the contrary, the Tatar stories are the Âryan tales themselves, or, at most, the Hindoo ones, a little modified by a few peculiarities which are specifically of a Tatar character.

It is unnecessary that I should insist upon the great importance of the Scandinavian and German traditions, after the distinguished labours of learned Germans, who, for half a century, by the publication of their investigations, have already created for the use of the student a complete literature on the subject. The myths, the legends, the nursery tales, the songs, proverbs, and popular customs of the Scandinavo-Germanic race have had a whole host of faithful expounders and affectionate illustrators, who have scarcely left a single foot unexplored of that vast and interesting field of tradition.

There is a whole mine, however, of mythical wealth which, on account of our own carelessness more especially, has remained hitherto unwrought, and that is the store of legend which, deep-hidden and far-reaching, is still to be dug up from the classic soil of Italy. It is only during the last few years that one or two students have perceived the existence of this wealth, and taken some notice of it; it will therefore be my care in this comparative study to bring before the reader's attention as far as possible some little of the unknown and unwritten part of our popular tradition. The result of my inquiries will, perhaps, go far to prove that, notwithstanding the splendour of our Christian art, and the fame of our civilisation, the basis of Italian belief has till now remained pagan; so that those of our housewives who are most assiduous in their attendance at the great spectacles of the Church, and their observance of its ritual, are, at bottom, the most jealous custodiers and guardians of devilish superstitions and pagan fables. There is, indeed, a tendency in Tuscany to furbish up the ancient tales with the lascivious pleasantries of Boccaccio, and to place, as was this author's custom, the ancient legends in modern scenes, to trick them up in modern garnitures, and ascribe their action to modern characters; but besides that this tendency belongs to but a few story-tellers, even their re-composition, in other hands, never alters the base of the old and universal story, but leaves it intact. Therefore, if in Italy, notwithstanding the sceptical civilisation of the Romans, notwithstanding incessant foreign invasions, and in spite of the incubus of the Roman Catholic Church, such a great portion of ancient tradition has been preserved, and that vitally, it is impossible not to recognise the exceptional character of this tradition, as an heirloom of our blood, and as a characteristic of the race from which we are descended, and to which we are linked by the lively remembrance of words which have become living images, and images which have become epical figures and superstitious beliefs.

Amongst these images or figures, those of animals, amongst these beliefs, those which relate to animals, are the most lively and persistent. The most material and sensible forms of the primitive mythology are preserved among us almost intact; the Âryan is become indifferent to the celestial phenomena, and has turned all his attention to the earth, which he peoples with the same deities that he formerly venerated in the sky. Hence, as he finds it sufficient to bow down before the idols representing the god who has come down to the earth, he endows the animals of the earth with the same magical qualities which he once attributed to the animals of heaven; notwithstanding all which, however, he cannot help sometimes perceiving the presence of two distinct persons in one animal—the real and permanent one which he knows from experience, and the fictitious and traditional one of which his ancestors have told him. This fictitious character of the traditional faith would easily be perceived by the ignorant common people, if they did but observe how the same virtues are sometimes attributed to animals of the most diverse nature, and how the same medicinal virtues are indiscriminately supposed to exist in an indeterminate number of animals. The infinite contradictions contained in the popular zoological system of medicine cannot be explained otherwise than by referring them to the extremely changeful celestial zoology, where the metamorphoses of animals are almost continuous, and where we pass with the rapidity of lightning, for instance, from the image of the horse to that of the bird, from the image of the wolf to that of the serpent, according to almost immediate physical and moral analogies, applicable to only a small part of the animal's habits or structure, which are found in mythology, and which suffice to form a new variety of myth and different beliefs, whilst certainly no single analogy would be sufficient to induce a classifying naturalist to assign to the same class, or to the same order, animals of diverse organisations, in spite of some accidental resemblance.

To the Vedic poet it is enough to know that the horse (açvaḥ) properly means the swift, in order that, transported into the sky, it may take the form of a well-winged one (suparṇaḥ), a bird, a hawk (çyenaḥ). To the Vedic poet the idea of a rapacious wolf (vṛikaḥ), a perfidious and voracious thief, who carries off prey, and keeps it in his obscure den, is enough to suggest, with various poetical images, that of a constrictor serpent (ahiḥ), perfidious, gloomy, voracious, and grasping. But that which is natural in the imagery of the poets, cannot stand before the reality of things and physical science, which searches it ; hence, what in the Vedic poetry is a happy image, is become a prejudice, a superstition, and a fatal error in our popular belief.

But before such prejudices could have so universally and deeply imbued the minds of the people, the first impression made by the myths must have been extremely vivid. Of such an impression we still find sporadic traces in some families of shepherds ; but to understand it well, I know no better method than to take an ingenuous child into the open country, under the vault of heaven, to observe a curious sunset, or the first dawn of day. The children of to-day will repeat the experiences of the ancient ones—that is, our ancestors in the youth of humanity—and will enable us to understand certain illusions which may appear impossible to the perception, or even imagination, of the erudite and sceptical modern. I myself, to realise more thoroughly the simplicity of our ancestors, am obliged to remember that one of the most vivid impressions ever made on me was received when, a child of scarcely four years of age, I was looking up into the sky. My family was living in a remote part of Piedmont: one autumn evening, towards night, one of my elder brothers pointed out to me, over a distant mountain, a dark cloud of a rather strange shape, saying, "Look down there; that is a hungry wolf running after the sheep." I do not know whether my brother was then repeating what he had heard the villagers say, or whether that heavenly scene had presented itself so to his own imagination; but I well recollect that he convinced me so entirely of that cloud being really a hungry wolf running upon the mountains, that fearing it might, in default of sheep, overtake me, I instantly took to my heels, and escaped precipitately into the house. The reader will kindly pardon this personal allusion. I recall and refer to it now to explain how the credulity which we always find in children may give us an idea of the credulity of infant nations. When Faith was pure, when Science did not exist, such illusions must have been continually awakening enthusiasm or fear in the breasts of our ingenuous forefathers, who lived in the open air with their herds of cattle, and stood with earth and sky in constant relation, and in continual communion. We busy dwellers in great cities, held back by a thousand social ties, oppressed by a thousand public or private cares, never happen to raise our eyes towards the sky, except it be to consult it on the probability of fine or wet weather; but evidently this is not sufficient to enable us to comprehend the vast and complicated epic poem transacted in the heavens.

Therefore, in beginning the separate lives of the mythological animals, I shall invoke but one unaccustomed Muse to aid and inspire me—the holy ingenuousness of infancy; I shall go back to my nurse for fairy tales; I shall begin again to dream of winged coursers, of birds that speak, and cows that spin; I shall believe everything possible and natural: and then I shall go forth into the open air to observe again the heavens; I shall take with me my little Cordelia and her friends, and let them explain in their own way the various and changing phenomena of the sky. Having thus taken my first inspiration from virgin infancy, I shall within myself ask pardon from their innocence, if into the paradise of their dreams I carry the foul malice of Satan; and if, after having taken account of their poetic and gentle impressions and of their ideal presentiments, I am obliged to return and descend amongst the brutes to seek out their sensual instincts, to find again in the dust our beloved deities disguised or fallen, then must my little children go far from me; my words, unavoidably bold, would be poison to their hearts; or else, begging them to take refuge in the sanctuary of their happy innocence, I would say one word alone to them—MYSTERY!

ANGELO DE GUBERNATIS.

FLORENCE, *September* 1872.

CONTENTS.

Part First.

THE ANIMALS OF THE EARTH.

PAGE

CHAPTER I.

THE COW AND THE BULL, ... 1

SECT. I.—THE COW AND THE BULL IN THE VEDIC HYMNS, . 1

SECT. II.—THE WORSHIP OF THE BULL AND OF THE COW IN INDIA, AND THE BRAHMANIC LEGENDS RELATING TO IT, ... 41

SECT. III.—THE BULL AND THE COW IN IRANIAN AND TURANIAN TRADITION, ... 90

SECT. IV.—THE BULL AND THE COW IN SLAVONIC TRADITION, 171

SECT. V.—THE BULL AND THE COW IN THE GERMANICO-SCANDINAVIAN AND FRANCO-CELTIC TRADITIONS, 221

SECT. VI.—THE BULL AND THE COW IN GREEK AND LATIN TRADITION, ... 261

CHAPTER II.

THE HORSE, ... 283

CHAPTER III.

THE ASS, ... 358

CHAPTER IV.

THE SHEEP, THE RAM, AND THE GOAT, ... 400

ZOOLOGICAL MYTHOLOGY;

OR

THE LEGENDS OF ANIMALS.

First Part.

THE ANIMALS OF THE EARTH.

CHAPTER I.

THE COW AND THE BULL.

SECTION I.—THE COW AND THE BULL IN THE VEDIC HYMNS.

SUMMARY.

Prelude.—The vault of Heaven as a luminous cow.—The gods and goddesses, sons and daughters of this cow.—The vault of Heaven as a spotted cow.—The sons and daughters of this cow, *i.e.* the winds, Marutas, and the clouds, Pṛiçnayas.—The wind-bulls subdue the cloud-cows.—Indras, the rain-sending, thundering, lightening, radiant sun, who makes the rain fall and the light return, called the bull of bulls.—The bull Indras drinks the water of strength.—Hunger and thirst of the heroes of mythology.—The cloud-barrel.—The horns of the bull and of the cow are sharpened.—The thunderbolt-horns.—The cloud as a cow, and even as a stable or hiding-place for cows. Cavern where the cows are shut up, of which cavern the bull Indras and the bulls Marutas remove the stone, and force the entrance, to reconquer the cows, delivering them from the monster; the male Indras finds himself again with his wife.—The cloud-fortress, which Indras destroys and Agnis sets on fire.—The cloud-forest, which the gods destroy.—The cloud-cow; the cow-bow; the bird-thunderbolts; the birds come out of the cow.—The monstrous cloud-cow, the wife of the monster.—

Some phenomena of the cloudy sky are analogous to those of the gloomy sky of night and of winter.—The moment most fit for an epic poem is the meeting of such phenomena in a nocturnal tempest. —The stars, cows put to flight by the sun.—The moon, a milk-yielding cow.—The ambrosial moon fished up in the fountain, gives nourishment to Indras.—The moon as a male, or bull, discomfits, with the bull Indras, the monster.—The two bulls, or the two stallions, the two horsemen, the twins.—The bull chases the wolf from the waters.—The cow tied.—The aurora, or ambrosial cow, formed out of the skin of another cow by the Ṛibhavas.—The Ṛibhavas, bulls and wise birds.—The three Ṛibhavas reproduce the triple Indras and the triple Vishṇus; their three relationships; the three brothers, eldest, middle, youngest; the three brother workmen; the youngest brother is the most intelligent, although at first thought stupid; the reason why.—The three brothers guests of a king.—The third of the Ṛibhavas, the third and youngest son becomes Tritas the third, in the heroic form of Indras, who kills the monster; Tritas, the third brother, after having accomplished the great heroic undertaking, is abandoned by his envious brothers in the well; the second brother is the son of the cow.—Indras a cowherd, parent of the sun and the aurora, the cow of abundance, milk-yielding and luminous.—The cow Sîtâ.—Relationship of the sun to the aurora.—The aurora as cow-nurse of the sun, mother of the cows; the aurora cowherd; the sun hostler and cowherd.—The riddle of the wonderful cowherd; the sun solves the riddle proposed by the aurora.—The aurora wins the race, being the first to arrive at the barrier, without making use of her feet.—The chariot of the aurora.—She who has no feet, who leaves no footsteps; she who is without footsteps of the measure of the feet; she who has no slipper (which is the measure of the foot).—The sun who never puts his foot down, the sun without feet, the sun lame, who, during the night, becomes blind; the blind and the lame who help each other, whom Indra helps, whom the ambrosia of the aurora enables to walk and to see.—The aurora of evening, witch who blinds the sun; the sun Indras, in the morning, chases the aurora away; Indras subdues and destroys the witch aurora.—The brother sun follows, as a seducer, the aurora his sister, and wishes to burn her.—The sun follows his daughter the aurora.—The aurora, a beautiful young girl, deliverer of the sun, rich in treasure, awakener of the sleepers, saviour of mankind, foreseeing; from small becomes large, from dark becomes brilliant, from infirm, whole, from blind, seeing and protectress of sight.—Night and aurora, now mother and daughter, now sisters.—The luminous night a good sister; the gloomy night gives place to the aurora, her elder or better sister, working, purifying, cleansing.—The aurora shines only when near the sun her husband, before whom she dances splendidly dressed; the aurora Urvaçî.—The wife of the sun followed by the monster.—The husband of the aurora subject to the same persecution.

We are on the vast table-land of Central Asia; gigantic mountains send forth on every side their thousand rivers; immense pasture-lands and forests cover it; migratory tribes of pastoral nations traverse it; the *gopatis*, the shepherd or lord of the cows, is the king; the gopatis who has most herds is the most powerful. The story begins with a graceful pastoral idyll.

To increase the number of the cows, to render them fruitful in milk and prolific in calves, to have them well looked after, is the dream, the ideal of the ancient Aryan. The bull, the *fœcundator*, is the type of every male perfection, and the symbol of regal strength.

Hence, it is only natural that the two most prominent animal figures in the mythical heaven should be the cow and the bull.

The cow is the ready, loving, faithful, fruitful Providence of the shepherd.

The worst enemy of the Aryan, therefore, is he who carries off the cow; the best, the most illustrious, of his friends, he who is able to recover it from the hands of the robber.

The same idea is hence transferred to heaven; in heaven there is a beneficent, fruitful power, which is called the cow, and a beneficent *fœcundator* of this same power, which is called the bull.

The dewy moon, the dewy aurora, the watery cloud, the entire vault of heaven, that giver of the quickening and benignant rain, that benefactress of mankind,—are each, with special predilection, represented as the beneficent cow of abundance. The lord of this multiform cow of heaven, he who makes it pregnant and fruitful and milk-yielding, the spring or morning sun, the rain-giving sun (or moon) is often represented as a bull.

Now, to apprehend all this clearly, we ought to go back, as nearly as possible, to that epoch in which such conceptions would arise spontaneously; but as the imagination so indulged is apt to betray us into mere fantastical conceits, into an *à priori* system, we shall begin by excluding it entirely from these preliminary researches, as being hazardous and misleading, and content ourselves with the humbler office of collecting the testimonies of the poets themselves who assisted in the creation of the mythology in question.

I do not mean to say anything of the Vedic myths that is not taken from one or other of the hymns contained in the greatest of the Vedas, but only to arrange and connect together the links of the chain as they certainly existed in the imagination of the ancient Aryan people, and which the *Ṛigvedas*, the work of a hundred poets and of several centuries, presents to us as a whole, continuous and artistic. I shall indeed suppose myself in the valley of Kaçmîra, or on the banks of the Sindhus, under that sky, at the foot of these mountains, among these rivers; but I shall search in the sky for that which I find in the hymns, and not in the hymns for that which I may imagine I see in the sky. I shall begin my voyage with a trusty chart, and shall consult it with all the diligence in my power, in order not to lose any of the advantages that a voyage so full of surprises has to offer. Hence the notes will all, or nearly all, consist of quotations from my guide, in order that the learned reader may be able to verify for himself every separate assertion. And as to the frequent stoppages we shall have to make by the way, let me ask the reader not to ascribe these to anything arbitrary on my part, but rather to the necessities of a voyage, made, as it is, step by step, in a region but little known, and by the help of a guide, where nearly everything indeed is to be found, but where, as in a rich inventory, it is easier to lose one's way than to find it again.

The immense vault of heaven which over-arches the earth, as the eternal storehouse of light and rain, as the power which causes the grass to grow, and therefore the animals which pasture upon it, assumes in the Vedic literature the name of Aditis, or the infinite, the inexhaustible, the fountain of ambrosia (*amṛitasya nabhis*). Thus far, however, we have no personification, as yet we have no myth. The *amṛitas* is simply the immortal, and only poetically represents the rain, the dew, the luminous wave. But the inexhaustible soon comes to mean that which can be milked without end—and hence also, a celestial cow, an inoffensive cow, which we must not offend, which must remain intact.[1] The whole heavens being thus represented as an infinite cow, it was natural that the principal and most visible phenomena of the sky should become, in their turn, children of the cow, or themselves cows or bulls, and that the *fœcundator* of the great mother should also be called a bull. Hence we read that the wind (*Vâyus* or *Rudras*) gave birth, from the womb of the celestial cow, to the winds that howl in the tempest (*Marutas* and *Rudrâs*), called for this reason children of the cow.[2] But, since this great celestial cow produces the tempestuous, noisy winds, she represents not only the serene, tranquil vault of the shining sky, but also the cloudy and tene-

[1] Mâ gâm anâgâm aditiṁ vadhishṭa; *Ṛigv.* viii. 90, 15.

[2] Gomâtaraḥ; *Ṛigv.* i. 8, 1, 3.—Aditis, called "mâtâ rudrâṇâm;" *Ṛigv.* viii. 90, 15.

brous mother of storms. This great cow, this immense cloud, that occupies all the vault of heaven and unchains the winds, is a brown, dark, spotted (*pṛiçnis*) cow; and so the winds, or Marutas, her sons, are called the children of the spotted one.[1] The singular has thus become a plural; the male sons of the cloud, the winds, are 21; the daughters, the clouds themselves, called the spotted ones (*pṛiçnayas*) are also three times seven, or 21: 3 and 7 are sacred numbers in the Aryan faith; and the number 21 is only a multiple of these two great legendary numbers, by which either the strength of a god or that of a monster is often symbolised. If *pṛiçnis*, or the variegated cow, therefore, is the mother of the Marutas, the winds, and of the variegated ones (*pṛiçnayas*), the clouds, we may say that the clouds are the sisters of the winds. We often have three or seven sisters, three or seven brothers in the legends. Now, that 21, in the *Ṛigvedas* itself, involves a reference to 3, is evident, if we only observe how one hymn speaks of the 3 times 7 spotted cows who bring to the god the divine drink, while another speaks of the spotted ones (the number not being specified) who give him three lakes to drink.[2] Evidently here the 3, or 7, or 21 sister cows that yield to the god of the eastern heavens their own nutritious milk, and amidst whose milky humours the winds, now become invulnerable, increase,[3] fulfil the pious duties of benevolent guardian fates.

[1] Tubhyaṁ (to Vâyus, to the wind), dhenuḥ sabardughâ viçvâ vasûni dohate aǵanayo maruto vakshaṇâbhyaḥ; *Ṛigv.* i. 134, 4.

[2] Imâs ta indra pṛiçnayo ghṛitaṁ duhata âçiram; *Ṛigv.* viii. 6, 19.—Trir asmâi sapta dhenavo duduhre satyâm âçiram pûrvye vyomani; *Ṛigv.* ix. 70, 1.—Trîṇi sarâṅsi pṛiçnayo duduhre vaǵriṇe madhu; *Ṛigv.* viii. 7, 10.—In the *Râmâyaṇan*, i. 48, the Marutas also appear in the number of 7.

[3] Pra çaṅsâ goshv aghnyaṁ krîḻaṁ yać ćhardho mârutam ǵambhe rasasya vâvṛidhe; *Ṛigv.* i. 37, 5.

But if the winds are sons of a cow, and the cows are their nurses, the winds, or Marutas, must, as masculine, be necessarily represented as bulls. In reality the Wind (*Vâyus*), their father, is borne by bulls—that is, by the winds themselves, who hurry, who grow, are movable as the rays of the sun, very strong, and indomitable;[1] the strength of the wind is compared to that of the bull or the bear;[2] the winds, as lusty as bulls, overcome and subdue the dark ones.[3] Here, therefore, the clouds are no longer represented as the cows that nurse, but with the gloomy aspect of a monster. The Marutas, the winds that howl in the tempest, are as swift as lightning, and surround themselves with lightning. Hence they are celebrated for their luminous vestments; and hence it is said that the reddish winds are resplendent with gems, as some bulls with stars.[4] As such—that is, as subduers of the clouds, and as they who run impetuously through them—these winds, these bulls, are the best friends, the most powerful helpers, of the great bellowing bull; of the god of thunder and rain; of the sun, the dispeller of clouds and darkness; of the supreme Vedic god, Indras, the friend of light and ambrosia—of Indras, who brings with him daylight and fine weather, who sends us the beneficent dew and the fertilising rain. Like the winds his companions, the sun Indras—the sun (and the luminous sky) hidden in the dark, who strives to dissipate the

---

[1] Ime ye te su vâyo bâhvoǵaso 'ntar nadî te patayanty ukshaṇo mahi vrâdhanta ukshaṇaḥ dhanvań ćid ye anâçavo ǵirâç, ćid aǵirâukasaḥ sûryasyeva raçmayo durniyantavo hastayor durniyantavaḥ; *Ṛigv.* i. 135, 9.

[2] Ṛiksho na vo marutaḥ çimîvâṇ amo dudhro gâur iva bhîmayuḥ; *Ṛigv.* v. 56, 3.

[3] Te syandrâso nokshaṇo 'ṭi shkandanti çarvarîḥ; *Ṛigv.* v. 52, 3.

[4] Tvam vâtâir aruṇâir yâsi; *Tâittiriya Yaǵurvedas*, i. 3, 14.—Ańgibhir vy ânaǵre ke cid usrâ iva stṛibhiḥ; *Ṛigv.* i. 87, 1.

shadows, the sun hidden in the cloud that thunders and lightens, to dissolve it in rain—is represented as a powerful bull, as the bull of bulls, invincible son of the cow, that bellows like the Marutas.[1]

But in order to become a bull, in order to grow, to develop the strength necessary to kill the serpent, Indras must drink; and he drinks the water of strength, the *somas*.[2] "Drink and grow,"[3] one of the poets says to him, while offering the symbolical libation of the cup of sacrifice, which is a type of the cup of heaven, now the heavenly vault, now the cloud, now the sun, and now the moon. From the sweet food of the celestial cow, Indras acquires a swiftness which resembles that of the horse;[4] and he eats and drinks at one time enough to enable him to attain maturity at once. The gods give him three hundred oxen to eat, and three lakes of ambrosial liquor[5] to drink, in order that he may be able to kill the monster serpent. The hunger and thirst of the heroes is always proportioned to the miracle they are called upon to perform; and for this reason the hymns of the *Ṛigvedas* and of the *Atharvavedas* often represent

---

[1] Vṛishâ vṛishabhih; *Ṛigv.* i. 100, 4.—Gṛishṭiḥ sasûva sthaviraṁ tavâgâm anâdhṛishyaṁ vṛishabhaṁ tumram indram; *Ṛigv.* iv. 18, 10.—Sa mâtarâ na dadṛiçâna usriyo nânadad eti marutâm iva svanaḥ; *Ṛigv.* ix. 70, 6.

[2] Vṛishâyamâṇo vṛiṇita somam; *Ṛigv.* i. 32, 3.—Pituṁ nu stosham maho dharmâṇam tavishîm yasya trito (Tritas, as we shall see, is an *alter ego* of the god Indras) vy oǵasâ vṛitram viparvaṁ ardayat; *Ṛigv.* i. 187, 1.

[3] Pibâ vardhasva; *Ṛigv.* iii. 36, 3.

[4] Indro madhu sambhṛitam usriyâyâm padvad viveda çaphavan name goḥ; *Ṛigv.* iii. 39, 6.

[5] Trî yać ćhatâ mahishâṇâm agho mâs trî sarâṇsi maghavâ somyâpâḥ kâraṁ na viçve ahvanta devâ bharam indrâya yad ahim ǵaghâna; *Ṛigv.* v. 29, 8.

the cloud as an immense great-bellied barrel (*Kabandhas*), which is carried by the divine *bull.*[1]

But when and how does the hero-bull display his extraordinary strength? The terrible bull bellows, and shows his strength, as he sharpens his horns:[2] the splendid bull, with sharpened horns, who is able of himself to overthrow all peoples.[3] But what are the horns of the bull Indras, the god of thunder? Evidently the thunderbolts; Indras is, in fact, said to sharpen the thunderbolts as a bull sharpens his horns;[4] the thunderbolt of Indras is said to be thousand-pointed;[5] the bull Indras is called the bull with the thousand horns, who rises from the sea[6] (or from the cloudy ocean as a thunder-dealing sun, from the gloomy ocean as a radiant sun—the thunderbolt being supposed to be rays from the solar disc). Sometimes the thunderbolt of Indras is itself called a bull,[7] and is sharpened by its beloved refulgent cows,[8] being used, now to withdraw the cows from the darkness, now to deliver

---

[1] Vasoḥ kabandhamṛishabho bibharti; *Atharvavedas*, ix. 4, 3.

[2] Sruvati bhîmo vṛishabhas tavishyayâ çṛiñge çiçâno hariṇî vićakshaṇaḥ; *Ṛigv.* ix. 70, 7.

[3] Yas tigmaçṛiñgo vṛishabho na bhîma ekaḥ kṛishṭîç ćyâvayati pra viçvâḥ; *Ṛigv.* vii. 19, 1.—Idaṁ namo vṛishabhâya svarâǵe satyaçushmâya tavase 'vâći; *Ṛigv.* i. 51, 15.

[4] Çiçîte vaǵraṁ teǵase na vaṅsagaḥ; *Ṛigv.* i. 55, 1.

[5] Abhy enaṁ vaǵra âyasaḥ sahasrabhṛishṭir âyatârćano; *Ṛigv.* i. 80, 12.

[6] Sahasraçṛiñgo vṛishabho yaḥ samudrâd udâćarat; *Ṛigv.* vii. 55, 7.

[7] Vi tigmena vṛishabheṇa puro 'bhet; *Ṛigv.* i. 33, 13.

[8] Priyâ indrasya dhenavo vagraṁ hinvanti sâyakaṁ vasvîḥ; *Ṛigv.* i. 84, 10, 11, 12. The root, HI, properly signifies to *distend, draw out;* here, to *draw out* the arm of Indras seems to me to mean to elongate it, to render it as fine as a thread—to sharpen it (in Italian, *affilare*); the cows that sharpen (It. *affilanti*), are a variety of the cows that *spin* (It. *filanti*).

them from the monster of darkness that envelops them,[1] and now to destroy the monster of clouds and darkness itself. Besides the name of Indras, this exceedingly powerful horned bull, who sharpens his horns to plunge them into the monster, assumes also, as the fire which sends forth lightning, as that which sends forth rays of light from the clouds and the darkness, the name of Agnis; and, as such, has two heads, four horns, three feet, seven hands, teeth of fire, and wings; he is borne on the wind, and blows.[2]

Thus far, then, we have heavenly cows which nurture heavenly bulls, and heavenly bulls and cows which use their horns for a battle that is fought in heaven.

Let us now suppose ourselves on the field of battle, and let us visit both the hostile camps. In one we find the sun (and sometimes the moon), the bull of bulls Indras, with the winds, Marutas, the radiant and bellowing bulls; in the other, a multiform monster, in the shape of wolves, serpents, wild boars, owls, mice, and such like. The bull Indras has cows with him, who help him; the monster has also cows, either such as he has carried off from Indras, and which he imprisons and secretes in gloomy caverns, towers, or fortresses, or those which he caresses as his own wives. In the one case, the cows consider the bull Indras as their friend and liberating hero; in the other,

[1] Yuǵaṁ vaǵraṁ vṛishabhaç ćakra indro nir ǵyotishâ tamaso gâ adukshat; *Ṛigv.* i. 33, 10.

[2] Çiçîte çṛiñge rakshase vinikshe; *Ṛigv.* v. 2, 9.—Ćatvâri çṛiñgâ trayo asya pâdâ dve çîrshe sapta hastâso asya; *Ṛigv.* iv. 58, 3.—Tapurǵambho vana â vâtaćodito yûthe na sâhvân ava vâti vaṅsagaḥ abhi vraǵann akshitam pâǵasâ raǵaḥ sthâtuç ćaratham bhayate patatriṇaḥ; *Ṛigv.* i. 58, 5. In this stanza, however, *Vaṅsagaḥ* may probably signify rather *the stallion* than *the bull*, as we find in the second stanza this same Agnis already compared to a radiant horse (atyo na pṛishṭham prushitasya roćate).

those with the monster are themselves monsters and enemies of Indras, who fights against them. The clouds, in a word, are regarded at one time as the friends of the rain-giving sun, who delivers them from the monster that keeps back the rain, and at another as attacked by the sun, as they who wickedly envelop him, and endeavour to destroy him. Let us now go on to search, in the *Ṛigvedas*, the proofs of this double battle.

To begin with the first phase of the conflict, where in the sky does Indras fight the most celebrated of all his battles?

The clouds generally assume the aspect of mountains; the words *adris* and *parvatas*, in the Vedic language, expressing the several ideas of stone, mountain, and cloud.[1] The cloud being compared to a stone, a rock, or a mountain, it was natural,—1st, To imagine in the rock or mountain dens or caverns, which, as they imprisoned cows, might be likened to stables;[2] 2d, To pass from the idea of a roçk to that of citadel, fortress, fortified city, tower; 3d, To pass from the idea of a

---

[1] *Adris* and *parvatas* properly mean mountain, but, in the Vedâs, often cloud; and among their many meanings there is also that of tree; *agas* (properly that which does not move) expresses equally tree and mountain. Hence perhaps the Italian proverb: *Le montagne stanno ferme, ma gli uomini s'incontrano,* Mountains stand still, but men meet; hence the cry of Râmas in the *Râmâyaṇam,* ii. 122, that the Himâlayas would move before he should become a traitor; hence the assurance with which Macbeth, after the celebrated prophecy of the witches, can say: "That will never be; who can impress the forest; bid the tree unfix his earth-bound root?" *Shakspeare* (*Macbeth,* iv. 1.) Nevertheless the forest moved, as it not unfrequently does in the myths, where the tree-clouds walk, and fill all with terror wherever they go, where heroes and monsters often fight, by unrooting the trees of a whole forest. Cfr. *Râmâyaṇam,* iii. 3, 5, and the chapters of this work which treat of the Horse, the Bear, and the Monkey.

[2] Vraǵam gaćha gosthânam; *Tâittir. Yaǵúr.* i. 1, 9; cfr. *Çatapathabrâhmaṇam,* i. 2, 3, 4.

mountain, which is immovable, to that of a tree which, though it cannot move from its place, yet rears itself and expands in the air ; and from the idea of the tree of the forest to the shadowy and awe-inspiring grove. Hence the bull, or hero, or god Indras, or the sun of thunder, lightning, and rain, now does battle within a cavern, now carries a fortified town by assault, and now draws forth the cow from the forest, or unbinds it from the tree, destroying the *rakshas*, or monster, that enchained it.

The Vedic poetry celebrates, in particular, the exploit of Indras against the cavern, enclosure, or mountain in which the monster (called by different names and especially by those of Valas, Vṛitras, Cushṇas, of enemy, black one, thief, serpent, wolf, or wild boar) conceals the herds of the celestial heroes, or slaughters them.

The black bull bellows; the thunderbolt bellows, that is, the thunder follows the lightning, as the cow follows its calf;[1] the Marutas bulls ascend the rock—now, by their own efforts, moving and making the sonorous stone, the rock mountain, fall;[2] now, with the iron edge of their rolling chariots violently splitting the mountain;[3] the valiant hero, beloved by the gods, moves the stone;[4] Indras hears the cows: by the aid of the wind-bulls he

[1] Krishṇo nonâva vṛishabhaḥ; *Ṛigv.* i. 79, 2.—Vâçreva vidyun mimâti vatsaṁ na mâtâ sishakti; *Ṛigv.* i. 38, 8.

[2] Açmânaṁ ćit svaryam parvataṁ girim pra ćyâvayanti yâmabhiḥ; *Ṛigv.* v. 96, 4.

[3] Pavyâ rathânâm adrim bhindanty oǵasâ; *Ṛigv.* v. 52, 9. *Pavis*, in general, is the iron part, the iron end (of a dart, or a lance); here it would appear to be the iron tire of the chariot's wheels, which, driving furiously over the mountain, break it,—thunder, in fact, often suggests the idea of a noisy chariot making ruin in heaven.

[4] Vîraḥ karmaṇyaḥ sudaksho yuktagrâvâ ǵâyate devakâmaḥ; *Ṛigv.* iii. 4, 9.

finds the cows hidden in the cavern; he himself, furnished with an arm of stone, opens the grotto of Valas, who keeps the cows; or, opens the cavern to the cows; he vanquishes, kills, and pursues the thieves in battle; the bulls bellow; the cows move forward to meet them; the bull, Indras, bellows and leaves his seed in the herd; the thunder-dealing male, Indras, and his spouse are glad and rejoice.[1]

In this fabled enterprise, three moments must be noted: 1st, The effort to raise the stone; 2d, The struggle with the monster who carried off the cows; 3d, The liberation of the prisoners. It is an entire epic poem.

The second form of the enterprise of Indras in the cloudy heavens is that which has for its object the destruction of the celestial fortresses, of the ninety, or ninety-nine, or hundred cities of Çambaras, of the cities which were the wives of the demons; and from this undertaking Indras acquired the surname of *puramdaras* (explained as destroyer of cities); although he had in it a most valuable companion-in-arms, Agnis, that is, Fire, which naturally suggests to our thoughts the notion of destruction by fire.[2]

In a hymn to Indras, the gods arrive at last, bring their axes, and with their edges destroy the woods, and burn

---

[1] Ayaṁ çriṇve adha ǵayann uta ghnann ayam uta pra kriṇute yudhâ gâḥ; *Ṛigv.* iv. 17, 10.—Viḷu ćid ârugatnubhir guhâ ćid indra vahnibhiḥ avinda usriyâ anu; *Ṛigv.* i. 6, 5.—Tvaṁ valasya gomato 'pavar adrivo bilam; *Ṛigv.* i. 11, 5.—Vi gobhir adrim âirayat; *Ṛigv.* i. 7, 3.—Ukshâ mimâti prati yanti dhenavaḥ; *Ṛigv.* ix. 69, 4.—Yad anyâsu vṛishabho roravîti so anyasmin yûthe ni dadhâti retaḥ; *Ṛigv.* iii. 55, 17.—Pûshaṅvân vaǵrint sam u patnyâmadaḥ; *Ṛigv.* i. 82, 6.

[2] Indrâgnî navatim puro dâsapatnîr adhûnutam sâkam ekena karmaṇâ; *Ṛigv.* iii. 12, 6; *Tâitt. Yaǵurv.* i. 1, 14. Cfr. chap. on Serpent.

the monsters who restrain the milk in the breasts of the cows.[1] The clouded sky here figures in the imagination as a great forest inhabited by *rakshasas*, or monsters, which render it unfruitful—that is, which prevent the great celestial cow from giving her milk. The cow that gives the honey, the ambrosial cow of the Vedâs, is thus replaced by a forest which hides the honey, the ambrosia beloved by the gods. And although the Vedic hymns do not dwell much upon this conception of the cloudy-sky, preferring as they do to represent the darkness of night as a gloomy forest, the above passage from the Vedâs is worthy of notice as indicating the existence at least during the Vedic period of a myth which was afterwards largely amplified in zoological legend.[2]

In this threefold battle of Indras, we must, moreover, remark a curious feature. The thunder-dealing Indras overpowers his enemies with arrows and darts; the same cloud which thunders, bellows, and therefore is called a cow, becomes, as throwing darts, a bow: hence we have the cow-bow, from which Indras hurls the iron stone, the thunderbolt; and the cord itself of that bellowing bow is called a cow; from the bow-cow, from the cord-cow, come forth the winged darts, the thunderbolts, called birds, that eat men; and when they come forth, all the world trembles.[3] We shall come upon the same idea again further on.

Thus far we have considered the cow-cloud as a victim of the monster (that Indras comes to subdue). But it is

[1] Devâsa âyan paraçûṅr abibhran vanâ vṛiçćanto abhi viḍbhir âyan ni sudrvaṁ dadhato vakshaṇâsu yatrâ kṛipîṭam anu tad dahanti; *Ṛigv.* x. 28, 8.

[2] Cfr. the chapter on the Bear and the Monkey.

[3] Vṛikshe-vṛikshe niyatâ mîmayad gâus tato vayaḥ pra patân pûrushâdaḥ viçvam bhuvanam bhayâte; *Ṛigv.* x. 27, 22.—Tvam âyasam prati vartayo gor divo açmânam; *Ṛigv.* i. 121, 9.

not uncommon to see the cloud itself or the darkness, that is, the cow, the fortress, or the forest represented as a monster. Thus, a Vedic hymn informs us that the monster Valas had the shape of a cow;[1] another hymn represents the cloud as the cow that forms the waters, and that has now one foot, now four, now eight, now nine, and fills the highest heaven with sounds;[2] still another hymn sings that the sun hurls his golden disc in the variegated cow;[3] they who have been carried off, who are guarded by the monster serpent, the waters, the cows, are become the wives of the demons;[4] and they must be malignant, since a poet can use as a curse the wish that the malign spirits, the demons, may drink the poison of those cows.[5] We have already seen that the fortresses are wives of demons, and that the demons possessed the forests.[6]

It is in the beclouded and thundering heavens that the warrior hero displays his greatest strength; but it cannot be denied that the great majority of the myths, and the most poetical, exemplify or represent the relation between the nocturnal sky (now dark, tenebrous, watery, horrid, wild, now lit up by the ambrosial moonbeams, and now bespangled with stars) and the two glowing skies—the two resplendent ambrosial twilights of

[1] Brihaspatir govapusho valasya nir maǵǵânaṁ na parvaṇo ǵabhâra; *Ṛigv.* x. 68, 9.

[2] Gâurîr mimâya salilâni takshaty ekapadî dvipadî sâ ćatushpadî—ashṭâpadî navapadî babhûvushî sahasrâksharâ parame vyoman; *Ṛigv.* i. 164, 41.

[3] Utâdaḥ parushe gavi sûraç ćakraṁ hiraṇyayam; *Ṛigv.* vi. 56, 3.

[4] Dâsapatnîr ahigopâ atishṭhan niruddhâ âpah paṇineva gâvaḥ; *Ṛigv.* i. 32, 11.

[5] Vishaṁ gavâṁ yâtudhânaḥ pibantu; *Ṛigv.* x. 87, 18. The same passage can, however, be also translated: "The demons of the cows may drink the poison."

[6] *Ṛigv.* iii. 12, 6; x. 27, 22.

morning and evening (of autumn and spring). We have here the same general phenomenon of light and darkness engaged in strife; here, again, the sun Indras is hidden, as though in a cloud, to prepare the light, to recover from the monster of darkness the waters of youth and light, the riches, the cows, which he keeps concealed; but this conquest is only made by the hero after long wandering amidst many dangers, and is finally accomplished by battles, in which the principal credit is often due to a heroine; except in those cases, not frequent but well worthy of remark, in which the clouds, hurricanes, tempests of lightning and thunderbolts, coincide with the end of the night (or of winter), and the sun Indras, by tearing the clouds, at the same time disperses the darkness of night and brings dawn (or spring) back to the sky. In such coincidences, the sun Indras, besides being the greatest of the gods, reveals himself to be also the most epic of the heroes; the two skies, the dark and the clouded, with their relative monsters, and the two suns, the thundering and the radiant, with their relative companions, are confounded, and the myth then assumes all its poetical splendour. And the most solemn moments of the great national Aryan epic poems, the *Râmâyaṇam* and the *Mahâbhâratam*, the *Book of Kings*, as well as those of the *Iliad*, the *Song of Roland* and the *Nibelungen*, are founded upon this very coincidence of the two solar actions—the cloudy and shadowy monster thunderstruck, and the dawn (or spring) delivered and resuscitated. In truth, the *Ṛigvedas* itself, in a passage already quoted,[1] tells us that the clouds—the three times seven spotted cows—cause their milk to drop to a god (whom, from another similar passage,[2]

[1] *Ṛigv.* ix. 70, 1.

[2] viii. 6, 19. Cfr. the chapters on the Horse and the Cuckoo.

we know to be Indras, the sun) in the eastern sky (*pûrve vyomani*), that is, towards the morning, and sometimes towards the spring, many of the phenomena of which correspond to those of the aurora. The *Pṛiçnayas*, or spotted ones, are beyond doubt the clouds, as the Marutas, sons of Pṛiçnis, or the spotted one, are the winds that howl and lighten in the storm cloud. It is therefore necessary to carry back the cloudy sky towards the morning, to understand the Pṛiçnayas feeding the sun Indras in the eastern heavens and the seven *Angirasas*, the seven sunbeams, the seven wise men, who also sing hymns in the morning;—it seems to me that the hymn of these fabled wise men can be nothing else than the crash of the thunderbolts, which, as we have already seen, are supposed to be detached from the solar rays. Allusions to Indras thundering in the morning are so frequent in the Vedic hymns, that I hope to be excused for this short digression, from which I must at once return, because my sole object here is to treat in detail of the mythical animals, and because the road we have to take will be a long one.

Even the luminous night has its cows; the stars, which the sun puts to flight with his rays,[1] are cows: the cows themselves, whose dwellings the dwellings of the sun's cows must adjoin, are called the many-horned ones.[2] These dwellings seem to me worthy of passing remark,

[1] Vi raçmibhiḥ sasṛiġe sûryo gâḥ; *Ṛigv.* vii. 36, 1.

[2] Ta vâm (the gods Vishṇus and Indras) vâstûny uçmasi gamadhyâi yatra gâvo bhûriçṛiñgâ ayâsaḥ; *Ṛigv.* i. 154, 6. Here all the stars or cows together form *many horns;* but perhaps each star or cow in itself was supposed to have but *one horn;* for the stars, like the moon, shed but one ray of light, but one light. This, it appears to me, may be inferred from the name of *Ekaçṛiñgâs* or *unicorns*, given, in the later mythology of the Indians, to an entire order of Mani, of whom the stars are represented as the supreme habitations, and even purest forms.

they are the celestial houses that move, the enchanted huts and palaces that appear, disappear, and are transformed so often in the popular stories of the Aryans.

The moon is generally a male, for its most popular names, *Ćandras*, *Indus*, and *Somas* are masculine; but as Somas signifies ambrosia, the moon, as giver of ambrosia, soon came to be considered a milk-giving cow; in fact, moon is one among the various meanings given in Sanskrit to the word *gâus* (cow). The moon, Somas, who illumines the nocturnal sky, and the pluvial sun, Indras, who during the night, or the winter, prepares the light of morn, or spring, are represented as companions; a young girl, the evening, or autumnal, twilight, who goes to draw water towards night, or winter, finds in the well, and takes to Indras, the ambrosial moon, that is, the Somas whom he loves. Here are the very words of the Vedic hymn:—"The young girl, descending towards the water, found the moon in the fountain, and said: 'I will take you to Indras, I will take you to Çakras; flow, O moon, and envelop Indras.'"[1] The moon and ambrosia in the word indus, as well as somas, are confounded with one another; hence, Indras, the drinker *par excellence* of *somas* (somapâtamas), is also the best friend and companion of the ambrosial or pluvial moon, and so the sun and moon (as also Indras and Vishṇus) together come to suggest to us the idea of two friends, two brothers (Indus and Indras), two twins, the two Açvinâu; often the two twilights, properly speaking, the morning and the evening, the spring and the autumn, twilights, the former, however, being especially associated with the red sun which appears in the morning (or in the spring), and the latter with the

[1] Kanyâ vâr avâyatî somam api srutâvidat astam bharanty abravîd indrâya sunavâi tvâ çakrâya sunavâi tvâ.—Indrâyendo pari srava; *Ṛigv.* viii. 80, 1, 3.

pale moon which appears in the evening (or in the autumn, as a particular regent of the cold season). Indras and Somas (*Indrâsomâu*) are more frequently represented as two bulls who together discomfit the monster (*raksho-haṇâu*), who destroy by fire the monsters that live in darkness.[1] The word *vṛishaṇâu* properly means the two who pour out, or fertilise. Here it means the two bulls; but as the word *vṛishan* signifies stallion as well as bull, the two stallions, the vṛishaṇâu Indras and Somas, are, by a natural transition, soon transformed into two horses or horsemen, the two Açvinâu. Hence, in popular tales, we find near the young princess the hero, who now leads out the cows to pasture, and now, as hostler or groom, takes excellent care of the horses. But we must not anticipate comparisons which we shall have to make further on. Having noticed that, in the *Ṛigvedas,* we find the moon represented either as a bull or a cow (the masculine, *Indus, somas, ćandras,* is always a bull; while the feminine, *râkâ,* suggests more naturally the idea of a cow), let us now consider the bull Indras in relation to the cow Aurora (or spring).

Five bulls stand in the midst of the heavens, and chase out of the way the wolf who crosses the waters;[2] the luminous Vasavas unbind the cow that is tied by its foot.[3]

How now is this cow brought forth?

This ambrosial cow is created by the artists of the gods, by the three brothers *Ṛibhavas,* who draw it out of the skin of a cow; that is, they make a cow, and,

---

[1] Indrâsomâ tapataṁ raksha ubǵataṁ ny arpayataṁ vṛishaṇâ tamo-vṛidhaḥ; *Ṛigv.* vii. 104, 1.—The following stanzas reproduce and develop the same argument.

[2] Pańćokshaṇo madhye tasthur maho divaḥ — Te sedhanti patho vṛikaṁ tarantaṁ yahvatîr apaḥ; *Ṛigv.* i. 105, 10, 11.

[3] Vasavo gâuryaṁ ćit padi shitâm amuńćatâ yaǵatrâh; *Ṛigv.* iv. 12, 6.

to give it life, cover it with the skin of a dead cow.[1] It being understood that the cow Aurora (or Spring) dies at even (or in the autumn), the Ṛibhavas, the threefold sun Indras, *i.e.*, the sun in the three watches of the night, prepares the skin of this cow, one Ṛibhus taking off the skin from the dead cow, another Ṛibhus preparing it during the night (or winter), and the third Ṛibhus, in the early morning (or at the end of winter) dressing the new cow, the aurora (or the spring) with it. Thus it is that Indras, in three distinct moments, takes the skin from off the girl that he loves, who had become ugly during the night, and restores her beauty in the morning.[2] And the three Ṛibhavas may, it seems to me, be the more easily identified with the triple Indras, with Indra-Vishṇus, who measures the world in three paces, since, as Indras is called a bull, they also are called bulls;[3] as Indras is often a falcon, they also are named birds;[4] and their miracles are sometimes also those of Indras. This identification of the bulls Ṛibhavas, whom we speak of here as producers of the cow Aurora (the same sterile cow of the sleeping hero Çayus, that which the Açvinâu, the two horsemen of the twilight, restored to youth by the

[1] Takshan dhenuṁ sabardugham; *Ṛigv.* i. 20, 3.—Niç ćarmaṇo gâm ariṇîta dhîtibhiḥ; *Ṛigv.* i. 161, 7, e, iv. 36, 4.

[2] This interesting particular is more fully developed in the chapters which treat of the Wolf, the Pig and the Wild Boar, *q. v.*—To avoid useless and troublesome repetitions, I must observe here that the myths of morning and evening are often applied to spring and autumn, and the myths of night to winter.

[3] Rayim ṛibhavaḥ sarvavîram â takshata vṛishaṇo mandasânâḥ; *Ṛigv.* iv. 35, 6.

[4] Rayim ṛibhavas takshatâ vayaḥ; *Ṛigv.* iv. 36, 8.—Here again we have the cow in relation to the birds, since the riches given by the Ṛibhavas consist above all in cows. (Ye gomantaṁ vâǵavantaṁ suvîraṁ rayiṁ dhattha vasumantam purukshuṁ te agrepâ ṛibhavo mandasânâ asme dhatta ye ća râṭiṁ gṛiṇanti; *Ṛigv.* iv. 34, 10.)

Ṛibhavas, rendered fruitful again),[1] with the bull, or hero Indras, appears to me to be of the greatest importance, inasmuch as it affords us the key to much that is most vital to the Aryan legends.

The Ṛibhavas, then, are three brothers. They prepare themselves to procure the cups which are to serve for the gods to drink out of. Each has a cup in his hand; the eldest brother defies the others to make two cups out of one; the second defies them to make three out of one; the youngest brother comes forward and defies them to make four. The victory is his, and the greatest workman of heaven, the Vedic Vulcan, *Tvashtar*, praises their wonderful work.[2] The youngest of the three brothers is therefore the most skilful. We find in the *Ṛigvedas* the name of *Sukarmas*, or maker of fine works, good workman, given to each of the three brothers; and though only one of them, who is properly called Ṛibhus, or *Ṛibhukshâ*, is said to serve the god Indras in the quality of a workman (whence Indras himself sometimes received the name of Ṛibhukshâ, Ṛibhvan, or Ṛibhvas), yet the other two brothers, *Vâǵas* and *Vibhvan*, are in the service, one of all the gods, the other of Varuṇas, the god of night.[3] It would seem natural to recognise in Ṛibhus, the protégé of Indras, the most skilful of the three brothers, who, as we have seen above, was the youngest; yet, as we cannot infer anything from the order in which the hymns name the three brothers—as,

---

1 Çayave ćin nâsâtyâ çaćibhir ǵasuraye staryam pipyathur gâm; *Ṛigv.* i. 116. 22.—Yâ ǵarantâ yuvaçâ tâkṛiṇotana; *Ṛigv.* i. 161, 7.

2 Ǵyeshṭha âha ćamasâ dvâ kareti kanîyân trîn kriṇavâmety âha kanishṭha âha ćaturas kareti tvashṭa ṛibhavas tat panayad vaćo vaḥ; *Ṛigv.* iv. 33, 5.

3 Vâǵo devânâm abhavat sukarmendrasya ṛibhukshâ varuṇasya vibhvâ; *Ṛigv.* iv. 33, 9.

in one, Vâǵas is first named, then Ṛibhukshâ, and finally Vibhvan; in another, Vâǵas first, Vibhvan second, and Ṛibhus third;[1] in another, again, Ṛibhus is invoked first, then Vibhvan, and lastly Vâǵas; and as we also find all the Ṛibhavas saluted under the common epithet of Vâǵas, and Vâǵas himself by the name of Indras, or rather Indras saluted in his triple form of Ṛibhus, Vibhvan, and Vâǵas,[1] it remains uncertain which of these was the proper name of the third brother of the Ṛibhavas. But what seems to be sufficiently clear is, that Indras is identified with the Ṛibhavas (*Indravantas*), that the third brother is the most skilful, and that the three brothers serve the lords of heaven as workmen. And here we meet with an interesting element. In two hymns of the *Ṛigvedas*, the host of the Ṛibhavas appears as one only, Indras himself, or the sun (Savitar), under the name of *Agohyas* (*i.e.*, who cannot be hidden). During the twelve days (the twelve hours of the night, or the twelve months of the year) in which they are the guests of Agohyas, they bring as they sleep every species of prosperity to the land, by making the fields fertile, causing the rivers to flow, and refreshing the grass of the field. In this, however, let us not forget that they are the beneficent sons of *Sudhanvan*, the good archer, and archers themselves, representatives of the great celestial archer, of the thunder-dealing and rain-giving Indras; and that therefore their sleep is only a figure of speech to express their latent existence in darkness and the clouds of night.

---

[1] Te vâǵo vibhvân ṛibhur indravantaḥ; *Ṛigv.* iv. 33, 3.

[2] Ṛibhur vibhvâ vâǵa indro no aćhemaṁ yaǵńaṁ ratnadheyopa yâta; *Ṛigv.* iv. 34, 1.—Pibata vâǵâ ṛibhavo; *Ṛigv.* iv. 34, 4.

[3] Dvâdaça dyûn yad agohyasyâtithye raṇann ṛibhavaḥ sasantaḥ sukshetrâkṛiṇvann anayanta sindhûn dhanvâtishṭhann oshadhîr nimnam âpaḥ; *Ṛigv.* iv. 33, 7.—Cfr. *Ṛigv.* i. 161, 11-13.

But the *Ṛigvedas* introduces the three brothers under other names, and especially in one, and that an important aspect. The third brother is called *Tritas,* or the third, and as such, is also identified with Indras. Thus, for instance, the moments of Indras in the sky are three—evening, night, and towards morning; and the horse of Tritas (the horse that Tritas has received from *Yamas*) is now mysteriously Yama himself, now the son of Aditis (whom we have already seen to be the cow, or the son of the cow), now Tritas himself, whom Tritas alone can yoke, and Indras alone ride upon, a horse bedewed with ambrosia, which has three relationships in heaven, three in the waters, three in the ocean;[1] that is to say, one relation is Yamas, the elder brother; the second is the son of the cow, or the second brother; the last is Tritas himself, or the youngest brother. This Tritas is called intelligent; he therefore corresponds to the third brother, who makes four cups out of one. How then does he appear sometimes stupid? The language itself supplies the explanation. In Sanskrit, *bâlas* means both child and stolid; and the third brother is supposed to be stolid, because, at his first appearance especially, he is a child,—and we constantly see him as a child do wonderful things, and give proofs of superhuman wisdom. With this key, the meaning of the myth is obvious. The eldest brother, Yamas, the dying sun, with all his wisdom and experience, is unable of himself to recover the ravished or missing princess; the son of the cow Âditis, that is, Âdityas, the sun in the middle of the night, gives often

[1] Yamena dattam̀ trita enam âyunag indra eṇam prathamo adhy atishṭhat; *Ṛigv.* i. 163, 2.—Asi yamo asy âdityo arvann asi trito guhyena vratena asi somena samayâ viprikta âhus te trîṇi divi bandhanâni trîṇi ta âhur divi bandhanâni trîṇy apsu trîṇy antaḥ samudre; *Ṛigv.* i. 163, 3, 4.

proof of strength great enough to disperse the darkness and the clouds, and break the incantation; but, generally it is the the third sun, the morning sun, Indras in his third moment, Vishṇus taking his third step,[1] the third brother, Tritas, who seems to obtain the victory, and deliver the young aurora from the monster of night. All this seems to me to be very evident.

Tritas, like Indras, drinks the water of strength, and thereupon tears the monster in pieces;[2] the victory of the young hero must be achieved in the same way in which it is accomplished by Indras, his more splendid and grandiose impersonation. But Tritas, or *Trâitanas,* after having killed the monster of the waters, is afraid that the waters themselves may devour him; after cuting off the head of the monster, some enemies have lowered him down into the waters.[3] The sun has vanquished the monster that kept the fountain of waters shut—he has unchained the waters, but he himself has not been able to break through the cloud; he has delivered from the dark and cloudy monster the princess, the dawn that was to have been its prey, but he himself does not yet come forth—is still invisible. Now, who are the enemies here that have placed the young hero in the cistern, down into the well, in the sea? We have already seen that Tritas has two brothers; and it is these two brothers who, in a fit

[1] Vishṇus the three-faced is already spoken of in the *Ṛigvedas* and in the *Yaǵurvedas.* The third step of Vishṇus is taken among the cows with the great or many horns: Gamadhye gâvo yatra bhûri-çriñgâ ayâsaḥ atrâ 'ha tad urugâyasya vishṇoḥ paramam padam ava bhâti bhûreḥ; *Tâittiriya Yaǵurv.* i. 3, 6.

[2] *Ṛigv.* i. 187, 1, the passage already cited, when speaking of the water of strength.

[3] Na mâ garan nadyo mâtṛitamâ dâsâ yad îm susamubdham avâdhuḥ çiro yaḍ asya trâitano vitakshat; *Ṛigv.* i. 158, 5. We shall have occasion to return more than once to an analogous myth referring to Indras.

of jealousy, on account of his wife, the aurora, and the riches she brings with her from the realm of darkness, the cistern or well, detain their brother in the well,—all which is told us in a single but eloquent verse of the Vedas. The intelligent Tritas in the well calls out (*rebhati*) on account of his brothers;[1] and the two horsemen of the twilight, the Açvinâu, come to deliver the invoker (*rebhas*) covered and enveloped by the waters.[2] In another hymn, the deliverer appears to be Bṛihaspatis, the lord of prayer, who having heard how Tritas, thrust down into the well, was invoking the gods, made the large from the small;[3] that is to say, opened for the young hero a way to escape from the well and show himself in his glory.

Having seen how in the Vedic hymns Tritas, the third brother, and the ablest as well as best, is persecuted by his brothers, it is interesting to note the form of the myth in popular Hindoo tradition:—"Three brothers, *Ekatas* (*i.e.*, the first), *Dvitas* (*i.e.*, the second), and *Tritas* (*i.e.*, the third), were travelling in a desert, and distressed with thirst, came to a well, from which the youngest, Tritas, drew water and gave it to his seniors. In requital, they threw him into the well, in order to appropriate his property, and having covered the top with a cart-wheel, left him within it. In this extremity he prayed to the gods to extricate him, and by their favour he made his escape."[4]

Thus have we brought the three brothers, of whom Tritas is the youngest, into close affinity with the three

[1] Tritas tad vedâptyaḥ sa ǵâmitvâya rebhati; *Ṛigv*, i. 105, 9.—*Ǵâmitvâ* is properly the relation of brotherhood, and also relationship in general. *Rebhas*, or the invoker, represented as a hero, is no other than our *Trita âptyas*.

[2] Rebham nivṛitaṁ sitam adbhyaḥ; *Ṛigv*. i. 112, 5.

[3] Tritaḥ kûpe 'vahito devân havata ûtaye taé ćhuçrâva bṛihaspatiḥ kṛiṇvann aṅhûraṇâd uru; *Ṛigv*. i. 105, 17.

[4] *Nîtimaṅǵarî*, quoted by Wilson, *Ṛigvedas-Saṁhitâ*, vol. i.

Ṛibhavas, and both the former and the latter into an equally close connection with the three moments of Indras. We have already said that the Ṛibhavas created the cow; in the same way *Uçanâ Kâvyâs*, the desiring wise one protected by Indras, another name for the sun-hero of the morning, sends the cows together before him;[1] and Indras himself is the only lord of the cows, the only real celestial shepherd;[2] or, rather, it is he that begets the sun and the aurora,[3] or, as another hymn says, who gives the horses and the sun and the cow of abundance.[4]

Here, therefore, the aurora is explicitly the cow of abundance; she is still also the milk-giving and luminous cow, in which is found all sweetness;[5] and finally, *usrâ* or *ushâ* are two words, two appellations, which indiscriminately express aurora and cow as the red or brilliant one. The identification of the aurora with the cow, in the mythical sky of the Vedas, is therefore a certainty.

Another of the names which the milk-yielding cow assumes in the *Ṛigvedas*, besides the ordinary one of *Ushâ*, is *Sîtâ*, whom Indras also causes to descend from heaven, like the aurora, and who must be milked by the sun-god *Pûshan*,[6] the nourisher, the *fœcundator*, compared in one hymn to a pugnacious buffalo.[7] This Indras, protector and friend of Sîtâ, prepares therefore Vishṇus, the protector, in the form of Râmas, of his wife Sîtâ. And

[1] Â gâ âǵad uçanâ kâvyaḥ saćâ; *Ṛigv.* i. 83, 5.

[2] Patir gavâm abhavad eka indraḥ; *Ṛigv.* iii. 31, 4.

[3] Ǵaǵâna sûryam ushâsam; *Ṛigv.* iii. 32, 8.

[4] Sasânâtyâṅ uta sûryaṁ sasânendraḥ sasâna purubhoǵasam gâm; *Ṛigv.* iii. 34, 9.

[5] Mahi ǵyotir nihitaṁ vakshaṇâsu âmâ pakvaṁ ćarati bibhratî gâuḥ viçvaṁ svâdma sambhṛitam usriyâyâm; *Ṛigv.* iii. 30, 14.

[6] Indraḥ sîtâm ni gṛihṇâtu tâm pûshânu yaćhatu sâ naḥ payasvatî duhâm uttarâm-uttarâṁ samâm; *Ṛigv.* iv. 57, 7.

[7] Mṛidha ushṭro na; *Ṛigv.* i. 138, 2.

even the Ṛibhavas are the protectors of the cow, as well as the producers.[1]

But Indras, whose special function it is to lighten, to thunder, to fight the monster of darkness, and to prepare the light, generally figures in the popular imagination, at dawn (aurora), as the sun, under his three names of *Sûryas*, of *Ṛitas*, and of *Savitar*.

The sun, with respect to the aurora, is now the father, now the husband, now the son, and now the brother. As begotten of Indras simultaneously with the aurora, he is the brother; as following and embracing the aurora, he is the husband; as simply coming after the aurora, he is the son; and as sending the cow or the aurora before him, he is the father. These four relationships of the sun to the aurora or dawn are all mentioned in the *Ṛigvedas*.

In one of the hymns, the pure effulgence with which the aurora chases away the shadows of night is said to resemble the milk of a cow;[2] that is, the whitish light of the daybreak precedes in the eastern heavens the rosy light of aurora. The aurora is the cow-nurse, and the oriental mother of the old sun; at the sound of the hymn in praise of the dawn, the two horsemen of twilight, the Açvinâu, awaken.[3] Two cows—[*i.e.*, the two twilights, that of the evening and that of the morning, related to the two horsemen, the evening one and the morning one, whom we also find together in the morning, the one white and the other red, the one in company with daybreak and the other with the aurora, and who may

[1] Yat saṁvatsam ṛibhavo gâm arakshan yat saṁvatsam ṛibhavo mâ apiṅçan; *Ṛigv.* iv. 33, 4.

[2] Ushâ nâ râmîr aruṇâir aporṇute maho ǵyotishâ çućatâ goarṇasâ; *Ṛigv.* ii. 34, 12.

[3] Dhenuḥ pratnasya kâmyaṁ duhânântaḥ putraç ćarati dakshiṇâyâḥ-â dyotaniṁ vahati çubhrayâmoshasaḥ stomo açvinâv aǵigaḥ; *Ṛigv.* iii. 58, 1.

therefore be sometimes identified with the two morning dawns, the white dawn (alba) or daybreak, and the red dawn (aurora), and, from another point of view, the lunar dawn and the solar one]—drop milk towards the sun, in the heaven.[1] The aurora is the mother of the cows.[2]

As the sun approaches, the heavenly cows, who walk without covering themselves with dust, celebrate him[3] with songs. The red rays of the high sun fly and join themselves to the sun's cows.[4] The seven wise *Añgirasas* (the seven solar rays, or else the Angiras, the seven-rayed or seven-faced sun, as another hymn[5] represents him) celebrate in their songs the herds of cows which belong to the aurora, who appears upon the mountain.[6] Let us notice more particularly what is said of the aurora that appears with the cows upon the mountain. It is the sun that enables the Añgirasas to split the mountain, to bellow along with the cows, and to surround themselves with the splendour of the aurora.[7] The aurora, the daughter of the sky, the splendid one, appears; at the same time, the sun draws up the cows.[8] The aurora is carried by red luminous cows, whilst the

1 Ṛitâya dhenû parame duhâte; *Ṛigv.* iv. 23, 10.

2 Gavâm mâtâ; *Ṛigv.* v. 45, 2.

3 Areṇâvas tuǵa â sadman dhenavaḥ svaranti tâ uparatâti sûryam; *Ṛigv.* i. 151, 5.

4 Ud apaptann aruṇâ bhânavô vṛithâ svâyuǵo arushîr gâ ayukshata; *Ṛigv.* i. 92, 2.

5 Yenâ navagve añgire daçagve saptâsye revatî revad ûsha; *Ṛigv.* iv. 51, 4.—The sun is also said to be drawn by seven fair horses; *Ṛigv.* i. 50, 9.—Cfr. the following chapter.

6 Ta usho adrisâno gotrâ gavâm añgiraso gṛiṇanti; *Ṛigv.* vi. 65, 5.

7 Ṛiteṇâdriṁ vy asan bhidantaḥ sam añgiraso navanta gobhiḥ çûnaṁ naraḥ pari shadann ushâsam; *Ṛigv.* iv. 3, 11.

8 Praty u adarçy âyaty uǵhantî duhitâ divaḥ—Ud usriyâḥ sṛiǵate sûryaḥ saǵâ; *Ṛigv.* vii. 81, 1, 2.

sun, the hero-archer, kills the enemies.[1] The aurora breaks open the prison of the cows; the cows exult towards the aurora;[2] the aurora comes out of the darkness as cows come out of their stable.[3] As the solar hero, Indras, is the guardian or shepherd of horses and of cows,[4] so the auroras are often celebrated in the *Ṛigvedas* as *açvâvatîs* and *gomatîs*, that is, as provided with and attended by horses and cows. The aurora keeps together the herd of red cows, and always accompanies them.[5]

Thus have we passed from the pastor-hero to the pastoral heroine upon the mountain. The pastoral aurora, unveiling her body in the east, follows the path of the sun;[6] and the sun is represented to us in the following riddle as a wonderful cowherd:—"I have seen a shepherd who never set down his foot, and yet went and disappeared on the roads; and who, taking the same and yet different roads, goes round and round amidst the worlds."[7] The sun goes round in the ether, and never puts down a foot, for he has none; and he takes the same, yet different, roads in the sky, *i.e.*, luminous by day, and gloomy by night. The puzzle of the riddle lies in its self-contradiction; and the beautiful girl is the prize appointed for him who, by his actions, resolves it. A similar

1 Vahanti sîm aruṇâso ruçanto gâvaḥ subhagâm urviyâ prathânâm apeǵate çûro asteva çatrûn bâdhate; *Ṛigv.* vi. 64, 3.

2 Ruǵad drilhâni dadad usriyâṇâm prati gâva ushasaṁ vâvaçanta; *Ṛigv.* vii. 75, 7.

3 Gâvo na vraǵaṁ vy ushâ avar tamaḥ; *Ṛigv.* i. 92, 4.

4 Yo açvânâṁ yo gavâṁ gopatiḥ; *Ṛigv.* i. 101, 4.

5 Yuñkte gavâm aruṇânâm anîkam; *Ṛigv.* i. 124, 11.—Esha gobhir aruṇebhir yuǵânâ; *Ṛigv.* v. 80, 3.

6 Avishk Kṛinvânâ tanvam purastat ṛitasya panthâm anv eti; *Ṛigv.* v. 80, 4.

7 Apaçyam gopâm anipadyamânam â ća parâ ća pathibhiç ćarantaṁ sa sadhrîćîḥ sa vishûćir vasâna â varîvarti bhuvaneshv antaḥ; *Ṛigv.* x. 177, 3.

riddle is, in the *Ṛigvedas* itself, proposed to *Mitras*, the sun, and to *Varuṇas*, the night. The riddle is as follows: —"The first of them who walk afoot (*padvatînam*) comes without feet (*apâd*);" and the two divine heroes are asked, "Which of you two has guessed it?"[1] He who solves this enigma we may be sure is Mitras, the sun, who recognises the aurora, the girl who comes making use of feet, although she seem to have none, for she comes borne in a chariot, of which the wheels appear to be feet, which is the same luminous chariot that rolls well,[2] given by the Ṛibhavas to the two horsemen Açvinâu (represented sometimes as two old men made young again by the Ṛibhavas, and sometimes simply as two handsome youths), into which chariot she mounts by the help of the Açvinâu; and the daughter of the sun is, in the race, the first to come to the winning-post, amid the enthusiastic plaudits of the gods.[3] Then the hymns to the aurora sometimes represent that vast chariot as belonging to the eastern aurora, who guides a hundred chariots, and who, in turn, helps the immortal gods to ascend into the chariot beside her.[4] The aurora, as the first of those who appear every day in the eastern sky, as the first to know the break of day,[5] is naturally represented as one of the swiftest

[1] Apâd eti prathamâ padvatînâṁ kas tad vâm ćiketa; *Ṛigv.* i. 152, 3.

[2] Ratham ye ćakruḥ suvṛitam; *Ṛigv.* iv. 33, 8.—Takshan nâsatyâbhyâm pariǵmânaṁ sukhaṁ ratham; *Ṛigv.* i. 20, 3.

[3] Yuvo rathaṁ duhitâ sûryasya saha çriyâ nâsatyâvṛiṇîta; *Ṛigv.* i. 117, 13.—Â vâm rathaṁ duhitâ sûryasya kârshmevâtishṭhad arvatâ ǵayantî viçve devâ anv amanyanta hṛidbhih; *Ṛigv.* i. 116, 17.

[4] Yuktvâ ratham upa devân ayâtana; *Ṛigv.* i. 161, 7.—Pṛithû ratho dakshiṇâyâ ayogy âenam devâso amṛitâso asthuḥ; *Ṛigv.* i. 123, 1.—Devî ǵirâ rathânâm; *Ṛigv.* i. 48, 3.—Çataṁ rathebhiḥ subhagoshâ iyaṁ vi yâty abhi mânushân; *Ṛigv.* i. 48, 7.

[5] Ǵânaty ahnaḥ prathamasya; *Ṛigv.* i. 123, 9.

among those who are the guests of the sun-prince during the night; and like her cows, which do not cover themselves with dust (this being an attribute which, in the Indian faith, distinguishes the gods from mortals, for the former walk in the heavens, and the latter upon earth), she, in her onward flight, leaves no footsteps behind her. The word *apâd* (*pad* and *pada*, being synonymous) may, indeed, mean not only she who has no feet, but also she who has no footsteps (that is, what is the measure of the foot), or, again, she who has no slippers, the aurora having, as appears, lost them; for the prince Mitras, while following the beautiful young girl, finds a slipper which shows her footstep, the measure of her foot, a foot so small, that no other woman has a foot like it, an almost unfindable, almost imperceptible foot, which brings us back again to the idea of her who has no feet. The legend of the lost slipper, and of the prince who tries to find the foot predestined to wear it, the central interest in the popular story of Cinderella, seems to me to repose entirely upon the double meaning of the word *apâd*, *i.e.*, who has no feet, or what is the measure of the foot, which may be either the footstep or the slipper; often, moreover, in the story of Cinderella, the prince cannot overtake the fugitive, because a chariot bears her away.

The word *apâd*, which we have heretofore seen applied to the heroine, was applied, moreover, to the hero, giving rise to another popular legend, of which the *Ṛigvedas* offers us the mythical elements. We have already seen the sun as *anipadyamanas*, *i.e.*, the sun who never puts his foot down; but this sun who never puts down his foot easily, came to be conceived of and represented as a sun without feet, or as a lame hero, who, during the night, by the perfidy of the witch, the dusk of evening, became also blind. In one hymn, the blind and the lame are not one, but two, whom propitious Indras guides;[1] in another, the blind-lame is one person, with the name of *Pâravṛig*, whom the two horsemen Açvinâu, the two friends of the dawn, enable to walk and to see.[2] The lame one who sees, shows the way to the blind who is able to walk, or the lame carries the blind; Indras, the hidden sun, guides the blind and the lame; or, the blind and the lame, lost in the forest, help each other; in the morning, the Açvinâu, the two horsemen, friends of the aurora, with the water of sight and of strength (that is, Páravṛig, the blind-lame having discovered the hidden fountain of the young girls of the dawn,[3] with the ambrosia of the aurora, with the aurora itself), make the blind see, and him who has no feet, the lame, walk; that is, they burst forth into the upper air again, transfigured now into the luminous sun who sets out on his heavenly voyage. I have said above that the hero becomes blind and lame through the perfidy and magic of the evening aurora: nor was the assertion unfounded; for the Vedic hymn in which Indras guides the blind and the lame, *i.e.*, himself or the sun, in the gloomy tardy night, is the very same hymn in which is celebrated his heroic and manly enterprise of the destruction of the daughter of the sky. The sun Indras revenges himself in the morn-

[1] Anu dvâ ǵahitâ nayo 'ndhaṁ çroṇaṁ ća vṛitrahan; *Ṛigv.* iv. 30, 19.

[2] Sakhâbhûd açvinor ushâḥ; *Ṛigv.* iv. 52, 2.—Parâvṛiǵam prandhaṁ çroṇaṁ ćakshasa etave kṛithaḥ; *Ṛigv.* i. 112, 8.—I here explicitly abandon the hypothesis I advanced six years ago in the "Life and Miracles of the God Indras in the Ṛigvedas," pp. 22 and 24, to the effect that the hero Pâravṛiǵ is the lightning flashing from the dark cloud; whereas the blind-lame seems now to me the sun in the darkness of night or winter.

[3] Sa vidvâṅ apagohaṁ kanînâm âvir bhavann udatishṭhat parâvṛik prati çronaḥ sthâd vy aṇag aćashṭa; *Ṛigv.* ii. 15, 7.

ing upon the aurora of the morning, for the wrong done him by the aurora of the evening, beautiful, but faithless.

For the aurora counts among her other talents that of magic; when the Ṛibhavas created the aurora cow of morning, investing her with the skin of the aurora cow of evening, they endowed her with Protean qualities (*Viçvarûpâm*), and on this account the aurora herself is also called witch or enchantress (*Mâjinî*).[1] This aurora, this virago, this Amazon, this Vedic Medea, who, treacherously plunging her husband, or brother, the solar hero, into a fiery furnace, blinds and lames him, is punished in the morning for her crime of the evening. The hero vanquishes her, overcomes her incantations, and annihilates her. The Vedic hymn sings—"A manly and heroic undertaking thou hast accomplished, O Indras, for an evil-doing woman, the daughter of the heavens, thou hast smitten; the growing daughter of the heaven, the aurora, O Indras, thou hast destroyed; from the chariot, broken in pieces, fell the aurora, trembling, because the bull had struck her."[2] Here the mythical animal reappears on the same stage with the heroes, and for the image of the hero and the heroine there is substituted that of the cow and the bull.[3]

The sun and the aurora, therefore, do not always seek each other from promptings of affection only, nor is the hateful part always played by the aurora. The sun, also appears as a perverse persecutor in his turn.

[1] *Ṛigv.* v. 48, 1.

[2] Etad ghed uta vîryam indra ćakartha pâuṅsyam striyaṁ yad durhaṇâ yuvaṁ vadhîr duhitaram divaḥ divaç ćid ghâ duhitaram mahân mahîyamânâm ushâsam indra sam piṇak aposhâ anasaḥ sarat sampishṭâd aha bibhyushî ni yat sîm çiçnathad vṛishâ; *Ṛigv.* iv. 30, 8-11.

[3] The two arms of Indras are said to vanquish the cow (or the cows); Goǵitâ bahû; *Ṛigv.* i. 102, 6.

One Vedic hymn advises the aurora not to stretch out the web she works at too far, lest the sun, like a robber, with hostile intention, set fire to and burn her.[1] Another hymn tells us that the handsome one follows the beautiful one, the brother the sister, like a lover,[2]—the aurora fleeing from the sun, her brother, out of shame, and her brother following her, actuated by a brutal instinct. Finally, a third hymn shows us the Vedic Vulcan, the blacksmith of the gods, the sun Tvashṭar, called also the omniform sun (*Sâvitâ Viçvarûpah*), as father of Saraṇyû, another name for the aurora, omniform herself, like her father (and, like the cow, undergoing the triple transmutation at the hands of Tvashṭar, *i.e.*, the three brothers, the Ṛibhavas), creating another form of himself, that is, the sun *Vivasvant*, to be able to espouse the aurora. Saraṇyû, perceiving perhaps that Vivasvant is her father under another shape, creates another woman like herself, and flees away on the chariot that flies of itself, and that was before given her by her father; and thereupon Vivasvant, in order to overtake her, transforms himself into a horse.[3]

But sometimes the alienation the sun and the aurora, the young husband and wife, is not due to evil propensities in themselves, but the decree of fate working through the machinations of monsters. The two beautiful ones are at bottom united by love and reciprocal gratitude; for now it is the sun who delivers the aurora, and now the aurora

[1] Vy ućhâ duhitar divo mâ ćiraṁ tanuthâ apaḥ net tvâ stenaṁ yathâ ripuṁ tapâti sûro arćishâ; *Ṛigv.* v. 79, 9.—Cfr. the chapter which treats of the Spider.

[2] Bhadro bhadrayâ saćamâna âgât svasâraṁ ǵâro abhy eti paçćat; *Ṛigv.* x. 3, 3.

[3] Cfr. *Ṛigv.* x. 17, and Max Müller's "Lectures on the Science of Language," second series, 481–486.

who liberates the sun; and we have already seen the aurora making the ambrosial milk drop for the sun from her cows, and the sun drawing up and delivering the cows of the aurora. There is a hymn in which the divine girl, the aurora, comes up in the east, with a lascivious air, smiling, fresh, uncovering her bosom, resplendent, towards the god who sacrifices himself,[1] that is to say, towards the sun, towards *Çunahçepas* (the sun), who, in three verses of another hymn,[2] invokes her, the well-known legend of which, narrated in the *Âitareya-Brâhmaṇam*, I shall briefly relate. The aurora has also the merit of having, with her pure and purifying light, opened the gates of the gloomy cavern, discomfited the enemies, the shades of night, and exposed to view the treasures hidden by the darkness (and here we have Medea again, but this time in a benignant form); she awakens to activity the sleepers and everything with life (and therefore, among the living sleepers, the sun, her son, whom one of the hymns represents as sleeping profoundly in the bosom of the darkness of night); she is the saviour of mortals,[3] that is to say, she protects mortals from death, and resuscitates them; she sees and foresees everything.[4] The awakener is also the awakened; the illu-

---

1 Kanyeva tanvâ çâçadânâṅ (arepasâ tanvâ çâçadânâ; *Ṛigv.* i. 124, 6), eshi devi devam iyakshamâṇam saṁsmayamânâ yuvatiḥ purastâd âvir vakshâṅsi kṛiṇushe vibhâtî; *Ṛigv.* i. 123, 10.

2 *Ṛigv.* i. 30, 20-22.

3 Vy û vraǵasya tamaso dvâroćhantîr avran ćhućayaḥ pâvakâḥ; *Ṛigv.* iv. 51, 2.—Apa dvesho bâdhamânâ tamâṅsy ushâ divo duhitâ ǵyotishâgât; *Ṛigv.* v. 80, 5.—Spârhâ vasûni tamasâpagûḻhâ âvish kṛiṇvanty ushaso vibhâtîḥ; *Ṛigv.* i. 123, 6.—Sasato bodhayantî; *Ṛigv.* i. 124, 4.—Viçvaṁ ǵivaṁ ćarase bodhayantî; *Ṛigv.* i. 92, 9.—Martyatrâ; *Ṛigv.* i. 123, 3.

4 Viçvâni devî bhuvanâbhićakshyâ; *Ṛigv.* i. 92, 6.—Praǵânatî; *Ṛigv.* i. 124, 3.

minator is also the illumined, or the wise; and the illumined or luminous one is also the beautiful one. From being small, she is become large[1] (the heroes and heroines of mythology are only small at birth, and pass at once into fulness of stature); from being infirm and sombre-visaged, by the grace of Indras and of the Açvinâu, she is cured and restored to strength and clearness.[2] But why was she dark at first? Because her mother, the night, is the black one; she, the white one, is born of the black one.[3]

During the night, the young girl was blind, and she recovers her sight by the grace of a wise one, one who, protected by Indras, another shape of Indras, has become enamoured of her. We have seen above that it is the Açvinâu who, with the aurora, give back to the sun his sight; here it is the sun who makes the aurora see, it is the sun who gives her light; and she who, having been blind, recovers her sight, becomes the protectress of the blind and preserver of vision,[4] like St Lucia, virgin and martyr, in the Christian Mythology. Physical truth and the mythical narration are in perfect accordance.

The night is now the mother, now the sister of the aurora; but the gloomy night is sometimes her step-mother, sometimes her half-sister. There is a riddle which celebrates the luminous night and the aurora, as two diversely beautiful ones who go together, but of whom

---

[1] Arbhâd îshate na maho vibhâtî; *Ṛigv.* i. 124, 6.

[2] As to Ghoshâ, cured by the Açvinâu (*Ṛigv.* i. 117, 7), and Apalâ, cured by Indras (*Ṛigv.* viii. 80), see the same subject discussed more in detail in the chapter which treats of the Hog.

[3] Çukrâ krishṇâd aǵanishṭa çvitîćî; *Ṛigv.* i. 123, 9.

[4] Yasyânakshâ duhitâ ǵâtvâsa kas tâṁ vidvâṅ abhi manyâte andhâm kataro menim prati tam mućâte ya îm vahâte ya îm vâ vareyât; *Ṛigv.* x. 27,11.—Vṛitrasya kanînikâ 'si ćakshushpâ asi; *Tâittir. Yagurv.* i. 2, 1.

one goes while the other comes.[1] Another hymn sings of them thus: "The brilliantly-decked one approaches, the white aurora comes; the black one prepares for her her rooms. The one immortal having joined the other, the two appear alternately in the heavens. One and eternal is the path of the two sisters; they follow it, one after the other, guided by the gods; they do not meet, and they never stand still—the two good nurses, night and aurora, one in soul yet different in form."[2] The two good nurses, night and aurora, whose hues alternate eternally, nourish between them one and the same child (the sun).[3] But the *Ṛigvedas* itself tells us that the night is not always the legitimate sister of the aurora; the latter "abandons now the one that is, now the one that is not, properly its sister."[4] Here probably we must understand by the proper sister of the aurora the luminous or moonlight night, and by the half-sister, the gloomy night, the night without a moon. This is the sister whom, in a hymn, the aurora removes, sends far away from her, while she shines to be seen of her husband;[5] and her half-sister, the night, is obliged to resign her place to her elder or better sister,[6] the word *ǵyeshṭhas* meaning not only the eldest, but the

---

1 Apânyad ety abhy anyad eti vishurûpe ahanî saṁ ćarete; *Ṛigv.* i. 123, 7.

2 Ruçadvatsâ ruçatî çvetyâgâd ârâig u kṛishṇâ sadanâny asyâḥ samânabandhû amṛite anûćî dyâvâ varṇaṁ ćarata âminâne samâno adhvâ svasror anantas tam anyânyâ ćarato devaçishṭe na methete na tasthatuḥ sumeke naktoshâsa samanasâ virûpe; *Ṛigv.* i. 113, 2, 3.

3 Naktoshâsâ varṇam âmemyâne dhâpayete çiçum ekaṁ samîćî; *Ṛigv.* i. 96, 5.

4 Nâǵâmiṁ na pari vṛiṇakti ǵâmim; *Ṛigv.* i. 124, 6.

5 Vyûrṇvatî divo antân abodhy apa svasâraṁ sanutar yuyoti praminatî manushyâ yugâni yoshâ ǵarasya ćakshasâ vi bhâti; *Ṛigv.* i. 92, 11.

6 Svasâ svasre ǵyâyasyâi yonim ârâik; *Ṛigv.* i. 124, 8.

best. We have already seen that the aurora is the first to appear; as such, and as she who in the evening precedes the night (the evening aurora), she is the first-born, the eldest, the most experienced, the best; while, from another point of view, she is represented to us as the little one who becomes great, and, in this case, as younger sister of the night (the morning dawn). The dawns, or auroras, are saluted with the epithet of workwomen,[1] just as the good sister, with respect to the bad one, is always she who works, doing wonderful work, that is, spinning or weaving the rosy cloth. But the auroras are not only the workers, they are also the pure purifying and cleansing ones;[2] hence one can understand how one of the tasks imposed upon the youngest sister was that of purifying, purging, or separating the grain during the night, taking from it all that is impure, in which task she is assisted sometimes by a good fairy, sometimes by the Virgin Mary, who, according to all probability, is the moon.

One of the singular qualities of the younger sister is that she displays her beauty only before the eyes of her husband. The wife aurora manifests herself in the sight of her husband;[3] united, in her splendour, with the rays of the sun,[4] like a wife she prepares the dwelling of the sun.[5] Very brilliant, like a wife cleansed by her mother, she uncovers her body;[6] like a bather who shows

---

[1] Nârîr apasaḥ; *Ṛigv.* i. 92, 3.

[2] Çućayaḥ pâvakâh; *Ṛigv.* iv. 51, 2.

[3] Yoshâ ǵârasya ćakshasâ vibhâti; *Ṛigv.* quoted above, i. 92, 11.

[4] Yatamânâ raçmibhiḥ sûryasya; *Ṛigv.* i. 123, 12.—Vyućhantî raçmibhiḥ sûryasya; *Ṛigv.* i. 124, 8.

[5] Ritasya yoshâ na minâti dhâma; *Ṛigv.* i. 123, 9.

[6] Susaṁkâçâ mâtṛimṛishṭeva yoshâvis tanvaṁ kriṇushe dṛiçe kam; *Ṛigv.* i. 123, 11.

herself, the shining one unveils her body;[1] she adorns herself like a dancer, uncovering, like a cow, her breast;[2] she displays her luminous garments;[3] all-radiant, with beautiful face, she laughs;[4] and he who has made the aurora laugh, her, the beautiful princess, who, at first, that is, during the night, did not laugh, espouses her; the sun espouses the aurora.

The celestial nuptials take place, and the ceremony is minutely described in the 85th hymn of the 10th book of the *Ṛigvedas.* But the marriage of the two celestials is never consummated except under conditions; these conditions are always accepted and afterwards forgotten, and it is now the husband who, by forsaking his wife, now the wife who, by abandoning her husband, violates the promise given. One of these estrangements, these temporary alienations of husband and wife, is described in the *Ṛigvedas* by the poetical myth of the dawn *Urvaçî* and her husband *Purûravas,* one of the names given to the sun. Urvaçî says of herself, "I have arrived like the first of the auroras;"[5] thereupon Urvaçî suddenly abandons her husband Purûravas, because he breaks an agreement made between them. We shall see further on in this chapter what this agreement was. Besides, having given him a son before her departure, she consoles him by permitting him to come and find her again in heaven, that is, by endowing the sun with the immortality she possesses herself. In the morning the aurora precedes

---

1 Eshâ çubhrâ na tanvo vidânordhveva snâtî dṛiçaye no asthât; *Ṛigv.* v. 80, 5.

2 Adhi peçâṅsi vapate nṛitûr ivâporṇute vaksha usreva barǵaham; *Ṛigv.* i. 92, 4.

3 Bhadrâ vastrâ tanvate; *Ṛigv.* i. 134, 4.

4 Smayate vibhâtî supratîkâ; *Ṛigv.* i. 92, 6.

5 Prâkramisham ushasâm agriyeva; *Ṛigv.* x. 95, 2.

the sun; he follows her too closely, and she disappears, but leaves a son, *i.e.*, the new sun. In the evening the aurora precedes the sun; he follows her again, and she loses herself, now in a forest, now in the sea. The same phenomenon, a divorce of husband from wife, or a separation of brother and sister, or the flight of a sister from her brother, or again, that of a daughter from her father, presents itself twice every day (and every year) in the sky. Sometimes, on the other hand, it is a witch, or the monster of nocturnal darkness, who takes the place of the radiant bride, or the aurora, near the sun; and in that case the aurora, the beauteous bride, is spirited away into a wood to be killed or thrown into the sea, from both of which predicaments, however, she always escapes. Sometimes the witch of night throws the brother and sister, the mother and son, the sun and the aurora, together into the waves of the sea, whence they both escape again, to reappear in the morning.

All these alternative variations of a mythical representation become each in turn a legend by itself, as we shall see again more in detail, when the study of the different animals that take part in them shall furnish us with opportunities of doing so. In the meantime, we have here finished our enumeration of all that in the hymns of the *Ṛigvedas* refers in any way to the bull and the cow,—to the wind, moon, and sun bulls, to the cow-cloud, moon, spring and aurora,—leaving it, however, to be understood how natural it is to pass from the bull to the handsome hero-prince, and from the cow to the beautiful girl, the rich princess, the valiant heroine, or the wise fairy. For though in the mythical hymns of the *Ṛigvedas* we have little more than hints or foreshadows of the many popular legends which we have thus referred to, often without naming them, these are so many and so precise that it seems to me to be almost impossible not to recognise them. To demonstrate this, however, it will be necessary for me to show further what form the mythological ideas and figures relating to the animals dispersed in the Vedic hymns afterwards assumed in the Hindoo traditions.

SECTION II.

The Worship of the Bull and of the Cow in India, and the Brâhmanic Legends relating to it.

SUMMARY.

The princes called bulls.—The bull the symbol of the god Çivas.—The cow was not to be killed.—Exchange of the bull and the cow for other animals; the bull and the cow, considered as the greatest reward desired by the legislating priests of India.—The cow's hide in nuptial usages a symbol of abundance; its elasticity and power of extension; the cow and its hide during the pregnancy of women an augury of happy birth, and in funeral ceremonies an augury of resurrection.—Cows sent to pasture with auguries.—Cows seen by night in a dream are a sinister omen; meaning of this Hindoo superstition.—The black cow which produces white milk in the Vedic hymns.—The reins of the cow or black goat sacrificed in funerals given as a viaticum or provision to the dead man, that they may contribute to his resurrection.—The variegated cow comes again in a brâhmaṇam, and is interpreted as a cloud.—The coming out of the cow-dawns feasted.—The cornucopia.—The milk of the cows is the serpent's poison.—The salutary herb.—The enchanted gem, the ring of recognition.—The moon, as a female, a good fairy who works for the aurora, and who entertains and guides the hero.—The moon, as a male, a white bull.—The city of the moon.—Indras consoles and nourishes the unhappy Sîtâ.—Râmas assimilated to Indras.—The coadjutors of Râmas are those of Indras.—The bull Râmas.—The names of the monsters and the names of the heroes in the Râmâyaṇam.—Râmas, the Hindoo Xerxes, chastises the sea.—The celestial ocean; the cloud-mountains carried by the heroes; the bridge across the sea made of these mountains; while the bridge is being made, it rains.—The battle of Râmas is a winter and a nocturnal one, in a cloudy sky.—The monster barrel again; the monster trunk with a cavity; Kabandhas.—The dying monster thanks the hero, who delivers him from an ancient malediction, and becomes again a handsome luminous youth.—The dawn Sîtâ sacrificed in the fire.—Sîtâ daughter of the sun.—The Buddhist legend of Râmas and Sîtâ.—Sîtâ predestined as the reward of valour.—An indiscretion of the husband Râmas causes him to lose his wife Sîtâ.—The story of Urvaçî again, the first of the auroras; the wife flees because her husband has revealed her secret, because her husband has looked at another woman, because he has let himself be seen naked; the fugitive wife hides herself in a plant.—The wife stays with her husband as long as he says nothing displeasing to her.—The wife kills her sons; the husband complains and the wife flees.—The contrary.—The story of Çunaḥçepas again.—The god Varuṇas, who binds; the son sacrificed to the monster against his will by his father.—The hero-hunter.—The middle son sold, the son of the cow.—The cow herself, Aditi, or Çabalâ, or Kâmadhuk, wife of Vasishṭas, sacrificed instead of the son of Viçvâmitras.—Indras delivers the bound hero, *i.e.*, he delivers himself. The aurora, or the daughter of the black one, liberates Çunaḥçepas, bound by the black one, that is, she delivers the sun her husband.—The fetters of Varuṇas and of Aǵigartas are equivalent to the bridle of the horse and to the collar of the dog sold to the demon in European fairy tales.—The golden palace of Varuṇas on the western mountain.—Monstrous fathers.—Identification of Hariçćandras, Aǵigartas, and Viçvâmitras.—The contention of Viçvâmitras and Vasishṭas for the possession of the cow Çabalâ.—Demoniacal character of Viçvâmitras.—The sister of the monster-lover or seducer of the hero.—The cloud drum.—The cloudy monster Dundubhis, in the form of a buffalo with sharpened horns, destroyed by the son of Indras.—The buffalo a monster, the bull a hero.—Krishṇas the monster becomes a god.—The god Indras fallen for having killed a brâhman monster.—The three heads of the monster cut off at a blow.—The three brothers in the palace of Lañkâ; the eldest brother has the royal dignity; the second, the strong one, sleeps, and only wakens to eat and prove his strength; the third is good and is victorious.—The three brothers Pâṇdavas, sons of Yamas, Vâyus and Indras in the Mahâbhâratam; the first is wise, the second is strong, the third is handsome and victorious; he is the best.—Again the three working brothers entertained by a king.—The three disciples of Dhâumyas.—The blind one who falls into the well.—The voyage of Utañkas to hell.—He meets a bull.—The excrement of the bull, ambrosia.—The stone uplifted with the help of the lever, of the thunderbolt of Indras.—The earrings of the queen carried off; their mythical meaning.—Indras and Kṛishṇas also search for the earrings.—The three Buddhist brothers.—The eldest brother frees the younger ones by his knowledge in questions and riddles.—The hero and the monster ill or vulnerable in their feet.—The two rival sisters.—The good sister thrown into the well by the wicked one.—The prince comes to deliver her.—The wicked sister takes the place of the good one.—The three brothers again.—The sons make their father and mother recognise each other.—The third brother, Pûrus, the only good one, assists his aged father Yayâtis, by taking his old age upon himself.—The old blind man, Dîrghatamas, thrown into the water by his sons.—Yayâtis and Dîrghatamas, Hindoo King Lears.—The queen Sudeshnâ makes her maid or foster-sister take her place; a Hindoo form of Queen Berta.—The blind and the crooked or lame, or hunchbacked, again with the three-breasted princess.—They cure each other.—The bride disputed by the brothers.—The aurora and the sun flee from each other.—The beautiful girl, the daughter of the sun, flees after having seen the prince upon the mountain.—The prince cannot overtake her; the third time, at last, the prince marries the daughter of the sun.—The marvellous cow of Vasishṭhas.—The hero Vasishṭhas wishes to kill himself, but cannot; he is immortal; he throws himself down from the mountain and does not hurt himself; he goes through fire and is not burnt; he throws himself into the water and does not drown; mythical signification of these prodigies.—The wind runs after women.—Conclusion of the study of the myth and of the legends which refer to the bull and the cow of India.

Just as the importance of the cattle to primitive and pastoral Aryan life explains the propensity of the Aryan mind to conceive of the mobile phenomena of the heavens, at first considered living beings, as bulls and cows, so the consecration of these animals, associated and identified with the celestial phenomena and the gods, naturally gave rise to the superstitious worship of the bull and the cow, common to all the Aryan nations, but particularly, through the intervention of the brâhmanic priests, to the Hindoos.

It is a remarkable fact that the words *ṛishas, ṛishabhas,* and *ṛishabhas,* which mean the bull as the one who pours out, the *fœcundator,* is often used in Sanscrit to denote the best, the first, the prince; and hence the bull, that is to say, the best *fœcundator,* is in India the most sacred symbol of royalty. For this reason the phallic and destroying god, the royal *Çivas,* who inhabits *Gokarṇas* (a word which properly means cow's ear), has both for his steed and his emblem a brâhmanic bull, *i.e.*, a bull with a hunch on its back; the *nandin,* or joyful attribute, being given to Çivas himself, inasmuch as, being the *Deus phallicus,* he is the god of joyfulness and beatitude.[1]

Still more honour is paid to the cow (like the Vedic dawn *anavadyâ,* innocent or inculpable[2]), which therefore it was a crime to kill.[3] An interesting chapter of the *Âitareya-brâhmaṇam,*[4] on the sacrifice of animals, shows us how, next to man, the horse was the supreme sacrifice offered to the gods; how the cow afterwards took the place of the horse; the sheep, of the cow; the goat, of the sheep; and, at last, vegetable products were substituted for animals;—a substitution or cheating of the gods in the sacrifice, which, perhaps, serves to explain even more the fraud of which, in popular stories, the simpleton is

[1] I must, however, observe that competent authorities, such as Professor Weber, consider the phallical worship of Çivas to have originated in the beliefs of the indigenous tribes of Dravidian race.

[2] *Ṛigv.* i. 123, 8.

[3] Vidique saepe, sed cumprimis anno 1785 in Malabaria ad flumen templo celebri Ambalapushe proximum, extra oppidum Callureàta in silvula, sententia regis Travancoridis Ráma Varmer, quinque viros arbori appensos et morti traditos, quod, contra regni leges et religionis præscripta, voluntarie unicam vaccam occiderint; *Systema Brahmanicum,* illustr. Fr. Paullinus a S. Bartholomæo, Romæ, 179.—Cfr. *Mânava-Dharmaçâstram,* xi. 60, and *Yâgńavalkya-Dharmaçâstram,* iii. 234.

[4] ii. 1, 8.

always the victim ; the simpleton here being the god himself, and the cheater man, who changes, under a sacred pretext, the noblest and most valued animals for common and less valuable ones, and finally for vegetables apparently of no value whatever. In the Hindoo codes of law we have the same fraudulent substitution of animals under a legal pretext. "The killer of a cow," says the code attributed to *Yâǵńavalkyas*,[1] "must stay a month in penitence, drinking the *pańćagavyam* (*i.e.*, the five good productions of the cow, which, according to Manus,[2] are milk, curds, butter, urine, and dung), sleeping in a stable and following the cows ; and he must purify himself by the gift of another cow." Thus, according to *Yâǵńavalkya*,[3] the killer of a parrot is purified by giving a two-year-old calf ; the killer of a crane by giving a calf three years old ; the killer of an ass, a goat, or a sheep, by the gift of a bull ; the killer of an elephant by the gift of five black bulls (*nîlavṛishâp*). And one need not be astonished to find these contracts (which remind one of that between Jacob and Laban) in the Hindoo codes of law, when, in the Vedic hymns themselves, a poet offers to sell to whoever will buy it, an Indras of his, that is to say, a bull, for ten cows.[4] Another interesting verse of *Yâǵńavalkyas*[5] tells us they die pure who are killed by lightning or in battle for the sake of the cows or the brâhmans. The cow was often the object heroes fought for in heaven ; the Brâhman wished to be the object heroes should fight for upon earth.

[1] Pańćagavyaṁ piban goghno mâsam âsîta saṁyataḥ goshṭreçayo go 'nugâmî gopradânena çudhyati ; *Dharm.* iii. 263.

[2] *Dharm.* xi. 166.

[3] Ibid. iii. 271.

[4] Ka imaṁ daçabhir mamendraṁ krîṇâti dhenubhiḥ ; *Ṛigv.* iv. 24, 10.

[5] *Dharm.* iii. 27.

We learn from the domestic ceremonies referred to by *Gṛihyasûtrâni* with how much respect the bull and the cow were treated as the symbols of abundance in a family. In *Âçvalâyanas,*[1] we find the bull's hide stretched out near the nuptial hearth, the wife seated upon it, and the husband, touching his wife, saying, "May the lord of all creatures allow us to have children;" —words taken from the Vedic nuptial hymn.[2] We have seen above how the Ṛibhavas, from the hide of a dead cow, formed a new and beautiful one, or, in other words, how, from the dusk of evening, by stretching it in the night, they formed the dawn of morning. This cow's hide plays also an important *rôle* in the popular faith; an extraordinary elasticity is attributed to it, a power of endless expansibility, and for this reason it is adopted as a symbol of fecundity, upon which the wife must place herself in order to become a mother of children. The cow's hide (*goćarman*), in the *Mahâbhâratam,*[3] is the garment of the god Vishṇus; and the goćarman divided into thongs, and afterwards fastened to each other, served formerly in India to measure the circumference of a piece of ground;[4] hence the cow's hide suggested the idea of a species of infinity. Further on we shall find it put to extraordinary uses in western legend; we find it even in the hymns of the Vedic age used to cover the body of a dead man, the fire being invoked not to consume it, almost as if the cow's hide had the virtue of resuscitating the dead.[5]

---

[1] *Gṛihyasûtrâṇi*, i. 8, 9.—It was, moreover, on the occasion of a marriage, the custom to give cows to the Brâhmans; in the *Râmâyaṇam*, i. 74, the King Daçarathas, at the nuptials of his four sons, gives 400,000 cows.

[2] Â naḥ praǵâm ǵanayatu praǵâpatiḥ; *Ṛigv.* x. 85, 43.

[3] Goćarmavasano hariḥ; xiii. 1228.

[4] Cfr. Böhtlingk u. Roth's, *Sanskrit Wörterbuch* s. v. *goćarman.*

[5] Âçvalây. *Gṛihyasû.* iv. 3.

The cow, being the symbol of fruitfulness, was also the companion of the wife during pregnancy. *Âçvalâyaṇas*[1] tells us how, in the third month, the husband was to give his wife to drink of the sour milk of a cow that has a calf like itself, and in it two beans and a grain of barley; the husband was then to ask his wife three times, "What drinkest thou?" and she was to answer three times: "The generation of males." In the fourth month, the wife, according to *Âçvalâyaṇas*, was to put herself again upon the bull's hide, near the fire of sacrifice, when they again invoked the god *Praǵâpatis*, lord of all creatures, or of procreation; the moon, like a celestial bull and cow, was invited to be present at the generation of men;[2] and a bull, during the Vedic period, was the gift which sufficed for the priest. In the Vedic antiquity, neither bulls nor cows were allowed to go to pasture without some special augury, which, in the domestic ceremonials of *Âçvalâyaṇas*,[3] has been also handed down to us; the cows were to give milk and honey, for the strength and increase of whoever possessed them. Here we have again the cows not only as the beneficent, but as the strong ones, they who help the hero or the heroine who takes them to pasture.

But although beautiful cows, when seen by day, are a sign of good luck, seen in dreams they are of evil omen; for in that case they are of course the black cows, the shadows of night, or the gloomy waters of the nocturnal

---

[1] *Gṛihyasû.* i. 13.—The commentator *Nârâyaṇas*, quoted by Professor Stenzler, in his version of *Âçvalâyanas*, explains how the two beans and grain of barley express by their form the male organs of generation.

[2] *Gṛihyasû.* i. 14.

[3] *Gṛihyasû.* ii. 10.—The St Antony, protector of animals, of the Vedic faith was the god Rudras, the wind, to whom, when the cattle were afflicted by a disease, it was necessary to sacrifice in the midst of an enclosure of cows.—Cfr. the same, *Âçvalây.* iv. 8.

ocean. Already in the *Ṛigvedas*, the dawn, or the luminous cow, comes to deliver the fore-mentioned solar hero, Tritas Aptyas, from the evil sleep which he sleeps amidst the cows[1] of night. *Âçvalâyaṇas*, in his turn, recommends us when we have an evil dream, to invoke the sun, to hasten the approach of the morning, or, better still, to recite the hymn of five verses to the dawn which we have already referred to, and which begins with the words, "And like an evil dream amidst the cows." Here the belief is not yet an entirely superstitious one; and we understand what is meant by the cows who envelop us in the sleep of night, when we are told to invoke the sun and the dawn to come and deliver us from them.

A cow (probably a black one), often a black goat, was sometimes also sacrificed in the funeral ceremonies of the Hindoos, as if to augur that, just as the black cow, night, produces the milky humours of the aurora, or is fruitful, so will he who has passed through the kingdom of darkness rise again in the world of light. We have already seen the black night as the mother of the white and luminous aurora; I quote below yet another Vedic sentence, in which a poet ingenuously wonders why the cows of Indras, the black ones as well as the light-coloured (the black clouds, as well as the white and red ones), should both yield white milk.[2] And even the gloomy nocturnal kingdom of Yamas, the god of the dead, has its cows of black appearance, which are nevertheless milk-yielding; and thus the black cow of the funeral sacrifices comes to forebode resurrection.

---

[1] Yać ća goshu dushvapnyaṁ yać ćâsme duhitar divaḥ tritâya tad vibhâvary âptyâya parâ vahânehaso va ûtayaḥ suûtayo va ûtayaḥ; *Ṛigv.* viii. 47, 14.

[2] Payaḥ kṛishṇâsu ruçad rohiṇîshu; *Ṛigv.* i. 62, 9.—Cfr. *Ṛigv.* i. 123, 9.

In the same way the viaticum, or provision of food for his journey, given to the dead man is a symbol of his resurrection. The journey being considered as a short one, the provision of food which is to sustain the traveller to the kingdom of the dead is limited, and each dead hero carries it with him, generally not so much for himself, as to ensure a passage into the kingdom of the dead. For this reason we read, even in the domestic ceremonials of *Âçvalâyaṇas,* that it is recommended to put into the hands of the dead man,[1] what is the greatest symbol of strength, the reins of the animal killed in the funeral sacrifice (or, in default of an animal victim, at least two cakes of rice or of flour), in order that the dead man may throw them down the throats of the two Cerberi, the two sons of the bitch *Saramâ,* so that they may let the deceased enter scatheless into the death-kingdom, the mysterious kingdom of Yamas; and here we find the monster of the popular tales, into whose house the hero, having passed through many dangers, enters, by the advice of a good fairy or of a good old man, giving something to appease the hunger of the two dogs who guard its gate.

They who return from the funeral must touch the stone of Priapus, a fire, the excrement of a cow,[2] a grain of barley, a grain of sesame and water,—all symbols of that fecundity which the contact with a corpse might have destroyed.

The Vedic hymns have shown us the principal mythical aspects and functions of the cow and the bull; we have also seen how the brâhmanic codes confirmed, by the sanction of law, the worship of these animals, and how jealously the domestic tradition of the Hindoos has

[1] *Gṛihyasû.* iv. 3.

[2] Âçvalây; *Gṛihyasû.*

guarded it. Let us now see from the *Âitareya-brâhmaṇam*, how the Brâhmans themselves, those of the era immediately following that of the Vedâs, interpreted the myth of the cow.

We have recognised in the Vedic heavens, as reflected in the hymns of the *Ṛigvedas*, three cows—the cow-cloud, the cow-moon, and the cow-aurora. These three cows, and especially the first and the third, are also quite distinct from one another in the *Âitareya-brâhmaṇam*.

It tells us how the *gâuh pṛiçnih*, the variegated cow, or spotted cow, of the *Ṛigvedas*, must be celebrated to make the earth fruitful[1] (or that one must sing to the cloud that it may fertilise the pastures and fields with rain), and how one must sacrifice a bull to *Viçvakarman* (or the one that does all), who is transformed into the god Indras when killing the demon Vṛitras,[2] or the monster who keeps the rain in the cloud.

It shows us the full moon, *Râkâ*, joined to the aurora, as a source of abundance,[3] and the aurora with the cow.[4] It tells us explicitly that the characteristic form of the aurora is the red cow, because she moves with the red cows.[5] The gods, after having discovered the cows in the cavern, open the cavern with the third libation of the morning;[6] when the cows come out, the gods, the *Âdityâs*, also come out; hence the coming

[1] v. 4, 23.

[2] Indro vâi vṛitraṁ hatvâ viçvakarmâbhavat; iv. 3, 22.

[3] iii. 2, 37.

[4] Ushase ćaruṁ yoshâḥ sâ râkâ so eva trishṭup gave ćarum ya gâuḥ sâ sinîvâlî (the new moon) so eva ǵagati; iii. 2, 48.

[5] Abhûd ushâ ruçatpaçur ityushaso rûpam; i. 2, 18.—Gobhiraruṇâir ushâ âǵimadhâvat tasmâd ushasyagatâyâm aruṇam ivaeva prabhátyushasorûpam; iv. 2, 9.—Abhûd ushâ ruçatpaçur ityushaso rûpam; i. 2, 18.

[6] *Âit.-brâhm.* vi. 4, 24.

forth of the gods (*Âdityânâm ayanam*) is equivalent to the coming forth of the cows (*gavâm ayanam*). The cows come out when they have their horns, and adorn themselves.[1]

The aurora is a cow; this cow has horns; her horns are radiant and golden. When the cow aurora comes forth, all that falls from her horns brings good luck; hence in the *Mahâbhâratam*,[2] the benefits received from a holy hermit, called Matañgas, are compared to those of a *gavâm ayanam*, *i.e.*, a coming out of cows. To understand this simile, besides a reference to the Vedic texts, it is necessary to compare it with the modern usages of India, in which, in celebration of the new solar year, or the birth of the pastoral god Kṛishṇas (the god who is black during the night, but who becomes luminous in the morning among the cows of the dawning, or among the female cowherds), it is customary, towards the end of December, to give cows to the Brâhmans, exchange presents of cows and calves, besprinkle one another with milk, to adorn a beautiful milch cow, crown her with flowers, gild her horns, or paint them various colours, to deck her to overloading with flowers, fruit, and little cakes, and then hunt her from the village to the sound of drums and trumpets, in order that, full of terror, she may flee away with distraction and impetuosity. The cow loses her ornaments in her flight, and these, being estimated as propitious treasures, are eagerly picked up by the faithful, and preserved as sacred relics.[3]

In the *Âitareya-brâhmaṇam*,[4] the sun is born of the cows (*goǵâ*), is the son of the cow aurora; as the sun's

---

[1] *Âit.-brâhm.* iv. 3, 17. [2] iii. 8080.

[3] Cfr. Weber's *Über die Kṛishṇaǵamâshtamî*, Berlin, 1868; *L'Inde Française*, par Eugène Burnouf, Paris, 1828; *The Hindoos*, London, 1834, vol. i. [4] iv. 3, 20.

mother she naturally nourishes him with her milk ; hence the same *Âitareya*[1] tells us that the gods Mitras and Varuṇas, by means of the curdled milk, took from the drink of the gods the inebriating poison which the long-tongued witch (*Dîrghaǵihvî*) had poured into it. This curdled milk is the same milky sea, with health-giving herbs scattered in it, and which the gods agitate to form ambrosia, in the *Râmâyaṇam*, the *Mahâbhâratam*, and the Puranic legends ; a sea and herbs which we find already spoken of together in a Vedic hymn.[2] But in the sky, where the ambrosial milk and the health giving herbs are produced, there are gods and demons ; and the milk, which is at one time the rain, at another ambrosia, is now in the cloud, now in the moon (called also *Oshadhipatis*, or lord of herbs), now round the dawn. Hanumant, who, in the *Râmâyaṇam*, goes in quest of the health-giving grass to restore their souls to the half-dead heroes, looks for it now between the mountain bull (*ṛishabhas*) and the heavenly mountain *Kâilasas*, now between the Mount Lunus (*Çandras*) and the mountain cup (*Droṇas*) ; and the mountain which possesses the herb for which Hanumant is searching is itself called herb (*oshadhis*), or the one that causes to rejoice with perfumes (*Gandhamâdanas*[3]), which two words are used

---

[1] i. 3. 22.

[2] Mahînâm payo 'sy oshadhînáṁ rasaḥ; *Taittir. Yagurv.* i. 1, 10.—Kshîrodaṁ sâgaraṁ sarve mathnîmaḥ sahitâ vayaṁ nâuâushadhîḥ samâhṛitya prakshipya ća tatastataḥ; *Râmây.* i. 46.—Cfr. Kuhn's *Die Herabkunft des Feuers und des Göttertranks*, Berlin, 1859.

[3] The *Gandhamâdanas* is especially defended by the *Gandharvâs*, a word which seems to be composed of *gandha*, perfume, and *arvas*, the one who goes on (and afterwards the horse), from the root *arv*, expansion of *ṛiv ;* according to this, they would therefore be those who go in the perfumes, as the nymphs beloved and guarded by them are they who go in the waters (ap-sarasas). Cfr. the chapter on the Ass.

synonymously. Here the milky, ambrosial, and healthful humour is supposed to be produced, not by a cow, but by an herb. And the gods and demons contend in heaven for the possession of this herb, as well as for the ambrosia; the only difference being that the gods enjoy both one and the other without corrupting them, whilst the demons poison them as they drink them; that is to say, they spread darkness over the light, they move about in the darkness, in the gloomy waters, in the black humour which comes out of the herb itself, which, in contact with them, becomes poisonous, so that they in turn suck the poison. On the other hand, the *Gandharvâs*,[1] an amphibious race, in whom at one time the nature of the gods predominates, at another that of the demons, and who consequently take now the side of the gods, now that of the demons, are simply guards who, as against theft, keep watch and ward over the perfumes and healthful herbs, which are their own property, and the healthful or ambrosial waters, the ambrosia which belongs to their wives, the nymphs; they are, in a word, the earliest representatives of the enjoying and jealous proprietor. We have already heard, in the *Ṛigvedas*, the demoniacal monsters call on each other to suck the poison of the celestial cows; and we have seen that the *Âitareya-brâhmaṇam* accuses a witch of being the poisoner of the divine ambrosia; we have, moreover, noticed that a Vedic hymn already associates together the ambrosial milk and the healthful herb, and that, in the brâhmanic cosmogony, the milk and the herb which produces it are manifested together, which herb or grass is beneficent or the reverse according as the gods or the demons enjoy it; from all which it will be easy to understand this

[1] Cfr. *Râmây.* vi. 82, 83.

interesting Hindoo proverb, "The grass gives the milk to the cows, and the milk gives the poison to the serpents."[1] It is indeed the milk of the cow of the dawn and of the cow of the moon which destroys the serpents of darkness, the demoniacal shadows of night.

But the idea of the healthful herb is incorporated in another image, very familiar to the popular Indo-European legends, and which is contained even in the Vedic hymns. The cow produces the sun and the moon; the circular shape, the disc of sun and moon, suggests variously the idea of a ring, a gem, and a pearl; and the sun, *Savitar*, he who gives the juice, and the generator, is introduced in a Vedic hymn, as the one who has immortal juice, who gives the pearl.[2] The humours of the cow have passed to the herb, and from the herb to the pearl; and the naturalness of this figure recommends itself to our modern conception, for when we would describe a diamond or other gem as of the purest quality, we say it is a diamond or gem of the first water. Even the pearl-moon and the pearl-sun, from their ambrosial humours, have a fine water. In the *Râmâyaṇam*,[3] at the moment of production of ambrosia from the stirring up of the milky sea, we see, near the healthful herb, the gem *Kâustubhas*, the same which we afterwards find on the breast of the sun-god Vishṇus, and which is sometimes his navel; whence Vishṇus, in the *Mahâbhâratam*,[4] is saluted by the name of *ratnanâbhas*—that is to say, he who has a pearl for his navel; as the sun is in like manner saluted by the name of *Maṇiçṛiñgas*—*i.e.*,

---

[1] Böhtlingk's *Indische Sprüche*, 122, erster Theil; 2te Aufl. S. Petersburg, 1870.—Cfr. *Mahâbhâratam*, i. 1143-1145.

[2] Abhi tyaṁ devaṁ savitâram ûṇyoḥ kavikratum arćâmi satyasavasam ratnadhâm abhi priyam matim; *Tâittir. Yagurv.* i. 2, 6.

[3] i. 46.

[4] xiii. 7034.

who has horns of pearls.[1] In the *Râmâyaṇam*,[2] the bright-shining grass and the solar disc appear together on the summit of the mountain Gandhamâdanas; no sooner does he smell its odour than the solar hero *Lakshmaṇas*, delivered from the iron that oppressed him, lifts himself up from the ground; *i.e.*, scarcely has the sun formed his disc, and begun to shine like a celestial gem, than the sun-hero, whom the monsters had vanquished during the night, rises in victory. And it is on the summit of the mountain that, with a mountain metal of a colour similar to that of the young sun,[3] the sun *Râmas* imprints a dazzling mark on the forehead of the dawn Sîtâ, as if to be able to recognise her—that is to say, he places himself upon the forehead of the aurora or dawn. When the sun Râmas is separated from the dawn Sîtâ, he sends her in recognition, as a symbol of his disc, his own ring, which appears again in the famous ring given by King *Dushmantas* to the beautiful *Çakuntalâ*, the daughter of the nymph, and by means of which alone the lost bride can be recognised by the young and forgetful king; and Sîtâ sends back to Râmas, by the hands of Hanumant, as a sign of recognition, the dazzling ornament which Râmas had one day placed upon her forehead in an idyllic scene among the mountains known to them alone. This ring of recognition, this magic pearl, often turns up in the Hindoo legends. It is enough for me to indicate here the two most famous examples.

The aurora who possesses the pearl becomes she who

---

1 Hariv., 12,367.

2 Âruhya tasya çikhare so 'paçyat paramâushadîṁ dṛishṭvâ ćotpâtayâmâsa viçalyakaraṇîṁ çubhâm.—Viçalyo nirugaḥ çîghramudatishṭhanmahîtalât; vi. 83.

3 Sa nighṛishâñgulim râmo dhâute manaḥçilâgirâu ćakara tilakaṁ patnyâ lalâṭe rućiraṁ tadâ bâlârkasamavarṇena tena sâ giridhâtunâ lalâṭe vinivishṭhe na sasaṁdheva niçâbhavat; *Râmây.* ii. 105.

is rich in pearls, and herself a source of pearls; but the pearl, as we have already seen, is not only the sun, it is also the moon. The moon is the friend of the aurora; she comforts her in the evening under her persecutions; she loads her with presents during the night, accompanies and guides her, and helps her to find her husband.

In the *Râmâyaṇam*, I frequently find the moon as a beneficent fairy, who succours the dawn Sîtâ; for the moon, as *râganîkaras* (she who gives light to the night), assumes a benignant aspect. We have already said that the moon is generally a male in India; but as full moon and new moon it assumes, even in the Vedic texts, a feminine name. In a Vedic hymn, *Râkâ*, the full moon is exhorted to sew the work with a needle that cannot be broken.[1] Here we have the moon personified as a marvellous workwoman, a fairy with golden fingers, a good fairy; and in this character we find her again in the *Râmâyaṇam*, under the form of the old *Anasûyâ*, who anoints the darkened Sîtâ (for Sîtâ, like the Vedic girl, is dark and ugly during the night, or winter, when she is hidden) in the wood, with a divine unguent; gives her a garland, various ornaments, and two beauteous garments, which are always pure (as, *i.e.*, they do not touch the earth, like the cows of the Vedic dawn, who do not cover themselves with dust), and similar in colour to the young sun;[2] in all which the fairy moon appears as working during the night for the aurora, preparing her luminous garments—the two garments, of which the one is for the evening and the other for the morning, one lunar and of

[1] Sîvyatu apaḥ sûćyâćhidyamânayâ dadâtu vîraṁ çatadâyam ukthyam; *Ṛigv.* ii. 32, 4.

[2] Tataḥ çubhaṁ sâ taruṇârkasaṁnibhaṁ gataklamâ vasrayugaṁ sadâ malaṁ sraǵo 'ñgarâgaṁ ća vibhûshaṇâni ća prasannaćetâ ǵagṛihe tu mâithilî; *Râmây.* iii. 5.

silver, the other solar and of gold—in order that she may please her husband Râmas, or the sun Vishṇus, who is glad when he sees her thus adorned. In the *Svayamprabhâ*, too, we meet with the moon as a good fairy, who, from the golden palace which she reserves for her friend Hemâ (the golden one), is during a month the guide, in the vast cavern, of Hanumant and his companions, who have lost their way in the search of the dawn Sîtâ. To come out of this cavern, it is necessary to shut the eyes, in order not to see its entrance; all Hanumant's companions are come out, but Taras, who shines like the moon,[1] would wish to return. The same moon can be recognised in the benignant fairies *Triǵâtâ*, *Suramâ*, and *Saramâ*, who announce to Sîtâ that her husband will soon arrive, and that she will soon see him. The first, while the arrival of Râmas is imminent, dreams that the monsters, dressed in yellow, are playing in a lake of cow's milk;[2] at the time when Suramâ announces to Sîtâ the approach of Râmas, Sîtâ shines by her own beauty, like the opening dawn;[3] finally, Saramâ (who seems to be the same as Suramâ), whom Sîtâ calls her twin-sister (*sahodarâ*), penetrating underground, like the moon Proserpine, also announces to Sîtâ her approaching deliverance at the hands of Râmas.[4] As to Triǵaṭâ, it is not difficult to recognise in her the moon, when we remember that Trǵiaṭas is a name which is frequently given to the evening sun, or rising moon, *Çivas*, who is represented with the moon for a diadem, whence his

[1] *Râmây.* iv. 50-53.

[2] Pîtâirnivâsitâ vastrâiḥ krîdanto gomaye hrade; *Râmây.* v. 27.—Cfr. vi. 23.

[3] Sîtâmuvâća ha dîpyamânâm svayâ lakshmyâ sandhyâmâutpâtikîmiva; *Râmây.* v. 52.

[4] Samarthâ gatanaṁ gantumapivâ tvaṁ rasâtalam—Aćirammokshyase sîte; *Râmây.* vi. 9, 10.

other name of *Çandraćûḍas* (having the moon for his diadem). Suramâ I believe to be, not a mythical, but only an orthographical variation, and more incorrect one, of Saramâ, whose relation to the moon we shall see in detail when we come to the chapter which treats of the mythical dog.

Thus far we have a moon fairy; but we find the moon designated at other times in the *Râmâyaṇam* by its common masculine name. The guardian of the forest of honey, *Dadhimukhas,* in which forest, with its honey, the heroes who accompany Sîtâ enjoy themselves, is said to be generated by the god Lunus.[1] And the moon, who assists Hanumant in his search of Sîtâ, is said to shine like a white bull with a sharpened horn, with a full horn;[2] in which we come back to the moon as a horned animal, and to the cornucopia. Moreover, we find the same lunar horn again in the city of *Çṛiñgaveram,* where first the solar hero Râmas, and afterwards his brother Bharatas, are hospitably received when the sun is darkened,[3] by *Guhas,* king of the black *Wishâdâs,* who also is of the colour of a black cloud;[4] and Râmas and Bharatas take their departure in the morning from Guhas, who is said to wander always in the forests.[5] Now, this Guhas, who, though always hidden, yet wishes to entertain the solar hero during the night with presents of the town of Çṛiñgaveram, appears to me to be just another form of the solar hero himself, who enters and hides himself in the night, hospitably received in the lunar habitation, another form of the god Indras, whom we have seen in the *Ṛigvedas*

[1] Sâumyaḥ somâtmagáḥ; *Râmây.* vi. 6.

[2] Sitaḥ kakudvâniva tîkshṇaçṛiñgo rarâga ćandraḥ paripûrṇaçṛiñgaḥ; *Râmây.* v. 11.—Cfr. v. 20.

[3] Babhâu nashṭaprabhaḥ sûryo raǵanî ćâbhyavartata; *Râmây.* ii. 92.

[4] Nishâdarâgo guhaḥ sanîlâmbudatulyavarṇaḥ; *Râmây.* ii. 48.

[5] Sadâ vanagoćaraḥ; *Râmây.* ii. 98.

united during the night to Indus or Somas—that is, to the moon—and who, in the *Râmâyaṇam*[1], when Sîtâ is in the power of the monster, comes down during the night to console her, lulls her keepers to sleep, and nourishes her with the ambrosial milk (with Soma, the moon, the same moon which, in the *Ṛigvedas*, the dawn, the girl beloved of Indras, and whom therefore he does good to, brings him as a present), encouraging her with the prospect of the near advent of Râmas, the deliverer.

But it remains to us to adduce clearer evidence to show that in the *Râmâyaṇam* Râmas is the sun, and Sîtâ the dawn, or aurora.

Without taking into account that Râmas is the most popular personification of Vishṇus, and that Vishṇus is often the solar hero (although he is not seldom identified with the moon), let us see how Râmas manifests himself, and what he does in the *Râmâyaṇam* to vindicate especially his solar nature.

It is my opinion that the best way to prove this is to show how Râmas performs the very same miracles that Indras does. Râmas, like Indras, gives, while still young, extraordinary proofs of his strength ; Râmas, like Indras, achieves his greatest enterprises while he is himself hidden ; Râmas, like Indras, vanquishes the monster, reconquers Sîtâ, and enjoys of right the company of his wife. Till Râmas goes into the forests, as Indras into the clouds and shadows, his great epopee does not begin. Indras has for assistants the winds (the Marutas) ; Râmas has for his greatest help Hanumant, the son of the wind (*Mârutâtmagah*) ;[2] Hanumant amuses himself with the monsters, as the wind with the archer-clouds of the thousand-eyed Indras ;[3] and it is said that Râmas gets on

[1] iii. 63. [2] *Râmây.* iv. 1.
[3] Sahasrâkshadhanushmadbhis toyadâiriva mârutaḥ ; *Râmây.* v. 40.

Hanumant's back, as Indras does on the elephant *Âiravatas.* The elephant with a proboscis is not unfrequently substituted, in the brâhmanic tradition, for the horned bull of the Vedâs.[1] But the bull Indras is reproduced in the bull Râmas, and the monkeys who assist Râmas have kept at least the tail of the Vedic cows, the helpers of Indras, whence their generic name of *golâñgulâs* (who have cows' tails).[2] The bow with which Râmas shoots the monsters is made of a horn, whence his name of *Çârngadhanvant* (he who shoots with the horn);[3] Râmas receives the shower of hostile darts, as a bull upon its horns the abundant rains of autumn.[4] Sîtâ herself calls both her Râmas and his brother Lakshmaṇas by the name of *siṇharshabhâu,*[5] or the lion and the bull, which are conjoined so frequently in the mythology, on account of equal strength; hence the terror of the lion when he hears the bull bellow in the first book of the *Pañćatantram,* and in all the numerous Eastern and Western variations of that book. Indras has his conflicts in the cloudy, rainy, and gloomy sky; these are also the battle-fields of Râmas. The names of the monsters of the *Râmâyaṇam,* as, for instance, *Vidyuǵǵivas* (he who lives upon thunderbolts), *Vaǵrodarî* (she who has thunderbolts in her stomach), *Indraǵit* (who vanquishes Indras with magical arts), *Meghanâdas* (thundering cloud),[6] and others, show

[1] *Râmây.* v. 73.—In the *Râmâyaṇam* itself, Râmas, overpowered with grief, is compared now to a bull (v. 34), now to an elephant tormented by a lion (v. 37).

[2] *Râmây.* vi. 105.

[3] *Râmây.* vi. 102.

[4] Çâradaṁ sthûlapṛishataṁ çṛiñgâbhyâm govṛisho yathâ; *Râmây.* iii. 32.

[5] *Râmây.* v. 28.—The monster Kabandhas salutes them both with the name of *Vṛishabhaskandhâu,* or they who have bulls' shoulders; *Râmây.* iii. 74.

[6] *Râmây.* vii. 36–38.

us the nature of the battle. In the battle-field of Râmas, instead, the assisting hero is now a bull (*ṛishabhas*), now an ox's eye (*gavâkshas*), now *gavayas* (*bos gavæus*), and beings of similar appellations, which remind us of the Vedic deities. Indras strikes with lightning the celestial ocean; Râmas, an Indian Xerxes, chastises the sea with burning arrows.[1] Indras, in the *Ṛigvedas*, crosses the sea and passes ninety-nine rivers; Râmas crosses the ocean upon a bridge of mountains, in carrying which Hanumant, the son of the wind, shows himself peculiarly skilful; the winds carry the clouds, which we have seen, in the language of the Vedâs, represented as mountains. And that clouds, and not real mountains, are here spoken of, we deduce from observing, as we read, that while the animal army of Râmas carries the bridge on to the ocean, or the winds carry the clouds into the sky, the sun cannot burn the weary monkey-workers, because that clouds arise and cover it, rain falls, and the wind expires.[2] The field of this epic battle is evidently the same as that of the mythical battle of Indras. And in the *Râmâyaṇam* we find at every step the similarity of the combatants to the dark clouds, the bellowing clouds, the clouds carried by the wind. The forest which Râmas goes through is compared to a group of clouds.[3] The name of wanderer by night (*rağanîćaras*), afterwards given frequently in the *Râmâyaṇam*, to the monster whom Râmas combats, implies, of course, that the battle is fought by night. The fact that, as we read, the witch *Çûrpaṇakhâ* comes in winter to seduce Râmas whilst he is in the forest,[4] and

[1] *Râmây.* v. 93.

[2] Çrantâṅstu na tapet sûryaḥ kathaṅćidvânarânapi abhrâṇi ğağnire digbhyas ćhâdayitvâ raveḥ prabhâṁ pravavarsha ća parğanyo mârutaçća çivo vavâu; *Râmây.* v. 95.

[3] *Râmây.* iii. 77.

[4] *Râmây.* iii. 23.

the monster *Kumbhakarṇas* awakens after six months' sleep, like a rainy cloud which increases towards the end of summer (*tapânte*),[1] shows us that the epic poem of Râmas embraces, besides the nightly battle of the sun over darkness, also the great annual battle of the sun in winter to recover and rejoin the spring. Anyhow, it is always a battle of the sun against the monster of darkness. Râmas, in the very beginning of the great poem, says to his brother Lakshmaṇas :—" See, O Lakshmaṇas, Mârićas is come here with his followers, making a noise like thunder, and with him the wanderer by night Subâhus; thou wilt see them to-day, like a mass of dark clouds, dispersed by me in a moment, like clouds by the wind."[2] Here we find almost the whole battle of Indras.

And similar battles in the clouds are found in several other episodes of the *Râmâyaṇam*. The dart of Râmas falls upon the monster *Kharas* (the monster ass), as upon a great tree falls the thunderbolt hurled by Indras.[3] Heroes and monsters combat with stones and rocks from the great mountain, and fall, overthrown on the earth, like mountains. The monster Râvaṇas carries off Sîtâ with the magic of the wind and the tempest.[4] Heroes and monsters fight with trunks of trees from the great forest; moreover, the trunks themselves, having become monsters, join the fray, stretch out their strange arms, and devour the hero in their cavities. And here we come upon the interesting legend of *Kabandhas,* in which we

[1] *Râmây.* vi. 37.

[2] Paçya lakshmaṇa mârîćaṁ mahâçanisamasvanam sapadânugamâyântaṁ subâhuṁ ća niçâćaraṁ etâvadya mayâ paçya nîlâńćanaćayopamâu asmin kshaṇe samâdhûtâvanilenâmbudâviva; *Râmây.* i. 33.

[3] Çakreṇeva vinirmukto vaǵrastaruvaropari; *Râmây.* iii. 35.

[4] Mâyâmâçrîtya vipulâṁ vâtadurdinasaṁkulâm; *Râmây.* iii. 73.

find again the forests and trees combating, and the barrel of the Vedâs carried by the divine bull. The *Dânavâs* or demons also appear, in the *Mahâbhâratam*,[1] in the forms of sounding barrels. In the *Râmâyaṇam*, the highest of the demons (*dânavottamah*) is called by the name of *Kabandhas* (barrel and trunk), compared to a black thundering cloud, and represented as an enormous trunk, having one large yellowish eye, and an enormous devouring mouth in his chest.[2] In Tuscany, we say of water that gushes copiously out of a reservoir, that it pours as from a barrel's mouth. The monster Kabandhas draws towards himself, with his long arms, the two brothers Râmas and Lakshmaṇas (compared several times in the *Râmâyaṇam*[3] to the two Açvinâu, who resemble each other in everything). Râmas and Lakshmaṇas, *i.e.*, the two Açvinâu, the morning and evening, the spring and autumn suns, the two twilights, who, in a passage of the *Râmâyaṇam*, are called the two ears of Râmas, cut off the two extremities, the two long arms, of the monster *Kabandhas;* upon which the trunk, able no longer to support itself, falls to the ground. The fallen monster then relates to the two brothers that he was once a beautiful demon; but that, by a malediction, Indras one day made his head and legs enter his body; his arms having been lacerated

[1] Te nikṛittabhuǵaskandhâs kavandhâkṛiti ekadarçanâḥ nadanto bhâiravânnâdânnâpatanti sma dânavâs; *Mbh.* iii. 806.

[2] Atha tatra mahâghoraṁ vikṛitaṁ tam mahoććhrayaṁ vivṛiddhamaçirogrîvaṁ kabandhamudare mukham romabhirnićitaṁ tikshṇâirmahâgirimivoććhritam nîlameghanibhaṁ ghoraṁ meghastanitanisvanam mahatâ ćâtipiñgena vipulenâyatenaća ekenorasi dîrgheṇa nayanenâtidarçinâ; *Râmây.* iii. 74.—The one yellowish eye of Kabandhas reminds us of Vâiçravaṇas with only one yellowish eye (*ekapinghekshaṇas*), his other eye having been burnt out by the goddess Parvatî; *Râmây.* vii. 13.

[3] i. 49; ii. 7, *et passim.*

by the two brothers, the monster is disenchanted from this malediction, and having resumed his form of a splendid demon, he ascends to heaven in a luminous form. Here we have the all-radiant sun shut up in the cloud, he being the yellow eye, the burning mouth, of Kabandhas, and, in union with the cloud, forming a hideous monster; the hero comes to destroy his monstrous form, and the monster thanks him, for thus he becomes the glorious god, the splendid being, the handsome prince he was before. Râmas who delivers Kabandhas from his monstrous form by cutting off his two arms, is the sun Râmas coming forth from the gloomy forest, and uncovering the sky in the east and in the west. Râmas delivering Kabandhas is simply the sun delivering himself from the monster of gloom and cloud that envelops him. And, indeed, the greater part of the myths have their origin in the plurality of appellations given to the same phenomenon. Each appellation grows into a distinct personality, and the various personalities fight with each other. Hence the hero who delivers himself becomes the deliverer of the hero, viewed as a different person from the hero; the monstrous form which envelops the hero is often his own malediction; the hero who comes to kill this monstrous form is his benefactor.[1]

This theory of the monster who thanks the hero that kills him, agrees with what we find on several other occasions in the *Râmâyaṇam,* as in the case of the stag *Marîćas,*[2] which, after being killed by Râmas, re-ascends to heaven in a luminous form; of the sea-monster, which Hanumant destroys, and restores to its primitive form, that of a celestial nymph; of the old Çavarî, who, after having seen Râmas, sacrifices herself in the fire, and

[1] Cfr. the chapter on the Wolf. [2] iii. 40, *et seq.*

re-ascends young and beautiful to heaven (the usual Vedic young girl, the dawn whom, ugly during the night, Indras, by taking off her ugly skin, restores to beauty in the morning); an episodical variation of what afterwards happens to Sîtâ herself, who, having been ugly when in the power of the monster Râvaṇas, recovers her beauty by the sacrifice of fire, in order to prove her innocence to her husband Râmas, and shines again a young girl, like the young sun, adorned with burning gold, and wearing a red dress;[1] and when Râmas comes near (like the young dawn, when she sees her husband), she resembles the first light (Prabhâ), the wife of the sun.[2] This Sîtâ, daughter of Ǵanakas (the generator), whom the *Tâittiriya Brâhmaṇam* calls Savitar[3] or the sun, seems to me to be no other than the dawn, the daughter of light, the daughter of Indras, the god of the Vedic texts. These, indeed, sometimes represent Sûryâ, the daughter of the sun, as the lover of the moon (who is then masculine); but we find more frequently the loves of the dawn and the sun, of the beautiful heroine and the splendid solar hero, while the moon is generally the brother, or the pitying sister of the hero and the heroine, the beneficent old man, the foreseeing fairy, the good hostess, who aids them in their enterprises; although we also find the dawn as a sister of the sun and his succourer. In fact, the Buddhist tradition of the legend of Râmas, illustrated by Weber,[4] represents Sîtâ to us as the sister of the two

[1] Taruṇâdityasaṁkâçâm taptakâńćanabhûshitâṁ raktâmbaradharâm bâlâm; *Râmây.* vi. 103.—Of the dress of Sîtâ we read in another place that it shines "like the light of the sun upon the summit of a mountain" (Sûryaprabheva çâilâgre tasyâḥ kâusheyamuttamaṁ; iv. 58).

[2] *Râmây.* vi. 99.

[3] Cfr. Weber's *Ueber das Râmâyaṇa*, Berlin, 1870, p. 9.

[4] Ibid. p. 1.

brothers Râmas and Lakshmaṇas, who go into banishment for twelve years to escape the persecutions of their cruel step-mother (of whom the *Kâikeyî* of the *Râmâyaṇam* offers a confused image), in the same way as the Vedic dawn is united to the twin Açvinâu; and the same tradition makes Râmas, at the termination of his exile, end with marrying his own sister Sîtâ, as the sun marries the dawn. And the fact of Sîtâ being not born from the womb, but produced from the ground, a girl of heavenly beauty, destined to be the reward of valour,[1] not only does not exclude her relationship with the dawn, but confirms it; for we have seen the dawn rise from the mountain, as the daughter of light and the sun, whom the young sun wins for his bride, as a reward for his wonderful skill as an archer against the monsters of darkness; and we have seen that the dawn marries only her predestined husband, and her predestined husband is he who performs the greatest miracles, restores her lost gaiety, and most resembles her. We have just seen the old Çavarî and the ugly Sîtâ, at the sight of the sun Râmas, deliver themselves in the fire from every mortal danger, and become beautiful and happy once more.

But the concord between the mythical husband and wife is not more steadfast than that of mortal couples. Râmas is very apt to be suspicious. Having returned to his kingdom of Ayodhyâ, he allows himself to brood upon what his subjects may say of him for having taken back his wife, after she had been in the hands of the monster (they were not present at the first fire-sacrifice of Sîtâ); Râmas reveals his suspicions to Sîtâ, and blames the evil-speaking of the citizens for originating them; she sub-

[1] Vîryaçulkâ ća me kanyâ divyarûpâ guṇânvitâ bhûtalâdutthitâ pûrvaṁ nâmnâ sîtetyayoniġâ; *Râmây.* i. 68.

mits a second time to the trial by fire, but, offended by his continual suspicions, she flees from her husband, and on a car of light, drawn by serpents (*Pannagâs*), goes down again underground (which appears to mean simply this—the dawn, or spring, marries the sun in the morning, or she stays all day, or all summer, in his kingdom, and in the evening, or in the autumn, goes down into the shades of night, or of winter).[1] It is an indiscretion of the husband which causes his wife to abandon him.

Thus, in the *Ṛigvedas*, we have seen *Urvaçî*, the first of the dawns, flee from the sun *Purûravas*. In *Somadevas*,[2] the king Purûravas loses his wife Urvaçî, because he has let it be known in heaven that she was with him; in Kâlidâsas's drama of *Vikramorvaçî*, the king Purûravas, having helped Indras in the fight, receives from him Urvaçî to wife, with whom he engages to stay till a child is born to them; the king, shortly after having espoused Urvaçî, looks at another nymph, Udakavatî (the watery). Urvaçî, offended, flees; she enters a wood to hide herself, and is transformed into a creeper. In the brâhmanic tradition of the *Yaġurvedas*, referred to at length by Professor Max Müller, in his "Oxford Essays," Purûravas loses sight of Urvaçî, because he has let himself be seen by her without his regal dress, or even naked.

We find yet another similar legend in the *Mahâbhâratam*.[3] The wise and splendid Çântanus goes to the chase on the banks of the Gañgâ, and there finds a beautiful nymph whom he becomes enamoured of. The nymph responds to his suit, and consents to remain with him, on condition that he will never say anything displeasing

[1] *Râmây.* vii. 104, 105.

[2] *Kathâ sarit sâgaras*, iii. 17.

[3] i. 3888–3965.

to her, whatever she may do or meditate; and the enamoured king assents to the grave condition. They live together happily, for the king yields to the nymph in everything; but in the course of time, eight sons are born to them; the nymph has already thrown seven into the river, and the king, although inwardly full of grief, dares not say anything to her; but when she is about to throw the last one in, the king implores her not to do it, and challenges her to say who she is. The nymph then confesses to him that she is the Gañgâ itself personified, and that the eight sons born to their loves are human personifications of the eight divine Vasavas, who, by being thrown into the Gañgâ, are liberated from the curse of the human form: the only Vasus who is pleased to remain among men is Dyâus (the sky), in the form of the eunuch Bhîshmas, whom Çântanus would not allow to be thrown into the waters. The same curse falls upon the Vasavas for having ravished the cow of abundance from the penitent Apavas. We shall find a legendary subject analogous to this one of Çântanus in several of the popular tales of Europe, with this difference that, in European tradition, it is generally the husband who abandons his indiscreet partner. The Hindoo tradition, however, also offers us an example of the husband who abandons his wife, in the wise Ǵaratkarus, who marries the sister of the king of the serpents, on condition that she never does anything to displease him.[1] One day the wise man sleeps; evening comes on; he ought to be awakened in order to say his evening prayers; if he does not say them, he does not do his duty, and she would do wrong did she not warn him. If she awaken him, he

[1] "Apriyańća na kartavyaṁ kṛite ćâinâm tyaǵâmyaham," says Ǵaratkarus; *Mbh.* i. 1871.

will be enraged. What is to be done? She takes the latter course. The wise man awakes, becomes enraged, and abandons her, after she had given him a son.[1]

The glowing aspect of the sky, morning and evening, suggested the idea, now of a splendid nuptial feast, now of a fire. In this fire, sometimes the witch who persecutes the hero and heroine is burnt, and sometimes the hero and heroine themselves are immolated. The sacrifice of Çavarî and of Sîtâ, who are delivered by the sun Râmas, is only a variation of that of Çunaḥçepas, liberated by the dawn in the *Ṛigvedas.* The story of Çunaḥçepas has already been made known by Professor Rodolph Roth,[2] and by Professor Max Müller,[3] who translated it from the *Âitareya-brâhmaṇam;* and I refer the reader to these translations, as well as to the English version which Professor Martin Haugh has given us of all the *Âitareya.* I shall, therefore, here give but a short account of it, with a few observations apropos to the subject in hand.

The king Hariçćandras has no sons; the god Varuṇas the coverer, the gloomy, the watery, the king of the waters,[4] obliges him to promise that he will sacrifice to him whatever is born to him. The king promises; a child is born, who is named the red (Rohitas). Varuṇas

---

[1] *Mbh.* i. 1870–1911.

[2] *Indische Studien*, vol. i. pp. 457-464, vol. ii. pp. 111–128.

[3] *History of Ancient Sanskrit Literature.*

[4] Varuṇas, the god of night, has, like the night, a double aspect; now he is the gloomy ocean, now the luminous milky ocean without a moon. He is represented under the latter aspect in the 7th book of the *Râmâyaṇam* (canto 27), in which the solar hero, having entered the celestial city of Varuṇas, finds the cow which always yields milk (payaḥ ksharantâm satataṁ tatra gâṁ ća dadarça saḥ), whence the white-rayed moon emerges, whence also the ambrosia and the nectar (yataçćandraḥ prabhavati çîtaraçmiḥ—yasmâdamṛitamutpannaṁ sudhâ ćâpi).

claims him; the father begs him to wait till the child has cut his teeth, then till his first teeth are cast, then till he is able to bear armour. It is evident that the father wishes to wait till his son be strong enough to defend himself against his persecutor, Varuṇas. Varuṇas thereupon claims him in a more resolute manner, and Hariçćandras informs the son himself that he must be given up in sacrifice. Rohitas takes his bow and flees into the woods, where he lives by the chase. This first part of the legend corresponds with those numerous European popular tales, in which, now the devil, now the aquatic monster, now the serpent, demands from a father the son who has just been born to him without his knowledge. The second part of the story of Çunaḥçepas shows us the hero in the forest; he has taken his bow with him, and hence, like Râmas in the *Râmâyaṇam*, who has scarcely entered the forest than he begins to hunt, Rohitas turns hunter, and hunts for the six years during which he remains in the forest. But his chase is unsuccessful; he wanders about in quest of some one to take his place as the victim of Varuṇas; at last he finds the brâhmaṇas Aġigartas, who consents to give his own second son, Çunaḥçepas, for a hundred cows. The first-born being particularly dear to the father, and the third being especially beloved by the mother, cannot be sacrificed; the second son, therefore, is ceded to Varuṇas, the gloomy god of night, who, like Yamas, binds all creatures with his cords. We have already observed how the middle son is the son of the celestial cow Aditis, the hidden sun, the sun during and covered by the darkness of night, or, in other words, bound by the fetters of Varuṇas—and it is his own father who binds him with those fetters. His sacrifice begins in the evening. During the night he appeals to all the gods. At last Indras, flattered by the praise heaped upon him, concedes to him a golden chariot, upon which, with praises to the Açvinâu, and help from the dawn, Çunaḥçepas, unbound from the fetters of Varuṇas, is delivered. These fetters of Varuṇas, which imprison the victim, bound and sacrificed by his own father, help us to understand the second part of the European popular tale of the son sacrificed against his will to the demon by his father; for Çunaḥçepas, towards the end of the European story, takes the form of a horse, Varuṇas that of a demon, and the fetters of Varuṇas are the bridle of the horse, which the imprudent father sells to the demon, together with his son in the shape of a horse;[1] the beautiful daughter of the demon (the white one, who, as usual, comes out of the black monster) delivers the young man transformed into a horse; as in the Vedic story of Çunaḥçepas, it is explicitly the dawn who is the young girl that delivers.[2] Varuṇas is called in the *Râmâyaṇam* the gôd who has in his hand a rope (*pâçahastas*); his dwelling is on Mount Astas, where the sun goes down, and which it is impossible to touch, because it burns, in an immense palace, the work of Viçvakarman, which has a hundred rooms, lakes with nymphs, and trees of gold.[3] Evidently, Varuṇas is here, not a different form, but a different name of the god Yamas, the pâçin, or furnished with rope, the constrictor *par excellence;* for we are to suppose the magic display of golden splendour in the evening heavens not so much the work of the sun itself, as produced by the

[1] Cfr. the chapter on the Horse.

[2] In the *Râmâyaṇam*, i. 63, the deliverer is Indras, who, even in the *Âitareya*, does much for Çunaḥçepas.

[3] Teǵasâ gharmadah sadâ—Prâsâdaçatasambâdhaṁ nirmitaṁ viçvakarmanâ çobhitaṁ padminîbhiçća kâńćanâiçća mahâdrumâiḥ nilayaḥ pâçahastasya varuṇasya mahâtmanaḥ; *Râmây*. iv. 43.

gloomy god who sits on the mountain, who invests and surprises the solar hero, and drags him into his kingdom. As to Hariçćandras and Aǵigartas, Rohitas and Çunaḥçepas, they appear, in my opinion, to be themselves different names for not only the same celestial phenomenon, but the same mythical personage. Hariçćandras is celebrated in the legends as a solar king; Rohitas, his son, the red one, is his *alter ego*, as well as his successor Çunaḥçepas. Hariçćandras, moreover, who promises to sacrifice his son to Varuṇas, seems to differ little, if at all, from Aǵigartas, who sells his own son for the sacrifice. The *Râmâyaṇam*,[1] has given us a third name for the same unnatural father,[2] in Viçvâmitras, who asks his own sons to sacrifice themselves, instead of Çunaḥçepas, who is under his protection, and as they refuse to obey, he curses them.

The variation of the same legend which we find in the *Harivanças*[3] proves these identities, and adds a new and notable particular. The wife of Viçvâmitras designs, on account of her poverty, to barter her middle son for a hundred cows, and with that view already keeps him tied with a rope like a slave. The grandfather of Rohitas, Hariçćandras's father, Triçañkus, wanders through the woods, and delivers this son of Viçvâmitras, whose family he thenceforth protects and maintains. The deeds of Triçañkus, who begs of Vasishṭas to be allowed to ascend to heaven bodily, and who, by grace of Viçvâmitras, obtains instead the favour of remaining suspended in the

[1] i. 64.

[2] The Puranic legend gives an instance of such another father in Hiraṇyakaçipus, who, persecuting his own son Prahlâdas, tries to destroy him in several ways, and finally throws him into the sea; Prahlâdas praises Vishṇus, and is delivered.—Cfr. *The Vishṇu Purâṇa*, translated by H. Wilson, i. 17–20. London: Trübner, 1864.

[3] Chap. xii. 13.

air like a constellation, are also attributed to his son Hariçćandras; whence we may affirm, without much risk of contradiction, that as Triçañkus is another name for his son Hariçćandras, so Hariçćandras is another name for his son Rohitas, and that, therefore, the Triçañkus of the *Harivañças* is the same as the Rohitas of the *Âitareya*, with this difference, that Triçañkus buys the son destined to the sacrifice in order to free him, while Rohitas buys him to free himself. But the first hundred cows given by Triçañkus to Viçvâmitras do not suffice for him, and the fruits of his hunting in the forest are not enough to maintain the family, a circumstance which weighs upon him almost as much as if the family were his own; upon which, in order to save Viçvâmitras, in order to save Viçvâmitras's son, and, we can perhaps add, to save himself, he resolves to sacrifice, to kill the beautiful and dearly-prized wife of Vasishṭas (the very luminous). I have said the wife of Vasishṭas, but the *Harivañças* says, speaking strictly, it was the cow of Vasishṭas who was killed. But we know from the *Râmâyaṇam*[1] that this cow of Vasishṭas, this kâmadhuk or kâmadhenus, which yields at pleasure all that is wished for, this cow of abundance, is kept by Vasishṭas, under the name of Çabâlâ, as his own wife. Viçvâmitras is covetous of her; he demands her from Vasishṭas, and offers a hundred cows for her, the exact price which, in the *Harivañças*, he receives from Triçañkus for his own son. Vasishṭas answers that he will not give her for a hundred, nor for a thousand, nor even for a hundred thousand cows, for Çabâlâ is his gem, his riches, his all, his life.[2] Viçvâmitras carries her off; she returns to the feet of Vasishṭas,

[1] i. 54–56.

[2] Etadeva hi me ratnametadeva hi me dhanam etadva hi sarvasvam etadeva hi ǵivitam; *Râmây.* l. c.

and bellows; her bellowing calls forth armies, who come out of her own body; the hundred sons of Viçvâmitras are burned to ashes by them. These armies which come out of the body of Vasishṭas's cow remind us again of the Vedic cow, from which come forth winged darts, or birds, by which the enemies are filled with terror. Vasishṭas is a form of Indras; his cow is here the rain-cloud. Viçvâmitras, who wishes to ravish the cow from Vasishṭas, often assumes monstrous forms in the Hindoo legends, and is almost always malignant, perverse, and revengeful. His hundred sons burned to cinders by Vasishṭas remind us, from one point of view, of the hundred cities of Çambaras destroyed by Indras, and the hundred perverse Dhṛitarâshtrides of the *Mahâbhâratam;* whence his name, Viçvâmitras, which may also mean the enemy of all (*viçva-amitras*), would agree well with his almost demoniacal character.

This story of the cow of Vasishṭas, whose relationship with the legend of Çunaḥçepas cannot be doubted, brings us back to the animal forms of heroes and heroines from which we started. In the story of Vasishṭas, the cow-cloud, the cow çabâlâ, or the spotted-cow, plays in the epic poem the part of the cow Aditis, the cow pṛiçnis (spotted, variegated), with which we are already familiar in the Vedic hymns. This cow is benignant towards the god, or the hero, or the wise Vasishṭas, as the pṛiçnis is to the god Indras. But we have seen in the *Ṛigvedas* itself the cloud as the enemy of the god, and represented as a female form of the monster, as his sister. This sister generally tries to seduce the god, promising to deliver into his hands the monster her brother, and she sometimes succeeds, as the witch Hidimbâ of the *Mahâbhâratam*, who gives up her brother, the monster Hidimbas, into the hands of the hero Bhîmas, who thereupon espouses her. On the other hand, Çûrpaṇakhâ, the sister of the monster Râvaṇas, does not succeed in her intent; making herself beautiful, she endeavours to win the affection of the hero Râmas; but being ridiculed by him and by Lakshmaṇas, she becomes deformed, and sends forth cries like a cloud in the rainy season,[1] exciting her brothers to annihilate Râmas.

The same cloud-monster is found again in the *Râmâyaṇam*, under the name of Dundubhis, in the form of a terrible buffalo with sharpened horns.[2] The buffalo, as a wild animal, is often chosen to represent the principle of evil, in the same way as the bull, increaser of the bovine herds, is selected as the image of good. This bellowing buffalo, whence his name of Dundubhis (drum), strikes and knocks with his two horns at the door of the cavern[3] of the son of Indras (Bâlin), the king of the monkeys. But Bâlin takes Dundubhis by the horns, throws him on the ground, and destroys him.

Dundus is also a name given to the father of Kṛishṇas, or the black one, who in the *Ṛigvedas* is still a demon, and only later becomes the god of cows and cowherds, a govindas, or pastor *par excellence*.[4] Indras, his enemy in the Vedas, having fallen from heaven, he became one of

---

[1] Nanâda vividhân nâdân yathâ prâvṛishi toyadaḥ; *Râmây.* iii. 24.

[2] Dhârayan mâhishaṁ rupaṁ tîkshṇaçriñgo bhayâvahaḥ; *Râmây.* iv. 9.—Further on, instead (iv. 46), the buffalo is said to be the brother of Dundubhis, and to have the strength of a thousand serpents (balaṁ nâgasahasrasya dhârayan) or elephants, for the word *nâgas* is equivocal.

[3] Çṛiñgâbhyâmâlikhan darpat taddvâram; *Râmây,* iv. 9.—Cfr. the two chapters which treat of the Horse and the Monkey.

[4] I do not insist upon this brâhmanic god, because his legend is now popular.—Cfr., for the rest, for the relationship of Kṛishṇas with the cows, the cowherds, and the cow-maiden, the whole 5th book of the *Vishṇu Purâna,* translated by H. Wilson, and the *Gîtagoviṅdas* of Gayadevas, edidit Lassen, Bonn, 1836.

the most popular gods, and even sometimes the most popular form of the deity. In the *Mahâbhâratam*, for instance, he is almost the *deus ex machina* of the battles between the Pâṇḍavas and the Dhârtarâshṭrâs, and presents many analogies to the Zeus of the Iliad; whereas Indras plays only a part in the episodes, the rain-giver and thunderer being often forgotten for the black one who prepares and hurls the light. But the fall of Indras begins in the Vedâs themselves. In the *Yaǵurvedas*, Viçvarûpas, the son of Tvashṭar, whom Indras kills, appears as no less than the purohitas or high-priest of the gods, and son of a daughter of the Asurâs; he has three heads, of which one drinks the ambrosia, another the spirituous drink, while the third eats food. Indras cuts off Viçvarûpas's three heads, in revenge of the one which drinks his ambrosia; he is therefore charged with having killed a Brâhman, and decried as a brâhmanicide.[1] In the *Âitareya-brâhmaṇam*,[2] the criminality of Indras in this regard is confirmed, to which the *Kâushîtaki-Upanishad* also refers. In the seventh book of the *Râmâyaṇam*, even the multiform monster Râvaṇas is represented as a great penitent, whom Brâhman fills with supreme grace; in the sixth book, the son of the wind, Hanumant, cuts off the three heads of the Râvanide monster Triçiras (having three heads), as one day Indras cut off the three heads of the monster Vṛitras, son of Tvashṭar;[3] and he cuts all the three heads off together (*samas*), as the hero of the

[1] Viçvarûpo vâi tvâshṭraḥ purohito devânâm âsît svasriyo 'surâṇâm tasya trîṇi çirshâny asant—Indras tasya vaǵram âdâya çîrshâny aćhinad yat somapânam—Brahma-hatyam upâ 'grihṇat—Tam bhûtâny abhy akroçan brahmahann iti; *Tâittirîya Saṁhitâ*, ed. Weber. ii. 5, 1–6.

[2] vii. 5, 28.

[3] Sa tasya khañgena mahâçirâṅsi kapiḥ samas tâṁ sukuṇḍalâṁ kruddhaḥ praćiććheda tadâ hanûmâns ṭvâshṭrâtmaǵasyeva çirânsi çakrah; *Râmây.* vii. 50.

European popular tales must cut off, at a blow, the three heads of the serpent, the wizard, otherwise he is powerless, and able to do nothing. The monster, like the hero, seems to have a special affinity for the number three: hence the three heads of Triçiras, as also the three brothers of Lañkâ—Râvaṇas, the eldest brother, who reigns; Kumbhakarṇas, the middle brother, who sleeps; Vibhishaṇas, the third brother, whom the two others do not care about, but who alone is just and good, and who alone obtains the gift of immortality.[1] We have evidently here again the three Vedic brothers; the two eldest in demoniacal form, the youngest a friend of the divine hero, and who, by the victory of Râmas over the monster Râvaṇas, obtains the kingdom of Lañkâ. As to the brothers Râmas and Lakshmaṇas, and the brothers Bâlin and Sugrîvas, their natural place is in the story of the two twins, which will be referred to in the next chapter, although Hanumant, the son of the wind, figures second to them in the character of strong brother.

The three interesting heroic brothers come out more prominently in the *Mahâbhâratam*, where of the five Pâṇdavas brothers, three stay on one side, and are Yudhishṭhiras, son of the god Yamas, the wise brother; Bhîmas (the terrible), or Vṛikodâras (wolf's belly), son of Vâyus (the wind), the strong brother (another form of Hanumant, in company with whom he is also found in the *Mahâbhâratam*, on Mount Gandhamâdanas); and Argunas (the splendid), the son of Indras, the genial, dexterous, fortunate, victorious brother, he who wins the bride. The first brother gives the best advice; the second shows proof of greatest strength; the third brother wins, conquers the bride. They are precisely the three Vedic brothers Ṛibhavas, Ekatas, Dvîtas, and

[1] *Râmây.* vii. 10.

Tritas, in the same relationships to one another and with the same natures; only the legend is amplified.[1] As to their other brothers, twins, born of another mother, Nakulas and Sahadevas, they are the sons of the two Açvinâu, and feebly repeat in the *Mahâbhâratam* the exploits of the two celestial twins. Bhîmas or Vṛikodâras, the second brother, is considered the strongest, (balavatâṁ çreshthaḥ), because immediately after birth, *i.e.*, scarcely has he come forth out of his mother (like the Vedic Marutas), than he breaks the rock upon which he falls, because he breaks his fetters as soon as he is bound with them (like Hanumant when he becomes the prisoner of Râvaṇas), because he carries his brothers during the night (as Hanumant carries Râmas), as he flees from the burning house prepared by the impious Duryodhanas (*i.e.*, from the burning sky of evening), and because in the kingdom of serpents, where Duryodhanas threw him down (that is, the night), he drinks the water of strength. A serpent, wishing to benefit Bhîmas, says to Vasukis, king of the serpents—"Let there be given to him as much strength as he can drink from that cistern in which is placed the strength of a thousand serpents."[2] Bhîmas, at one draught, drinks the whole cisternful; and with similar expedition, he drains consecutively eight cisterns.[3] The first-born of the Pâṇḍavas is dear to his father Yamas, the god of justice, Dharmarâǵas,—and is

---

[1] *Mbh.* i. 4990.—Cfr. also the three phallical and solar brothers of the story of Çunaḥçepas (him with the luminous tail or phallus).

[2] i. 4775.

[3] Balaṁ nâgasahasrasya yasmin kuṇḍe pratishṭhitaṁ yâvatpivati bâlo 'yaṁ tâvad asmâi pradîyataṁ—ekoććhvâsâttataḥ kuṇḍaṁ danaḥ; *Mbh.* i. 5030, 5032.—A similar legend is found again in the third book of the *Mahâbhâratam,* under the form of an impenetrable forest, in which the king of the serpents envelops Bhîmas.

himself indeed called Dharmarâǵas; and when he prepares himself to ascend into heaven, the god Yamas follows him in the form of a dog: by his skill in solving enigmas, he saves his brother Bhîmas from the king of the serpents. The third brother, Arǵunas, son of Indras, is the Benjamin of the Vedic supreme God. Indras welcomes him with festivals in heaven, whither Arǵunas had gone to find him. Arǵunas is an infallible archer, like Indras; like Indras, he several times regains the cows from the robbers or from the enemies; and, like Indras, he wins and conquers his bride; he is born by the assistance of all the celestials; he is invincible (*aǵayas*); he is the best son (*varaḥ putras*);[1] he alone of the three brothers has compassion on his master Droṇas and delivers him from an aquatic monster.[2]

But there is yet another particular which shows the resemblance between the three brothers Pâṇḍavas and the three brothers of the Vedas; it is their dwelling, hidden in the palace of the king Virâṭa, in the fourth book of the *Mahâbhâratam*. They are exiled from the kingdom, like Râmas; they flee from the persecution of their enemies, now into the woods, now, as the Ṛibhavas, disguised as workmen in the palace of Virâṭas, to whom their presence brings every kind of happiness.

We meet with these three brothers again, episodically, in the three disciples of Dhâumyas, in the first book of the *Mahâbhâratam*.[3] The first disciple, Upamanyus, takes his master's cows out to pasture, and, out of sensitive regard for his master's interest, refuses to drink not only their milk, but even the foam from their mouths, and fasts till, like to perish of hunger, he bites a leaf of arkapatrâ (properly, leaf of the sun, the *aristolochia indica*),

[1] *Mbh.* i. 4777. [2] i. 5300–5304. [3] i. 680–828.

when he instantly becomes blind. He wanders about and falls into a well; he there sings a hymn to the Açvinâu, and they come immediately to deliver him. The second brother, Uddâlakas, places his body, as a dike, to arrest the course of the waters. The third brother is Vedas, he who sees, he who knows, whose disciple Utañkas is himself in the form of a hero. Utañkas, like the Vedic Tritas, and the Pâṇḍavas Arǵuṇas, is protected by Indras. He is sent by the wife of his master to abstract the earrings of the wife of King Pâushyas. He sets out; on his way he meets a gigantic bull, and a horseman, who bids him, if he would succeed, eat the excrement of the bull; he does so, rinsing his mouth afterwards. He then presents himself to King Pâushyas and informs him of his message; the king consigns the earrings to him, but cautions him to beware of Takshakas, the king of the serpents. Utañkas says that he is not afraid of him, and sets out with the earrings; but as he puts down the earrings upon the shore, in order to bathe, Takshakas presents himself in the shape of a naked mendicant, whips them up, and flees away with them. Utañkas follows him, but Takshakas resumes his serpent form, penetrates the ground, and descends under it; Utañkas attempts to follow the serpent, but does not succeed in cleaving the entrance, which corresponds to the Vedic rock under which the monster keeps his prey. Indras sees him tiring himself in vain, and sends his weapon, in order that it may be for a help to Utañkas; that weapon, or club, penetrating, opened the cavern.[1] This club, this weapon of Indras is evidently the thunderbolt.[2] Utañkas

[1] Tam kliçyamânamindro 'paçyatsa vaǵraṁ preshayâmâsa—gaććhâsya brâhmaṇasya sâhâyyaṁ kurusveti—atha vaǵram daṇḍakâshṭhamanupraviçya tadvilamadârayat; *Mbh.* i. 794–795.

[2] In a legend of the Tibetan Buddhists, referred to by Professor

descends into the kingdom of the serpents, full of infinite wonders. Indras reappears at his side in the shape of a horse,[1] and obliges the king, Takshakas, to give back the earrings; having taken which, Utañkas mounts the horse, that he may be carried more swiftly to the wife of his master, from whom he learns that the horseman seen by him on the way was none other than Indras himself; his horse, Agnis, the god of fire; the bull, the steed of Indras, or the elephant Âiravatas; the excrement of the bull, the ambrosia, which made him immortal in the kingdom of the serpents. In another episode of the same (the first) book of the *Mahâbhâratam*,[2] we again find Indras busied in the search of the earrings, that is to say, of the excessively fleṣhy part hanging from the ears of Karṇas, the child of the sun, who, as soon as born, had been abandoned upon the waters. We have seen above how the two Açvinâu are also represented in the *Râmâyaṇam* as the two ears of Vishṇus Râmas (as the sun and moon are said to be his eyes); hence it seems to me that these mythical earrings, coveted by Indras, and protected by him, are nothing else than the two Açvinâu, the two luminous twilights (in connection with the sun and the moon), in which Indras, and, still more than he, the aurora, his wife, take such delight.[3]

Schiefner in his interesting work, *Ueber Indra's Donnerkeil* (St Petersburg), 1848, we find two valiant heroes who, upon Mount Gṛidhrakûṭa (the vulture's peak), strive, in presence of their master, to lift the vaǵram (that is, the arm in the form of a wedge, the lever-rod, the thunderbolt of Indras), but in vain; Vaǵrapâṇis alone succeeds in lifting the vaǵram with his right hand. Râmas makes a similar trial of strength in the *Râmâyaṇam*, when he lifts and breaks in pieces a bow, which no one had before been able even to move.

[1] Cfr. the following chapter. [2] i. 2772–2783.

[3] To the myth of the ravished earrings is almost always joined, even in the popular tales, the story of the horse, which is always especially

In the commentary of *Buddhagoshas* on the Buddhist Dhammapadam, we have the three brothers again; the two eldest are represented as fleeing from the persecution of their cruel step-mother; the third brother, Suriyas (Sûryas, the sun), goes to overtake them. The eldest counsels or commands, the second lends his aid, and the youngest fights. The second and third brothers fall into a fountain, under the power of a monster; the first-born saves them by his knowledge, as, in the *Mahâbhâratam*, Yudhishṭhiras, by his skill in solving riddles, delivers the second brother from the fetters of the forest of the monster serpent.

This mode of delivering the hero, by propounding a question or a riddle, is very common in the Hindoo legends. Even in the *Pańćatantram*,[1] a Brâhman who falls under the power of a forest monster who leaps on his shoulders, frees himself by asking why his feet are so soft. The monster confesses that it is because, on account of a vow, he cannot touch the earth with his feet. The Brâhman then betakes himself to a sacred pond; the monster wishes to take a bath, and the Brâhman throws him in; the monster orders him to stay there till he has bathed and said his orisons. The Brâhman profits by this opportunity to make his escape, knowing that the monster will not be able to overtake him, as he cannot put his feet to the ground. It is the usual vulnerability, weakness, or imperfection of the hero, or the monster, in the feet, and, if an animal is spoken of, in the tail.[2]

---

referred to the Açvinâu, as that of the bull to Indras. In the Puranic legends, Kṛishṇas receives from the earth the earrings of Aditis (whom we already know to be a cow), whilst he frees the princesses from the infernal Narakas.—Cfr. the *Vishṇu Purâṇa*, v. 29.

[1] v. 17.

[2] Cfr. the chapters which treat of the Wolf, the Fox, and the Serpent; and also the foregoing discussion on the Vedic riddles, where the sun is called *anipadyamânas.*

The *Mahâbhâratam* has shown us the three Vedic brothers, of whom the youngest has fallen into the well; it also presents to us, in the witch (*asurî*) Çarmishṭhâ, daughter of Vṛishaparvan, king of the demons, and in the nymph Devayânî, daughter of Çukras, who credits herself with the virtue of Indras as the rain-giver,[1] the two rival sisters of the Vedas, the good and the evil. In the *Râmâyaṇam*,[2] the witch Çûrpanakhâ, who seduces Râmas, in order to take the place of Sîtâ at his side, is compared to Çarmishṭhâ, who seduced Nâhushas. In the *Mahâbhâratam*, Çarmishṭhâ assumes the guise of Devayânî, whom she throws into a well. Yayâtis, son of King Nahushas, goes to the chase; feeling thirsty, he stops near the well; from the bottom of the well a young girl looks up, like a flame of fire.[3] The prince takes her by the right hand and draws her up; and because in the marriage ceremony, the bride is taken by the right hand,[4] the prince Yayâtis is said to marry Devayânî. But even after she is a wife, Çarmishṭhâ continues to seduce her husband, to whom she unites herself. Two sons are born of Devayânî, Yadus and Turvasas, similar to Indras and Vishṇus (a new form of the twins, of the Acvinâu); three are born of Çarmishṭhâ, Duhyus, Anus, and Pûrus; and here also the third brother is the most glorious and valiant. And in this way the episode is connected with the essential legend of the *Mahâbhâratam*, and one and the same general myth is multiplied into an infinity of particular legends. As the genealogy of the gods and heroes is infinite, so is there an infinite number of forms assumed by the same myth and of the names

---

1 Ahaṁ ǵalaṁ kimuńćâmi praǵânâm hitakâmyayâ; *Mbh.* i. 3317.

2 iii. 23, 24.

3 Dadarça râǵâ tâm tatra kanyâmagniçikhâmiva; *Mbh.* i. 3294.

4 *Mbh.* i. 3379–3394.

assumed by the same hero. Each day gave birth in the heavens to a new hero and a new monster, who exterminate each other, and afterwards revive in an aspect more or less glorious, according as their names were more or less fortunate.

It is for the same reason that the sons always recognise their fathers without having once seen them or even heard them spoken of; they recognise themselves in their fathers. Thus Çakuntalâ and Urvacî enable their mother to find again the husband that she has lost, and their father to recover his lost wife. Thus in the episode of Devayânî and Çarmishṭhâ, when the former wishes to know who is the father of the three sons of Çarmishṭhâ, so similar to the sons of immortals, she turns to them, and they tell her at once.

For this fault, Yayâtis, from being young, is fated to become old. He then beseeches the two eldest of the three sons that he had by Çarmishṭhâ to take on themselves the old age of their father; they refuse, but the third son, Pûrus, out of reverence for his father, consents to become old in his stead, to give up his youth to his father. After a thousand years, the king Yayâtis, satiated with life, restores to his son Pûrus his youth, and although he is the youngest, along with his youth, the kingdom, because he found him the only one of the three who respected the paternal will; and he expels the two eldest brothers.[1]

Sometimes, however, the blind old father is entirely abandoned by his sons. Thus the old Dîrghatamas (of the vast darkness), blind from birth, is deprived of food, and thrown into the water by his wife and sons,[2] but a heroic king saves him, in order, by his wife, to beget sons for

[1] *Mbh.* i. 3435–3545. [2] *Mbh.* i. 4193–4211.

him. We have in Dîrghatamas and Yayâtis, King Lear in embryo.

In the same legend of Dîrghatamas, we find an exchange of wives. Queen Sudeshnâ, instead of going herself, sends her servant-maid, her foster-sister, to be embraced by Dîrghatamas.[1] In the cunning Sudeshnâ we have an ancient variation of Queen Berta.

Other blind men occur frequently in the Hindoo legends. I shall here cite only Andhakas (the blind one) and Vṛishṇis (the sheep, as the lame one),[2] who appear in the *Harivanças*[3] as the two sons of Mâdrî. But we know from the *Mahâbhâratam*, that the two sons of Mâdrî are a human incarnation of the celestial twins, the Açvinâu ; and here we come again upon the blind-lame one of the Vedas, the solar hero in his twin forms, the two Açvinâu protected by Indras, and companions of the dawn.

The *Pańćatantram*[4] represents the blind and the crooked, or hunchbacked,[5] in union with the three-breasted princess (*i.e.*, the triple sister, the aurora in the evening, the aurora in the night, the aurora in the morning ; the breast of the night nourishing the defective, the monstrous, which the morning sweeps away). The crooked guides the blind with a stick ; they both marry the three-breasted

---

[1] *Mbh.* i. 4211–4216.

[2] We shall find the lame goat in the chapter which treats of the Lamb and the Goat.

[3] 1908.

[4] v. 12.

[5] The word *badhiras* means here the crooked, the crippled one, and not the deaf (from the root *badh* or *vadh*, to wound, to cut) ; the more so that here the name of the blind man's companion is Mantharakas, a word which properly means the slow one. The curved line and the slow line correspond ; and the curved one, who cannot stand upright, may be the hunchback just as well as the cripple, the crooked, the lame.—Cfr. The chapter on the Tortoise.

princess. The blind recovers sight by the steam of the poison of a black serpent, cooked in milk (the darkness of night, or of winter, mixed with the clearness of day, or of the snow); he then, being a strongly-built man, takes the hunchback by the legs, and beats his hunch against the third and superfluous breast of the princess. The anterior prominence of the latter, and the posterior one of the former, enter into their respective bodies;[1] thus the blind, the crooked, and the three-breasted princess help and cure each other; the two Açvinâu and the aurora (or the spring) reappear together in beauty. The Açvinâu and the aurora also come forth together from the monstrous shades of night; the Açvinâu contend for the aurora; as we shall see soon, and in the next chapter, the delivered bride disputed for by the brothers.

The sun and the aurora flee from each other; this spectacle has been represented in different ways by the popular imagination; and one of the most familiar is certainly that of a beautiful young girl who, running more quickly than the prince, escapes from him. This incident, which is already described in the *Ṛigvedas*, occurs again in the *Mahâbhâratam*,[2] in the legend of the loves of the virgin Tapatî, daughter of the sun (the luminous and burning aurora, and also the summer season, ardent as Dahanâ), with the king Saṁvaraṇas, son of the bear (*ṛikshaputras*, a kind of Indras). The king Saṁvaraṇas arrives on horseback with his retinue at the mountain, in order to hunt; he ties his horse up and begins the chase, when he sees on the mountain the beautiful girl, the daughter of the sun, who, covered with ornaments, shines like the sun; he declares his love and wishes to make her

[1] For the incident of the hunchback who betrays the blind man, in the same popular tale, cfr. next chapter.

[2] i. 6527.

his own; she answers not a word, but flees and disappears like the lightning in the clouds;[1] the king cannot overtake her, because his horse, while he was hunting, has died of hunger and thirst; he searches in vain through the forest, but not seeing her, he throws himself almost breathless to the ground. As he lies there the beautiful girl appears again, approaches and wakens him; he again speaks to her of love, and she answers that he must ask her father the sun, and then, still quite innocent, she disappears swiftly on high (*ûrdhvam*). The king again faints; his minister sprinkles him with the water of health, and makes him revive, but he refuses to leave the mountain, and having dismissed his hunting company, he awaits the arrival of the great purohitas Vasishṭhas, by whose mediation he demands from the sun his daughter Tapatî to wife; the sun consents, and Vasishṭhas reconducts to Saṁvaraṇas, for the third time, the beautiful girl as his legitimate wife. The husband and wife live together happily on the mountain of their loves; but as long as King Saṁvaraṇas remains with Tapatî upon this mountain, no rain falls upon the earth; wherefore the king, out of love for his subjects, returns to his palace, upon which Indras pours down the rain, and begins again to fructify the earth.[2]

We said a little ago that Vasishṭhas himself caused it to rain (*abhyavarshata*); and the mention of Vasishṭhas reminds us of the particularly rain-giving, cloudy, and lunar function of his cow Kâdmadhenus, whose wonderful productions are again described in the *Mahâbhâratam*.[3] Besides milk and ambrosia, she yields herbs and gems, which we have already referred to, as analogous products

[1] Sâudâminîva ćâbhreshu tatrâevântaradhîyata; *Mbh.* i. 6557.

[2] Tasminnṛipatiçârdûle pravishṭe nagaraṁ punaḥ pravavarsha sahasrâkshaḥ çasyâni ǵanayanprabhuḥ; *Mbh.* 6629, 6630.

[3] i. 6651–6772.

in mythology. The cow of Vasishṭhas is, besides her tail, celebrated for her breasts, her horns, and even her ears ending in a point; whence her name of *çañkukarṇâ* (the masculine form of which is generally applied to the ass). And in the *Mahâbhâratam*, also, the wise Viçvâmitras is covetous of this wonderful cow; the cow bellows and drops fire from her tail, and radiates from every part of her body armies which disperse those of the son of Gadhis. Viçvâmitras then avenges himself in other ways upon the sons of Vasishṭhas; having, *e.g.*, become a cannibal, he eats them.

Vasishṭhas cannot endure the pain this causes him: he tries to throw himself down from the summit of Mount Merus, but he falls without hurting himself; he throws himself into the fire, but does not burn himself; and, finally, he leaps into the sea, but is not drowned. These three miracles are accomplished every day by the solar hero, who throws himself down from the mountain into the gloomy ocean of night, after having passed through the burning sky of evening.

Vasishṭhas ends by freeing, with the help of charmed water, the monster Viçvâmitras from his curse; and the latter is no sooner delivered from the demon who possessed him, than he begins again to illumine the forest with his splendour, as the sun illumines a twilight cloud. The friendships, enmities, and rivalries of Vasishṭhas and Viçvâmitras seem to be another version of those of the two Açvinâu, whom we shall particularly describe in the next chapter.

Meanwhile, it is high time, as the reader will think, to conclude this part of our study, which treats of the mythical cow of India. We might easily, indeed, have made it much larger, had our design been to chain together, link by link, all the traditions and legends in which the cow plays a primary or subordinate part. But it is better to stop short, lest, by expatiating further, we should lose sight of the essential aim of our work, and be tempted into digressions from the legends relating to beasts to those relating to men; besides, we think that we have sufficiently proved the thesis of this chapter, and shown how the principal mythical subjects of the Vedic hymns are not only preserved, but developed, in the posterior Hindoo traditions. It is not entirely our fault if, from cows, we pass so often to princesses, and from bulls to princes; the myth itself involves and indicates these transformations. Hence we find the bull Indras, the winner of the cows, become a winner and a seducer of women; we see the bull Wind, who aids Indras in the conquest of the cows, become the violator of a hundred damsels;[1] we read of the bull and god Rudras, as husband of Umâ, given up to sensual indulgence for a hundred years without a pause; that the son of the bull, or of the wind, Hanumant, does prodigies of valour and strength for the sake of a beautiful woman, and receives, as a reward for his zeal, from the king Bharatas, a hundred thousand cows, sixteen wives, and a hundred servant-maids.[3] What could Hanumant have done with so many wives and maids, if he were simply a bull? or what could he have done with so many cows, if he had been an ape? It is these inconsistencies which have caused mythology to be condemned by the crowd of old but prolific pedants, as a vain science; whereas, on the contrary, it is precisely these inconsistencies which raise it, in our esteem, to the rank of a valid science.

[1] The hundred daughters of King Kuçanabhas, and of the nymph Ghṛitâći, who walks in curdled milk, recalling to us the mythical cow. —Cfr. *Râmây.* i. 35.

[2] Cfr. Virgil, *Ænëid*, I. 65-75, where Juno gives the nymph Deiopea to Æolus.

He who handed down to us the feats of Hanumant, took care also to tell us how he had the faculty of changing his form at will; and this faculty, attributed to this impersonation of a celestial phenomenon, is the fruit of one of the most *naïve* but just observations of virgin and grandiose nature.

SECTION III.

The Bull and the Cow in Iranian and Turanian Tradition.

SUMMARY.

The bull the first created in Persian tradition.—The bull of Mithra.—Mithra and Yamas.—The excrements of the celestial cow and bull.—Exorcisms for chasing the evil one away from the beasts of the stable.—The salutary herb, rue.—The heavenly cypress and the mythical forest.—The mountain and the gem.—The mountain of the heroes.—The defenceless soul of the bull recommends itself to the mercy of the gods.—The moon, as a cow or bitch, guides the hero over the funereal bridge.—The many-eyed god.—The golden-hoofed bull.—The spinners of the sky.—Friendship between sun and moon.—The Geusurva is the full moon.—The purifying moon.—Ardhvî-Çûra-Anâhita, the Persian aurora, has all the characteristics of the Vedic aurora, elevated, luminous, discomfiter of the demons, deliverer of the hero Thraetaona from the water, having golden shoes, swift, the first to arrive with her chariot, guesser of riddles, revered at the break of day.—The aurora sung to by her own name, the cow-aurora.—Mithra, the shepherd-god.—Mithra, the hero who fights to recover his cows.—The bull Veretraghna.—Thrita and Thraetaona.—The three brothers in the Avesta.—The two brothers.—The three sisters.—The strength of the solar hero consists in the wind.—The winds have golden shoes and an especial foible for women, as the women have for them.—Indras envious of the Marutas.—Kereçâçpa envious of the wind.—The wind, with its whistling and wailing, makes everything tremble; the hero presses him tightly and forces him to be silent.—The bound hero.—The bow-cow, and the birds coming out of the cow in the Avesta.—The darts, horns of the cow.—The rich brother and the poor one.—The poor one, who has a lean ox and a lean horse, makes his fortune.—Ashis Vaĝuhi, another equivalent of the aurora who also frees the hero Thraetaona.—Other names of the three Persian brothers.—Importance of the Avesta on account of its mythical contents.—The hero exposed on the mountain.—The hero-shepherd, the wonderful child, Cyrus.—Feridun.—The three brothers, sons of Feridun; the third brother is the best, and is murdered by the two elder ones. —Sal, with white hair, the hero exposed and nourished by a bird, solves riddles, and receives in reward the daughter of the king.—The hero Rustem, with the mace of a bull's head, with the strong horse that vanquishes the lion, the strong hero, the Persian Orlando, kills and binds demons, monsters, and giants, who fight with rocks.—From black comes white.—The prince Kawuṣ recovers his sight after the death of the monster.—The demon in the mountain, who keeps back the waters, is the same as the demon in the mill.—The hero Rustem unites himself with the daughter of the demoniacal and hostile king.—Sohrab is born of this union, with a demoniacal nature.—Gurdaferid, the Persian amazon princess, assailed in her white castle by the hero-demon Sohrab.—Rustem fights, wins, and kills his son Sohrab; he then retires from warfare.—Explanation of this myth.—The end of Rustem in an ambuscade.—Sijavush persecuted by his stepmother, whose love he had disdained; the young prince submits to the trial by fire, and comes out safely: the cruel stepmother was to have undergone the same trial, but Sijavush intercedes for her; she continues to persecute him; Sijavush dies in the country of his demoniacal father-in-law, and is avenged by Rustem, who kills the cruel stepmother.—The child-hero Kai Khosru consigned to the care of shepherds; during his childhood he performs prodigies of valour, and passes a river with dry feet.—The strength of the hair of the hero Firud.—The two hero-brothers again; one brother avenges the other.—The old hero becomes a penitent, and disappears in a tempest upon a mountain.—The seven heroic undertakings of Isfendiar.—The legend of Iskander.—The Tuti-Name. —The hero who wishes to kill himself for the king's sake; the deity prevents the sacrifice.—The story of the poor man and the rich one again.—The beautiful woman persecuted by her brother-in-law the seducer; the oriental Crescentia or Geneviève. —The sea, invited to the wedding, brings pearls and gold.—The maiden who discovers the thief by means of a riddle.—The girl who gives his eyesight back to the blind man against her will.—The lovers flee upon the bull's back.—The lover forsakes his mis-

FORSYTH LIBRARY
FORT HAYS KANSAS STATE COLLEGE

tress on the shore after having despoiled her.—The three brothers deliver the beautiful maiden and dispute for her; the maiden takes refuge in a convent.—The wise child who distinguishes false from true, honest from dishonest.—The money of the dead man.—The adulterer condemned to death who bites off the nose of his companion in guilt and dissoluteness.—The wife despoiled of her riches by her husband and thrown into the water. —Romeo and Juliet in the East.—The three brothers: the seer; the strong carrier, or Christophoros; the victorious one.—The disputed bride again.—The little pipkin of abundance; Perrette in the East.—The small porringer of abundance, which the two brothers contend for.—The shoes which take one in an instant wherever one wishes to go.—The little purse which is filled as fast as it is emptied.—The sword which makes a city rise.—The animals which contend for the division of the prey, and the third comer who profits between two disputers.—The four mines of the four brothers.—Why old men have white hair. —Calmuc and Mongol tradition.—The six companions are the same as three.—The bride torn in pieces.—A man unites himself with a cow, which brings forth a Minotaur of a good nature, who fights against the demons in favour of the gods.—The gem in the cow's litter.—The bull lost.—The three sisters; the third sister marries the monster bird; she loses him, because she has burned the aviary.—The painter and the woodman in Paradise; the painter is burned.—The two brothers, the rich one and the poor one; the rich brother ends badly.—The husband who despoils his wife and hides her in a chest in the sand of the desert.—The gem of the prince falls to the ground; his nose bleeds and he dies; explanation of this myth.—The wonderful hammer, which, when used, brings one whatever is wished for.—The rich and poor brothers; the poor one becomes rich.—The lengthened nose and the corresponding Italian proverb.—The wife kills her husband with the hammer, wishing to knock a protuberance off his nose. —The old man who eats his last cow; his wife continues, even after its death, to nourish and protect him until the wild beasts in the cavern devour him.—The woman disguised as a solar hero. —The lion and the bull friends, or foster-brothers; their friendship is put an end to by the fox.—The projects of Perrette again.—The horns of the dead buffalo.—The grateful animals.—The laughing princess.—The wise herd-children.—The wise puppets.—The prince born of a cake.—The boy learns in the forest every art, even devilish ones.—The son of the wolves who understands their language.—Heroes and demons cut in pieces multiply themselves.—The hero has good luck, because he has performed funeral services to the dead.—Four young shepherds, a new form of the Ṛibhavas, make a beautiful maiden of wood, and then dispute for her.—The wife throws her husband into the fountain out of jealousy, having heard another voice, perhaps the echo of her own.—The princess Light of the sun, who must be seen by no one, and who is visited by the minister Moon.—Turanian tradition in Siberia.—The three brothers dream upon the mountain; the third brother is persecuted on account of his dream; he finds the blind woman and lame man, and induces them to adopt him; he hunts, fights against the devil, and vanquishes him; from the body of the demon come forth animals, men, and treasures; he fishes up in the sea of milk the casket which contains the eyes of the blind woman; receives extraordinary gifts, and above all the faculty of transforming himself; wins his predestined bride, and kills his own cruel father.—The hero who solves enigmas.—Ancient and modern riddles.—The cow devours the wolf, and the wolf devours the cow.—The bow of horn.—The wolves fastened to the calf's tail.—The soul of the black bull in the rainbow, the bridge of souls, wounded by the young hero, who then espouses the daughter of the sky, after attaining the third heaven, and accomplishing heroic undertakings to merit her.—The sleeper in the cup, the gem in the fish.—The Argonauts and Medea in Turan.—The Finnish Diana.—The Finnish thundering God, Kave Ukko.—The little sun, the Finnish dwarf-hero.—The second of the three brothers.—The strong bear.—The monster giant darkness or cloud.—The Orpheus and the lyre of the Finns; grief the inspirer of song.—Finnish and Aryan myths.—The Sampo.—Esthonian tradition.—The three sisters; the third is the most beautiful, and is persecuted by her stepmother, and delivered by the prince.—The bird of light.—The maiden transformed into a pond-rose, and delivered by her husband in the shape of a shrimp.—The witch is burned in the form of a cat.—The gold of the witch.—Explanation of several myths.—The third brother is the swiftest.—The wise maiden.—The golden fairy.—The puppet.—The magical rod makes the cock come out of the mountain.—The fairy is good towards the good, and punishes the wicked.—The cow lost.—The old hospitable dwarf.—The leaf which carries the hero across the waters.—Heroic undertakings against the serpent and the tortoise.—The third brother, expelled from home, travels and solves riddles on the way.—The rod which makes a bridge.—In heaven and in hell time passes quickly.—The hero under-cook.—The golden birds and the voyages to hell.—The brothers punished, and the bride won by the magical sword.—The son of thunder.—The weapon carried off from the god of thunder.—The weapon recovered.—The fisherman-god.—The marvellous musical instrument; the magical flute.—The three dwarfs.—The hat that makes its owner invisible, made of men's nails; the shoes which carry one where-ever one wishes, and the stick which fights of itself.—The proverb of the third who profits between two disputers again.—The third brother is the son of a king, exposed when a child; he awakens the princess who sleeps in the glass mountain; *non est mortua puella, sed dormit.*—Passage from the dawn of the day to the dawn of the year.—The child sold by his father without the latter's knowledge.—The boy exchanged.—The boy sets out to deliver the maiden from the demon.—The pea, the kidney-bean, the cabbage, and the pumpkin of funerals accompany the solar hero in his nocturnal voyage.—The symbol of abundance, of generation, of stupidity.—The nuptial beans.—Meaning of the myth concerning vegetables.—The region of silence.—The region of noise.—The wise girl helps the hero.—The cow milked and the calf bound.—The luminous ball comes out of the calf.—The antithesis of white and of black.—Hungarian proverbs.—The luminous ball comes out of the stone.—The luminous ball and the ring.—The fearless hero frees the castle from spirits.—The Esthonian story of Blue Beard.—The charivari in the nuptials of widowers.—The widow who burns herself.—The hero exposed, and then brought up among cowherds, feels himself predestined to reign, and learns the art by guiding herds.—The German (or Western) witch endeavours to take the red strawberries from the Esthonian hero.—The boy avenges this injury by causing her to be devoured by wolves, who will not touch her heart.—The gardener's daughter.—The broken ring; the two parts of the ring unite again; the husband and wife find each other once more.—The maiden born of the egg in the shape of a puppet.—The casket which brings good luck disappears when the young couple are married.

Moving now from India westwards, we find on one side the Iranian, and on the other the Turanian traditions. We cannot pass into Europe without at least indicating the general character of each.

In the Persian cosmogony, the bull (*gâus aevo dâto*) is

one of the first of created existences, being as old as the elements. It is, moreover, well known how much importance was ascribed to the bull among the Persians in the mysteries of the solar god Mithra, who is represented as a beautiful youth, holding the horns of a bull in his left hand, and having the knife of sacrifice in his right. Mithra sacrificing the bull is just the solar hero sacrificing himself in the evening. Indeed, in the Persian tradition, Mithra, like the Hindoo Yamas, holds the office of god of the dead, and as such, like Yamas, is of a monstrous aspect, and is found in the *Yaçna* represented with a thousand ears and ten thousand eyes.

As in India, so in Persia, the urine of the cow is used in ceremonies of purification, during which it is drunk.[1] We have already seen in the story of Utañkas how the excrement of the bull, upon which Utañkas fed, was ambrosia itself; and, indeed, all is beneficial which is given by the cow of abundance (the moon, the cloud, and the aurora), and by the divine bull (the moon and the sun). The mythical belief was natural, however disgusting when we insist on literal interpretation.

And even in the Persian tradition itself, a distinction already exists between common bulls or oxen and sacred or privileged ones. This distinction appears in the legend of Gemshid, whose bulls were all devoured by the devil, as long as they were protected by no magical rites; whilst, when he was given a red ox (or bull) cooked in old, that is strong, vinegar, to which was added garlic and rue (famous for its potency in exorcism), he disappeared and was never seen again.[2] The rue is probably the

[1] *Anquetil du Perron, Zendavesta*, ii. p. 545.

[2] Misit itaque Deus justissimus citissime Angelum Behman quasi esset fumus (jubendo): Ito et bovem rubrum accipiens mactato in nomine Dei qui prudentiam dat; eumque coquito in aceto veteri, et

fabulous plant which the Zend tradition surmises to have sprung from the sea *Vouru-Kasha,* whence Ahura Mazda draws the clouds, from which all healthful water is derived, and which corresponds to the sea of milk of Hindoo tradition, in which the ambrosia is agitated.

Thus the funereal cypress of Kishmar (planted by Zarathustra, with a branch from the tree of Paradise), under which more than two thousand cows and sheep could pasture, and the innumerable birds of which darkened the air, obscuring the light of the sun, reminds us of the celestial forest of the Vedâs, in which the shepherd-hero and the hunter-hero wander and are lost.

The idea of the funereal tree recalls to us that of the Persian mountain Arezûra or Demâvend, where the demons met together to plot evil, and where was the gate of hell.[1]

The Zend word *açma,* which signifies stone and heaven, yields us, in its double meaning, the key to the interpretation of the myth. This stone, inasmuch as it is dark, is of evil omen ; inasmuch as it shines, it is a gem, or gives the gem (the moon or the sun) ; whence, according to the *Minokhired,* the sky is the progeny of a precious stone.[2]

Thus to the mountain of the demons (where the sun goes down), is opposed in Persian tradition the glorious mountain, out of which are born the heroes and the kings

---

cave accurate facias, allio ac rutâ, superadditis ; et in nomine Dei ex olla effundito : deinde coram eo adpone ut comedat. Cumque portiunculam panis in illud friasset, Diabolus ille maledictus inde aufugit, abiit, evanuit et disparuit, nec deinde, illum aliquis postea vidit ; *Sadder,* p. 94.—The Russian peasants still believe that a household devil, the damavoi, enters into the stable, who, during the night, mounts on horses and oxen and makes them sweat and grow lean.—Cfr. also, on the *Damavoi,* Ralston's *Songs of the Russian people,* London, 1872, pp. 119-139.

[1] Cfr. Spiegel's *Avesta,* vol. ii. ; *Einleitung,* vii.

[2] Cfr. Spiegel's *Avesta,* vol. ii. 21.

(or from which the sun rises and the moon); because Haoma is born there (the Hindoo Somas), the ambrosial, golden, and health-bringing god, who gives them the divine nourishment, and because the sacred bird, which stays on that mountain, feeds them with ambrosia, whence the *Yaçna*[1] invites Haoma to grow on the road of the birds.

In a rather obscure passage of the *Gâthâ Ahunavaiti*, confirmed by the *Bundehesh*, the soul of the bull (or of the cow, as the case may be), despoiled of his body by the evil one, complains to the Supreme Creator that he is without defence against the assaults of his enemies, and that he has no invincible protector. Ahura Mazda seems to wish only to give him spiritual help, but the bull continues to declare himself unsatisfied, until Zarathustra, the defender, accords it, and he receives the gift of efficacious favours which Ahura Mazda alone possesses.[2] Zarathustra is himself also born upon a mountain;[3] while his son Çaoshyańç, the deliverer, comes out of the waters.

A sacred cow, or at least a bitch which guards the cows (*paçuvaiti*), seems, besides a good fairy, to be, in the *Vendiad* itself,[4] the conductor of the souls across the bridge Ćinvat, created by Ahura Mazda, to the kingdom of the blessed. The cow, as the guide of the souls[5] lost in the kingdom of the dead, and placed upon the bridge, is probably the moon; the bitch (also the moon) reminds us of the Hindoo Saramâ, the bitch which aids the heroes

[1] x. 11. [2] xxix.

[3] Cfr. Spiegel's *Avesta*, vol. ii. p. 8.

[4] xix. 99–101. Professor Spiegel translates "Mit dem Hunde, mit Entscheidung, mit Vieh, mit Stärke, mit Tugend, diese bringt die Seelen der Reinen über den Harabezaiti hinweg: über die Brücke Chinvat bringt sie das Heer der himmlischen Yazatas."

[5] Cows and calves, as a funeral gift, are spoken of in the *Khorda Avesta*, li. 15, Spiegel's version.

who have lost themselves in the nocturnal forest, grotto, or darkness. In the same chapter, after accounts of the bridge, we read the praise of the good Çaoka, who has many eyes (like the brâhmanic Indras, disguised as a woman, having a thousand eyes, and, after the adventure of Ahalyâ, a thousand wombs—the god hidden in the night, who looks at the world through a thousand stars); after Çaoka, of the splendid Veretraghna (who corresponds to Vṛitrahan, properly the discomfiter of the all-covering darkness); and after him, of the luminous star Tistar, which seems a bull with golden hoofs,[1] which again must refer to the moon; as the Gâhs, who, according to Anquetil, "sont occupées à filer des robes pour les justes dans le ciel," like the cows and Madonnas in our popular tales, cannot be very different from the fairy, or at least from the stars which form her crown. The *Khorda Avesta*, in its hymns in praise of Mithra, celebrates the perfect friendship which reigns between the sun and the moon, and sings of the moon immediately after singing of the sun Mithra, and the splendid Tistar immediately after the moon, whose light is said to come from the constellation Tistrya.

We can thus divine the meaning of Geusurva (the soul of the bull or the cow), of which, besides the soul, the

[1] Cfr. also the Tistrya with a whole eye of the *Khorda Avesta* of Spiegel, p. 9, and all the *Tistar Yast* in the *Khorda Avesta*, xxiv. If Tistar is the moon, Tistrya would appear to perform the same duties as the good fairy—that is, of showing, by means of her good eyes, her good eyesight, and her splendour, the way to the lost heroes. The Hindoo cow of Vasishṭhas, which yields every good thing, and which then fights in the clouds against Viçvâmitras, would sometimes appear to be the moon veiled by the rainy cloud; thus we can explain the rain-giving character of the star Tistṛya, which, according to the *Bundehesh*, by raining ten days and ten nights, destroyed the monsters of dryness created by the demon Aġro-maiṇyus.

body also is invoked in the *Yaçna.*[1] The Geusurva appears in the *Yaçna* itself[2] as the protectress of the fourteenth day of the month, or of the full-moon, viewed as a full cow. And when it is said in the *Khorda Avesta*[3] that one must not sacrifice to the Geusurva at the time when the Daevas, or demons, are practising their evil-doings, it seems to me to indicate clearly enough that the sacrifice was to take place while the moon was increasing, and not while it was diminishing. Thus Asha Vahista, who reminds us of the Hindoo Vasishṭhas and his marvellous cow, has the power of conjuring away illness, north winds—in a word, evil of every kind—only when Ag̃ro-mainyus appears without help.[4]

We have seen in the legend of Utañkas how, as the youth is on his way to take the queen's earrings, he meets a bull, upon the excrement of which he feeds, as upon ambrosia; that this ambrosial bull stays near Indras, as Indras and Somas are invoked together; and we noticed that from this mythical belief was derived the superstitious Hindoo custom of purifying one's self by means of the excrement of a cow. The same custom passed into Persia; and the *Khorda Avesta*[5] has preserved the formula to be recited by the devotee, whilst he holds in his hands the urine of an ox or cow, preparatory to washing his face with it:—"Destroyed, destroyed be the demon Ahriman, whose actions and works are cursed. His actions and works do not come to us. May the thirty-three Amshaspands (the immortal saints, who correspond to the thirty-three Vedic devâs), and Ormazd,

[1] xxxix. 1. [2] xvii. 25.

[3] Spiegel's version, p. 149.—Cfr. the three litanies for the body and soul of the cow, in the fragments of the same vol. p. 254.

[4] *Khorda Avesta,* Spiegel's version, *Einl.* x.

[5] Spiegel's version, p. 4.

be victorious and pure!" It is said this remedial formula was used for the first time by Yima, when, from having touched Ahriman, in order to extricate from his body, by fraud, Takh mo Urupa, whom the demon had devoured, he had an eruption on his hand. Finally, it is interesting to learn that one of the Zend names of the moon is *gaoćithra*, which means he that contains the seed of the bull, since, according to the *Bundehesh*, the seed of the primitive bull passed into the moon, who, having purified it, used it to procreate other cattle (*pôuru çaredho*).

As to the aurora, there seems to be no doubt but that she was represented in ancient Persia by Ardvî Çûra Anâhita, the elevated, the strong, the innocent or pure, according to the interpretation of Professor Spiegel; she also drives a chariot drawn by four white horses, which she guides herself; she has a veil, a diadem, and bracelets of gold, beautiful earrings (the Vedic Açvinâu), a dress of beavers' skin, and prominent breasts; she is beautiful, and she is a good young girl who protects men and women. She is often invoked in the *Khorda Avesta*, like the Vedic aurora, to exorcise the demons, and to help the heroes who combat them; she herself has the strength of a thousand men, and is a marvellous heroine, like the Vedic amazon whom Indras fought with; her body is girt round with a girdle. The probability of this comparison seems to pass into certainty after reading a hymn of the *Khorda Avesta*,[1] even in the version of Professor

[1] These are the exact terms used by Spiegel:—"Dieser opferte der frühere Vifra-navâza, als ihn aufrief der siegreiche, starke Thraetaona, in der Gestalt eines Vogels, eines Kahrkâça. Dieser flog dort während dreier Tage und dreier Nächte hin zu seiner eigenen Wohnung, nicht abwärts, nicht abwärts gelangte er genährt. Er ging hervor gegen die Morgenröthe der dritten Nacht, der starken, beim Zerfliessen der Morgenröthe und betete zur Ardvî Çûra, der fleckenlosen; Ardvî Çûra, fleckenlose!

Spiegel, who perhaps would have introduced some little variation if he had recognised the aurora in Ardvî Çûra Anâhita. In this hymn, the victorious and mighty Thraetaona, in the form of a bird, flies for three days and three nights, which reminds us of the fugitive Indras of the *Ṛigvedas,* who wades across the rivers after his victory; at the end of the third night he arrives near the aurora, and beseeches Ardvî Çûra Anâhita (that is, as it seems to us, the aurora herself, elevated, mighty, and innocent) to come and help him, that he may pass the waters and touch the ground at her habitation. Then Ardvî Çûra Anâhita appears in the shape of a beautiful, strong, and splendid girl, having a golden diadem and wearing shoes of gold (cfr. the *Yast,* xxi. 19) on her feet (this is perhaps another feeble foreshadow of Cinderella's slippers); the beautiful girl takes him by one arm (the bird has, it seems, become a hero), and gives him back health and strength. But the certainty increases still more when, as the Vedic aurora is the first of those who arrive, winning the race in her chariot, the so-called Ardhvî Çûra Anâhita appears in the *Khorda Avesta* as "the first who guides the chariot;"[1] and we are recommended to offer up sacrifices to her at break of day, be-

eile mir schnell zu Hülfe, bringe nun mir Beistand, ich will dir tausend Opfer mit Haoma und Fleisch versehene, gereinigte, wohl ausgesuchte, bringen hin zu dem Wasser Ragha, wenn ich lebend hinkomme zu der von Ahura geschaffenen Erde, hin zu meiner Wohnung. Es lief herbei Ardvî Çûra, die fleckenlose, in Gestalt eines schönen Mädchens, eines sehr kräftigen, wohlgewachsenen, aufgeschürzten, reinen, mit glänzendem Gesichte, edlen, unten am Fusse mit Schuhen bekleidet, mit goldnem Diadem auf dem Scheitel. Diese ergriff ihm am Arme, bald war das, nicht lange dauerte es, dass er hinstrebte kräftig zu von Ahura geschaffenen Erde, gesund, so unverletzt als wie vorher, zu seiner eignen Wohnung;" *Khorda Avesta,* pp. 51, 52.

[1] Welche zuerst den Wagen fährt; *Khorda Avesta,* Spiegel's version, p. 45.

fore the sun rises.[1] We have seen the Vedic aurora and the sun propose and solve riddles; we have seen the Hindoo solar hero free himself from the monster by proposing or solving insoluble enigmas; in the same way, in the *Avesta*, the hero Yaçto Fryananamm asks Ardvî Çûra Anâhita to help him to solve ninety-nine enigmas, in order that he may free himself from the monster Akhtya.

Add to this that Ardvî Çûra Anâhita, like the Vedic aurora, is a giver of cows and horses, and that these animals are offered to her by her devotees. The aurora herself, in the invocation made to her in the sixth prayer of the *Khorda Avesta*, is also called "elevated," and furnished with swift and splendid horses.[2] The fact of finding the Anâhita drawn by four white horses, like the sun Mithra, enhances the evidence of this identity. And if the aurora is not explicitly represented in the *Avesta* as a cow, we infer that it was so conceived of, from the worship of Mithra, who was adored from the first streak of daylight till midday. Mithra often receives the epithet of "he who possesses vast pasture-lands;" the morning sun is therefore a pastoral god; and if so, we are constrained to think of the Persian aurora too as, if not a cow, at least a female cowherd.

---

[1] Professor Spiegel says, however, "Vom Aufgang der Sonne bis Tagesanbruch," which in a note he explains, "Vom Sonnenaufgang bis Mitternacht," which it appears to us cannot stand scrutiny, any more than the conclusion inferred from this, that the sacrifice was to be made "den ganzen Tag hindurch." Zarathustra would not have been obliged to ask the precise time at which to sacrifice to the goddess, if she was to answer him in such a general way. What occasion is there to pray in midday, in full daylight, that the darkness may be dispersed?—If there be any equivoque, it can only be, in my opinion, in the rather frequent exchange of the maiden Aurora and the fairy Moon.

[2] Cfr. *Khorda Avesta*, Spiegel's version, pp. 7, 27.

But Mithra is not a god of mere idyllic exploits, he is also a hero; the *Vendidad*[1] salutes him as "the most victorious of the victors." The booty of his victory [essentially due to his immediate predecessors Veretraghna (Vṛitrahan) and Çraosha][2] must have been the cows of the aurora, without which his immense pasture-lands would have been of no use to him. Indeed it is said that Mithra enables owners of herds to recover their lost oxen.[3]

But Mithra is not the only prominent hero of the *Avesta*. Besides him, the above-cited Veretraghna, with all his secondary and tertiary reflections, plays an important part in it. Now, this Veretraghna, who offers numerous analogies to the Vedic Indras, killer of Vṛitras, is, like Indras, now a hero, now a horse, now a bird, now a sheep, now a wild boar, and now a bull.[4] As the bull Indras assists Tritas, Trâitanas, and Kavya Ućanas[5] in the *Ṛigvedas*, so the bull Veretraghna in the *Avesta*, partaking of the nature of one Thrita[6] who is rich, splendid, and strong, and who, like Indras, cures maladies by the help of the guardian of the metals (the usual co-relation between the hero and the magic pearl), assists Thraetaona, the killer of the serpent Duhâka (Azhi Dahâka)

[1] xix. 52.

[2] Cfr. the chapter which treats of the Cock.

[3] Cfr. *Khorda Avesta*, Spiegel's version, *Einl.* xxv., and all the important *Mirh Yast*, or collection of hymns in honour of Mithra, in the *Khorda Avesta*, xxvi.

[4] Cfr. *Khorda Avesta*, Spiegel's version, *Einl.* xxxiii., and the *Bahrâm Yast* in the *Khorda Avesta*, xxx. 7, Spiegel's version. It is then that he says of himself, "As to strength, I am the strongest." Further on it is said that strength belongs to the bull (or the cow).

[5] In a hymn, Indras even calls himself Uçanâ, with the added denomination of kavis; Ahaṁ kaviruçanâ: *Ṛigv.* iv. 26, 1.

[6] *Vendidad*, xxii. 11.

and the hero Kava Uça, of which Kava Haoçrava is another name rather than another form. The Thrita and Thraetaona of the *Zend* are peculiarly interesting, because they remind us, though vaguely, of the Vedic myth of the three brothers. Only the *Avesta* names Thrita and Thraetaona as two distinct divine heroes; it attributes to Thraetaona the second place among the three brothers; and as in the *Mahâbhâratam*, it is the second brother, the strong Bhîmas, who falls into the waters, whilst the third brother, Arǵunas, delivers others from the marine monster by his valour, so in the *Avesta* it is Thraetaona who comes out of the waters, or who is the son of Athvya (-Âptya). But every one can see the point of contact, connection, or identification between the two hero-brothers. It is Bhîmas who comes out of the waters, and Arǵunas who extricates him, that is, who extricates his own strength, expressed in Bhîmas (the subject, and his virtue, become the object, being inclosed in one person). They are confounded together, inasmuch as Thraetaona, son of him who stays in the waters, or of the watery one, or he who comes out of the waters, and kills the demon, must be the same as Thrita, the third one, who has the virtue of curing demoniacal diseases. Thraetaona, the killer of the serpent, and Thrita, who destroys the evil-doing ones, are found again, with a different splendour, in the same heroic adventure. Scarcely an instant transpires between the time when the hero was a victim and that in which Veretraghna, or Thraetaona, or Thrita, the hero, triumphs in his own liberation.

In the *Yaçna*,[1] we find three men who, by their piety, win the favour of the god Haoma (Soma, the lunar god, the moon, the good magician, the good fairy). The first

[1] Chap. ix.

is Vivaghâo, the second Âthvya, and the third Thrita; from which we are led to conclude that Vivaghâo is the eldest brother, Âthvya the second, and Thrita the youngest. On account of their piety, they obtain sons; the son of Vivaghâo is Yima (the Vedic Yamas), the wise, the happy, the heavenly; the son of Âthvya is Thraetaona, the warrior who discomfits the monster; the third, Thrita, called the most useful, has two sons, Urvâksha and Kereçâçpa, who remind us of the Açvinâu. Âthvya's son and Thrita being confounded in one person, Thraetaona, or Thrita, forms a new triumvirate with Urvâksha and Kereçâçpa, as the Vedic Indras with the two Açvinâu. The story of the three brothers and that of the two brothers seem to be interwoven even in the myth, as they certainly are afterwards in the legend. To the three brothers, moreover, correspond, in the *Avesta*, the three sisters, the three daughters of Zarathustra and of Hvôvi: Freni, Thriti, and Pourućiçsta.[1] The first seems to correspond to Yamas, the second to Âptya and his son Thraetaona (or Thrita), the third, the luminous, the beautiful (as being the aurora), to the two handsome brother horsemen, Urvâksha and Kereçâçpa (the Açvinâu).

The solar hero comes out of his difficulties, and triumphs over his enemies, not only by force of arms, but by his innate strength and prowess. This extraordinary strength, by which he moves and is borne along, and which renders him irresistible, is the wind, invoked by the heroes in the *Avesta* under the name of Râman. The wind, according to the *Avesta*, is not only the swiftest of the swift, but the strongest of the strong (like the Marutas, Hanumant, or Bhîmas, Hindoo winds, or sons of the wind). Even in

---

[1] Cfr. *Farvardin Yast* in the *Khorda Avesta*, xxix. 30, Spiegel's version.

the *Avesta*, he fights and assures the heroes of victory, and is dear to woman and girls. (In the same way, Sîtâ has a leaning for Hanumant, and Hidimbâ, of all the Pâṇḍavas, gives the preference to Bhîmas.) Moreover, in the *Avesta*, girls invoke the wind in order to obtain a husband.[1]

A hymn of the *Ṛigvedas*, however, celebrates a kind of quarrel between the winds Marutas and the god Indras, prompted by rivalry; a quarrel which ends in Indras having the advantage. It is interesting to find in the Persian tradition[2] the same rivalry between the wind (vâta) and the son of Thrita, the hero Kereçâçpa. An evil genie informs the wind that Kereçâçpa boasts of being superior to him in strength. Thereupon the wind begins to howl and rage in such a terrifying manner that nothing can resist him, and the very trees are cleft in two or torn up, till Kereçâçpa comes and squeezes him so tightly in his arms that he is obliged to cease. This interesting mythical incident is a prefigurement of the loud whistle of the heroes and the monsters in fairy tales, which is brought to an end in a summary fashion, similar to that of the Persian legend; which also leads us to suppose that Thraetaona vanquished the serpent Dahâka, merely by tying him to the demoniacal mountain Demâvend.[3] This style of vanquishing the enemy by binding him occurs often enough in the Persian

[1] Cfr. *Khorda Avesta*, Spiegel's version, *Einleit.* xxxiv., and the *Râm Yast* in the *Khorda Avesta*, xxxi. 40.—The 57th strophe appears to be a real Vedic hymn to the Marutas; the wind is celebrated as the strongest of the strong, the swiftest of the swift, having arms and ornaments of gold, a golden wheel and a golden chariot; his golden shoes and his girdle of gold besides show his sympathy and relation with the Ardvî Çûra Anâhita, who, in the form of aurora, is referred to in the 55th strophe.

[2] Cfr. *Khorda Avesta*, p. lxix.

[3] Cfr. ibid. p. lxi.

legends and in the *Avesta* itself;[1] and is also mentioned in the Hindoo traditions. The arrows of the monsters hurled against the heroes of the *Râmâyaṇam* bind them; the god Yamas and the god Varuṇas bind their victims; the first draws tight, tightens the reins (*i.e.*, the evening sun shortens his rays); the second envelops, covers and binds with the darkness that which Yamas reined in. The solar ray which shortens itself, the shadow which advances, are images of the ensnarer of heroes; whereas the solar ray which lengthens itself, the thunderbolt which traverses all the heavens, surrounded by clouds and darkness, represents the hero who grasps around, presses tightly, and strangles the monster.

The bow of Mithra is formed of a thousand bows, prepared from the tough hide of a cow; these bows, in the *Avesta*, also hurl a thousand darts, which fly with winged vultures' feathers.[2] This carries us back again to the Vedic myth of the birds which come out of the cow.

The bow being considered a cow, this cow sharpens its horns; whence the *Khorda Avesta* celebrates the horned darts of the bow of Mithra, *i.e.*, the horns of the cow, which have become weapons[3] or the thunderbolts.

The legend of the two brothers is connected more with the myth of the horse than with that of the cow or the ox. But inasmuch as it presents the two brothers to us as the one poor and the other rich, the riches are symbolised by the ox. However, if I am not mistaken,

[1] Denn Verethraghna, der von Ahura geschaffene, hält die Hände zurück der furchtbaren Kampfesreihen, der verbündeten Länder und der mithratrügenden Menschen, er umhüllt ihr Gesicht, verhüllt ihre Ohren, nicht lässt er ihre Füsse ausschreiten, nicht sind sie mächtig; *Khorda Avesta.* xxx. 63, Spiegel's version.

[2] Cfr. the *Mihr Yast* in the *Khorda Avesta,* xxvi. 128, 129.

[3] Cfr. ibid.

there are two heroes, celebrated in the *Avesta* one after the other (and whom I therefore suppose to be brothers), who derive their origin from this legend; one is called Çrîraokhsan (or who has a fine ox), the other Kereçaokhsan (or who has a lean ox). As the *Avesta* does not go on to develop this subject more in detail, I dare not insist upon it; nevertheless it is gratifying to me to remark that, of the two brothers, Kereçaokhsan was the most valiant, as of the two brothers Urvâksha (a word which may perhaps signify the one who has the fat horse, and which is perhaps synonymous with Urvâçpa [1]) and Kereçâçpa (he of the lean horse), it is the second who is the glorious hero; as in the Russian popular tales, we shall find the third brother, though thought to be an idiot, despised by the others, and riding the worst jade of the stable, yet becoming afterwards the most fortunate hero. Kereçâçpa avenges his brother Urvâksha against Hitâçpa, whom Professor Spiegel [2] interprets to mean the bound horse, but which can also be rendered he who keeps the horse bound, which would bring us back again to the story of the bridle and of the hero-horse, whom the demon keeps bound to himself, which we have already noticed above in the story of the sacrifice of Çunaḥcepas, delivered by the aurora.

It is uncertain whether we must recognise the aurora or the moon, in the *Avesta*, in the so-called Ashis Vag̃uhi, the elevated (like Ardvî Çûra Anâhita), who appears upon the high mountain, rich, beautiful, splendid, golden-eyed, beneficent, giver of cattle, posterity, and abundance, who discomfits the demons, guides chariots, and is invoked by

[1] Urvâksha is also called the accumulator; *Khorda Avesta*, xl. 3, Spiegel's version.

[2] *Khorda Avesta*, p. 155.

the son of the watery one, Thraetaona, in the *Ashi Yast,*[1] in order that she may help him to vanquish the three-headed monster-serpent Dahâka. Now, Thraetaona, the victorious and rich in oxen,[2] being a well-known form of the solar hero Mithra, it is interesting to learn how the heroine, the so-called Ashis Vaǧuhi (the aurora, or the moon, as the three words Ardvî Çûra Anâhita are simple names of the aurora), having the same supreme god for her father, has three brothers, of whom the first is Çraosha, the pious; the second, Rashnus, the strong; and the third, Mithra, the victorious.

She is, moreover, herself represented as being pursued by enemies on horseback; and it is now a bull, now a sheep, now a child, anon a virgin who hides her from her pursuers. Not knowing where to go, whether to ascend into heaven, or creep along the earth, she applies to Ahura Mazda, who answers that she must neither ascend into heaven nor creep along the earth, but betake herself to the middle of a beautiful king's habitation.[3] How is it possible not to recognise in her the moon, or the aurora, who follows the path of the sun her husband, the moon, or the aurora, who appears on the summit of the high mountains?

Other facts not devoid of mythological interest might perhaps be found in the *Avesta,* which, on account of the

---

[1] *Khorda Avesta,* xxxiii., Spiegel's version.

[2] Mögest du reich an Rindern sein wie (der Sohn) de Athvyânischen (clanes); *Khorda Avesta,* xl. 4, Spiegel's version.

[3] Soll ich zum Himmel aufsteigen, soll ich in die Erde kriechen? Darauf entgegnete Ahura Mazda: Schöne Ashi, vom Schöpfer geschaffene! steige nicht zum Himmel auf, krieche nicht in die Erde; gehe du hieher in die Mitte der Wohnung eines schönen Königs; *Khorda Avesta,* xxxiii. 59, 60, Spiegel's version.—Cfr. xxxiv. 3, and following, where are celebrated the handsome husband of the beautiful Ashis and his rich kingdom.

uncertainty attending the translation of the original texts, has hitherto been, it seems to me, utterly neglected by mythologists. And yet, though Anquetil, Burnouf, Benfey, Spiegel, Haugh, Kossowicz, and all who have turned their talents and science to the interpretation of the Zendic texts, disagree in the more abtruse passages, there are many of which the interpretation is certain, in which the learned translators agree, which offer interesting mythological data, and permit us, in any case, to extract from the *Avesta* an embryo of mythology, in the same way as an embryo of grammar has already been extracted from it. The brief references which I have now made to the myth of the cow and the bull in the *Avesta*, anyhow appear to me sufficient to warrant the conclusion I draw, that the cow and the bull presented the same aspects, and generated the same myths and the same beliefs in Persia as in India, albeit in a form far more feeble and indeterminate.

The solar hero of Persia occurs again in the costume of historical legend in the Cyrus (Κῦρος) of Herodotus and Ktesias, the first of which represents to us the child exposed by his parents, saved and educated during his infancy (like the Hindoo Karṇas, child of the sun, and Kṛishṇas) among the shepherds, where for some time he gives extraordinary proofs of his valour; the second shows us the young hero who wins his own bride, Amytis, daughter of Astyages.

Finally, the same hero appears in several splendid and glorious forms in the *Shahname*.

As in the *Ṛigvedas*, Tritas or Trâitanas, and in the *Avesta*, Thraetaona (of whom Thritas is a corresponding form), accomplish the great exploit of killing the monster, and more especially the serpent, so Feridun, the Persian synonym (by means of the intermediate form Phreduna) for the Zendic Thraetaona is, in subsequent Persian tradition, the most distinguished hero in the struggle against the monster. I shall not insist upon the deeds of Feridun and his mythical valour, after the learned paper written upon the subject by Professor R. Roth, which appears in the Transactions of the Oriental Society of Leipzig, and the able and highly-valued essay by Professor Michael Bréal on the myth of Hercules and Cacus. I shall therefore content myself with quoting from the legend of Feridun the episode of his old age, which reminds us of the Vedic myth of the three brothers.

The great king Feridun has three sons, Selm, Tûr, and Ireǵ (Selm, Tûr, and Er are also the sons of Thraetaona); he divides the world into three parts and gives the west to the first-born, and the north to the second, whilst he keeps Iran for the youngest. The two eldest are jealous, and announce to their father their intention of declaring war against him, unless he expels their younger brother Ireǵ from the palace. Feridun replies to their impious threat with haughty reproofs, and meanwhile warns the young Ireǵ of the danger he is in. The youth proposes to go in person to his brothers, and induce them to make peace; his father is unwilling to let him go, but finally consents, and gives him a letter for the two brothers, in which he commends him as his best-loved son to their care. Ireǵ arrives at his brothers' dwelling; their soldiers see him, and cannot take their eyes off him, as though they already recognised him for their lord. Then Selm, the eldest, advises Tûr, the second, the strong one, to kill Ireǵ; Tûr thereupon assaults the defenceless Ireǵ, and transfixes his breast with a dagger. Ireǵ is afterwards avenged by the son of his daughter (born after his death of a maid whom he had left pregnant), the hero Minućehr, who kills Selm and Tûr.

The hero who succeeds Minućehr is Sal, the son of Sam, whom, because born with white hair, his father had exposed upon Mount Alburs, where the bird Simurg nourished and saved him. Sal proves his wisdom before Minućehr by solving six astronomical riddles which King Minućehr proposes to him. The king, satisfied, orders him to be dressed in festive clothes; he then, to prove his strength, challenges him to run a tilt with the horsemen; Sal is victorious, and obtains another robe of honour and innumerable royal gifts; after which he espouses Rudabe, daughter of King Mihrab.

Sal distinguishes himself, like Minućehr, in his wars against the perverse Turanians, the dragons and the monsters, in which he takes along with him as his chief helper the mighty hero Rustem, whose weapon is a club surmounted with the head of a bull[1] or a horned mace (the hero is the bull, the thunderbolts are his horns), and whose horse is so powerful as by itself to fight and vanquish a lion while Rustem is asleep. The hero himself kills a dragon, and a witch transformed into a beautiful woman, but who resumes her monstrous shape as soon as the hero pronounces the name of a god. He thunders like a cloud, is dark, and describes himself as a thunder-cloud which hurls the thunderbolt.[2] He binds the warrior Aulad, and obliges him to reveal where the demons detain in prison King Kawus, who is become blind in their kingdom of darkness. Kawus then informs Rustem that to recover his sight his eyes must be anointed

[1] Die Stierkopfkeule in der Rechten schwingend; Schack, *Heldensagen von Firdusi*, iv. 2.—Cfr. viii. 9.

[2] Die Donnerwolke bin ich, die Blitzeskeule schleudert; Schack, *Heldensagen von Firdusi*, v. 5.

with three drops of blood from the slain demon Sefid; upon which Rustem sets out to kill the demon. The demons can be vanquished only by day; when it is light, they sleep, and then they can be conquered, says Aulad to Rustem; for this reason, Rustem does not begin the enterprise till the sun is in mid-heaven;[1] then he thunders and lightens at the demons. Like a sun, he sets out towards the mountain (no doubt, towards sunset), where the demon Sefid sits, and arrives at the mouth of a deep and gloomy cavern, from which Sefid sallies forth in the form of a black giant just awakened from his sleep. The giant himself, like an enormous mountain assaulting the earth, hurls a rock like a millstone at Rustem; Rustem strikes the monster on the feet, and lops away one of them; the lame giant continuing the fight, Rustem at last wrestles with him, lifts him into the air, then beats him several times furiously against the ground, and so takes his life. He throws the body of Sefid into the mountain cavern, whilst his blood saturates the earth, and gives back to the prince Kawus his eyesight and his splendour. The myth is a beautiful and an expressive one. As from the black venomous serpent comes white healthy milk, so from the black monster, at his death, comes blood, which gives back his eyesight to the blinded prince; the red aurora is here represented as the blood of the nocturnal monster, discomfited by the solar hero.

Let me ask the reader to notice the Persian comparison of the rock thrown by the demon to a millstone, as it is important to explain a superstition still extant in the

[1] Die Diwe (the demons) pflegen um Mittagszeit zur Ruhe sich zu legen; das ist die Stunde sie zu besiegen. Nicht eher schreitet Rustem zu der That, bis sich die Sonne hoch erhoben hat; *Schack, Heldensagen von Firdusi*, v. 5.

West, to the effect that the devil goes under the millstone to carry out his evil designs. The stone or mountain fractured by the waters was naturally compared to a millstone moved by the waters; the demons inhabit the cavernous mountain to guard the waters; thus the devil, the evil one, the hobgoblins, prefer mills as their dwellings.

Rustem fights, in the *Shahname*, many other victoriously successful battles against Afrasiab the Turanian, and other demoniacal beings, in the service of sundry heroic kings, with epic incidents to boot, which are nearly all uniform. His struggle against his son Sohrab, however, is of an entirely different character.

Rustem goes to the chase. In the forest, Turkish bandits rob him of his invaluable horse while he sleeps; he then sets out, alone and sad, towards the city of Semengam, following the track left by his horse. When he appears, emerging from the wood, the king of Semengam and his courtiers note the phenomenon as though it were the sun coming out of the clouds of morning.[1] The king receives Rustem with great hospitality, and, as if to fill to the full the measure of his courtesy, he sends at night to the room where he sleeps his exceedingly beautiful daughter Tehmime. The hero and the beauty separate in the morning; but Rustem, before parting from Tehmime, leaves her a pearl of recognition. If a daughter is born to their loves, she is to wear it as an amulet in her hair; if a son, he is to wear it on his arm, and he will become an invincible hero. After nine months, Tehmime gives birth to Sohrab; at the age of one month he seems a year old, at three years of age he amuses himself with

[1] Ist's Rustem? ist es nicht die Sonne, die durch Morgenwolken bricht? *Schack, Heldensagen von Firdusi*, vii. 2.

arms, at five he gives proof of a lion's courage, and at ten he vanquishes all his companions, and asks his mother to inform him of his father, threatening to kill her if she does not tell him. Scarcely does Sohrab learn that he is the son of Rustem, than he conceives the desire of becoming king of Iran and supplanting Kawus; he then commences his persecution of the Iranian heroes by assaulting the white castle (the white morning sky, the alba), defended by a beautiful warrior princess, Gurdaferid, dear to the Iranian warriors. Sohrab conquers and destroys the white castle, but in the moment of triumph, the warrior maiden disappears. The old hero Rustem then moves against his own son Sohrab; the latter throws him down, but Rustem, in his turn, mortally wounds Sohrab. In the old Rustem thrown down on the mountain it is not difficult to recognise the setting sun; in Sohrab mortally wounded by Rustem, the sun itself, which dies; and in fact, the dying sun has a different appearance from the new sun which rises and triumphs in the heavens: these two appearances might give rise to the idea of a struggle between the old and the young sun, in which both are sacrificed. Indeed, Rustem feels, when he mortally wounds Sohrab, that he is wounding himself; he curses his work and immediately sends for a healing balsam; but in the meantime Sohrab dies. The only one who could destroy the young sun was the old sun; the sun grows old and dies; Rustem alone could kill Sohrab. With the death of Sohrab the glory of Rustem is also eclipsed; he retires unto solitude, and the most grandiose period of his epic life comes to an end. After this he only reappears in episodic battles or enterprises; as, for instance, in his setting fire to Turan, in which he resembles Hanumant, burner of Lañkâ; in the liberation of the young hero Bishen, who had been taken prisoner and incarcerated by the Turanians; in the killing of the powerful and perverse Turanian Afrasiab; and in his own death in an ambuscade set by young rivals of the old lion, who dies taking vengeance on his enemies.

In the very palace of Kawus (he who was protected by Rustem), a notable legendary drama takes place. Sijavush, son of King Kawus, is seduced by the queen-mother Sudabe, who burns with love for him. The youth spurns this love, upon which she accuses him to King Kawus as her seducer. The father, after hearing his son's defence in proof of his innocence, cannot believe the queen; and thereupon she devises another method for destroying the young Sijavush. She concerts with a slave she has, who is a sorceress, and persuades her to create two little venomous monsters, which she straightway proclaims aloud are the children of Sijavush. Then Sijavush, to prove his innocence, submits willingly to the trial by fire; he enters the flames upon his black horse, after having embraced his trembling father; both horse and horseman come out of the immense fire, amid the plaudits of all the spectators. Then the king gives orders to strangle the unnatural queen; but his son Sijavush intercedes in her favour, and Sudabe is allowed to live by grace of the young prince, whom, however, she continues to persecute, till, on the death of Sijavush, Rustem, who bewailed him as his own son, or as his other self, avenges him first by killing Sudabe, on account of whom Sijavush had been obliged to repair to Turan, and afterwards by carrying the war into Turan, where, after a very agitated life, Sijavush had fallen into the power of his father-in-law, Afrasiab, and been put to death.

The wife of Sijavush, Ferengis by name, being pregnant, is hospitably entertained by Piran, and gives birth to the hero Kai Khosru; and no sooner is he born than he is consigned to the shepherds of the mountain. As early as seven years of age, his favourite amusement is that of drawing the bow; at ten, he confronts wild boars, bears, lions, and tigers with only his shepherd's staff. When Afrasiab sees the young shepherd, he inquires at him about his sheep and the peaceful pursuits of shepherds; the boy replies with stories of lions having sharp teeth, and of other wild animals, of which he is not afraid. As soon as he comes to manhood, he flees from Turan, followed by the Turanians; he arrives at the banks of a river, where the ferryman asks impossible conditions to take him over; upon which, like Feridun, he crosses the river safely, but without a boat, and on dry feet (it is the sun traversing the cloudy and gloomy ocean without wetting himself);[1] arrived at length in Iran, he is feasted and fêted as the future king. His reign begins; he then assigns different tasks to different heroes, among whom is his brother Firud, born of another mother, of whom it is said that a single hair of his head has more strength in it than many warriors (one ray of the sun is enough to break the darkness). One evening, however, at sunset, Firud is killed in his castle upon the mountain, being surrounded by a crowd of enemies, after having lost his horse, and after his mother Cerire had dreamt that a fire had consumed both mountain and castle. His mother Cerire (the evening aurora) throws herself among the flames with her maids, and dies also. Kai Khosru bewails the loss of his brother Firud all the night through,

[1] Indeed, this undertaking seems to the ferryman himself so supernatural, that he says these cannot be called men: "In Wahrheit, Menschen kann man sie nicht heissen." *Schack, Heldensagen von Firdusi*, x. 27.

till the cock crows; when morning comes he thinks of avenging him.

After this, the life of Kai Khosru is consumed in battles fought by his heroes against the Turanians. Only towards the end of his days does he become a penitent king; he will no longer allow his subjects to fight, and his only occupation is prayer; he takes leave of his people and his daughters in peace, ascends a mountain, and disappears in a tempest, leaving no trace of himself. In a similar manner the heroes Yudhishṭhiras, Cyrus, and Romulus disappear (not to speak of the biblical Moses, still less of Christ, as we do not wish to complicate a comparison of which the materials are already so extensive, by mixing up the Aryan elements with those of Semitic origin; although the legends of the serpent, of Noah, of Abraham and his regained wife, of Abraham and his son Isaac, of Joseph and his brethren, of Joshua, of Job, and other and more recent biblical heroes, by their mythical or astronomical import, present numerous analogies with the Indo-European legends); in a similar manner, the old sun, weary of reigning in the heavens and fighting for his life, becomes invisible every evening on the mountain-peaks.

The *Shahname* contains numerous other legends besides those which we have thus far briefly described; and one of the most notable is, beyond a doubt, that of Isfendiar, who goes with his brother Bishutem to deliver his two sisters, imprisoned in a fortress by the Turanian king Ardshasp. The seven adventures of Isfendiar, *i.e.*, his meeting with the wolf, the lion, the dragon, the witch (who makes herself beautiful, but who is no sooner bound with the enchanted necklace of Isfendiar [the solar disc] than she becomes old and ugly again), the gigantic bird, the tempest and the river, all of which dangers he victoriously overcomes, are reproductions, in an analogous form too, of the seven adventures of Rustem.

Finally, the legend of Iskander or Iskender (the name of Alexander of Macedon), full of extraordinary adventures, became exceedingly popular in Persia, and thence, no doubt, passed with all its charms into Europe. The audacity and good fortune, the glory and the power of the great conqueror were the reasons why there grouped round his name so many extraordinary stories, which wandered dispersedly through the world without epic unity. To make up one glorious and never-to-be-forgotten hero, were combined together the achievements of many anonymous or nearly forgotten ones. The Persian *Iskendername* of Nishâmi, is, as its name denotes, entirely taken up with the celebration of the deeds of the Macedonian hero, of which the most illustrious are the liberation of the princess Nushâbe (taken prisoner by the Russians), and the voyage in search of the fountain of life and immortality, which, however, Iskander cannot find. From Persia the same legend afterwards passed, with new disguises, into Egypt, Armenia, and Greece, whence it was diffused during the middle ages over almost the whole of Western Europe.[1]

As a bridge of transition between the Hindoo and Persian, and the Turk or Tartar traditions, we shall make use of three works: the Turkish version[2] of the Persian *Tuti-Name*, itself a translation and in part a paraphrase of the Hindoo *Çuka-Saptatî*, *i.e.*, the seventy (stories) of the parrot; the Mongol stories of *Siddhi-kûr*, and the

[1] Cfr. Spiegel's *Die Alexandersage bei den Orientale*, Leipzig, 1851; and Zacher's *Pseudocallisthenes, Forschungen zur Kritik und Geschichte der ältesten Aufzeichnung der Alexandersage*, Halle, 1867.

[2] Georg Rosen's version, Leipzig, Brockhaus, 1858, 2 vols.

Mongol history of *Ardshi-Bordshi Khân,*[1] the first being a paraphrase of the Hindoo *Vetâla-Pańćavinçatî, i.e.*, the twenty-five of the Vetâla (a kind of demon), and the second of the Hindoo *Vikrama-ćaritram* (the heroic action).

We have seen in the *Âitareya Brahmânam* the father who prepares to offer up his son, and in the *Mahâbhâratam,* the son who forfeits youth that his father may live. In the *Tuti-Name,*[2] the faithful Merdi Gânbâz prepares to sacrifice his wife and sons, and afterwards himself, to prolong the life of the king; but his devotion and fidelity being proved, he is arrested by God before he can accomplish the cruel sacrifice, and receives numberless benefits from the king.

In the story of the goldsmith and the woodcutter, the *Tuti-Name*[3] reproduces the two brothers or friends, of whom one is wicked, rich, and avaricious, while the other is defrauded of the money due to him, because, though, in reality intelligent, he is supposed to be an idiot. The woodcutter avenges himself upon the goldsmith by a plan which we shall find described in the legend of the bear, and recovers, thanks to his craftiness, the gold which his brother or friend had kept from him.

In the interesting story of Merhuma,[4] we read of the wife who is persecuted by the seducer her brother-in-law. To avenge her refusal, he causes her to be stoned during the absence of his brother; being innocent, she rises again from under the stones; being sheltered by a Bedouin, a monster of a slave seduces her; being repulsed, he accuses her of the death of the Bedouin's

[1] Bernhard Jülg's version, Innsbruck, 1867–1868.

[2] i. 5.

[3] i. 6.

[4] *Tuti-Name*, i. 7.

little son, whom he had himself killed; the beautiful girl flees away; she frees a youth who was condemned to death, and who in his turn seduces her. She then embarks in a ship; while she is at sea all the sailors become enamoured of her and wish to possess her; she invokes the god who caused Pharaoh to be drowned and who saved Noah from the waters. The waves begin to move; a thunderbolt descends and burns to ashes all who are in the ship, with the exception of the beautiful girl, who lands safe and sound upon the shore (it is the aurora coming out of the gloomy ocean of night, and the monsters who persecute her are burned to ashes by the thunderbolts and the sun's rays); she thence escapes into a convent, in which she ministers to the unfortunate, cures the lame, and gives eyesight to the blind. Among the latter is her persecutor, the brother of her husband; she pardons him and gives him back his eyesight; in the same way she cures all her other persecutors. It is scarcely necessary for me to remind the reader how this oriental tale, which developed itself from the myth of the persecuted and delivering aurora which we have seen in the Vedic hymns, reappears in numerous very popular western legends, of which Crescentia and Geneviève are the most brilliant types.

The aurora comes out of the gloomy ocean and is espoused by the sun; these heavenly nuptials in proximity to the sea gave rise to the popular tale[1] of the king who wishes the sea with its pearls to be present at his nuptials; the pearls of the bride-aurora are supposed to come out of the sea of night. The sea sends as gifts to the king a casket of pearls, a chest of precious dresses, a

[1] *Tuti-Name,* i. 13.

horse that goes like the morning wind, and a chest full of gold.

The wise aurora figures again in the story of the ingenious princess[1] who discovers, by means of a story-riddle, the robbers who, during the night, stole the precious gem destined for the king.

The aurora imparts splendour and eyesight to the blinded sun. The story of the three-breasted princess who, while she meditates poisoning the blind man, in order that she may enjoy unrestained the affections of her young and handsome lover, relents and gives him back his sight, reappears in a rather incomplete form in the *Tuti-Name.*[2]

The girl who has been married to a monster, whom she flees from to follow a handsome young lover, who, arriving at the banks of a river, despoils her of her riches, leaves her naked and passes over to the other side, after which she resigns herself to her fate and resolves to return to her husband the monster,[3] represents the evening aurora, who flees before the monster of night to follow her lover the sun, who, in the morning, after adorning himself with her splendour, leaves her on the shore of the gloomy ocean and runs away, the aurora being thereupon obliged in the evening to re-unite herself to her husband the monster. It is interesting, moreover, as bearing upon our subject, to note the expression of which the youth who flees with the beautiful woman makes use to express his fear of discovery. He says that the monster-husband will follow them, and that should he sit upon the horns of the bull (the moon) he would be sure to recognise him.

[1] *Tuti-Name*, i. 14.—Cfr. Afanassieff, *Narodnija ruskija skaski*, vi. 23.

[2] iii. 27.

[3] ii. 17.

The story of two young people fleeing upon a bull, and followed by the monster, occurs again in the Russian popular tales. By the horns of the bull, the youth means the most prominent and visible situation; and he knows, moreover, that if the monster overtakes them, he will be sure to demonstrate the truth of the brave proverb which advises us in arduous undertakings to take the bull by the horns.

It is also the aurora who is represented by the beautiful maiden[1] whom her father, mother, and brother have, without each other's knowledge, severally affianced to three youths of different professions. The three young men contend for her person, but while the quarrel is undecided, the girl dies. The three then go to visit her tomb; one discovers her body, the second finds that there is still some life in her, and the third strikes her and raises her up alive, upon which the quarrel is resumed. She flees from them, and withdraws into another living tomb, a convent. In the most popular form of this legend the three companions, or three brothers, fighting for the bride, divide her; the aurora is torn into pieces as soon as the sun, her true lover and rightful suitor, appears.

From darkness comes forth light; from the old, the young; from death, life; from the dust of a dead man's skull, tasted by a virgin, is born a wonderful child, who knows how to distinguish false pearls from real, dishonest women from honest ones[2] (the morning sun can distinguish between light and darkness); the wise boy (the young sun) is the brother of the wise girl (the young aurora). The flesh of a killed Brâhman is turned into gold in another story of the *Tuti-Name.*[3]

---

[1] *Tuti-Name,* ii. 19. [2] ii. 21. [3] ii. 28.

We have seen that the aurora and the sun are mother and son, brother and sister, or lover and mistress. The sun in the evening dies ignominiously, is sacrificed and hanged upon a gibbet, and with himself sacrifices his mother or his mistress. The legend is popular and ancient which speaks of the robber son, when about to end his life upon a gibbet,[1] biting the nose off his mother, who gave birth to him and brought him up badly. In the *Tuti-Name*,[2] it is the young adulterer (and robber too) who, condemned to death for his adultery, asks to see his mistress once more before his death and kiss her, and who, as she does so, gratifies his revenge by inflicting upon her a like indignity. It is remarkable how, even in the Hindoo popular tale, the story of the adulterer is confounded with that of a thief; the adulterer ends by being thrown into the water (the sun and the aurora fall into the gloomy ocean of night).

In the next story it is the wicked husband who, travelling with his rich wife for change of dwelling-place, despoils her of her clothes, and then throws her into a well in order to ensure possession of her jewels and wardrobe. These riches, however, do not last long; he becomes poor and goes begging alms, dressed as a mendicant, until he finds his wife again, who had been saved by divine intervention from the well, and provided anew with clothes and jewels of equal gorgeousness. The husband passes some time with his wife, and then sets out again on a voyage with her; he arrives at the same well, and throws her in as before to enjoy alone her stripped-off garnitures and riches. (The meaning of the myth is evi-

[1] This story was current in Italy as early as the fifteenth century, having been related to her son by the mother of the philosopher and man of letters Pontano, as I find from his biography, published last year by Professor Tallarigo (Sanseverino-Marche).

[2] ii. 21.

dent; it is the sun throwing the splendid aurora into the gloomy waters of the night.)

A king becomes enamoured of the beauteous Mahrusa;[1] his councillors tear him from his love, upon which he pines away in solitude and dies. The beautiful girl unites herself to him in the grave (Romeo and Juliet, the evening aurora and the sun die together).

The story of the three brothers, the Ṛibhavas, occurs again in the *Tuti-Name*,[2] with other particulars which we already know. The first brother is the wise one; the second is a maker of talismans (amongst other things he can make a horse which will run in one day over a space of ground that would take other horses thirty); the third and youngest brother is the victorious archer. They set out to search for the beautiful maiden who has fled by night from the house of her father. The first brother discovers, by his wisdom, that the maiden was carried off by the fairies into an island-mountain which men cannot reach. The second creates a wonderful animal upon which to traverse the intervening waters (Christophoros or Bhîmas). Having arrived at the island-mountain, the third and youngest brother fights the demon, the lord of the fairies, vanquishes him, and frees the beautiful girl, who thereupon is conducted back to her father. Then there arises the usual quarrel between the three brothers as to who is to possess the bride.

In the Vedâs, we have the sky and the moon represented as a cup. From the little cup of abundance (the moon) it is easy to pass to the miraculous little pipkin (the moon), in which the kind-hearted but poor housekeeper of the Pâṇḍavas, in the *Mahâbhâratam*, still finds abundance of vegetables, after her powers of hospi-

[1] *Tuti-Name*, ii. 25. [2] ii. 24.

tality had been exhausted on the god Kṛishṇas disguised as a beggar—to the pipkin from which can be taken whatever is wished for. In the *Tuti-Name,*[1] a woodcutter finds ten magicians round a pipkin, and eating out of it as much and whatever they want; they are pleased with the woodcutter, and, at his request, give him the pipkin. He invites his acquaintances to a banquet at his house, but not able to contain himself for joy, he places the pipkin upon his head, and begins to dance. The pipkin falls to the ground and is broken to pieces, and with it his fortune vanishes (the story of Perrette).

A variation of the small cup is the wooden porringer (the moon), which two brothers (the Açvinâu) dispute for, in the history of the king of China,[2] and from which can be taken whatever drink and food is wished for; as, in the same story, we find the enchanted shoes which carry us in an instant wherever we wish to go;—which brings us back to the fugitive Vedic aurora, the swiftest in the race, and to the popular tales relating to Cinderella, who is overtaken and found again by the prince only when she has lost her enchanted slipper. With the porringer and the enchanted shoes we find, in the popular tales, the little purse full of money which fills again as fast as it is emptied (another form of the cup of abundance), and a sword which, when unsheathed, causes a fine, rich, and great city to arise in a desert, which city disappears when the sword is put back into the sheath (the solar ray is the drawn sword, which makes the luminous city of the rich aurora arise; scarcely does the sun's ray vanish, or scarcely is the sword sheathed, than the marvellous city vanishes). The rest of the story is also

[1] ii. 26.

[2] ii. 28.

interesting, because it applies to three men a double and well-known fable of the animals which contend for the prey (as the three brothers contend for the beautiful maiden whom they have found again). The animals cannot divide it equally; they refer to the judgment of a man passing by; he divides it so well that the animals are ever after grateful to him, and help him in every danger. The story of the *Tuti-Name* touches upon this form of the myth, but soon abandons it for another equally zoological, and a more familiar one, that of the third who comes in between two that quarrel, and enjoys the prey. The young adventurer undertakes to put an end to the dispute of the two brothers as to the division of the purse, the porringer, the sword and the wonderful shoes; he does so by putting the shoes on his feet and fleeing away with the other three articles contended for (the two brothers Açvinâu, the two twilights, contend for the moon and also for the aurora, as we shall see better in the next chapter; the sun puts an end to their quarrel by espousing her himself).

We are already familiar with the Vedic Ṛibhavas who out of one cup make four. Probably upon this legend depends that of the four brothers of the *Tuti-Name*,[1] who, as they let each a pearl fall from their forehead upon the ground, see four mines open, one of copper, the second of silver, the third of gold (the third brother is here again the favourite), the fourth only of iron. The gem appears to be the sun itself. The four mines seem to me to represent respectively the coppery sky in the evening, the silver sky in the moonlight night, the sky in the morning, golden with the dawn, and the iron sky, the grey or azure, of the day. The word *nîlas* in Sanskrit

[1] ii. 29.

means azure, as well as black, and between azure and black is grey, the colour of iron.

Of the three brothers, the most learned, he who solves the enigmas, is often the eldest; and in the story of the *Tuti-Name*,[1] the eldest of the three brothers explains why old men have white hair, saying that this whiteness is a symbol of the clearness of their thoughts.

Let us now pass to the Calmuc and Mongol stories of *Siddhi-kûr*, which, as we have said above, are also of Hindoo origin.

In the first story, the three companions, forming at first three groups of two, have resolved into six. The night-time is divided into three, into six, into seven (six, *plus* an extraordinary one, born afterwards), into nine (three groups of three), into twelve (three groups of four). Hence, near the monster with three, six, seven, nine, or twelve heads, we find sometimes three, sometimes six, seven, nine, twelve brother-heroes. The last head (or the last two, three, or four heads) of the monster, the decisive one, is the most difficult, and even dangerous, to cut off; the last of the brothers is he who, by cutting it off, is victorious. In the first Calmuc story of *Siddhi-kûr*, six brothers or companions separate where six rivers take their rise, and go in search of fortune. The first-born perishes; the second, by means of his wisdom (he partakes of the wisdom of the first-born, with whom he is grouped), discovers the place where the dead one is buried; the third, the strong one, breaks the rock under which the eldest is hidden; the fourth resuscitates him by means of a health-bringing drink, as Bhîmas, the strong hero of the *Mahâbhâratam*, arises again when he

[1] ii. 29.

drinks the water of health and strength; the fifth brother creates a bird, which the sixth colours; this bird flies to the bride of the eldest brother, and brings her among his companions, who, finding her exceedingly beautiful, become, one and all, enamoured of her; they fight for her, and, that each may have a part, end by cutting her to pieces. We already know the mythical meaning of this legend.

The third and fourth Calmuc tales introduce explicitly the bull and the cow. In the third, a man who possesses but one cow unites himself to her, in order to make her fruitful. Of this union a tailed monster is born, having a man's body and a bull's head. The man-bull (Minotauros) goes into the forest, where he finds three companions—one black, one green, and one white—who accompany him. The man-bull overcomes the enchantments of a dwarf witch; his three companions lower him into a well and leave him there, but he escapes. He meets a beautiful maiden drawing water, at whose every footstep a flower arises; he follows her, and finally finds himself in heaven; he fights against the demons, in favour of the gods, and dies in this enterprise. This story, of Hindoo origin, where the bull and the cow take the place of the hero and the maiden, appears to me to justify the amplitude of the comparisons.

We have already seen the beneficial qualities of the excrement of the cow. In the fourth story, it is under the excrement of a cow that the enchanted gem, lost by the daughter of the king, is found. It is of the cow that the pearl is the secretion. The moon-cow and the aurora-cow are rich in pearls; they are pearls themselves, like the sun; the sun comes out of the aurora, the pearl comes out of the cow.

The subject of the seventh tale is the three sisters who,

taking the cattle to pasture, lose a buffalo, or black bull. In their search for it, they came across an enchanted castle, tenanted by a white bird, who offers to marry them. The third sister consents, and marries him. The bird turns out then to be a handsome cavalier (a form of Lohengrin). But having, by the advice of a witch, burned the aviary, she loses him, and cannot recover him till the aviary is restored. We shall see the sun as a bird in the Vedic hymns; the aurora is the aviary, made of flames, of this divine bird. When the aviary is burned at morn, the aurora and the sun separate; they meet again in the evening, when the aviary is reconstructed.

Another beautiful myth of analogous import occurs again in the eighth story. A woodman and a painter envy each other; the painter makes the king believe that the woodman's father, who is in heaven, has written ordering his son to repair to paradise, in order to build him a temple, and to take the route that the painter shall indicate. The king orders the woodman to set out for paradise. The painter prepares a funeral pyre, by way of exit; from this the woodman succeeds in escaping, and, going back to the king, he tells him that he has been to paradise, and presents a letter which his father has given him, ordering the painter to come by the same road, and paint the temple. The king requires the summons to be obeyed, and the perfidious painter perishes in the flames. The morning sun emerges safe and sound from the flames of the morning aurora; the evening sun passes through those flames, and dies.

The tenth Calmuc tale gives us the myth of the two brothers; the rich one avaricious and wicked, and the poor one virtuous. The story ends in a manner analogous to that of the dying adulterer, who, as we have seen in the *Tuti-Name,* bites off his mistress's nose.

The eleventh story is a variation of that of the lover, or husband, who abandons or kills his wife, after having despoiled her of her riches; but instead of the waters of the sea, we have here the sea of sand, the sandy desert, in a cavity of which is deposited the young girl, shut up in a chest, the same chest which in other popular tales drifts about on the surface of the water.[1] But into the place where it was laid, the chest having been taken away by a young prince, a tiger enters; the unworthy husband turns up himself to abstract the chest, and is torn to pieces by the tiger. The sterile night is a vast desert, a sea of waters, a sea of sand; the sun-prince frees the aurora from the waters, out of the well, or the cavern of the desert; the tiger kills the monster-husband.

In the twelfth tale, a thief steals the enchanted gem from the prince; he throws the gem to the ground, the consequence of which is that the prince's nose bleeds so excessively that he dies. The nose is the most prominent part of the face, the most conspicuous and splendid part; it is the gem of the sun-prince. The sun falls at night upon the mountain; the gem falls to the ground; the prince's nose bleeds; he has struck his nose against the ground, and it bleeds. The sun-prince dies, and the evening sky is tinged red, blood-colour; the sun, who loses his blood in the evening, dies.

The thirteen Calmuc stories are followed by ten Mongol tales; in all, twenty-three, of which the sixteenth, however, is lost.

The fourteenth tells us of the rich and avaricious man whose poor brother goes in despair into the forest to die upon a rock; but his presence not being known to the

[1] Cfr. also the chapter on the Hog, where we shall expound the myths and legends relating to disguises.

spirits, he has the good luck to come upon a hammer and a sack, of which the former, when struck against an object, produces whatever is desired by the owner, the latter being used to carry away the objects thus obtained, this hammer and this sack having been left there by the hobgoblins. Thus the poor brother becomes rich, and is envied by the other, who goes to the same place, in hopes of experiencing the same good fortune; but as he does not hide himself, the hobgoblins see him, and believing him to be the man who stole the hammer and the sack, avenge themselves upon him by lengthening his nose, and covering it with protuberances. To this myth may perhaps be referred the origin of the Italian expression, "Restare con uno o due palmi di naso," to remain with one or two spans of the nose; that is to say, to be laughed at, and with the gesture by which derision is accompanied, and which is addressed to the man who is laughed at, by applying one or sometimes both hands to the end of one's nose. The poor brother, now rich, visits the miserly brother, who has a long nose covered with protuberances, and knocks them off with his hammer. He had already knocked off eight, and only one remained, when, at his wife's request, he desisted and left the last one on. The rich man's wife, seeing how the protuberances had been taken off by striking them, tries herself to remove the last one, and strikes it with a hammer; but not calculating her aim accurately, she splits her husband's head open, and he dies.

In the seventeenth Mongol story, an old man and an old woman have nine cows. The old man is fond of meat, and eats all the calves; the old woman, on the other hand, has a great liking for milk and butter, with which she satiates herself. When the old man has eaten all the calves, he thinks that one cow more or less will not affect his wealth ; reasoning thus, he eats all the cows except one, which he spares out of respect for the whim of his old wife. But one day that the old woman is out, the old man cannot resist the temptation, and kills the last cow. His wife returns, is angry, and abandons him, upon which he throws after her one of the cow's breasts. The woman, in grateful memory of the milk and butter she liked so much, takes it up and goes up the mountain, where she strikes the cow's breast against the summit of the rock, and thereupon there flow out milk and butter in rivers. She satisfies her appetite, and then remembers that her husband is perhaps dying of hunger, feeding, as he does, upon ashes; she therefore, but secretly, throws butter into the house down the chimney, and then disappears. In this attention the old man recognises the love of his wife, and resolves upon the plan of following her footsteps during the night upon the snow. He comes to the mountain, sees the breast, and cannot resist the temptation it offers; he eats it, and takes the butter away with him. The old woman wanders about till she comes upon a herd of deer, who pasture freely, and who, instead of fleeing, let themselves be milked. Again, she thinks of her husband, and she throws deer's butter down the chimney. The old man follows her over the snow, finds her near the deer, and kills them in his inordinate passion for meat. The old woman continues to wander about, and stumbles this time upon a cavern of the wild beasts, guarded by a hare. The hare defends her from the wild beasts ; but she then conceives the idea of giving her husband a stick, and throws it down the chimney whilst he is taking the ashes up with a spoon. He follows her, and comes to the cave of the wild animals, who, seeing them arrive together, tear them to pieces. Here again we have the myth of the sun and the aurora (or the fine season); the hare who guards the cavern and tames the wild beasts is, as we shall see in the chapter which treats of it, the moon, the cows and the deer being the same. The ferocious animals of the cavern of night rend both sun and aurora (or fine season), both old man and old woman.

The eighteenth Mongol story is too indecent for me to relate, or for the reader to peruse; suffice it to say, that we have in it a comic variation of the Amazon heroine, and that this heroine calls herself Sûrya (the sun) Bagatur (to which corresponds the bagatír, or hero, of the Russians).

In the twentieth tale we have a calf and a lion's whelp brought up together by a lioness upon the same milk.[1] When grown, the lion goes and inhabits the forest, or the desert, and the bull, the mountain illumined by the sun, meeting as good friends and brothers to drink the same water. This good understanding is, however, put an end to by their perfidious uncle the fox, who persuades the lion to believe that the bull designs to kill him, and adds that when the bull in the morning strikes the ground with his horns, and bellows loudly, will be the sign that he is going to carry his purpose into effect; he then tells the bull that the lion has a similar design against him. In the morning, when the two brothers, bull and lion, go to drink the same water, they approach each other with suspicion, engage in battle and kill each other, the fox, or wolf, being the only one to benefit by the quarrel. This is a form of the story of the two twilights (the Açvinâu), which we shall illustrate in the following chapter.

The beginning of the twenty-first Mongol story offers a new analogy with the apologue of Perrette.[2] A poor

[1] Cfr. also the chapters on the Lion and the Fox.

[2] Cfr. on the story of Perrette, an interesting essay of Professor Max Müller in the *Contemporary Review*, 1870.

father and mother find a little lamb's-wool; they consult together, and resolve with the wool to make cloth, and with the cloth to buy an ass. Upon this ass they will place their little child, and go a-begging; by begging they will become yet richer, and buy another ass. Of the two, a young ass will be born. The youngster immediately exclaims that if a young donkey is born he will ride upon it; whereupon his mother answers, "You would break its back," when, accompanying these words with the movement of a stick, she strikes the youngster's head with it, and kills him; with him the fine projects of the poor parents also vanish.

In the last of the stories of *Siddhi-kûr*, which is joined to the three legends of the grateful animals, the disguises, and the laughing princess, a man uses the horns of his dead buffalo to grub up the roots upon which he lives in exile.

The history of *Ardshi-Bordshi* also contains several interesting stories.

It begins with a challenge among the children who keep the king's cows to run a race from the summit of a mountain. The first who comes to the winning-post is honoured as a king by his companions for that day, and acts and judges on the spot where the race takes place as a real king; indeed, he judges and decides as a court of final appeal on cases which have not been well examined by the great king of the country. He unmasks and convicts robbers and false witnesses acquitted by the king as innocent, and sends a missive to the king, recommending him to be more cautious in future in his judgments, or else to resign his royal dignity. The great king wonders at the extraordinary wisdom of the king of the children, and ascribes his preternatural sagacity to the magical influence of the mountain where the children who guard the cows play their games. On another occasion, the king of the children, by his craftiness, detects a demon in one whom the king had thought to be the legitimate son of his minister. The discovery is made by means of a challenge to the minister's real son and his demoniacal counterfeit to get into a small jug at hand. The real son cannot; but the supposititious makes himself small and enters the jug, in which the king of the children shuts him up with a diamond, and administers thereupon fresh reproof to the great king for his carelessness. The great king then visits the mountain of the children, and sees a golden throne with thirty-two steps emerge from the ground; upon each step there is a wooden puppet (the moon). The great king has the throne carried into his palace, and endeavours to ascend it; the puppets arrest him, and one of them tells him that this was once the throne of the god Indras, and afterwards of King Vikramâdityas. The great king inclines himself in reverence, and one of the puppets begins to narrate the history of Vikramâdityas.

The history of Vikramâdityas, narrated by the puppets, refers to a wise child, born of the wife of the king, after she had eaten a cake made of earth mixed with oil, and dissolved in water in a porcelain vase (of which cake the servant-maid eats the remainder). The young Vikramâdityas passes his infancy in the forests, where he learns all the arts, not excluding the art of thieving, taught him by the most experienced robbers, as well as every kind of mercantile fraud; by cheating, he becomes possessed of an enchanted gem which was in the hip of a dead man, and of a child who has the faculty of understanding the language of the wolves, and who calls himself son of the wolves, but was, in fact, born by the roadside of the maid who had eaten the rest of the cake; this child is nursed by his mother, and although at first ill-favoured, becomes in the long run very handsome. Vikramâdityas afterwards kills the king of the demons in battle, in which it is remarkable that as many new demons arise to combat him as there are pieces into which the hero cuts the demon, until the hero multiplies himself in his turn, and to every demon opposes a lion sprung from his own body. Vikramâdityas mounts upon a throne where those who had sat before him had all perished, each after a reign of twenty-four hours, because they had omitted to offer up funeral sacrifices to the dead during the night; Vikramâdityas, with his companion, the son of the wolf, fulfils the sacred duty, and escapes death.

In the same story, which reminds us of the *Ṛibhavas* and the four cups and the cow, four young shepherds, one after another, work at the same piece of wood; one gives it the general shape of a woman, the second colours it, the third imparts the features peculiar to the feminine form, and the fourth gives it life; they then dispute for her person. The case is referred to the king; a wise man pronounces that the two first who worked the wood are the father and mother, the third is the priest, the fourth, who gave it life, is the legitimate husband. Thus the four become three, by making a group of the first two.

Next comes the legend of the wife who, taking her husband by the feet, makes him fall into a fountain, because she hears a melodious voice, perhaps an echo of her own, which charms her; she sees a monster instead, and bewails her lost husband. In zoological mythology, the fable of the dog who, at the sight of his own shadow, lets the meat drop into the river, is analogous to this legend, which, however, we introduce here, only because of its relation to the similar stories of the wife who kills her husband, and of the husband who kills his wife by throwing her into the water, already vaguely hinted at in the Vedic hymns.

The last of the tales contained in the history of *Ardshi Bordshi* shows us, on the other hand, a far too complaisant wife. A king has a daughter, named Light of the sun, who is to be seen by no one. The daughter asks to be allowed to go out into the city to walk on the 15th of the month (at full moon); this granted, the king orders every one to stay that day in his house, and all the doors and windows to be shut; and capital punishment is the penalty of disobeying the king's command. (The like occurs again in the British legend of Godiva, the Countess of Mercia, in the eleventh century.) A minister, Ssaran by name (moon), cannot repress his curiosity, and observes her from a balcony; the girl makes signs to him, inviting him to join her; the wife of the inquisitive minister interprets the signs to him, and urges him to overtake the beautiful girl, giving him, at parting, a pearl of recognition. Light of the sun and Light of the moon meet at the foot of a tree, and spend the night until sunrise in amorous dalliance. One of the persons employed to guard the princess discovers this intrigue, and denounces it before the king; the wife of the minister Ssaran ascertains, by means of the pearl, that her husband is in danger; she rejoins him, disguises and disfigures him, suggesting a formula of oath by which Light of the sun swears that it was the monster, and the monster only she embraced; which seeming impossible to the king and courtiers, the minister Ssaran and Light of the sun are acquitted. (The aurora, or the sun, hides during the night, and no one sees, no one is allowed to see her; the god Lunus shows himself; he remains during the night with the sun, or with the solar aurora, whom no one can see during the night; the god Lunus then transforms and disfigures himself, so that he becomes unrecognisable, invisible; the guilty one glides away, and escapes; it then seems impossible that the god Lunus, who is no longer seen, can have been with the light of the sun; their loves having come to an end, the adulterers being separated, their guilt is no longer believed, their innocence is recognised, and the morality of the myth is left to take care of itself as best it can.)

But the Calmuc and Mongol stories of *Siddhi-kûr*, and the history of *Ardshi Bordshi*, being, as they are, only paraphrases of Hindoo tales, would not alone suffice to prove the derivation from the zoological legends of Aryan mythology of the oral Turco-Finnic tradition, properly speaking. We must, therefore, search for the proofs of their influence in other quarters as well.

A Turanian story of the south of Siberia[1] combines together several of the mythical subjects which we are already acquainted with.

A poor old man and woman have three sons; the three sons go upon the mountain to dream; the two eldest dream of riches, and the third dreams that his father and mother are lean camels, his brothers two hungry wolves running towards the mountains, while he himself, between the sun and the moon, wears the morning star upon his forehead. The father orders the brothers to kill him; they dare not do so; they only expel him from the house, and kill the dog instead, the blood of which they take to their father, who, thinking it is his son's, says they have done well. The young man wanders about till he comes to a hut where a lame old man and

[1] Radloff, *Proben der Volkslitteratur der Türkischen Stämme süd-Sibiriens.*

a blind old woman are eating out of a golden cup, which of itself fills with meat as they empty it (the moon). The hungry youth helps himself to some of this meat, but the old man finds, as he continues to eat the food, that some one has put his teeth into it; with a hook, which he whirls around him, he clutches hold of the young man, who begs for his life, pledging himself to be the eye of her who has no eyes, and the foot of him who has no feet. This proposal pleases the old couple, and they adopt him as their son; he makes himself a bow and a wooden arrow, and goes to hunt wildfowl for their support. The old man lends him his iron-grey horse, one day old, but advises him to ride him only by day; the young man, thinking that by night he conceals treasures, cattle, and people, disobeys, and rides by night. What the horse then does we shall see in the next chapter. The youth fights and vanquishes the demon, by fastening one of his lips to the heavens, and the other to the earth; the defeated demon advises him to rub himself with the fat of his stomach; inside his stomach he will find a casket of silver, inside that a casket of gold, and inside that another casket of silver; he is to take it and throw it into the sea of milk. From the monster's stomach, cut open, come forth innumerable animals, men, treasures, and other objects. Some of the men say, "What noble man has delivered us from the black night? what noble man has shown us the clear day?" The youth finds in the caskets money and a white handkerchief, which he puts into his pocket; from the last casket come forth more men, animals, and valuables of every kind; he drives the white cattle before him and returns home, where the old couple are asleep. He opens the handkerchief, and finds in it the old woman's eyes; whilst he is smoking near the fire, the old people waken, see him, and embrace him. The old man then endows him with the power of transforming himself into a fox, a wolf, a lion, a vulture, and other shapes, at will. He goes, to find for himself a wife, to the residence of the prince Ai-Kan ; the latter promises to give his daughter to whoever will bring him the necessary amount of gold. It is in the shape of a vulture[1] that the young man sets out to search for it ; he then wins the young maiden who has the gold, and she, who is herself the daughter of Ai-Kan, says to him, "Thou art my husband." After various other transformations, in one of which the two lean camels reappear, *i.e.*, his two parents, of whom he had dreamt, whom he loads with a sack, he ends by taking to himself another wife, the daughter of Kün-Kan, and he lives now with one, now with the other, to whom he gives the flesh of his own infanticide father to eat. Let us recapitulate the moments of this significant legend :—1st, We have the presage, the dream of the mountain-peak ; 2d, The three brothers, the third of whom, predestined to good fortune, the others wish to sacrifice ; 3d, The lame and the blind in the forest ; 4th, The hero's hunt ; 5th, The struggle with the monster of night ; 6th, The treasures, spiritual and material, which come out of the monster ; 7th, The cattle in conjunction with the sea of milk ; 8th, The passage of the hero from the milky sea to the fireside, from the alba to the aurora, from the whitish sky to the reddish one ; 9th, The awakening of the sleepers, and restoration of sight to the blind, whilst he sits by the fire, whilst the sun is united to the aurora ; 10th, The transformation of the hero himself ; 11th, Winning his bride, by procuring the necessary amount of gold ; 12th, His marriage of two

[1] Professor Schiefner has already compared with this passage a story published by Ahlquist in his *Versuch einer Mokscha-Mordwinischen Grammatik*, p. 97.

wives ; 13th, His revenge on his persecuting father. The legend is in itself an epic poem, and we can only regret that the Altaic story-tellers did not give it a more artistic form than that in which it appears in the excellent collection of Radloff.

Another interesting Turanian story, in the same collection, which preserves several traces of the primitive myth, is another version of the story of the hero who solves the riddle proposed by his father-in-law, and thus wins his wife. A father has three sons ; the first-born dreams that their cow has devoured a wolf ; he goes to see, and finds it is true (the aurora destroys the night). We have already seen that, as the third brother is the wise child, so the first-born of the three is often the one who possesses the secret of solving riddles. The father of the three brothers wishes to obtain a wife for his first-born son, and the bride's father, to give her up, demands that the bridegroom's father should come to take her, arriving, the first time, with a fur-coat and without one (in the morning the old man, by the advice of the eldest son, departs wearing a coat of fur which seems to be one, but is not, being in reality a coat of mail), and coming, the second time, without touching the road, yet not off the road, on horseback, yet without horses (the old man, by the advice again of his first-born son, arrives at the father-in-law's abode, going on the side of the road, and riding on a stick ; thus he obtains permission to take the bride away for his son).

Professor Schiefner gives a Finnic variation of the same story. A king orders the son of a peasant to come neither by day nor by night, neither by the road nor by the road-side, neither on horseback nor on foot, neither dressed nor naked, neither inside nor outside. The intelligent boy makes a robe of goat's skin, goes to the city lying in the bottom of a coffin, during the morning twilight, having a sieve fastened to one foot, and a brush to the other, and stops on the doorstep of the ante-chamber, with one leg out and the other in.

Such was the humour, and such the wisdom of our fathers; ingenuity was measured by skill in solving astronomical riddles. Now the riddles have taken another form; they are strokes of diplomacy, amorous hieroglyphs, ethical ambiguities, metaphysical nebulosities, which we, the men of progress, must solve; but not wishing to acknowledge our inferiority in acuteness to the children of the legends, we are fain to persuade ourselves that the new riddles are more obscure than the ancient.

In the Vedic riddles proposed to one another by the aurora and the sun, we have seen how they were solved in the morning by the nuptials of the guesser and the guessee. Thus in the two riddles which we have just described, the son of the old man and the child solve the riddle in the morning. As to the sieve, the brush, and the coffin, they are mythical furniture of great interest and obvious import. The nocturnal sky is the great coffin; to sweep the sky of night, we must have a brush; to sunder the good grain from the bad during the night, as the cruel mother-in-law commands, we must have a sieve; the child-sun arrives, in the twilight, in the bottom of the coffin, at the doorstep of the royal palace, and presents to the maiden aurora (the Vedic cleaner or purifier) the brush and the sieve. The sun, at twilight, is neither in nor out. In the second Scottish story of Mr J. F. Campbell, the giant commands the hero, among other things, to cleanse, in one day, the stables which had not been cleansed for seven years (Heraklés and Augeias).

But let us continue our subject, for the path is a long one.

A Mongol tradition, contained in the *Mongol Cresto-*

mathy of Papoff,[1] speaks of the boy who comes riding upon a black ox, instead of in a coffin.

We have seen above the cow who eats the wolf; in another Altaic legend we find an old woman who gives up her seven azure (dark-coloured) cows to be eaten by the seven wolves, in order that the latter may spare the child Kan Püdai, whom she had found at the foot of a tree; meanwhile the child, who has fed upon two hundred hares,[2] has become strong, and breaks his iron cradle (the iron sky of night is the cradle of the young sun); from the horns of six roebucks he makes himself a bow; from the skin of a colossal marine animal (the cloud, the gloomy one), he makes a string for the bow (the string of the Hindoo bow is also called *go*, *i.e.*, cow, as a cloud in the sky, and as being formed from the hide of a cow); he rides upon the azure calf (the dark calf, which recalls our attention to the black ox, and leads us to conclude the colossal animal to have been a cow), and subdues and tames it; he then comes to a field of snow, upon which he breathes a black and numbing wind, and where he finds the seven wolves; he ties them to the tail of his calf, and drags them along the ground till they die. The boy continues his wild beast hunt; he kills the black and fat ones, and leaves the yellow and lean ones alone. He goes into a black sea, and erects there a black castle, into which he receives both the old woman who had sustained him, and his azure (*i.e.*, dark-coloured) calf. Thereafter the young Kan Püdai, applying himself to warfare, forsakes or exchanges his calf for a horse. We shall see in the next

[1] Kasan, 1836, quoted by Professor Schiefner in the introduction to the *Proben*, &c., of Radloff.

[2] Cfr., for the meaning of this myth, the chapter which treats of the Hare.

chapter what he does with his horse ;—suffice it to notice here, that, in the end, he meets the black bull, who will one day be the king of the Altaï. The soul of the black bull takes refuge in a red thread in the middle of the rainbow (in the popular belief of the East the rainbow was supposed to be a bridge, a road traversed by the souls of mortals) ; the young Kan Püdai transfixes it with his arrows. He wins the white cattle, kills the monstrous Kara Kula, and, taking the latter's wife and daughter with him, returns home ; and for seven days there is eating, drinking, and festivity in the house of Kan Püdai. But up to this point it is not said that he has espoused the daughter and the wife of Kara Kula. Kan Püdai is, on the contrary, passionately enamoured of Tämän Ökö, the daughter of the sky (duhitar divas, or daughter of the sky, is the name usually given to the aurora in the Vedic hymns), and ascends, in order to secure her and make her his wife, to the third heaven (it is the third step of Vishṇus ; it is the third brother, the sun of the third night-watch, who carries off the palm against the gloomy monster). In order to become worthy of the daughter of the sky, Kan Püdai has to kill two monsters ; to scatter ashes on the field of victory, and lead away from it the white cattle ; to catch the three bears ; to take the three black bulls and make them swallow three hills ; to take the tiger and give it the grass of the three mountains to eat ; to kill the whale in the azure sea (all different forms of one and the same mythical and heroic battle) ; and, finally, to play upon the mountain-peak with the golden-haired monster Andalma. He then obtains his bride, and returns with her to his own country, where he hunts, and makes war, and vanquishes all his enemies, until he grows old ; he then renounces all except his old companion (the old sun and the old aurora meet again in the evening).

Here evidently the mythology is really zoological.

In the complicated legend of Ai-Kan, we have in the brother Altyn Ayak, who sleeps in the form of a golden cup, and who awakens to help Ai-Kan, a figure which, though not the same as, is similar to, that of the sleeping brother Kumbhakarṇas (conch-ear) in the *Râmâyaṇam*, who awakens to help Râvaṇas. We have the inebriating liquor which gives strength to the hero, who is resuscitated three times from death, after having been the food of dogs; the wolves who devour Sary-Kan, or the fair-haired prince; the hero (the sun) who beats the wife (the aurora) given him by the two brothers (the Açvinâu); the friendly dog and cat; the golden cup in which the brother of Ai-Kan is shut up asleep, and which falls into the sea; the grateful animals which search for the cup; the gem found in the stomach of a fish (from the whale of the nocturnal ocean the gem comes forth); and the consequent awakening of the sleeping Altyn Ayak.

The following is from an Altaic saga, in the collection of Radloff:—Beyond the sea, on a rock surrounded with treasures, a dwarf girl is brought up, against whom aggressive warriors can prevail nothing. She sends all enemies away, after loading them with gold and silver, and placing on their heads part of the hair of her forehead, which proves to be sufficient to cover seven men. In this marvellous hair, in this enchanted maiden, and in the warriors who come by sea, who does not recognise the veil of the maiden aurora of the Vedâs, who uncovers her bosom before the sun her husband, and the sea which the warrior-sun crosses, and from which he emerges to come to the aurora?—who does not recognise the golden fleece, Jason, Medea, the Argonauts of Hellenic tradition?

In the Finnic mythology of the *Kalevala*[1] also, we have upon the mountain a good and pure hostess, a generous giver, from the golden windows of whose house are observed the women who give the wildfowl; but in this Finnic representation, it is not the heroic girl-aurora, it seems to me, we recognise, but the moon, Diana the huntress (the German *Helljäger*), who also appears on the mountain-peak, surrounded by the stars of the nocturnal forest, where the wildfowl is found, which she can therefore lavish upon the hero.

The Finns worship a thundering god, united with the clouds, who has the thunderbolt for his sword, and who is called Ukko,[2] father of Väinämöinen, the valorous and wise hero, who speaks in the womb of his mother, who performs prodigies when yet a child, and who produces the sun and the moon.

This child-hero occurs again in their dwarf-god (*pikku mies*), who, although, like the Hindoo Vishṇus, he is but a span long, wields in his hand an axe the length of a man, with which he cuts down an oak-tree that no one had yet been able to bring to the ground. The sun-hero is little; but his ray, his thunderbolt, his weapon, his hand, lengthen themselves, extend themselves as far as the dwarf-hero can desire, in order to destroy the

---

[1] *Rune*, 7.—Cfr. Castren's *Kleinere Schriften*, Petersburg, 1862, and the French translation of the *Kalevala*, published in 1867 by Leouzon le Duc.

[2] I find combined in the *Kleinere Schriften* of Castren (p. 25) the same *Ukko* with the word *Kave* (*Kave Ukko*). I would with diffidence ask the learned Finnish philologists, whether, as *Ukko* is a Finnish form of the deity whom the Hindoos called Indras, and as the hero protected by Indras, the hero in whom Indras is reproduced, is called in the Vedic (and Iranian) tradition *Kâvya Uçanâ*, or even *Uçanâ Kavis*, the words *Kave Ukko* may not have some relation to the name given to the Vedic and Iranian hero?

enemy, who wears here the well-known aspect of the trunk of a tree, or of a dark forest. The woodcutter is therefore a favourite figure in popular tradition. And the fact that Väinämöinen, having grown old and truthful in speech, cuts down in the *Kalevala*,[1] by the help of the little god, the prodigious oak, shows us that this little god is a new and junior form, a younger and victorious brother, or self-reproduction of the erewhile child-hero Väinämöinen, who has lived his life of a day. The valiant child-sun of morning has become the experienced old sun of evening; but as this old sun is not strong enough to cut down the oak-tree, under whose shadow he loses himself, he is obliged to become a child again to develope the requisite amount of strength; he needs a younger brother, a hero or dwarf-god, to free him from the evil shades of the forest of night. To this end he also invokes the sun and the moon to illumine the forest, and also the bear (the middle brother)—(in the *Kalevala*, of the three heroes it is the bear Ilmarinen who shows the greatest strength, and who wins the virgin for his bride)—in order that by his strength he may root up the tree. But to root up the tree is all that bears can do, while Väinämöinen wishes it to be cut down; and so this victorious enterprise is intrusted to the dwarf-god. Thus, without explicit mention of their names, we find the three brothers described in the entirely mythical epopee of the Finns.

Alongside of the dwarf, by force of antithesis, there arises, even in the Finnic mythology, the idea of a giant, a Titan who amuses himself with uplifting and hurling rocks and mountains. The cloud, the monster of dark-

---

[1] Väinämöinen, alt und wahrhaft, konnt durch ihn die Eiche fällen; *Kal.* 24, in Castren's *Kleinere Schriften*, p. 233.

ness, being represented as a mountain, the monster inhabiting this country must fight by means of the mountain itself. The cloudy mountain moves; it is a giant monster that moves it; it is the second brother, the strong brother, the son of the cow, the bear, who amuses himself with it, who shakes, carries, and throws it like a weapon. And such mythical battles must have seemed so much the more natural in the age in which the greater number of the myths were conceived and produced, as we know it to have been the age which archæologists call the age of stone. The sun, as a dwarf, destroys the vast cloud, the vast darkness, viewed as a giant.

But battles are not always going on in the heavens; even the wild animals of the gloomy forest become tame and rest themselves; music fills the soul with calm sentiments. Therefore even the warrior Gandharvâs of the Hindoo Olympus are transformed into expert musicians, who entrance the very gods with wonder. The song of the Sirens attracts and seduces the traveller; the lyre of Orpheus draws after it mountains, trees, and animals; the harp of Väinämöinen, in the *Kalevala*, makes the wolf forget his ferocity, the bear his wildness, the fish his coldness. And it is grief which is the first inspirer of song; the first stanza of the poet Vâlmîkis had its origin in the sorrow he felt upon seeing a bird bereft of its companion. Orpheus (the Thracian sun) sings and plays for grief, when the serpent (the shade of night) has bitten and thrown into the gloomy regions his sweet bride Eurydice (the aurora), and moves the demons to pity; the harp of Väinämöinen is also born of sorrow.[1]

[1] Nur aus Trauer ward die Harfe, nur aus Kummer sie geschaffen; harten Tagen ist die Wölbung, ist das Stammholz zu verdanken, nur Verdruss spannt ihre Saiten, andre Mühsal macht die Wirbel; *Kanteletar*, i., quoted by Castren in the *Kleinere Schriften*, p. 277.

The epopee of the Finns contains, moreover, several other myths cognate with those of Aryan mythical tradition ;—such as the resuscitated hero ; the winning of the maiden by display of heroism ; the bride heroically won and afterwards cut in pieces ; the cup of abundance, or the cornucopia (the Sampo) ; the golden cradle ; the marvellous vessel in which the hero crosses the sea ; the three sisters, of whom one gives black milk, one white, and one red (night, the alba or moon, and aurora) ; the invulnerable shirt ; the magician who makes children of gold and silver ; and others of secondary importance,[1] but all tending to prove that formerly the Turanian and Aryan races, in their neighbouring abodes, were originally much more similar to each other than they now appear, on account of partly diversity of language, and partly their different degrees of civilisation.

I have just named the Finnish Sampo as a cup of abundance or cornucopia ; it does, in fact, yield marvellous abundance to whoever possesses it, and wherever it falls. It is made of the feather of a swan, or of a duck (the swan and the duck are, as we shall see, confounded together in tradition, and the duck, like the hen, is a symbol of abundance), of a tuft of wool, of a grain of corn, and of chips from a spindle, all evident symbols of abundance ; and it becomes so large that it has to be carried by a hundred-horned ox (reminding us of the horns of the cow which spin). The ox bears abundance upon its horns, it yields abundance from its horns. The cornucopia is, in my mind, unmistakably implied in these mythical data.

[1] The origin of the bad and poor mythical iron, described in the *Kalevala*, is one of these: the mythical iron is the cloudy or tenebrous sky. The description is original, but the myths to which it refers are known to Indo-Europeans ; as, for instance, the honey which becomes poison.

The same mythical correspondence which we have found to exist between the Finnic epos and the various legendary Aryan traditions is observable between the latter and the Esthonian popular tales. In the collection of Frederic Kreuzwald[1] we find numerous proofs of this correspondence.

In the first story we have, in a hut in the forest, three sisters, of whom the youngest is the most beautiful. The old witch, her step-mother, persecutes her, and always gives her filaments of gold to spin, hiding from time to time the gold she has spun in a secret room. During the summer the old woman goes out of the house, no one knows where, after having apportioned their respective tasks to the three sisters. While the old woman is out, a young prince, having lost himself in the forest, finds his way to the hut, and becomes enamoured of the youngest of the three sisters. The young couple speak to each other of love in the light of the moon and of the stars; while the old king, impatient at the absence of his son, falls into grief, and sends everywhere to look for him. After three days he is found; before going back to the palace, he secretly promises to the youngest sister that he will return. Meanwhile the old woman comes back, finds the work badly done, curses, threatens, and maltreats the girl. Early in the morning, while the old woman and the two elder sisters are slumbering, the maiden slips out, and leaves the house. During her childhood she had learned the language of birds; accordingly, when she meets a crow, she salutes him by the name of "bird of light," and sends him as a messenger to the young prince, to warn him not to come back to see

[1] *Ehsthnische Märchen* aufgezeichnet von Fried. Kreuzwald, aus dem Ehsthnischen, übersetzt von F. Löwe, with notes by A. Schiefner and R. Köhler, Halle, 1869.

her, on account of the fury of the old woman. The prince then names her another trysting-place, and the young couple meet under a tree, between the second and third crowing of the cock; and when the sun rises, they flee away together. The old witch causes them to be followed by a ball made of nine evil herbs, and carried by malignant winds. The fugitives are overtaken on the banks of a river, where the ball strikes the prince's horse; it rears up on its hind legs, and the girl falls off into the river, into the hands of a marine monster; upon which the prince is struck by a disease which no one can cure. By eating the flesh of a hog, the prince acquires a knowledge of the language of birds; he sends the swallows as messengers to the magician of Finland, that he may teach him the way to free a girl who has been transformed into a pond-rose (lotus-flower). The answer, instead of being brought by the swallows, is brought by an eagle. The prince must become a shrimp, in order to enter the water without being drowned; he must detach the lotus by its root, draw it along the surface of the water to the bank, near a stone, and pronounce these words, "From the pond-rose, a maiden—from the shrimp, a man." The crow confirms the eagle's words. The prince hears a song issue from the rose; he then determines to deliver the girl. The two young people emerge together from the water. The maiden is ashamed of being naked, and the prince goes to procure nuptial robes for her; after which he conducts her to the palace in a beautiful chariot, where a joyous and gorgeous wedding-festival is celebrated. Soon afterwards the old witch dies, to appear again in the form of a cat, which is taken by the tail and flung into the fire. In the witch's house are found mountains of spun gold, which serve for the dowry of the three sisters. We have already said that the three sisters correspond to the three brothers, and the youngest sister to the youngest brother. The epithet of *young* is often given to the Vedic aurora, whom the sun marries. Here the prince marries the youngest of the three sisters; the morning aurora is united to the sun. Towards night she falls into the water; it is the witch (night) who throws her in; the hog which the prince (the sun) eats we shall see to be a figurative representation of the nocturnal monster, or the moon. Eating the hog, staying in the forest of night, the prince learns the language of birds. The prince frees the maiden from the waters; the sun delivers the aurora from the gloomy ocean of night, and robes her in his splendour, causing the witch of night to be burned in the flames of the aurora, and taking from the witch's abode the spun gold or golden fleece.

In the third Esthonian story, a woman, called mother-of-gold, bears, by the favour of a dwarf, three dwarf-sons at the same time, who become three heroes. The first is the seer (the wise brother), the second has a ready arm (the strong brother), the third runs swiftly in the race (a quality distinctive of the third brother, Arǵunas, in the *Mahâbhâratam*, and which is applicable to the victorious sun of morning, who wins the race, together with the aurora).

A variation of the story relating to the youngest sister and the dwarf is that of the girl seven years old, the wise girl (the aurora), in the fourth Esthonian tale, who, being persecuted by her step-mother, retires into the forest (the night). While there, it seems to her that she is in heaven, where, in a house of crystal and pearls, she is received by a well-dressed woman of gold (the fair-haired moon). The girl asks the golden woman to be allowed to take care of the cattle, like the cowmaid aurora. In the history of *Ardshi Bordshi* we have seen the wise puppet. This form of the wise girl, the dressed girl of wood, occurs again in the Esthonian story; in which she is made of wood from the forest, of three anchovies, of bread, of a black serpent, and of the blood of the girl herself, to whom the image has a great likeness, and which may be beaten by the old step-mother without being hurt. From the forest-tree, wood, or wooden box of the night, with the juice of the black serpent of night and the blood of the girl aurora of evening, comes forth the maiden aurora of morning, the wise, the speaking puppet, the puppet who guesses the riddles. The girl who comes out of wood is represented as a wooden puppet; more frequently the puppet is the moon, the wise fairy who comes out of the forest. In the same story we have the magic rod which produces a cock upon the mountain, beside which a tablecloth spreads itself out, while the chairs range themselves in their places, and the dishes are filled of their own accord. The story ends with the usual marriage between the beautiful maiden, and a king's son returning from the chase (or the son who comes out of the forest of night, viewed as infested by ferocious animals).

In the sixth Esthonian tale, the poor girl finds a woman in a white robe (the moon), adorned with gold, upon a rock near a fountain, who announces her approaching marriage with a youth as poor as herself; but the good fairy godmother—for in the legends the godmother is represented as good, as the stepmother is wicked—promises to make them both rich and happy. She calls herself the lady of the waters, secret wife of the wind, and she judges the criminals who present themselves at her tribunal (Proserpina or Persephonê).

In the seventh tale, a boy nine years of age, the third

son of two poor people, goes out to be a cowherd; his master treats him well, but his mistress gives him more floggings than bread. One day the young cowherd is unfortunate enough to lose a cow; he searches for it all through the forest, but in vain. He re-enters the house with the cattle, after the sun has set some time. The observant eye of his mistress perceives at once that there is a cow missing; she beats the boy without pity, and sends him out to look for it, threatening to kill him if he returns without it. He wanders through the forest; but when the sun arises from out the bosom of the dawn, he resolves to stay out of the house, and not to return to his persecutor (the young morning sun flees from the old and perverse night). In the evening, the boy finds an old dwarf, who is his host during the night (the moon), and who says to him, "When the sun rises to-morrow, carefully observe the spot in which he rises. Thou must go in that direction, so that every morning thou may'st have the sun before thee, and every evening the sun behind thee. Thus thy strength will increase more and more every day." How can one indicate better the apparent course of the solar hero, or of the sun in the night? The hero, in order to go towards the morning sun, must necessarily have the sun of evening behind him. The old dwarf also gives him a sack and a little barrel, in which he will always find the food and drink he requires; but he recommends him never to eat or drink more than is necessary, that he may have to give to a hungry bird or a thirsty wild beast. He also leaves him a rolled-up leaf of burdock, upon which, by rolling it out, he will always be able to cross water (a new form of the cup). We know how the Hindoos represented their god as floating upon a lotus-leaf in the midst of the waters, and how Padmaǵas (born of the lotus-flower, or the rose of the waters, which shuts during the night) was one of the names of Brâhman; here we have the god or hero shutting himself up in the flower, from which he afterwards comes out. In the chapters on the Serpent and the Frog we shall again see how the god sometimes shuts himself up in a monstrous form in this flower, the rose, on account of a curse from which he is to be freed by a beautiful maiden. We have seen how the Esthonian girl, who was by the curse of the old woman thrown into the water, was transformed into a water-rose or lotus-flower, and delivered by the young prince. The Esthonian boy finds himself before a small lake; he throws the leaf in, and it becomes a magical boat, which carries him over. Meanwhile he has become strong. Upon the mountain he sees a serpent, a tortoise, and an eagle, all three of enormous dimensions, approaching to attack him, with a man upon a black horse, which has wings on its feet, in the rear of them. He kills the serpent and the tortoise, but the eagle flies away. The man with the black horse takes the boy into his house, and appoints him to look after the dogs, that they may not get loose from their chains, a danger against which the man provides by making twelve colossal oxen fetch rocks upon rocks, to repair the damage done by the dogs. The rocks, touched by a magical rod, arrange themselves upon the car drawn by the oxen. At last, by the advice of the eagle, he steals his master's horse, and departs to sojourn among mankind, taking a wife with him.

In the eighth Esthonian story too, the third brother is the cunning one. His two elder brothers, after the death of their father, despoil him of his share of the inheritance, and he is reduced to wander alone and impoverished about the world in quest of good fortune. He falls in with a woman who complains to him that her husband regularly beats her when she is unable to procure for him the things he wants, which he asks for in the form of a riddle. The third brother solves the enigma for the woman (the moon), who, in gratitude, gives him provisions for his travels. He then comes to a palace, where the king is engaged in celebrating a summer festival, and he undertakes to provide and prepare the feast. A magician presents himself at the festival in the shape of an old man, and asks to taste the food. The young man suspects him, but, seeing a ring upon his finger, he consents to allow him if he gives him a pledge. The magician vows that he has nothing to give. The youth asks for his ring, and the old man in his gluttony at once gives it up; upon which the youth, who, along with the ring, has taken all the magician's strength away, first binds and derides him, and then has him beaten by seven strong men. The old man breaks the ropes and disappears; however, the young man, having the ring in his hands, possesses the means of tracking his footsteps and making him his. (This is the usual disc, lasso, or bridle which is now in the hands of the hero, now in those of the monster.) The youth follows the magician underground. The latter, it appears, is served by three maidens, who, when they perceive that the sorcerer has lost his ring, and that they have a young man for companion, enjoy themselves with him while the magician is asleep. The youth learns from them that the old wizard also possesses a sword which can destroy armies, and a magical rod which can create a bridge to span the sea; these, therefore, he steals, and departs, returning by a wonderful bridge thrown over the sea to the palace whence he had started. It seems to him as if his journey had lasted only two nights, instead of which a year has passed.[1] He finds on his arrival his two brothers in the king's service, one as coachman and the other as a valet, both enriched because they have received the pay due to their younger brother for having prepared the great feast. The young man now engages himself in another capacity, in a species of service especially dear to the young hero, next to those of stable-boy and cowherd; that is to say, he becomes under-cook of the king. (In the *Vîrâṭa-Parvam* of the *Mahâbhâratam,* it is the second of the brothers who disguises himself as a cook, in order to prepare good sauces and substantial food for the king whose guest he is; the elder brother is disguised as a Brâhmanas, a wise adviser; the third brother, Arǵunas, the agile, the swift one, pretends to be a eunuch, is given in exchange for a woman, and teaches dancing, music, and singing in the gynecium. Of the two sons of the Açvinâu, one becomes a groom, the other a cowherd.) His brothers continue to dislike him, and because he boasts to them that he had seen in hell golden birds, they induce the king to send him to hell in order to procure them. He accomplishes this undertaking with great difficulty, and brings the birds in a sack made of spiders' webs, which is so strong that the birds enclosed in it cannot extricate themselves. In the same sack, during another expedition, the young man brings from hell many precious objects of gold and silver. In compensation, he only asks of the king to send the princess, his daughter, to listen for one evening to the conversation of his two brothers the coachman and the valet. Both boast of having enjoyed to satiety the favours of the princess. The latter, indignant and full of shame, runs to tell the king everything, upon which

[1] This is the phenomenon which occurs in the winter solstice on Christmas Eve and that of New Year's Day, in which we pass from one year to another; in one night we become older by a year.

he arraigns them before him and has them judged. The third brother is named Counsellor; with his enchanted sword he destroys an entire army of enemies, and obtains in reward for his services and his valour the king's daughter to wife.

The ninth Esthonian story presents to us the son of the thunder, who sells his soul to the devil, on condition that the latter serves him for seven years. The time agreed upon is nearly come to an end, and the son of the thunder wishes to escape from him, and profits by an opportunity which has chanced. The devil sees a black cloud, which is a sign of an approaching tempest; he is afraid, hides himself under a stone, and asks the son of the thunder to keep him company. The latter consents; but seeing that the devil is afraid, at each thunderclap he presses his ears and eyes in such a manner as to make him perspire and shiver all over. The devil, believing this to be the effect of the thunder, promises the son of the thunder that he will not only leave him his soul, but give him three other souls, if he will deliver him from the evils which he suffers on account of the thunder, by taking from the thundering god, the father of the clouds, his weapon (which is also a musical instrument). This weapon, having been ravished from the god, is taken by the devil into hell, into a chamber of iron, shut up within seven castles. A great drought coming upon the earth, the son of the thunder repents of having rendered such a service to the devil; he finds means, however, of informing the thunder-god where his weapon is concealed. The thunder-god then becomes a child, and engages himself in the service of a fisherman, near a lake which the devil is accustomed to visit to steal the fishes. He surprises him in the act of robbery, and by the help of a magician takes him prisoner, and has him beaten without pity, until he promises to pay a heavy ransom in money to be let free, the fisherman and his child to accompany him to hell itself to receive the sum of money. Arrived in hell, the devil entertains them like a gentleman. The child tells the fisherman to ask the devil to show them the musical instrument which he keeps enclosed in the iron room. The devil kindly consents, but cannot draw from the instrument anything more musical than the mewing of a cat or the grunting of a pig. The fisherman then laughs at the devil, and says that his boy can play better. The devil does not believe it, and laughingly gives the instrument, which he calls bagpipes, to the boy. The latter blows into them and makes such a noise that all hell resounds with it, and the devils fall to the earth as if dead. The child then becomes the god of thunder again, and returns to heaven, where by the noise of his instrument he opens the celestial reservoirs and lets out the beneficent rain. The description of the tempest which occurs in many Vedic hymns is the germ of this interesting myth. The drum or kettledrum thunder is a familiar image in Hindoo poetry, and the Gandharvâs, the musician-warriors of the Hindoo Olympus, have no other instrument than the thunder. The conch of the warrior Pâṇḍavâs in the *Mahâbhâratam*, and the famous horn of Orlando (which comes from the golden horn of Odin), are epical reminiscences of thunder. Orpheus, who in hell plays on his lyre and tames the animals, is a more lucid and more perfect form of this Esthonian thunder-god who plays the bagpipes in hell. It is also remarkable how, in harmony with the pastoral bagpipes, in the tenth Esthonian story, which is a variation of the preceding one, the god transformed into a powerful boy is called a little shepherd or cowherd—another interesting fact, which completes his identification with Orpheus.[1] The magic flute is a variation of the same celestial musical instrument. The magic flute, the bagpipes or wonderful pipe, occurs again in the twenty-third Esthonian story, in which the good Tiidu, by means of it and of his virtue, obtains riches. The magical harp of Gunnar in the Edda has the same marvellous effects.

Evidently the monster-dwarf is a favourite subject of Esthonian tradition, and it often occurs in the Hindoo and in the German traditions, as well as in the Franco-Latin tradition of Charlemagne. The eleventh story introduces us to three dwarf-brothers who contend for the inheritance left by their father, consisting of a miraculous hat, which enables its wearer to see everything, whilst he can himself be visible or invisible at pleasure (this hat is made of pieces of men's nails cut up);[2] of a pair of slippers which transport the owner in an instant wherever he wishes (we must not forget that Cinderella, when she loses the slipper, is overtaken by the prince bridegroom); and of a stick which strikes of itself, and destroys everything, even stronger than the thunderbolt (the thunderbolt itself). The three brothers maintain that these three articles, to be really useful,

[1] In a popular Swedish song, the maiden Gundela, who plays marvellously upon the harp, and, in order to play it, demands the king to marry her, is also a shepherdess.—Cfr. *Schwedische Volkslieder der Vorzeit*, übertragen von Warrens, Leipzig, Brockhaus, 1857.

[2] Cfr. the note of F. Löwe, illustrating this passage, in his version of the collection of Kreuzwald, pp. 144 and 145.—[This is also a myth of easy interpretation, if I am not mistaken: at evening, the sun loses his rays; the lion, the hero, loses his nails; these nails are picked up by the demoniacal monster, who forms out of them a hat (the gloom of night, or the clouds), by which the wearer has the gift of seeing without being seen. The magician who sees with his eyes shut is an interesting variation of this subject.]

must be the property of one; but who is to enjoy this privilege? A man comes up to put an end to the dispute, and feigns disbelief in the virtue of these three things, unless he proves it himself. The three simpletons give them to him that he may prove them. The man takes them off, and the three dwarfs are left to meditate upon the truth of the above-quoted proverb, "Between two disputers the third profits," or at least that variation of it which their own case suggests "Between three that dispute, the fourth profits."

In the thirteenth Esthonian story, the privileged character of the third brother is explained, as we are told that he is the son of a king, but was exchanged by a witch during his infancy for the child of a peasant. The latter died in the palace, whilst the king's son grew in the hut, showing in every action his royal pedigree. Here we have the story of the hero who is exposed on the mountains intimately connected with that of the third brother. To this third brother, who alone shows himself to be devoted to his father, and who alone makes a vow to watch by his grave, is also attributed the merit of having delivered, upon a high mountain of crystal, from a seven years' sleep, a princess, who then becomes his wife. We have seen the aurora-awakener in the Vedic hymns—the sun and the aurora arouse each other: the sun sends forth the aurora; the aurora draws out the sun. The myth reproduces itself every day, and expresses in its entirety a daily phenomenon of light in the heavens. In Northern countries, where the contrast is great between winter and spring, and therefore the impression is striking which is caused by the cessation of vegetation in autumn, the earth also assumed the aspect of a dead young princess; but an omniscient magician having said, *Non est mortua puella, sed dormit,* the third brother, predestined to the enterprise, lays down his poor robes, and dresses himself, on the first occasion, in the colour of bronze; on the second, the colour of silver; on the third, the colour of gold, and ascends the mountain of crystal, or ice, whence he brings forth the beautiful spring. The sky, grey in autumn, snowy in winter, and golden in spring, corresponds to the grey sky of evening, the silver one of night, and the golden one of morning. Spring is the dawn of the year; the primitive myth is but amplified; the last hour of the day awakens the aurora; the last month of the solar year awakens the spring. The application of the myth of the day to the year is one of the greatest simplicity.

In the fourteenth story, the king of the golden country loses himself in the forest full of ferocious animals, and cannot find his way out. A stranger (no doubt the devil) conducts him out, on condition that he will give him whatever first comes to meet him. The king promises. The first thing he sees on his return is his royal child, who, carried by his nurse, stretches out his arms to his father. The king exchanges him for a peasant's girl, whom he gives up to the stranger, allowing his own son to be brought up among the peasant's herds. The king's son, having grown to manhood, determines to go and deliver the poor girl. He disguises himself as a poor man, puts a sack of peas on his shoulders, and goes into the forest where his father was lost eighteen years before. He also loses himself, and meets the stranger, who promises to direct him if he will give him the peas which are in the sack, as they will serve, he alleges, to recompense the assistants at the funeral of his aunt, who died in poverty during the night.—This pulse in funeral ceremonies refers to a very ancient custom. The Vedic ceremonials already mention them in connection with funerals; and in the Greek belief, the dead carried vegetables with them to hell, either for the right of passage or as provisions for travelling. In Piedmont, it is still the custom on the second of November (All Soul's Day) to make a great distribution of kidney-beans to the poor, who pray for the souls of the dead. Vegetables, peas, vetches, and kidney-beans are symbols of abundance, and to this belief may be traced the numerous Indo-European stories in which mention is made of beans which multiply themselves in the pipkin, or of peas which grow up to the sky, and up the stalk of which the hero climbs to heaven. The vegetables necessary for being introduced into the kingdom of the dead, and the pea by means of which the hero enters heaven, are variations of the same mythical subject. In Hindoo tradition, besides the pea or kidney-bean, we have the pumpkin as a symbol of abundance, which is multiplied infinitely, or which mounts up to heaven. The wife of the hero Sagaras gives birth to a pumpkin, from which afterwards come forth sixty thousand sons. The kidney-bean, the pea, the vetch, the common bean, and the pumpkin are also symbols of generation, not only on account of the facility with which they multiply, but also on account of their form. We have seen in the Vedic ceremonials what organs are represented by the two kidney-beans; we shall also see, in the chapter on the Ass, how the names given to the organs of generation are also used to designate fools. Now, it is worthy of notice that the Sanskrit word *mâshas* (or kidney-bean) also signified the foolish, the stolid one, in the same way as in Piedmont a *bonus vir* is called a kidney-bean. Thus, too, the pumpkin, which expresses fecundity, also means, in Italian, idiocy or stupidity. As to beans, I have already remarked, in my work upon "Nuptial Usages," upon their symbolical meaning, and cited the Russian and Piedmontese custom of putting a black and a white bean into the cake eaten at Epiphany, one of which represents the male and the other the female, one the king and the other the queen. The two who find the beans kiss each other with joyful auguries. As all these vegetables personify the moon, which we know to be considered as a giver of abundance, and which, by its form of a turning ball, can well be represented by the turning pea, in this personification we must search for the solution of the principal myths relating to vegetables.—The young prince of the Esthonian story, having obtained the stranger's favour in the gloomy forest by means of the peas, engages himself in his service, with intent to deliver the girl who had freed him by taking his place with the stranger during eighteen years. He therefore follows him; but on the way he lets a pea fall to the ground from time to time, in order to know the way back. He is conducted by a strange and wild subterranean passage, where silence as of the tomb reigns—it is, in fact, the kingdom of the dead—where birds have the appearance of wishing to sing, dogs to bark, and oxen to low, but cannot, and where the water flows without a murmur. The young prince feels in his heart a kind of anguish; the universal stillness in the midst of animated beings oppresses him. Having passed the region of silence, they come to that of deafening noise. The young prince thinks he hears the excruciating din of twenty-four saws at work; but the old stranger tells him that it is only his grandmother who has fallen asleep, and is snoring. At last they come to the stranger's dwelling, where the prince finds the beautiful maiden, but the old stranger will not let him speak. He sees in the stable a white horse and a black cow, with a white or luminous-headed calf. This cow the young prince is ordered to milk until there is not a drop of milk in its breast; instead of milking it with his fingers, he, by the advice of the girl, uses for that purpose red-hot pincers. Another time the youth is told to lead away the enchanted calf with the white or luminous head. In order that it may not escape, the girl gives him a magic thread, of which one end is to be tied to the left leg of the calf, and the other to the little toe of the prince's left foot.—The little finger, although the smallest, is the most privileged of the five. It is the one that knows everything; and in Piedmont, when the mothers wish to make their children believe that they are in communication with a mysterious spy, who sees everything that they do, they are accustomed to awe them by the words, "My little finger tells me everything."—At last the two young people resolve to flee. Before starting, the prince splits open the forehead of the white-headed calf; from its skull comes forth an enchanted little red ball, which shines like a small sun. He wraps it up, leaving part of it uncovered to light the way, and flees away with the girl. Being followed by malignant spirits, who are sent by the old man to follow them, the two fugitives, by means of the enchanted little ball (or pearl), turned round three times, become, first the one a pond and the other a fish, then the one a rose-bush and the other a rose, then again the one a breeze and the other a gnat, until the stone which covers the entrance to the subterranean world having been lifted up, they arrive again safe and happy upon the earth; and by means of the little red ball, they show themselves to mankind in splendid and princely robes. I scarcely think it necessary to explain to the reader the sense of this lucid mythical story. The black cow which produces the calf with the white or luminous head is a Vedic antithesis which we have already seen;[1] the cow (night) produces the calf (the moon). The prince takes the little red ball out of the calf; by means of this ball, the girl is delivered from the regions of gloom. The little ball moves the stone; the sun and the aurora come out together from the mountain, after having travelled together in the kingdom of shadows; the sun delivers the aurora. This story unites together and puts in order several myths of an analogous character, but born separately.

The three next stories describe other voyages made by the solar hero to heaven, or in hell, and end by meaning the same thing. In the eighteenth story we again find the enchanted ring, called Solomon's ring, which the young hero goes to search for; when he finds it, by taking it from the daughter of hell, and puts it on his finger, he is of a sudden endowed with such strength that he can split a rock with one blow of his fist. The little red ball of the story just described, which lifts up the rock, and this ring which splits the stone, represent the same mythical object, *i.e.*, the sun, the sun's ball or disc.

The twenty-first story shows us the fearless hero who frees a castle from the presence of the demons, and who thus gains a treasure; riches are the reward of valour.

---

1 A similar antithesis is found in a Hungarian proverb, communicated to me by my learned friend Count Geza Kunn, together with other notices of Hungarian beliefs relating to animals. This proverb is as follows: "Even the black cow's milk is white." The black cow is spoken of in two other Hungarian proverbs; one says, "The black cow has not trodden upon his heel," meaning that no misfortune has happened to him; it is the usual vulnerable heel, the heel of Achilles, the posterior part, for which is substituted sometimes, as we shall see in the chapter on the Fox and the Serpent, the tail or extreme hind part. Another proverb is, "In the dark all cows are black;" but it does not seem to have any mythical importance.

The twentieth Esthonian story is a variation of the exceedingly popular tale of Blue Beard, the killer of his wives. The Esthonian monster-husband has already killed eleven, and is about to murder the twelfth, by way of punishing her for having, against his express prohibition, visited the secret room opened by the golden key (perhaps the moon), when a youth who takes care of the goslings, the friend of her childhood, comes to deliver her. From the subject itself, and the expressions used in this story, we can discover the origin of the terrible charivari in the nuptials of widowers or widows. This savage custom is intended not only to deride the lust of the old man or woman who marries again, but to warn the girl who marries the one, or the youth who marries the other, of the possibility of a fate similar to the first wife or husband. When, therefore, the wife *apatighnî* (who does not kill her husband) is praised to the Vedic husband, we must understand that the *patighnî* (or killer of her husband) is a widow, whom no one must marry, as being suspected of murder. Hence, to free herself from this suspicion, an honest Hindoo wife (like Gudrun in the Edda) was to throw herself into the fire after the death of her husband; the evening aurora, after the death of the sun, dies too.

In the twenty-second story we have once more the myth of the young pastoral hero; he is the son of a king. By the order of his step-mother, a witch, who carries off shepherds, steals him from the palace during his infancy, and abandons him in a solitary place, where he is brought up by cowherds, and becomes himself an excellent cowherd. An old man finds him and says, looking at him and at the cattle, "Thou dost not seem to me born to remain a cowherd." The boy answers that he knows he was born to command, and adds, "Here I learn the duties of a commander by anticipation. If things go well with the quadrupeds, I shall also prosper with bipeds." The shepherd is therefore a little king; a good shepherd will become a good king. The boy goes through several adventures, in which he displays his valour. A wicked German lady wishes to take from him the strawberries which he has plucked. He defends himself bravely; his mistress persecutes him; and he takes twelve wolves, shuts them up in a cavern, and each day gives them a lamb to eat, in order to avenge himself upon his wicked mistress, to whom he simply says that the wolves have devoured them. At last he causes her to be devoured herself by the wolves, who eat her all up, leaving only the heart (the sun) and the tongue, which are too full of venom for the wolves of the night, because they burn their mouths. At the age of eighteen, the youth has several other adventures. He becomes enamoured of a gardener's daughter, and is found again by the king his father, who, before allowing him to marry the beautiful gardener's daughter, wishes to prove that they are predestined to each other. He cuts a ring in two with his sword, and gives one part to the young prince and the other to the maiden; the two halves must be preserved by both, and one day they will meet of themselves and form again the whole ring, in such a manner that it will be impossible to find the place where it was broken.—In a Tuscan story, the beautiful maiden gives half her necklace to the third brother. The young couple lose each other; their meeting again and mutual recognition take place when the two parts of the necklace join each other. The use of the wedding-ring has a mythical origin. The solar (and sometimes the lunar disc) is the ring which unites the heavenly husband and wife.—When, after other adventures, the two young people of the Esthonian story join together the two halves of their ring, their misfortunes come to an end; they marry and live together happily, whilst the cruel step-mother, who meanwhile has become a widow, is expelled from the kingdom.

The last Esthonian story tells of the extraordinary births, in the same day, of a handsome prince and a beautiful princess. The princess is born in a bird's egg, laid like a pearl in the bosom of the queen; she has at first the form of a living puppet, and afterwards, when warmed in wool, she becomes a real girl. Whilst she undergoes this transformation, the queen also gives birth to a beautiful boy. The two children are considered as twins, and baptized together. To the baptism of the girl there comes as godmother, in a splendid chariot drawn by six horses, a young woman dressed in rose-coloured and golden robes, who shines like the sun, and who, as she lets her veil drop, like the beautiful Argive Helen, fills the bystanders with admiration. [The aurora, who, before appearing in the form of a beautiful girl, is enclosed in the wood of the forest, is a wooden puppet, and becomes a wooden puppet once more when, fleeing from the sun, she hides herself in a creeping-plant, like the Hindoo Urvaçî (the first of the dawns), or in a laurel-plant, like the Hellenic Daphne (the Vedic Dahanâ-aurora). The aurora is born together with the sun; the beautiful doll-maiden is born with the little prince. The mother and the beneficent godmother seem to be the moon, or a more ancient aurora.] The mother, dying, leaves her daughter, putting it upon her breast, a gem which is to bring her happiness; that is, the little basket which contained the bird's egg, with the eggshell itself. By means of the magical little basket, and by pronouncing some magic words, the maiden can find all that she searches or wishes for. The young man and woman end by marrying each other, having discovered that, although both born of a king, they are children of different fathers; they marry, and the little basket of happiness mysteriously disappears.

SECTION IV.

The Bull and the Cow in Slavonic Tradition.

SUMMARY.

The red cow and the black cow; what they prognosticate.—The red hue of evening.—The bull that drinks.—The bull corrupts the water.—The bull's hoofs.—The cow in the bartering of animals.—The hero ascends into heaven.—The bull sold to the tree; the tree, split open, yields gold.—The fool sells the bull.—Two bulls conduct the poor brother to riches.—The bull carries the fugitive home.—The bull is split in two, and is useful even after death.—Ivan and Helen, followed by the bear, flee upon the bull with their faces turned to the part whence the bear is likely to come.—The dwarf comes out of the bull's bones; the dwarf dies amid the flames.—The beasts of prey help the hero.—John and Mary, sun and aurora of the Christians.—The saviour-bull again.—From the dead bull an apple-tree springs up.—Ivan delivers Mary.—Mary, the step-daughter, and persecuted.—The cow that spins, the good fairy, the Madonna, the moon.—The maiden who combs the hair is the same as the purifier.—The demoniacal cow obliges men to kiss her under her tail.—The witch who sucks the beautiful girl's breast whilst the latter combs her hair.—The hide of the demoniacal cow taken off.—The eye which does not sleep and plays the spy.—From the cow, the apple-tree; from the apple-tree, the branches which wound the wicked sisters, and let the good one pluck their fruit; from the apple, the husband.—The maiden bows to the right foot of the beneficent cow; a tree springs up again from the killed cow.—The red apples which cause horns to grow, and the white ones which give beauty and youth.—Ivan, the sun, persecuted by the witch his sister, is saved by the sister of the sun, the aurora.—The mythical scales; the scales of St Michael.—The cows with golden horns and tails.—The black demoniacal bull strikes the ground with his horns, in order to prevent a wedding from taking place.—The hare and the crow put obstacles in the way of nuptials.—The demon blinded whilst drinking.—The third son of the peasant throws down the bull.—

The avaricious merchant.—The epidemic among the animals, and the bull killed because he has stolen some hay from a priest.—The bull in the forest.—The robber of cows and of oxen.—The black bull led away by Ivan, by means of a cock.—The hero comes out of the cow.—The intestines of the calf eaten by the fox.—Out of the calf come birds.—The son of the cow, the strongest brother.—The three brothers reduced to one with the qualities of the three.—The third brother mounts into heaven by means of the cow's hide.—He who ascends does not come down again.—Dreams.—The wife of the old man, carried to heaven in a sack, is let fall to the ground and dies.—The ascent into heaven by means of vegetables.—Turn-little-Pea, the third brother, the killer of monsters; Turn-little-Pea and Ivan identified.—Ivan followed by the serpent-witches.—The female serpent tries to file the iron gate with her tongue, which is caught by the pincers and burned.—The three brothers, the evening one, the midnight one, and the clearly-seeing one; the third is the victorious hero; he delivers three princesses out of three castles of copper, of silver, and of gold, and receives from them three eggs of copper, of silver, and of gold, new forms corresponding to those of the three brothers; the third brother, abandoned by his elders, after various vicissitudes, finds his bride again; explanation of this beautiful myth.—Ivan identified with Svetazór.—The mother of the birds, in gratitude, delivers the hero.—The third brother, the cunning one, despoils his two elder brothers of their precious objects.—Ivan of the dog is equivalent to Svetazór; the story of the goldsmith.—Ivan the great drinker.—Ivan the prince, Ivan the fool; Ivan and Emilius, foolish and lazy, are one and the same person.—The red shoes in the legend.—The sister kills her little brother to take his red shoes; a magical flute discovers the crime.—The slippers attract the bridegroom; corresponding nuptial usages.—The slipper tried on; the toe cut off.—The change of wives.—The ugly one becomes beautiful.—The grateful pike.—The barrel full of water, which walks of its own accord.—The forest which is cut down and walks of itself, the chariot which goes on by itself, the stove that moves and carries Emilius where he wishes, the cask in which the hero and heroine are shut up and thrown into the sea, all forms of the cloud and of the gloom of night; the ugly becomes beautiful; the poor, rich and pleasing.—The wine allowed to run out of the barrel, *i.e.*, the cloud which dissolves itself in rain.—Ivan, thought to be stupid, makes his fortune out of having watched by his father's grave.—Ivan, thought to be stupid, speculates upon his dead mother; his brothers try to do the same by their wives, and are punished.—The law of atavism in tradition.—The foolish mother and the cunning son.—The funereal storks.—The thief cheats the gentleman in several ways, and finally places him to guard his hat.—Ivan without fear; a little fish terrifies him.—Various heroical forms of Ivan in Russian tradition: Alessino, the son of the priest, invokes the rain against the monster-serpent; Baldak spits in the Sultan's face—the star under his heel; Basil and Plavaćek, who demand a gift from the monster; the fortunate fictitious hero; the cunning little Thomas; the third brother, who does not allow himself to be put to sleep; the thief Klimka, who terrifies the other thieves in order to rob them; tho Cossack who delivers the maiden from the flames, and receives precious gifts; Ilia Muromietz and his companions; the merchant's son educated by the devil; the boy who understands the language of birds; the virtuous workman, who prefers good advice to a large reward.—The flying ship; the protector of the unfortunate rewarded; eating and drinking.—The girl who solves the riddle of the prince, who comes with the hare and the quail, and obtains her husband.—The dwarf Allwis obtains the bride by answering the questions of his father-in-law.—The wonderful puppet (the moon), that sews for the priest's daughter (the aurora) the shirt destined for the prince.—The girl-heroine, protectress of her brother, helper of the young hero in dangers and trials of heroism.—The cowherd's daughter, who never says anything displeasing to her husband the king, whatever the latter does.—By contact with the monster, the heroine is perverted, and also becomes a persecutor of the hero, her brother or husband; analogous types of the perfidious woman.—Dangerous trials imposed on the hero.—The sister bound to the tree.—The wife subdued, and the magical belt.—The tooth of a dead man thrust into Ivan's head; the animals deliver him; the fox knows better than the rest how to manage it.—The towel which causes a bridge to spring up across the water; the hero's sister steals the towel, and unites herself to the monster-serpent; she demands from her brother Ivan wild beasts' milk, and the flour or powder of gold which is under a mill guarded by twelve gates.—The monster burned, and the hero's sister condemned to weep and to eat hay.—The exchange of the hero.—The crow brings the water of death and of life.—The stepmother who persecutes Ivan.—Ivan resuscitated by his two sons.—Ivan chaunts his death-song; the liberating animals appear to help him.—Ivan and his preceptor persecuted by his wife Anna.—The blind man, the lame man, and the beautiful girl whose breast is sucked by the witch.—The witch is forced to find the fountain of life and of health; the blind man sees, the lame walks, and the girl recovers her good health.—The maiden blinded; the wife changed; the dew which gives eyesight; the girl finds her husband; a Russian variety of the legend of Berta.

HAVING drawn so far the general outline of the Turanian boundaries of Slavonian tradition, it is now time to begin to study the tradition of the Slaves itself, as far as it concerns the myth and the legend of the bull and the cow.

The Russian peasants and shepherds are accustomed to remark that the weather will be fine when a red cow places herself at the head of the herd, and that it will rain or be bad weather when, on the contrary, the first of the cows to re-enter the stable at evening is a black one. We already know what the black and the red cow signify in the language of the Vedâs. The aurora of morning and evening, that is, the red cows promise fine weather; the cloud (or black cow) announces wet weather. In Piedmont, when a beautiful evening aurora is observed, it is the custom to say—

"Rosso di sera,
Buon tempo si spera."
(Red at eve, we hope for fine weather.)

Let us now follow the Russian tradition relating to the cow and the bull in two of the many invaluable collections of popular stories already printed in Russia, as well as in the celebrated fables of Kriloff.[1]

[1] These last have already been translated into English, and illustrated, by W. R. S. Ralston, M.A. The *Narodnija Skaski* sabrannija selskimi ućiteliami, isdanie A. A. Erlenwein (Moskva 1863), and the more voluminous N. Aphanasieva, *Narodnija ruskija skaski,* Isd. 2 (Moskva 1860, 1861), have not thus far been translated into other European languages. I have therefore thought fit to make copious quotations from them as well for the use of Western readers, as on account of the real importance of their mythical contents, whilst awaiting the publication of the competent work which Mr Ralston is expressly preparing upon Russian songs.

We shall begin with those stories and fables in which the cow or the bull is explicitly mentioned. They show us the bull who protects the hero and the heroine, the bull who enriches the hero, the bull that is sold, the grateful bull, the bull who sacrifices himself, the persecuted bull, the demoniacal bull; the cow who spins, the beneficent cow, the son of the cow, the birds that come out from the cow, the cow's hide which becomes a rope to mount up to heaven, the cow exchanged, the demoniacal cow, the cow's horns. Here, again, therefore, we have the double aspect of the Vedic cow; the dark-coloured one (cloud and darkness), generally monstrous, the luminous one (moon and aurora), usually divine and beneficent.

One of the special characteristics of the bull and of the cow is their capacity of drinking. We have already seen how much the bull Indras (the sun in the cloud) drank. In the third story of the first book of *Afanassieff*, when the good maiden, persecuted by the witch, stretches out a towel, and thus causes a river to arise, in order that the witch may not overtake her, the latter leads forward the bull to drink up the river (a form of the Hindoo Agastyas, who, in the *Mahâbhâratam*,[1] absorbs the sea). But the bull, who could dry up the river, refuses to do so on account of a debt of gratitude he owes to the good maiden. The water where this bull, or cow, belonging to the witch, drinks, has the property of transforming into a calf the man who drinks of it;[2] nay, to drink out of the hoof of the bull itself is enough to turn him into a calf.[3] The water which comes out of the hoof of the demoniacal bull is the opposite of the

[1] iii. 8805, and following.

[2] *Afanassieff*, ii. 29.

[3] iv. 45.

water of Hippokrene, which flows from the hoofs of the divine horse of the Hellenes, the Pêgasos.

In the second book of *Afanassieff*, there is a story which speaks of the exchange of animals in the very same order as in the *Âitareya-brâhmaṇam*, *i.e.*, the gold for a horse, the horse for a cow, the cow for a goat or sheep. The Russian peasant goes on with his unfortunate exchanges; he barters the sheep for a young pig, the young pig for a goose, the goose for a duck, the duck for a little stick with which he sees some children playing; he takes the stick home to his wife, and she beats him with it. In the twelfth story of the fifth book of *Afanassieff*, an old man also begins to barter the golden stockings and silver garters received in heaven from God for a horse, the horse for a bull, the bull for a lamb; his last exchange is for a little needle, which he loses. In the second story of the sixth book, the same foolish liberality is attributed to the third brother, the stupid one (who, in another Russian variation of the same story, is the cunning one), who, having learned that in heaven cows are cheap, gives his cow for a fly, his ox for a horse-fly, and mounts up to heaven.

But, generally speaking, the bull and the cow are the beginning of good luck for the heroes of popular tales.

In the fifty-second story of the fifth book of *Afanassieff*, the third brother, the truthful and fortunate fool, has, for his inheritance from his father, one bull alone; he goes to sell it, and passes a dry old tree, which rattles; thinking that the tree wishes to buy his bull, he gives it, promising to come back for the money. On his return the bull is gone; he asks the tree for the money, and, receiving no answer, proceeds to cut it down with his hatchet, when from the tree there drops out a treasure which some robbers had hidden in it;[1] the young man then takes it up and carries it home. In a variation of the same story, in the collection of *Erlenwein*,[2] the third son of the miller, before going to sell his bull, or ox, seeing the second son milking the cow, endeavours to milk the bull too; finding that his efforts are in vain, he resolves upon selling an animal which appears to him to be so utterly useless.

In the thirty-fourth story of the fifth book of *Afanassieff*, we meet again the two brothers, one rich and miserly, the other poor; the poor one borrows from a neighbour two bulls, and is conducted by Misery (gory) to a stone, under which he finds a cavity full of gold. The poor man fills his waggon, and, on coming out, tells Misery that there is plenty more inside. Misery turns in to see; the ex-pauper thereupon closes up the entrance with the stone, and returns home.[3]

But the bull and the cow do not only provide the hero with riches, they help him in danger. In the eleventh story of *Erlenwein*,[4] Ivan Tzarević, or the Prince John,—the name of the favourite hero of Slavonian popular tradition (he is the third brother, the strongest, the most fortunate, the victorious, the most intelligent, after having been the most foolish)—wishes to flee from the serpent, and, not knowing how, sits down on the trunk of a tree and weeps. The hare comes to carry him away, but is

[1] This subject is already given in *Æsop's Fables*, in the twenty-first fable (ed. Del Furia, Florence, 1809): the man prays to a wooden idol (xülinon theon) that it may make him rich; the statue does not answer; he breaks it to pieces, and gold comes out of it.

[2] Seventeenth story.

[3] Cfr. also in *Afanassieff*, the story, v. 19.

[4] Cfr. also, for the variations, the twenty-second of *Erlenwein*, and iii. 24, of *Afanassieff*.

killed by the serpent; the wolf comes, but is killed too. At last the ox or bull comes, and carries him off. Ivan having arrived at his dwelling, the ox has himself divided in two; one part must be placed under the sacred images, which ornament a corner of every room in Russian houses, the other part under the window; Ivan must then look out sharp till two dogs and two bears appear, who will serve him in the chase, and be his strength.

In the twenty-seventh story of the fifth book of *Afanassieff*, Ivan Tzarević and the beautiful Helen are pursued by a monstrous bear with iron bristles; they escape upon a bull (the moon), and Ivan, by the bull's advice, rides him with his face turned towards the place whence the pursuing bear is likely to come, in order that he may not take them by surprise. When Ivan sees that the bear is coming, the bull turns round and tears his eyes out; the blind bear follows them still, but the fugitives pass a river on the bull's back, in which the bear is drowned. Ivan and Helen feel hungry; the bull tells them to cut him to pieces and eat him, but to preserve his bones, and to strike them together; from the bones of the bull, when struck, a dwarf, the height of a finger-nail, but with a beard a cubit long, comes out; he assists Ivan in finding the milk of a wolf, a she-bear, and a lioness, until he is swallowed by the burning bird, whose eggs he wished to steal. (The bear is the night; the bull is the sun's steed in the night, the moon; the bull-moon is sacrificed; then comes forth a little sun with long rays, the dwarf with a long beard, an *alter ego* of Ivan, who ends his life in the burning furnace of the phœnix, or of the evening aurora.) Ivan is threatened with death when the dwarf dies, but he is at that moment helped by the wild beasts he had tamed and fed, who save him from danger These were, as we have seen before, given to him after the death of the bull, his deliverer, being born of the bull himself, cut in pieces (the wild animals of the forest of night are born as soon as the evening sun is sacrificed).

The same subject occurs again, with some variations, in the twenty-eighth story, which follows ; only instead of John and Helen, we have John and Mary, the sun and the aurora of the Christians. Near the abode of Ivan and Mary a funeral pile arises, on which the bull sacrifices himself. The bull's bones are sown in three furrows ; from the first furrow a horse comes forth, from the second a dog, and in the third an apple-tree grows up. Ivan mounts upon the horse, followed by the dog, and hunts wolves' whelps and young bears, which he afterwards tames and uses to kill the serpent, who has shut up his dog in a cavern, and carried off his sister ; he forces the entrance of the place where the dog is hidden, by striking the bolt of the door with three small branches of the apple-tree ; the bolt breaks into pieces, the door bursts open, and the dog is delivered ; dog, wolf, and young bear then worry the serpent, and Ivan liberates the Princess Mary.

In the sixth book of *Afanassieff*,[1] the young Mary, being persecuted, is miraculously assisted by a cow. An old woman has three daughters of her own (of whom one has one eye, another two, and the third three), and a step-daughter called Mary ; her own three do nothing, and eat much ; the step-daughter must work hard and eat little. Her step-mother gives her for one night alone, while she takes the cow to pasture, to spin, make into skeins, weave, and bleach, the weight of five pounds. The maiden goes to the pasture-ground, embraces her variegated cow, leans on her neck and bewails her fate. The cow says to her, " Beautiful girl, enter one of my

[1] Story 54.

ears, and come out by the other, and all will be done."—In the Italian variety of this story,[1] the cow spins with her horns for the good maiden, whilst she combs the head of the old woman or the Madonna. I think I have already said that I recognise in this good old woman, fairy, or Madonna, the moon. The moon, like the sun, is considered as in relation with the aurora, and especially the evening aurora, which she accompanies; she is the hostess, the guide, and the protectress of the hero and heroine of evening, lost and pursued in the night; after the evening aurora, the white moon comes out, in the same way as after the morning aurora the sun comes out in effulgence. We have seen that the name of purifier, cleanser, is given to the Vedic aurora; from this expression to the image of comber or cleanser of the head of the old Madonna the transition is easy;[2] from, *i.e.*, after, the aurora, the moon comes out shining and clean, in a beautiful and serene sky; and on this account pearls fall from the Madonna's head; but when, on the other hand, the beautiful maiden, the aurora, does not come, when the step-mother sends to the pasture-ground, near the old woman, one of her own daughters, foul lice fall from the head of the old fairy or Madonna, inasmuch as the moon cannot show herself in her splendour amid the shadows of the cloudy and black night. The Russian story shows us how the beneficent cow of the good maiden, who caresses her and serves her well, and the Madonna or good old woman grateful for

[1] Cfr. the first story of my collection of the *Novelline di Santo Stefano di Calcinaia*, Torino, A. F. Negro, 1869. I am also acquainted with a Piedmontese variation, differing but little from this Tuscan story.

[2] In the story, ii. 27, of the collection of *Afanassieff*, the beautiful princess, near the sea, combs the youngest son of the Tzar, who goes to sleep.

the careful combing of her hair of Italian tradition, are one and the same thing. In the thirty-fifth story of the fifth book of *Afanassieff*, on the contrary, where the cow appears in a demoniacal aspect, whom the hero Ivan, condemned from a prince to become a cowherd, must kiss under her tail, which she lifts with this intent, we meet with an old witch who sucks the white breasts of the beautiful girl, while the latter is obliged to hunt the vermin in her head; in the witch, as well as in the cow who insolently lifts up her tail, we can recognise the gloomy night, an explanation which is justified by the fact that the hero-shepherd Katoma, the adorned one, the agile-footed, ends by flaying the shameless cow (the morning sun, shepherd of the luminous cows, takes off the skin of the dark-coloured cow of the gloomy night). But, to return to the fifty-fourth story.—When the step-mother sees that the girl has done all the work assigned her, she begins to suspect that there is some one who helps her, and so sends next night her first daughter, who has but one eye, to watch the daughter-in-law, who goes to the pasture-ground. The young Mary then says to her, "Eye, sleep;" and immediately her step-sister falls asleep, thus allowing the cow to assist her without any one perceiving it. The second night, the second daughter, who has two eyes, is sent; Mary says twice to her, "Eye, sleep," and obtains, without being seen, the same favours from the cow. The third night, the third sister, who has three eyes, is sent; Mary does not remember the third eye, and only says twice, "Eye, sleep:" and so the third sister sees with her remaining eye [1] what the cow does with Mary, and in the morning tells everything to her mother, who gives orders that the

[1] Cfr. the chapter on the Goat.

cow be killed. Mary warns the cow; and the cow recommends her to eat none of her flesh, to keep the bones, sow them in the garden, and water them. The maiden does so; every day, however hungry she may be, she eats none of the meat, only collects the bones together. From the bones sown in the garden arises a marvellous apple-tree, with leaves of gold, and branches of silver, which prick and wound the three daughters of the stepmother, whilst, on the other hand, they offer apples to the beautiful maiden, in order that she may present one to the young and rich lord who is to make her his wife. In the following story, the fifty-fifth, which is a variation of the preceding one, the girl is named Mary, and her husband Ivan Tzarević; when she goes to the pasture, and when she returns, she is accustomed to make obeisance to the right foot of the cow. When the cow, being killed, revives again in the shape of a tree, it swarms with birds, which sing songs for kings and peasants alike, and make the sweet fruits fall upon Mary's plate.

The apples that cause horns to grow, and those which beautify and make young, mentioned in the thirty-sixth story of the fifth book, and again in the last book of the collection of *Afanassieff*, as well as in other European variations of the same subject, are connected, in my opinion, with the myth of the evening sky, and of the lunar night, in the shape of an apple-tree. In the fifteenth story of the collection of *Erlenwein*, the third brother, the usual Ivan, comes to an apple-tree which has red apples, and eats four of them, upon which four horns grow on his head, to such a height that he cannot enter the forest; he goes to an apple-tree that bears white fruit, eats four apples, and the four horns disappear. (The solar hero at evening approaches the tree with the red apples, the evening aurora, and immediately becomes deformed; horns grow on his head; he loses himself in the shades of night; in the moonlight and the alba, he approaches the tree with the white apples, loses his horns, and becomes young and beautiful again.)

In the fifty-seventh story of the sixth book of *Afanassieff's* collection, Ivan Tzarević is presented with the apples which restore youth to him who eats them, by the sister of the sun, to whose abode he is lifted in the following manner: Ivan (the sun) has for his sister (no doubt half-sister) a serpent-witch (night), who has already devoured his father and mother (the sun and the aurora of evening, which create the night, and are destroyed by it); the witch persecutes her little brother Ivan, and endeavours to eat him; he flees, and she overtakes him in the vicinity of the dwelling of the sister of the sun (the aurora, the true sister of Ivan). The witch makes a proposal to Ivan, that they be weighed together in the scales. Ivan accepts this proposal, upon which the one enters the one scale, and the other the other; no sooner does the witch put her foot on the scale than, as she weighs so much more than Ivan, he is lifted up to heaven, the dwelling of the sister of the sun, where he is welcomed and admitted. (A beautiful myth, of which the meaning is evident. Ivan is the sun, the aurora is his sister; at morning, near the abode of the aurora, that is, in the east, the shades of night go underground, and the sun arises to the heavens; this is the mythical pair of scales. Thus, in the Christian belief, St Michael weighs human souls: those who weigh much sink down into hell, and those who are light arise to the heavenly paradise.)

By means of the sister of the sun, Ivan saves himself from the witch. In another story in *Afanassieff*,[1] by

[1] v. 37.

means of the sister of the hero Nikanore, the same Ivan, running after the cows, causes them to have golden horns and tails, with sides formed of stars; and afterwards, with the assistance of the hero Nikanore in person (of the sun, that is, of himself), he kills the serpent.

We have already seen the cloudy and the gloomy sky represented in the Vedic poems, now as a black cow, now as a stable which encloses the bulls and cows. The black bull or cow of night is considered to be demoniacal. In a story given in *Afanassieff*,[1] we find the devil in the shape of a bull, which bellows, and throws up the earth with its horns, arresting a nuptial procession. From a bull he turns into a bear, then a hare, and then a crow, to put obstacles in the way of the marriage, until, having presented himself in the form of a devil, a soldier-hero blinds him while he is drinking. A variation of this soldier is the third son of the peasant,[2] who is so strong that with a snap of his fingers he makes the bull and the bear fall dead, and then by a single pinch strips off their skins. The same hero hires himself to a merchant, whom he engages to serve for two years, on condition of receiving as his reward, at the end of them, the permission to give him a snap with the fingers and a pinch. The merchant thinks he is getting the man's service for nothing, but pays for it with his life. The merchant seldom plays a good part in popular stories. He and the miser are synonymous,—the miser is the monster which keeps treasures hidden; and on this account, as we have already seen in the Vedic hymns themselves, the enemies of the gods, the monsters that ravish and conceal the treasures, are represented as paṇayas or merchants, cheats, robbers, or misers. The currency of this epithet

---

[1] v. 50.

[2] v. 9.

as a term of infamy must have been owing in part to the dislike with which the priestly sacrificers of the last Vedic period regarded the merchants, in whom they saw only a pack of misers, because, on account of their wandering life, they had neither cows nor bulls to give them for sacrifice, but carried with them all their fortune, and did not require the fertilising rain of the god Indras to multiply their gold and their silver.

The celestial bull comes out of the night or the nocturnal stables either, as we have seen, to help the hero, to be sacrificed, to flee from persecution, or because he has been stolen by a skilful thief.

In one of Kriloff's fables, God sends a terrible plague among the animals, of which they perish in great numbers. They are so terrified by it that they forsake their habits, and begin to wander aimlessly hither and thither. The wolf no longer eats the sheep; the fox leaves the hens unmolested; the turtle-doves no longer make love to each other. Then the lion holds a council of the animals, and exhorts them all to confess their faults. The cunning fox essays to quiet the lion-judge by assuring him that though he stole some sheep, he did not thereby commit a fault; and so he justifies his own ravages; as also do the bear, the tiger, the wolf, and all the most wicked of the animals. Then the simple bull comes forward, and, in his turn, confesses that he stole a little hay from the priest. This crime appears so heinous that the council of animals sentences the bull to be offered in sacrifice.[1]

Sometimes, on the contrary, the bull, either because he cannot bear the bad treatment that he receives from his masters, or in order to avoid the danger of being killed or sold by the stupid son, who is in need of money

---

[1] In Lafontaine, *Fables*, vii. 1, the animal sacrificed is the ass.

that he may marry a wife, a danger of which he has a presentiment, abandons the stable with other animals, constructs a hut or isbà and shuts himself up in it.[1] He has with him the lamb, the goose, the cock, or else some other tame animals. The fox passes by, hears the crowing of the cock, and goes to call his friends the bear and the wolf to help him. The bear opens the door, the fox enters, and the bull by goring him with his horns, the lamb by butting against his sides, and the cock by pecking his eyes out, put an end to the unwelcome intruder. The wolf, who goes in, curious to see what is going on, has the same fate, and the bear, who comes last, only succeeds with great difficulty, and after having been severely maltreated, in effecting his escape. In another variation of the same story, the bear dies of fear, and the stupid son takes his skin, sells it and makes money; then, the danger of being sold having passed by, the bull and his company return home. The battle between the tame and the savage animals, won by the former, is an expression in zoological form of the victory of the heroes (the sun and the moon) over the monsters of darkness.

The story of the hero-thief is generally connected with the carrying off of his master's horse; but not unfrequently the hero, like the monster, becomes a robber of cows and oxen.

The thief Ivan[2] is required to steal from his master a black bull or ox tied to the plough; if he succeeds, he is to have a hundred roubles for his reward; but if he does not, he is to receive instead a hundred bastinadoes. In

[1] *Afanassieff*, iv. 20–22.—In a Lithuanian song, which describes the nuptials of animals, the bull appears as a woodcutter or woodman. —Cfr. Uhland's *Schriften zur Geschichte der Dichtung und Sage*, iii. 75.

[2] *Afanassieff*, v. 6.

order to steal it, Ivan adopts the following device: he takes a cock, plucks it, and puts it alive under a clod of earth. The ploughmen come with the oxen; while they are ploughing, the cock starts up; they leave the plough to run after it, upon which Ivan, who was hidden behind a bush, comes out. He cuts off one ox's tail and puts it in another ox's mouth, and then leads away the black ox. The ploughmen, not having been able to overtake the cock, come back, and when they see only two animals instead of three, conclude that one ox has eaten the black ox and is beginning to eat the tail of the other, the variegated ox. In the twenty-first story of the fifth book of *Afanassieff*, the boy-dwarf steals an ox from the priest and eats its tripe.[1]

From the cow the hero is born; under a putrid cow thrown into a ditch lies Ivan Tzarević; a bird takes the water off and Ivan Tzarević comes forth.[2] In another story of *Afanassieff*, the fox-heroine, companion of the wolf, whilst the wolf is absent, eats the intestines of the calf, their common property (which they had received from cowherds in exchange for a certain cake contaminated by their excrement, the usual excrement which is the beginning of riches); she then fills the calf or cow with straw and sparrows, and departs. The wolf returns, is astonished that the calf should have eaten so much straw that it comes out, and draws out the straw. The birds fly away, the calf falls, and the wolf flees away terrified.[3] With these two myths are connected two more, that of the son of the cow and

[1] Cfr. the chapter which treats of the Wolf.

[2] *Afanassieff*, v. 41.

[3] *Afanassieff*, iv. 1.—In another variation of the same myth, which we have already referred to in the Vedic hymns, the birds come, on the contrary, out of a horse.

that of the ascent into heaven by means of the cow's hide.

The king has no sons; he catches a pike, which the cook washes, giving thereafter the dirty water to the cow to drink; the fish they give to the black girl to carry to the queen; the black girl eats a piece of it on the way, and the queen eats what remains. At the expiration of nine months, the cow, the maid, and the queen, give each birth to a son. The three sons resemble each other completely; but the son of the cow, the hero-tempest, is the strongest of the three brothers, and accomplishes the most difficult enterprises. In another variation of the same story, in *Afanassieff*,[1] instead of the cow we have the bitch giving birth to the strongest of the three brothers.[2] In the nineteenth story of *Erlenwein*, instead of the cow and the bitch, we have the mare; the strongest brother is here the son of the black girl, Burgh-raver or the hero-tempest (Burya-Bagatír). In the third story of *Erlenwein*, Ivan Tzarević appears as the son of the black girl. As in numerous other Russian stories, Ivan Tzarević, usually the third brother, appears not only (as) the most skilful, but the strongest of the brothers, we are driven to recognise in the three brothers, the son of the black girl, the son of the cow, and the queen's son, who alternately accomplish the same heroic undertakings, the same solar personage, whose mother, Night, is represented now as a queen, now as a cow (we have just seen Ivan Tzarević come out of the putrid cow), now as a black slave (the negro washerwoman, the Saracen woman of Italian stories [Holda]; the cleaned fish which is carried by the black girl may perhaps be a link connecting the imagery of Russian tradition with that of Italian legend).

[1] v. 54.

[2] Cfr. *Afanassieff*, v. 54, and the chapters on the Fish and the Eel.

In the second story of the fifth book of *Afanassieff*, the third brother, the cunning one, by means of the hides of his cows and oxen converted into thongs, ascends into heaven; thus, in a variation of the same story, the third brother thinks to let himself down by the cow's hide, cut into pieces and made into thongs, being fastened to the confines of heaven; but he perceives on the way that the thong is not long enough. Some peasants are threshing corn, and the chaff rises into the air; he tries to make a rope with this chaff, but the rope breaks and he falls to the ground. This successful ascent into heaven, followed by an unlucky descent, is often referred to, with curious details, in Russian popular legend; to which a play of words in the language must have not a little contributed. It is as follows, "He who mounts does not descend,"[1] *i.e.*, when one is doing one thing he cannot be doing the contrary. This elementary truth was afterwards altered by changing the tenses. "He who has been able to ascend will not be able to come down again;" which is only partly true, and means that while in dreams we require only a thin thread to mount up high, when we wish to come down from the world of dreams to that of reality, the fall is heavy; we come down with leaden wings, with that difficulty in breathing which oppresses us in dreams when we seem to fall from a height with painful slowness. And as at the end of the dream, after the

[1] I read in the travels of Olearius in Persia during the year 1638, French translation: "Les Persans disent que la montagne de Kilissim a une telle propriété que tous ceux qui y montent n'en descendent point; que le schach Abas obligea un jour un de ses chasseurs, en lui promettant une grosse somme d'argent, à monter sur cette montagne, et qu'il y monta effectivement, l'ayant fait connoître par le feu qu'il alluma; mais qu'il n'en descendit point, et que l'on ne sçait point ce qu'il devint avec son chien, qu'il menait avec lui."

painful fall from the sky, we awaken alive, so the story does not say of the hero who fell from heaven that he is dead, only that his dreams are dead. He is only unlucky when, the second time, he attempts the descent with a greater weight.

While reasonings such as these may have helped to diffuse the myths, I believe that the myths, at their formation, pleased more as images of nature than of reason, and as the images of mythology are almost all celestial, so in the third brother, or old man of other varieties of the story, who mounts up to heaven and comes down again by means of the cow's hide, I always recognise the sun. The old man who ascends into heaven, after the cow is dead, does so also by means of a vegetable of funereal omen which grows up in a marvellous manner.

An old man and an old woman have one daughter; she eats some beans and lets one fall to the ground; a plant (the moon) grows up till it reaches the sky. The old man mounts up and then comes back again. He tries to take his wife up in a sack, but unable to bear the weight, he lets her fall to the ground, when she dies.[1]

A cabbage grows up near an old man's dwelling, till in like manner it rises up to the sky. The old man climbs up, makes a hole in the sky, and eats and drinks to satiety. He then returns and narrates everything to his wife. She wishes to go up too; when they are half way, the old man lets the sack drop, the old woman dies, and her husband prepares her funeral, calling in the fox[2] as a mourner.

Other variations of the same story offer us, instead of

[1] *Afanassieff*, iv. 9.—In the well-known English story of *Jack and the Bean-stalk*, it is the giant who is killed by the fall from heaven, when Jack cuts the bean-stalk close to the ground.

[2] *Afanassieff*, iv. 7.—Cfr. the chapter on the Fox.

the cow's hide, the cabbage, and the beanstalk, the pea-plant, and even the oak-tree, which grows up to heaven.[1]

From the vegetable or funereal plant,—a symbol, as we have already remarked, at once of abundance and resurrection,—by which the hero ascends to heaven, where he finds riches and abundance of food, the transition was very natural to the pea which turns round, of which the hero Turn-little-Pea (the son of the king of the peas) is born.

In the second story of the third book of *Afanassieff*,[2] Turn-little-Pea appears as the third of the brothers, as the youngest brother, who delivers his sister and his two brothers from the monster. But the ungrateful brothers (perhaps covetous of the maiden, here called a sister, but, who is virtually the same, the bride delivered and disputed for by the three brothers in numerous Indo-European legends), tie him to an oak-tree and go home alone. Turn-little-Pea unroots the whole oak and goes off. He afterwards kills three more monster-serpents, and the she-serpents their wives.

In the thirtieth story of the second book of *Afanassieff*, this enterprise against the serpents, male and female, is attributed to the usual Ivan. He goes with his brothers against the serpent with twelve heads, and with his iron stick alone kills nine of them, and the three remaining ones by the help of his two brothers. Then the she-serpent and her three daughters persecute the three brothers, and

---

[1] *Afanassieff*, v. 12, and vi. 2.—Cfr. the chapters on the Goat, the Fox, the Wolf, and the Duck, where other episodes of this legend are found again.—In the twelfth story of the fifth book of *Afanassieff*, the old man goes up to heaven to call God to account for the peas that He has taken from the top of the pea-plant; God gives him in exchange stockings of gold and garters of silver.

[2] Cfr. also v. 24.

Ivan in particular. She causes them to find a beautiful cushion upon the ground; Ivan, who is suspicious of some trick, first beats the cushion, upon which blood gushes out of it (in the story of *Turn-little-Pea,* the young hero averts the danger by making the sign of the cross with his sword, when blood comes out). The serpent then tempts them by an apple-tree with gold and silver apples. The brothers wish to pluck some; Ivan, however, first strikes the tree, and blood flows from it. They then come to a beautiful fountain, where the brothers would like to drink; Ivan strikes the fountain, and again blood comes from it. The cushion, the apple-tree, and the fountain were the three daughters of the serpent. Then the serpent, having failed to deceive them, rushes upon Ivan; the latter escapes with his brothers into a forge shut by twelve iron gates; the serpent licks the doors with her tongue to force a passage, and her tongue is caught with red-hot pincers.

In the fourth story of *Erlenwein,* the three brothers occur again with interesting mythical names. A woman bears three sons; one at evening, who is on this account called Većernik, or the evening one; the second at midnight, whence he is named Polunoćnik, or the midnight one; the third at the aurora, who is named Svetazór, or the clearly-seeing. The three brothers become adults in a few hours. The most valiant of the three is Svetazór, the last one. To prove his strength, he goes to the blacksmith and orders an iron club that weighs twelve puds (480 pounds); he throws it into the air and catches it on the palm of his hand, the club breaks. He orders one of twenty puds (800 pounds), throws it up, catches it on his knee, and it breaks. Finally he orders one of thirty puds (1200 pounds), throws it up, and catches it on his forehead; it bends but does not break. Svetazór has it straightened and takes it with him, as he goes with his two brothers to deliver the three daughters of the Tzar, carried off by three magicians into the three castles of copper, silver, and gold. Svetazór, after having drunk the water of strength, and received from the first princess an egg of copper, from the second one of silver, and from the third a golden one, delivers the three princesses and brings them out. The two brothers, seeing that the third princess is more beautiful than the others, think that the youngest brother is reserving her for himself, and throw him into the water. Svetazór wanders about the subterranean world, and delivers the daughter of another Tzar by killing a monster and burying him under a rock. A soldier boasts before the Tzar of having accomplished this heroic act. Svetazór invites the soldier to prove his strength, and so the truth of his boast, by lifting the rock up. He does not succeed, and Svetazór wins the trial of strength, upon which the soldier is executed by order of the Tzar. After this, Svetazór, for having once spared the life of a crow, is carried by it into the world of the living, on condition that he gives it something to eat by the way. Svetazór has at length to feed the crow with his own flesh, yet is in the end set down again safe and sound, with all his flesh, in the world above, where, with the eggs of copper, silver, and gold, he causes the castles formed of these metals to arise, in which are found the ring, the slipper, and the robe demanded from their bridegrooms by the three princesses, who hoped by this expedient to see again their lost Svetazór. Then Svetazór begins to sweep out the terrace of the golden castle. The third princess expresses her intention to take him for her husband. The nuptials are celebrated, Svetazór pardoning his two elder brothers and giving them the two elder sisters of his bride. (The princess of the copper is the evening aurora, the princess of the silver is the silvery moon, and that of the gold is the morning aurora, to whom Svetazór, the clearly-seeing, the illumined, the sun, is married.)

In the sixth story of the first book of *Afanassieff*, the same undertaking is accomplished by the third brother, Ivan. The monster which carries off the three sisters is an aquatic one, an otter. Abandoned by his brothers in the nether world, Ivan is overtaken by a great tempest; he takes pity upon some young birds that are bathing, and saves them under his dress, upon which the grateful mother of the birds brings him back to the upper world. In the fifteenth story of *Erlenwein*, the third brother is the cunning one, who, by a stratagem, and by means of his purse, which is self-replenishing, steals from his two brothers the snuff-box out of which issue as many armies as are wished for, and the cloth which makes the wearer invisible (both figures to represent the cloud from which come forth riches, solar rays, thunderbolts, and weapons, and which hides the hero, that is, renders him invisible). In the fifty-fourth story of the fifth book of *Afanassieff*, Ivan of the dog, the hero sacrificed by his brothers, is the strong one, he who delivers the three princesses, who possesses the three rings, and gives them to the goldsmith from whom they were ordered, and who is not able to make them, by which means he is recognised.

Ivan Tzarević, inasmuch as he was born of a cow, as we have also seen above, was necessarily represented as a bull; the bull displays part of his strength by drinking; Ivan Tzarević drinks, at a gulp, whole barrels of wine of marvellous strength. In this capacity he resembles Indras, the great drinker of somas, and the drinker Bhîmas, the second brother of the Pâṇḍavas.

The third brother is now Prince Ivan (Ivan Tzarević, Ivan Karoliević, Ivan Kraliević), now the stupid Ivan (Ivan durak), Ivan the little fool (Ivan Duraćiok). But, as I have already remarked, the fool generally makes his fortune, either because the kingdom of heaven is for the poor in spirit, or because the stupidity of Ivan is feigned, or else because the fool becomes wise. In a story given in *Afanassieff*,[1] the fool is also lazy, and takes the name of Emilius.

Emilius is sent with a barrel to draw water; he only goes on account of the promise made him by his sister, that he will receive as a reward a pair of red boots.—This desire of the boy-hero, and of the girl-heroine, is spoken of in many popular songs, and among others, in a Piedmontese one, as yet unpublished. In the seventeenth story of the fifth book of *Afanassieff*,[2] the sister kills her brother, Little John, to possess herself of his red strawberries (as in the Esthonian tale), and his red little shoes. Upon his grave a fine cane grows; a shepherd makes a flute of it, and the flute, pressed to the lips, begins to emit the following lamentation:—

"Gently, gently, little shepherd, play;
Do not wound my heart!
My little sister, the traitress,
For the red little strawberries, for the red little shoes!"

When the flute is pressed to the sister's lips, instead of the word "little shepherd," it says, "Little sister, thou hast betrayed me,"[3] and her crime is thus discovered. These

[1] v. 55.—Cfr. also vi. 22.—Cfr. the *Contes et Proverbes Populaires recueillis en Armagnac*, par Bladé (Paris, 1867), where the foolish and lazy one occurs again under the name of Joan Lou Pigre.

[2] Cfr. also the two variations in *Afanassieff*, vi. 25.

[3] Po malu, malu, sestritze, grai
Nie vraszi ti mavó serdienká vkrai!
Ti-sz mini szradila
Sza kraşni yagodki, sza ćorvonni ćobotki!

Also cfr. the chapter on the Peacock.

little red shoes are simply a variation of the slippers which are lost by the fugitive aurora, and found again by the sun, and which both wish to wear. (I refer to this myth the origin of the nuptial custom in Europe of maidens, towards the new year, throwing the slipper to know whether, during the next year, they will be married, and who is to be their husband.)[1] The slipper lost by the maiden, Little Mary (Masha, the Marion of Piedmontese and French legends), and found by the prince, also occurs in the Russian tales. In the thirtieth of the sixth book of *Afanassieff*, Little Mary's elder sister begins by trying on the slipper; but it is too small; the foot will not go in. Seeing this, Little Mary's step-mother advises her daughter to cut off her great toe, which would not enter; then the foot goes in, and the messengers of the prince lead the eldest sister away; but two doves fly after them and cry out, "Blood on her foot, blood on her foot." The deceit is discovered, and the eldest sister sent back; the prince causes his true and predestined bride, Little Mary, to be carried off. (This is the usual exchange of wives, upon which I have remarked in my "Essay on the Comparative History of Nuptial Usages," and of which the

[1] In the Festival of the Epiphany, which is also a festival of the husband and wife, the good fairy is accustomed to bring to the child, husband, and wife, a boot or a stocking full of presents. This nuptial boot occurs again in the English custom of throwing a slipper after a newly-married couple. Another meaning was also given to the slippers which are thrown away in the popular belief. Instead of being the heroine's shoes which, having been abandoned, serve to attract and guide the predestined husband, they are also considered as the old shoes which the devil leaves behind him when he flees (his tail, which betrays itself). The Germanic wild huntress Gueroryssa, another form of the Frau Holle—the phantom of winter expelled at Epiphany—is represented with a serpent's tail. Hence in the German carnival the use of the *Schuh-teufel laufen*, or running in the devil's slippers.

legend of Queen Berta is one of the most popular examples. The Russian Little Mary, like Cinderella, is at first of ugly aspect, and then beautiful. In the Russian story, the maiden becomes beautiful by mounting upon the stove. Sîtâ comes forth, beautiful in her innocence, passing through the fire; the morning aurora only seems beautiful when it passes through the flames of the Eastern sky. The stove brings us back to the interrupted story of the foolish and lazy Emilius (or Ivan).—On account, therefore, of the promise made to him of the red boots, he goes to the fountain with the barrel to draw water. In the fountain he catches a pike, who beseeches him to set him at liberty, and promises in return to make him fortunate. Being lazy, the greatest favour that he wishes for at this moment is that he may be helped to carry the barrel; the grateful pike performs the miracle of the barrel full of water which walks of its own accord. (I have already endeavoured to explain this myth: the cloud is represented as a barrel in the Vedic hymns; it moves on of its own accord; the barrel does the same; the hero, as long as he is shut up in the cloud, remains foolish; the barrel of the fool walks of itself.) Emilius is then sent to cut wood; by favour of the grateful pike, it is enough for him to send his hatchet, which cuts the wood of itself; the wood piles itself upon the waggon, and the waggon, without being drawn by any one, advances, passing or crushing whatever it meets; they endeavour to arrest its progress, when the trunk of an oak-tree detaches itself from the waggon, and, like a stick, beating on every side, sweeps the road (these are all curious variations of the walking forest or cloud). The Tzar then sends to invite him to court, and knowing his weak penchant for things of a red colour, he promises him a red robe, a red hat, and red boots. When the

Tzar's envoys arrive, Emilius, like his *alter ego* Ivan Durak (Ivan the fool), is warming himself at the stove; grudging all trouble, he obtains from the pike the favour of being carried by the stove itself to the Tzar at court. The Tzar's daughter falls in love with him; the Tzar shuts the young couple up in a cask (the usual cloud-barrel, which occurs in the form of a little chest in other stories, a variation of the wooden dress), and has them thrown into the sea. Emilius, who was drunk in the cask, sleeps; the princess wakens him, and beseeches him to save her; by means of the pike, the cask comes to a beautiful island, where it breaks open; Emilius becomes handsome, rich, and happy in a beautiful palace with the young princess. (The aurora and the sun of evening are thrown together into the ocean of night, until they land on the happy isle of the east, where they re-appear again together in all their splendour.) One of the most popular stupidities of the fool is that of letting the wine contained in the barrel flow out upon the ground, when he is left alone at home; in the Russian story, too, Ivan the fool leaves the beer that is fermenting in the barrel open (Indras with his lightning makes a hole in the cloud-barrel, and the rain comes out).[1]

The fool Ivan takes his good luck from the living, but he also does so from the dead. On account of having watched three nights by the tomb of his father, his luck begins,[2] the shade of his father having blessed him; but, as the dead bring good luck (a belief which, at any rate, has always been entertained by the heirs of rich men deceased), the third brother speculates on the body of his own mother. We do not know whether he does so out

[1] Cfr. *Afanassieff*, v. 4, and the chapter on the Stork.
[2] Cfr. *Afanassieff*, ii. 25, ii. 28, iv. 47, v. 37.

of pure simplicity, or with some hidden and far-seeing design, presumable from the ease with which he exchanges the character of a fool for that of a cunning schemer (the first Brutus of popular tradition). In the seventeenth story of *Erlenwein,* after he has carried a treasure home, by selling his ox to the tree, and then cutting down the tree, which contains money, he always guards his money, and sleeps upon it. His brothers know this, and resolve to go and kill him. But that very night, the third, the foolish brother, leaves his mother in charge of the treasure ; the brothers come and kill his mother by mistake, instead of him. He turns up, and threatens to give them up to justice ; they bribe him with a hundred roubles to keep silence. Then the third brother takes his mother's body and carries it into the middle of the road, in order that a merchant's waggon may crush it ; when this happens, he accuses the merchant of murder, until the latter gives him a hundred more roubles to say nothing about it. He then comes to a village by night with his mother's corpse ; he places it against a peasant's door, and knocks at the window ; the peasant opens the door, the body falls, and the peasant treads upon it, upon which the so-called stupid son cries out that he has killed his mother, and receives another hundred roubles, on promise of silence. Then the two elder brothers, finding that it is possible to speculate upon corpses, and make one's fortune, kill their wives, and go to town with their bodies; they are immediately arrested and put into prison.

The law of atavism evolves itself in the generation of the heroes of mythical legends, no less than in that of simple mortals upon earth. Of a stupid father is born a wise son, and then the wise son in turn has a foolish one. I do not as yet know how to explain this singular fact of natural history ; its appearance in mythology, however, is not difficult to understand. To the luminous day succeeds the gloomy night, and then again to the dark night the luminous day; to summer succeeds winter, and to winter summer; to white black, and to black white; to heat cold, and to cold heat.

On this account, in legends, when the mother is intelligent, the son, generally speaking, is silly; whereas, when the mother is silly,[1] the son is usually intelligent.

In the fifth story of the sixth book of *Afanassieff*, a soldier enters the house of a woman, while her son is travelling, and induces her to believe that he has just returned from hell, where he had seen her son employed in taking the storks to pasture, and greatly in want of money; the soldier says that he is about to return to hell, and will be happy to take with him whatever the woman wishes to send to her son. The credulous woman gives him some money, directing him to take it immediately to hell, and give it to her poor child. The soldier disappears, and shortly afterwards the woman's son returns home; his mother is greatly astonished at his appearance, and tells him how she has been deceived; he gets angry and leaves the house again, swearing never to return till he finds some one more foolish than his mother. He is a skilful thief; he steals from a lady, whilst her husband is absent, a hog with its little pigs, and puts them in safe concealment; the husband returns, hears what has taken place, and follows the thief with a carriage and horses. The robber hears him coming; squats down on the ground, takes off his hat, and pretends to be covering

[1] The *mère sotte* has become proverbial in France, where, in the sixteenth century, Pierre Gringore wrote a satirical comedy with the title of *Le Jeu de Mère Sotte*, in which the Mère Sotte is the Catholic Church.

with it a bird or a falcon, which wishes to escape. The husband comes and asks him if he has seen the robber; the latter answers that he has seen him, but that he is a long way off, and that the roads by which he can be overtaken are many and winding. The husband, who, perhaps, does not know the proverb which says, "Who wishes, let him go; who wishes not, let him send," asks the robber to overtake the fugitive; the thief demurs, saying that he has under his hat a falcon, which cost his master three hundred roubles, and that it may escape. The gentleman promises to take care of it, and if the falcon escapes, to pay the three hundred roubles. The thief does not believe his promise, and desires the three hundred roubles in pledge of his good faith; the gentleman gives them, and the thief goes off with the carriage, the horses, and the three hundred roubles. The gentleman stays till evening looking at the hat, waiting for his friend to return; at last he loses patience, wants to see what there is under the hat, and finds nothing—but a proof of his own stupidity.[1]

Ivan (John), and oftener still Vaniusha (Little John, the Giovannino of Italian legends), distinguishes himself, not only by his thieving accomplishments, but also by his courage. In order to play the part of a thief, as Little John does in all the Indo-Europeans legends, not only industry, but courage must be called into requisition; hence he acquires, like the Chevalier Bayard, the good reputation of a hero without fear and without reproach. The hero Ivan is now the son of a king, now of a

[1] A similar story, which, on account of its indecent details, I was not able to publish in my collection of the *Novelline di Santo Stefano di Calcinaia*, is narrated upon the hills of Signa, near Florence. It is also told, with some variations, in Piedmont.—Cfr. a Russian variety of the same story in the chapter on the Hen.

merchant, and now of a peasant; the merchants wished, no less than the peasants, to appropriate to themselves the most popular hero of tradition. In the forty-sixth story of the fifth book of *Afanassieff*, neither the shades of night, nor brigands, nor death, can make the hero afraid; but he is terrified and dies, falling into the water, when the little *iersh* (the perch) leaps upon his stomach, whilst he is asleep in his fishing-boat. In the Tuscan story,[1] the fearless hero Giovannino, after having confronted every kind of danger, dies from the terror the sight of his own shadow inspires him with. In the same way, in the *Ṛigvedas*, the god Indras, terrified at his own shadow, or, probably, that of his dead enemy, takes to flight after the killing of the serpent Ahis.[2]

The following heroes are also variations of Prince Ivan, Ivan the son of the cow, Ivan the peasant's son, Ivan the merchant's son, and the cunning Ivan:—1st, Alessino Papović, the son of the priest (it is well known that the Russian priests are not bound to celibacy), who kills Tugarin, the son of the serpent, by prayer, that is, by praying to the Holy Mother of God, to order the black cloud to cause drops of rain to fall on the monster's wings, upon which the son of the serpent, like the Vedic Ahis, when Indras opens a way for the rivers to come out, instantly falls to the ground;[3] 2d, Baldak, son of Boris, the boy seven years old, who succeeds in spitting in the Sultan's face—(I have already remarked, in the preface to this work, that the king of the Turks is, in the Slavonic tradition, as well as in that of Persia, the representative of the devil; the demon, when the hero

[1] *Novelline di Santo Stefano di Calcinaia*, 22.

[2] Cfr. the chapter on the Fishes.

[3] *Afanassieff*, vi. 59.—But in the tale v. 11, he knows how to fight well.

approaches, smells the odour of human flesh in India, of Christian flesh in Western stories,[1] and of Russian flesh in Russian fairy tales)—but who afterwards becomes the Sultan's prisoner, because he appears to the third daughter of the latter with a star under his heel, or shows his heel (which is the vulnerable part of both hero and monster); 3d, Basil Bes-ćiastnoi, who goes, by his father-in-law's order, into the kingdom of the serpent, in order to receive a gift from him, with adventures similar to those of the young Plavaćek in Bohemian stories, when he goes to seek the three golden hairs of the old Vsieveda (the all-seeing, the Vedic sun Viçvavedas);[2] 4th, The third brother who exchanges two sacks of flies and gnats he has caught for good cattle.[3] The same hero takes the name of Little Thomas Berennikoff; being blind of one eye, he kills an army of flies, and boasts of having killed an army of heroes; he thus dishonestly gains the reputation of being a hero, and is fortunate in having an opportunity offered him of proving his bravery by killing a monster-serpent, who, out of foolhardiness, shuts both eyes when he sees that Thomas has but one; he afterwards destroys an army of Chinese with the trunk of a tree, rooted up by his indomitable horse, which a real hero had bound to the tree;[4] 5th, The cunning rogue, Little Thomas (Thomka; the quacks in Piedmont are accustomed to give the name of Tommasino to the little devil which they conjure out

[1] In England the monster smells the blood of an Englishman, as in the familiar lines in *Jack the Giant-Killer*—

> "Fe fo fum,
> I smell the blood of an Englishman;
> Be he alive or be he dead,
> I'll grind his bones to make my bread."

[2] Cfr. Teza, *The Three Golden Hairs of the Grandfather Know-all*, a Bohemian tale (*I tre Capelli d'oro del Nonno Satutto*, Bologna, 1866).

[3] *Afanassieff*, ii. 7.

[4] v. 11.

of a phial), who, by means of disguises, cheats and robs the priest;[1] 6th, The third brother who does not suffer himself to be put to sleep by the witch (as we have seen above the third sister who keeps one of her three eyes open);[2] 7th, The famous robber, Klimka,[3] who, by means of a drum (in Indian tales a trumpet), terrifies his accomplices, the robbers, and takes their money, and then steals from a gentleman his horse, his casket of jewels, and even his wife; 8th, The Cossack who delivers the maiden from the flames, and carries her to his golden house, where there are two other maidens (be it understood, the one in the silver house, and the other in that of copper); from which three maidens the Cossack receives a shirt which renders him invulnerable, a sword which produces the most marvellous effects in slaughtering men, and a purse which, when shaken, drops money;[4] 9th, The celebrated Ilia Muromietz (Elias of Murom), round whom, as also around Svetazór and Svyatogor (holy mount), Dobrynia Nikitić, and the heroes of Vladimir, is grouped an entire heroic Russian epic poem.[5]

---

[1] *Afanassieff*, v. 7, 8. [2] iv. 46.

[3] v. 6; *Erlenwein*, 7.

[4] *Erlenwein*, 5.—In the first story of *Erlenwein*, the last-born, Vaniusha (Little John), takes from disputing peasants, by a stratagem, first a marvellous arrow, then a hat which makes the wearer invisible, and, finally, a mantle which flies of itself. He promises to divide them equitably, and for this service makes them pay him beforehand, each of the three times, a hundred roubles; he then throws the objects far away and says, that he who is able to find them will have them; all search, but he alone finds them. (Thus Arǵunas, in the *Mahâbhâratam*, hides his wonderful arms in the trunk of a tree, in which he alone can find them.)

[5] Cfr. Schiefner, *Zur Russischen Heldensage*, Petersburg, 1861. This is how the hero Svyatogor is described in a Russian popular epic song cited by Ralston (*The Songs of the Russian people*): "There comes a hero taller than the standing woods, whose head reaches to the fleeting clouds, bearing on his shoulders a crystal coffer.

Other variations of the same hero are the son of the merchant given up to be educated by the devil, who teaches him every kind of craft; the boy Basil, who understands the language of birds, and who makes his parents serve him;[1] the merchant or son of a peasant,[2] who, because he prefers good advice to money, acquires a fortune; the virtuous workman, who receives by way of pay for his labour only three kapeika, which, spent in good works, enables him at last to marry the king's daughter, or the princess who did not laugh.[3]

The legend of the hero Ivan has yet other interesting forms, reflective of the beautiful Vedic myth of the Açvinâu, who into their flying chariot-vessel also take up the unhappy. In *Afanassieff*,[4] the third brother, thought to be foolish, is ill-treated by his parents, who dress and feed him badly. The king issues a proclamation, that whoever can make a flying vessel will obtain his daughter to wife. The mother sends forth her three sons in quest of the necessary enchantment; to her third son she gives a little brown bread and water, whilst the two eldest go provided with good white loaves and some brandy. The fool meets on the way a poor old man, salutes him, and begins to share with him his scanty store of food; the old man transmutes his brown bread into white, and his water into brandy, and then advises him to enter the forest, to make the sign of the cross upon the first tree he finds, and to strike it with his axe; then to throw himself on the ground and stay there until he wakens; he will see a vessel ready before him: "Sit down in it," added the old man, "and fly whither your behest requires you; and by the way take up beside you as

[1] *Afanassieff*, vi. 41.
[2] v. 31, and *Erlenwein*, 16.
[3] v. 32.
[4] vi. 27.

many as you meet." [1] This chariot is freighted with abundance, both to eat and to drink; the young man overtakes several needy beggars, and invites them up into the chariot; he receives only poor people, not a single rich man.[2] But these poor men afterwards show their gratitude to the hero, and help him in other adventures imposed upon him by the Tzar, who hopes by this means to get rid of a son-in-law of such vulgar origin. One of the new tasks imposed requires him to eat twelve oxen, and to drink at one gulp forty barrels of wine; in this he is helped by Eating (Abiédalo) and by Drinking (Apiválo), whom he had entertained in his chariot-ship, and who eat and drink instead of him.[3] At last he comes to claim and marry the young princess. (The hero-sun, taken up into the chariot of the Açvinâu, by the grace of the Açvinâu, invoked by him in danger, is delivered, and espouses the aurora.)

In a variation of this legend, a prince, fifteen years of age, who has been lost by his parents, is found again by means of a riddle which they propose, and which he alone can solve.[4] In the Vedic hymns it is now the aurora, the beautiful maiden, who delivers the hero-sun, and now the hero-sun who delivers the beautiful maiden, the aurora.

---

[1] Çadis v nievó, i leti kuda nadobno; da po daroghie zabirái k sebié vsiákavo vstriećnavo.

[2] Na karablié niet ni adnavó pána, a vsió córnie ludi.

[3] Cfr. *Afanassieff*, v. 23.—Ice, in the form of an old man, comes to try the boiling bath into which the king of the sea wishes to throw the young hero; when Ice has tried the bath, the youth enters it without suffering any harm.—The trial of drinking occurs again in a grandiose form in the combat between Loki and Thor to empty the cup in the Edda of Snorri, a different form of the Hindoo legend of Agastyas, who dries up the sea.—Odin, too, as Indras and as Bhîmas, at three gulps dries up three lakes of mead.

[4] *Afanassieff*, v. 42.

In the forty-first story of the sixth book of *Afanassieff*, a little girl, seven years old (semilietká), presents herself to the Tzar, who must marry her, inasmuch as she solves the riddle proposed by him, by arriving riding on a hare (an animal which represents the moon), with a quail (an animal which seems to represent the sun) tied to her hand.[1] She too, like the aurora, knows all; she too protects the poor against the rich, and the innocent against the guilty. The dwarf Allwis is a form of this child. Allwis is the omniscient man of the Edda, who solves all the questions put to him by the god Thor, in order to obtain his daughter; when he is done with answering these questions, day breaks, and the sun shines.

The wondrous girl of seven years of age (the aurora), brings us back to the marvellous puppet (generally, the moon). It is three puppets (the wooden chest of Marion d'bosch, or wooden little Mary of the Piedmontese story, the dark forest of night, the tree that hides the splendid treasures of the evening aurora; another variety of the same myth in relation to the sun) that hide the three splendid dresses of the stars, the moon and the sun, which belong to the beautiful maiden, the daughter of the priest (a variation of the Vedic aurora, duhitar divas, or daughter of the sky). It is the three puppets which enable the beautiful girl to descend through the ground, and so escape from the persecutions of her father and seducer (in other versions, of her brother), and which go down with her, dressed as old women, and enter a forest, where, near an oak-tree, there is the house of a princess, who has a young and handsome son.[2] In a

[1] Cfr. the chapters on the Hare and the Quail.
[2] *Afanassieff*, vi. 28, and ii. 31.

variation of this story,[1] the girl is persecuted, not by her father, but the well-known cruel stepmother, for whom she divides the wheat from the barley, and draws water at the fountain (like the Vedic maiden Apalâ); she goes three times splendidly dressed to church (which takes the place of the ball-room of other stories), where she is seen three times by a handsome prince; she is twice followed, and twice disappears; the third time the prince has gum (pitch, in other variations) put on the ground; the fugitive loses her golden slipper in consequence, which the prince picks up, and tries on all the maidens till he finds his bride. In another story,[2] where the relation of the aurora with the two Açvinau comes out in wonderful distinctness,[3] it is by means of her marvellous speaking puppet (*i.e.*, the moon, the Vedic Rakâ, very small, but very intelligent, enclosed in the wooden dress, in the forest of night) that the girl, persecuted by her step-mother, weaves a cloth so fine that it can pass like a thread through the eye of a needle (just as the girl's feet are very small, so also are the puppet's hands). The marvellous cloth is brought to the Tzar, but no one is found who is able to sew it into a shirt for the Tzar.[4] The maiden alone, by the help of her puppet, succeeds; the Tzar wishes to see the girl who prepared his extraordinary shirt, and goes to find her; he is astonished at her beauty, and marries her. In the *Ṛigvedas*, the aurora weaves a robe for her husband the sun.

---

[1] *Afanassieff*, vi. 20.—Cfr. i. 3, and ii. 31, where we have the same particular of the prince who strikes three times the disguised girl who serves him, as in the Tuscan story of the Wooden Top (the puppet), the third in my collection of the *Novelline di Santo Stefano di Calcinaia.*

[2] iv. 44.

[3] Cfr. next chapter.

[4] Cfr. the chapter on the Spider.

The same girl (the aurora) whom we have here only as a good, beautiful, intelligent, and skilful maiden, appears in other stories given in *Afanassieff* as a heroic damsel. In the seventh story of the first book she disguises herself as a man, and mocks the Tzar three times. In the fourteenth story of the first book, the same girl, under the name of Anastasia the beautiful, vanquishes and binds the serpent, and discovers the secret of how he can be killed. Under the name of Helen, or Little Helen, she is the protectress of her little brother, Ivanusca (Little John),[1] and his guide through the world; and when the boy, by the incantation of a witch, is transformed into a lamb or kid (in a story of the Canavese, in Piedmont, the seven monks, brothers of the courageous girl, are transformed into seven hogs), she recommends him to the care of the prince, her husband, in order that he may destroy the evil work of the witch. The same maiden is found again as the very wise Basilia (Vasilisa Premudraia), who succours the young hero, because, after stealing her dress while she was bathing in the sea, he restores it to her, agreeably to her prayer. For this favour she gratefully accomplishes for him the labours imposed upon him by the king of the waters, and ends, after many vicissitudes, by marrying him.[2] She appears once more as the royal maiden (Tzar-dievitza), who comes three times with her ships by sea to lead away the young Ivan, beloved by her;[3] and I also place among the girl-heroines the daughter of the shepherd in the twenty-ninth story of the fifth book of *Afanassieff*, of which this is an abridgment. There was once a king who could not find a maiden beautiful enough to suit his taste. One day,

[1] *Afanassieff*, ii. 29, and iv. 45. [2] v. 23.
[3] v. 42.

returning from the chase (the solar hero always meets the aurora, his bride, when returning from the hunt in the forest of night), he meets a shepherd's daughter, who is leading out the flock to pasture, so beautiful that her like would be sought for in vain over the world. He becomes enamoured of her, and promises to make her his wife, but only on condition that she will never say anything displeasing to him, whatever he may do; the poor enamoured maiden consents, the nuptials are celebrated, and the couple live together happily for a year. A boy is born to them; then the king says roughly to his wife that the boy must be killed, that it may never be said the heir to the throne is the son of a shepherdess. The poor woman resigns herself to her fate, remarking, "The will of the king must be done." Another year passes, and a daughter is born. The king informs his wife that she too must be killed, as she can never become a princess, but will always remain a peasant girl. The unhappy mother once more bows her head to the will of the king, who, however, consigns his son and daughter, not to an executioner, but to his sister, that they may receive all the attentions due to their royal pedigree and standing. Years pass away; the little prince and princess grow up beautiful, healthy, good, and happy, and pass adolescence. Then the king puts his wife to the last proof. He sends her back to her house in the dress of a shepherdess, signifying at the same time that she has lived with him long enough. Then he orders her to return, to put the rooms in order, and to wait upon the new bride whom he intends to take her place; the shepherd's daughter obeys again without a murmur. The new bride arrives, and is set down at the table; they eat, drink, and are merry; the shepherd's daughter is obliged to see and hear all, and to serve in silence; at last the king asks her, "Well, is not my bride beautiful?" To which the unhappy woman responds with a heroic effort, "If she seem beautiful to thee, still more does she seem so to me." Then the king, at the summit of his felicity, exclaims, "Dress thyself again in thy royal robes, and place thyself by my side; thou hast been, and shalt always be, my wife, my only wife; this, my supposed bride, is thy daughter, and this handsome youth is thy son." The poor heroine had undergone the last proof of her virtue, and triumphed.

But the virtue of the legendary heroine is not always so sound. Often the good wife, sister, maiden, or woman is corrupted by contact with the wicked. We have already seen how the beautiful aurora, the pitying and beneficent maiden, becomes, in the Vedic hymns themselves, the evil-doer, whom the god Indras overthrows and destroys. The Hellenic Amazons, the beautiful and proud warrior-women, were also pursued, fought with, and vanquished by the Hellenic heroes. Thus the Scandinavian warrior, Walkiries, has a double aspect, a good and a bad. The Russian stories also supply numerous instances of the ease with which the good degenerates into the demon, the hero into the monster, and the beautiful heroine into the powerful and mischief-working witch.

This good sister Helen or Little Helen, so careful a guardian of her brother John, ends, when she conceives a passion for the monster, with becoming his perfidious persecutor. (The evening aurora is represented as a friend of the monster of night, who conspires with him against her brother the sun; and whoever observes the sinister aspect often assumed by the reddish sky of evening, will find this fiction a very natural one. I have said above that a Piedmontese proverb predicts bad weather for the morrow from a red evening; but in

Piedmont the belief is also widely diffused that the red of evening signifies blood, and that this bloody redness signifies war. It certainly does mean war, but a mythical war—the war in which the hero, fighting against the monster, succumbs and sheds blood. It is a woman that is the hero's destruction. A counter-type of the biblical Delilah is found in all the popular Indo-European traditions; the Vedic aurora, the sister of Râvaṇas in the *Râmâyaṇam*, the sister of Hidimbas in the *Mahâbhâratam*, the Hellenic Dejanira, Ariadne, Medea, the Amazons, Helen, the Slavonic Helen, and Anna the Sabine woman, the Scandinavian Walkiries, Freya, Idun, Brünhilt, Gudrun, the Germanic Krîmhilt, are all forms of one and the same heroine, conceived now in the light of a saint, and now in that of a witch.

In the Russian story,[1] after the bull has saved from the bear the fugitive brother and sister, Ivan Tzarević and Helen the exceedingly beautiful (Prekraçna), they enter a brigand's house. Their bull, having become a dwarf, kills all the brigands, and shuts their bodies up in a room, which he forbids Helen to enter; the latter, not attending to the prohibition, enters, and seeing the head of the brigand chief, falls in love with him, resuscitates him by means of the water of life, and then conspires with him to destroy her brother Ivan, by requiring him to accomplish enterprises in which death seemed inevitable, or else by ordering him to bring her, first, the milk of a wolf, then that of a she-bear, and then that of a lioness. Ivan, by the help of his dwarf (or the sun grown small during the night, and perhaps also the moon), accomplishes all these undertakings. We have already seen how white comes from black; the milk of the wolf, the bear, and

[1] *Afanassieff*, v. 27.

the lioness is the *alba luna*, or the white morning sky brought back by the solar hero. Ivan is then sent to fetch the eggs of the burning bird (Szar-ptitza). Ivan goes with his dwarf (that is to say, the moon, or he makes himself a dwarf, in other words, renders himself invisible); the bird is enraged, and swallows the dwarf (*i.e.*, the red sky of evening, the burning bird, or phœnix, absorbs the moon or the sun in its flames.[1]) Ivan goes back to his sister without the eggs, upon which she threatens to burn him in the bath. Ivan, with the help of the wolf's, the bear's, and the lion's whelps, or Ivan, with the young wolf, bear, or lion (the moon), or Ivan the son of the wolf, Ivan the son of the bear, Ivan the son of the lion (Ivan born of the she-wolf Night, the she-bear Night, or the lioness Night), tears the brigand to pieces, and binds his sister (as the Vedic cow) to a tree (the aurora almost always loses herself in a tree or the water). Then Ivan wishes to marry a heroine. [Two myths are here united in the story, originating in one and the same phenomenon, which seems twofold, because observed at different, almost literally succeeding, instants. The morning sun comes and puts to flight his sister the aurora, driving her back into the forest of night, and binding her to the tree; the morning sun passes safe and sound through the flames (like Sîfrit in the *Nibelungen*), vanquishes and subdues the aurora, makes her his, and espouses her.] He fights with her first, and succeeds in throwing her with his lance from her horse, and subduing her. The first night—that is, when evening comes, she embraces and presses him so tightly, and with such strength, that he cannot succeed in extricating himself (the evening aurora envelops and surrounds the sun; it is the famous nuptial belt, the belt

[1] Cfr. the chapter which treats of the Eagle, the Vulture, and the Falcon.

of strength of the god Thor, the shirt of Nessus). At last, however, towards morning, Ivan vanquishes, subdues, and throws down (like Sîfrit in the *Nibelungen*) the girl-heroine (the morning sun, as Indras, throws down the aurora). He then thinks of liberating his sister Helen, who is bound to the tree, in order to take her with him; but she, under the pretext of combing his hair, thrusts a dead man's tooth into his head. Ivan is about to die. Here the primary myth of the sun and aurora, as brother and sister, reappears, and the secondary one of the husband and wife is forgotten. The lion's whelp comes forward and extracts the tooth; the lion is on the point of dying, when the young bear runs up and extracts it again. He is also about to die; the fox then comes up, who assumes towards the end of the story the part played in the middle by the young wolf (in the same way as in Indian tales the jackal is substituted for the fox), and, with more cunning, throws the dead man's tooth into the fire, and thus saves himself—*i.e.*, the solar hero, passing through the flames, comes out of the shadows which enveloped him during the night. Helen is attached to the tail of a horse (of Ivan's solar horse itself), and is thus made to perish (when the sun comes forth in the morning the aurora loses herself behind him).

The same story of Ivan's perfidious sister, of which the mythical sense appears to me more than usually evident, occurs again in other forms in Russian tales.

Whilst Ivan is travelling with his sister towards the kingdom where all the people die[1] (that is, towards the night), a fairy gives him a towel, by shaking which a bridge may be thrown across a river—(is this bridge the milky way, the bridge or road to be taken by the souls

[1] *Afanassieff*, vi. 52.

in the Persian and Porphyrian belief, as well as in the German ?)—but advises him never to let his sister see him shake it. Ivan arrives with his sister in the kingdom of the dead; they come upon a river on the further bank of which there is a serpent, who has the power of transforming himself into a handsome youth; Ivan's sister becomes enamoured of him, and he induces her to steal the towel from her brother and shake it. The sister, under the pretext of washing the dirty linen, takes off the fairy's towel and shakes it; a bridge rises, upon which the serpent crosses the river, and then conspires with the girl with intent to work Ivan's ruin. They demand the usual milk, which Ivan brings; then the flour which is shut up within twelve doors. Ivan goes thither with his beasts of prey, takes the flour and brings it away, but his beasts remain shut up inside; then his strength diminishes, and the serpent, boasting that he fears him no longer, prepares to devour him. Ivan, by the advice of a crow, prays for time, and procrastinates till his beasts of prey, gnawing the twelve doors through, come to his help, and tear the serpent in pieces. The serpent's bones are burned in the fire, its ashes are dispersed to the four winds, and the sister is bound to a stone pillar (to the rock or mountain upon which the aurora arises, fading away afterwards when the sun appears). Ivan places near her some hay and a vessel full of water, that she may have whereof to eat and drink, and another empty vessel, which she is to fill with her tears: when she has eaten the hay, drunk the water, and filled the vessel with her tears, it will be a sign that God has forgiven her; when Ivan too will forgive her. Meanwhile, Ivan goes into a kingdom where there is nothing but mourning, because a twelve-headed serpent is massacring all the people (the usual nocturnal sky, where it is now the hero-sun, now the heroine aurora that sacrifices itself), and the king's daughter is the next victim. Ivan, by the help of his hunting animals, cuts the serpent to pieces, and then goes to sleep on the knees of the king's daughter. While he sleeps, a water-carrier passes towards morning, cuts off his head, and presents himself to the king as the deliverer of the princess, whom he demands for his wife. The beasts of prey come up, descry the crow upon Ivan's corpse, and prepare to eat it, when the crow begs for its life; they consent, and in return require it to search for the water of life and death, by means of which Ivan is resuscitated; the water-carrier's deceit is found out, and Ivan marries the princess whom he had delivered from the monster. Then he goes to look for his sister, and finds she has eaten the hay, drunk the water, and filled half the vessel with tears; upon this he pardons her, and takes her away with him.

In another story,[1] instead of the perfidious sister, we have the perfidious mother (probably step-mother), who, to please her demon lover, feigns illness, and demands from Ivan the heart, first of the three-headed, then of the six-headed, and finally of the twelve-headed monster. Ivan accomplishes these undertakings. He is then sent to a hot bath, to weaken his strength. Ivan goes, and his head is cut off by the monster. But Ivan's two sons resuscitate him by rubbing a root upon his body; the demon lover of Ivan's mother dies as soon as the hero revives again. In the two sons of Ivan we recognise again the myth of the Açvinâu, the celestial physicians who resuscitate the solar hero.

In another story, Ivan Karolievié (king's son) is threatened with death by his own wife,[2] who, feigning illness,

[1] *Afanassieff*, vi. 63. [2] vi. 51.

demands the usual milk of a she-wolf, a she-bear, and a lioness, and then the enchanted powder (powder of gold or flour), which is under the devil's mill, barred behind twelve doors. Ivan comes out, but his beasts remain inside. He returns and finds his wife with the serpent, the son of the serpent; he chaunts the song of death—he sings it three times;[1] on hearing which the serpent is thrown down, and the beasts, regaining strength to deliver themselves, come out and tear the serpent, and with him the perfidious wife is put to death.

Ivan's perfidious wife occurs again in the thirty-fifth story of the fifth book of *Afanassieff*, under the name of Anna the very beautiful (Prekraçnaia). She has married Ivan Tzarević against her will, because she could not solve a riddle which he proposed to her; she does not love him, and endeavours to destroy him by requiring an extraordinary proof of his valour,[2] in which, by the help of his tutor, Katoma, Ivan is victorious, so that Anna falls into his hands. But, understanding that Ivan's strength is not in himself, but his tutor, she induces Ivan to send him away, after depriving him of his feet. Anna then sends Ivan to take the cows to pasture. The lame Katoma finds in the forest a blind man, also made so by Anna;[3] they become friends and consociate together, and carry off a beautiful maiden to be their sister; but a witch comes and makes the maiden comb her hair, whilst she sucks her

[1] In the story, vi. 52, Ivan, by playing in a marvellous manner on a flute, is recognised by the princess whom he had delivered from the monster.

[2] Cf. next chapter.

[3] We find the blind-lame man again in an epigram by Ausonius of Bordeaux, a writer of the fourth century:—

"Insidens cæco graditur pede claudus utroque,
Quo caret alteruter, sumit ab alterutro.
Cæcus namque pedes claudo gressumque ministrat,
At claudus cæco lumina, pro pedibus."

breast (we must remember that in the Indian story the girl has three breasts, or is defective in her breast, in the same way as the witch makes the Russian girl so by sucking her breast). The poor girl grows thin and ugly, until the old witch is surprised in her evil doings by the two heroes, fallen upon by them like a mountain of stone, and pressed so tightly that she cries for mercy. Then they demand to be shown where the fountain of life and healing can be found. The old woman conducts them into a dense forest, and shows them a fountain. They first throw a dry twig in, which immediately takes fire; they threaten to kill the old witch, and force her to lead them to another fountain, into which they throw another dry twig; it becomes green again. Then one rubs his eyes, and the other his feet, with the water, and both become healthy and strong again. They throw the witch into the fountain of fire. Katoma, in a shepherd's dress, goes to deliver the hero Ivan from the demon cow, which lifts up its tail and gives him back his strength and splendour. This is again the Vedic myth of the Açvinâu united to the aurora, who cure the blind and the lame, *i.e.*, themselves, and save the multiform solar hero.

Finally, such as we have found the blind girl in the Vedic hymns, so we meet her again in Russian tradition.[1] A servant-maid takes out the eyes of the maiden her mistress, after having put her to sleep by means of a herb, and marries the king in her stead. The girl awakens, hears but does not see; an old shepherd receives her into his house; during the night she, although blind, sews a crown for the Tzar and sends the old man to court to sell it for an eye (this is a variation of Queen Berta in the forest). The servant-

[1] *Afanassieff*, v. 39.

maid, now become queen, tempted by the beauty of this crown, takes one of the girl's eyes out of her pocket and gives it to the old man. The maiden arises at the aurora, washes her eye in her own saliva (*i.e.*, the dew. In Tuscany, the peasants believe that whoever washes his face in the dew before the sun rises on St John's Day, will have no illness all the year following), puts it in the socket and sees. She then sews another crown, and, in the same manner, recovers her other eye at the next aurora. Then the servant-queen learns that she is alive, and makes hired murderers cut her to pieces. Where the maiden is buried, a garden arises and a boy shows himself. The boy goes to the palace and runs after the queen, making such a din that she is obliged, in order to silence him, to give him the girl's heart, which she had kept hidden. The boy then runs off contented; the king follows him, and finds himself before the resuscitated maiden. He marries her, and the servant-girl is blinded, and then torn to pieces by being fastened to the tails of horses. Like the German Geneviève and the Hindoo Çakuntalâ, the Russian wife is recognised by her husband by means of a boy. This is the young sun, who enables the old one to be born again, to arise again and be young once more; this is the son who, in the Hindoo legend, gives his father his eyesight back, and by doing so, naturally imparts to him the means of recognising his wife, whom he had forgotten, or rejected, or lost, according to the various forms assumed by the celestial myth of the separation of husband and wife.

I might now carry on this comparison by entering the mythical field of the more Western Slavonic nations;[1]

[1] The student who wishes to extend his researches in Slavonic tradition may consult with profit, among others, the following works:—Schwenck, *Mythologie der Slaven;* Hanusch, *Slavische Mythologie;*

but it is not my intention to convert this modest volume into an entire library of legends; neither is it necessary for my purpose, as by so doing I should not add much more evidence to that which I have thus far attempted to collect, in order to prove how zoological mythology is the same in existing Slavonic tradition as it was in Hindoo antiquity. I have, moreover, gone rather minutely into the contents of Russian tradition in particular, because, on account of our ignorance of the language, which is beautiful and worthy of study, it is little known, and because it is of especial importance in our present inquiry. I believe, if I do no deceive myself, that I have, up to this point, given an account of all the more essential legends developed in the Eastern Aryan world relating to the myth of the cow and the bull; and now, in moving towards the West, I think I may venture to proceed with greater expedition, because we shall find ourselves in a region already familiar to us. It seemed to me that it was especially necessary, for a just comparison, to determine and fix the character of Oriental tradition, in order that it may be easy for the student to classify the interminable stories and traditions which have already been collected in Western Europe, and which are published in languages which are, certainly, different from each other, but all, comparatively speaking, readily accessible. If I have succeeded in imparting to the reader a understanding of the more authentic sources of legendary traditions and their most probable meanings, I shall go on with more courage and a greater confidence to the investigations that follow.

Woycicki, *Polnische Märchen;* Schleicher, *Littauische Märchen;* Wenzig, *Westslavischer Märchenschatz;* Kapper, *Die Gesänge der Serben;* Chodzko, *Contes des Paysans et des Pâtres Slaves;* Teza, *Itre Capelli d'oro del Nonno Satutto,* a Bohemian story; Miękievič, *Canti Popolari Illirici.*

SECTION V.

The Bull and the Cow in the Germanico-Scandinavian and Franco-Celtic Traditions.

SUMMARY.

The four bulls, sons of the virgin Gefion.—The bull which comes out of the sea.—The bull progenitor of royal races.—The bull who carries the maiden.—The cow of abundance, Audhumla, nurse and mother of heroes.—The three brothers of Scandinavian and German mythology.—The warrior-cow.—The sacred cow of Ögwaldr burned upon the hero's tomb.—The rod-phallos used to strike the cow, as an augury of abundance and fecundity.—The head of the ox used as a hook to catch the sea-serpent.—The Scandinavian cornucopia made of the horns of oxen.—The horn full of honey.—The horn-trumpet.—The daughter that milks.—The hero who eats oxen.—Atli eats the hearts of his sons, believing them to be the hearts of calves.—Hornboge.—To a wicked cow God gives short horns; to cut off the cow's horns; to take the bull or cow by the horns, three Germanic proverbs.—To dream of eagles announces the vicinity of cows; Scandinavian corresponding legend.—A red cow on a certain bridge announces a battle.—The Germanico-Scandinavian mythical bridge.—The red cow and the black cow yield white milk.—Digression upon mythical proverbs, and the explanation which seems to be the most likely.—To shut the stable after the cow has been stolen.—When the daughter is stolen, shut Peppergate.—He who has lost a cow and gets its tail back again has not much, but he has more than nothing.—To take by the horns.—Even if the cow's tail moves it does not fall.—The tails in the mud.—The virtues of the tail.—The ascent to heaven by means of the tails.—The hero in the sack made of a cow's hide thrown into the sea.—The punishment of the bull.—When the cow places herself upon the eggs, do not expect fowls.—The black cow has crushed him.—The sack of the wolf or of the black beast is his body itself.—The trial between hero and monster to take off their skins; the hero gives cows' skins, but the monster is obliged to give his own.—The cow's hide, when sold, is the beginning of good luck.—The daughter flees from her father, who wishes to seduce her; the story of the slipper again.—The cow can pass before the hare.—The cow jumped over the moon.—Tarde sed tute.—To take the hare with the chariot.—All those who blow the horn do not hunt hares.—As a blind cow finds a pea.—Marvellous pipkins and amphoræ.—The cow that laughs.—The princess who laughs.—The cow that speaks.—The language of animals.—Phallical mysteries.—What the king said in the queen's ear.—Because they have spoken, the husband and wife are separated.—Bulls that speak at Rome.—Women know everything, even how Zeus married Hêra.—The mythical laugh is in the sun's ray and in the lightning.—The fishes that laugh; Phallic meaning of the myth.—If the cow-maid must spin, there will be little yarn.—The cows that spin.—The spinning Berta.—Berchta and Holda.—The time is passed when Berta spun.—The times of King Pipino.—Berta with the large foot.—Berta with the goose's foot.—St Lucia and St Luke.—Virgins after parturition.—The old husband Pepin, a form of St Joseph.—The wife Berta changed.—The Italian proverbs dare la Berta and dare la Madre d'Orlando.—Continuation of the story of Berta persecuted in the forest.—Orlando and Charlemagne.—The bull-priest and the priest-bull.—The bull in funerals, in pregnancy, and as the food of the hero.—The dwarf and the giant.—A French dwarf explains a myth to us; a Scandinavian explains other myths to us.

I SHALL here combine under one category the Germanico-Scandinavian and Franco-Celtic traditions, as traditions which, in the Middle Ages especially, had a close and continual correlation of correspondence with each other.

The *Edda* of Snorri begins with the voyage of Gefion, with the four oxen, her sons (although she is a virgin), yoked to a plough. The king Gylfi concedes to her the right of occupying and possessing as much ground as she can plough in twenty-four hours. When they come to the western sea-board, the four oxen rush forward and drag Gefion with them into the sea, until they arrive at the land of Seelund (Seeland).[1] In which, it is obvious we have again the Vedic bull with a thousand horns

[1] *Les Eddas*, traduites de l'ancien idiome Scandinave par Mdlle. du Puget, 2ème édition, p. 16.

which comes out of the sea, and the bull which carries off the maiden. The bull which comes out of the sea is also found in Irish legends, and in German ones. According to a German legend, of which several variations exist, a shepherd received a dinner every day and a clean shirt every Sunday from a variegated bull that came out of the sea.[1] A bull on the seaside begets, by the sleeping queen, the king Meroveus, the first of the Merovingians; perhaps it is on this account that we find a golden bull's head represented on the tomb of King Childeric. Charles Simrock[2] found a similar legend also in Spain. The bull which carries the girl, which we have already met with in the Russian stories, occurs again in the Norse tale[3] of "*Katee Wooden Cloak* (Dasent), endowed with the powers of wish. In its left ear is a cloth (which reminds us of that spun on the cow's horns), which, when spread out, is covered with dainties of all kinds for the dawn-maiden, who has been thrust out of her father's house; but when the stepmother informs her that she cannot rest until she has eaten the dun bull's flesh, the animal, hearing her,

---

[1] Kuhn und Schwartz, *Norddeutsche Sagen, Märchen und Gebräuche*, p. 501.

[2] *Handbuch der Deutschen Mythologie*, mit Einschluss der nordischen, 2te. aufl. p. 437.—We find also in Eginhardus (*Vita Caroli Magni*): "Quocumque eundum erat, carpento ibat, quod bubus junctis et bubulco rustico more agente, trahebatur."—The bull is a symbol of generation; the man who fears the bull is a stupid and ridiculous eunuch. We find in Du Cange, Lit. Remiss. ann. 1397, "Le suppliant, lui dist, Eudet, vous avéz un toreau qui purte les gens et ne osent aler aux champs pour luy; lequel Eudet luy respondis: as tu nom Jehannot?" Faire Johan dicitur mulier, quæ marito fidem non servat (a variety of the Mongol Sûrya Bagatur).

[3] Recorded by Cox, *Mythology of the Aryan Nations*, vol. i. p. 438, when speaking of the Hellenic myth of Zeus and Eurôpâ.

engages to deliver her, and offers, if she so wills, to carry her away."

In the voyage of Gylfi in the *Edda* of Snorri, we find that the cow Audhumla, the cow of abundance, was the parent of the supreme Scandinavian god Odin, as it was of the supreme Vedic god Indras. The cow Audhumla nourishes with her milk Ymir, the first of the giants. She licks the salt mountain of ice (the Esthonian ice-mountain, the twelve glasses of the Russian princess, through which the young hero Ivan penetrates to kiss her). From the ice which the cow has licked, comes forth, first the hair, then the head, then the whole body, of the hero Buri. (The sun arises little by little from the mountain of the east, warmed, attracted by the cow-aurora, and shows, first a few rays, then his disc, and then himself in all his splendour and strength; and that which the sun does every day he repeats on a larger scale once a year, rising again from the ice of winter through the tepidity of spring.) Of Buri, who is at birth strong, is born Bör, who has, by Bestla, the daughter of the giant Bölthorn, three sons, Odin, Wili, and We (the usual three brothers of the legends), who correspond to the three sons of Mannus in German tradition, that is, Inguis, Istio, and Irminius. The Swedish king Eistein had a great veneration for the cow Sibilia, and used to take her with him to battle, that she might terrify the enemy by her lowing. (The lowing of cows plays an important part in the battles of the Vedic hero Indras. In the *Pańćatantram*, as we have noticed, the bellowing of the bull fills the lion with terror.) The Scandinavian king, Ögwaldr, was accompanied everywhere by a sacred cow, of which he drank the milk, and with which he desired to be buried. In the *Ṛigvedas*, as we have seen, the hero Indras makes the cow fruitful;

and the thunderbolt of the god, penetrating the cloud, takes the form of a phallos. Afterwards, as a symbol of the rod-phallos, the branch or rod of the tree palâças was adopted, with which the cow was struck to make it fruitful; such a magic rod is used in Germany to this day, where it is in many parts the custom to strike the cow, in the belief that it will render her fruitful.[1]

It is with the head of the most beautiful of the giant Hymir's oxen fastened to his hook that, in Snorri's *Edda*, the god Thor goes to fish up the immense serpent of Midgard from the bottom of the sea, and destroys it upon the sea-shore. (This myth, if I am not mistaken, has the following meaning:—The head of the solar, or lunar, bull is devoured by the monster of night; this same head, tossed about, draws up, towards morning as sun, and towards evening as moon, upon the shore of the sea of night, that is to say, on the eastern mountain, the monster-serpent: thus Hanumant, in the *Râmâyaṇam*, passes over to the opposite shore of the sea, crossing the body of the marine monster, which he causes to burst; thus Indras kills Ahis the serpent upon the mountain).

Nor is there the cow of abundance only. Scandinavian tradition, in the short poem on the dwarf Allwis, offers us the cornucopia in the cup formed of the defence of oxen (*i.e.*, with their horns), in which the god Thor drinks hydromel. Thus Sigurd offers to Brünhilt a horn

[1] Cfr. Kuhn, *Die Herabkunft des Feuers und des Göttertranks*, p. 181 and following.—In Du Cange, *Glossarium Mediæ et Infimæ Latinitatis*, s. v. Acannizare, we read an extract of a paper of Jacob. i. *Regis Arag.* fol. 16: "Quicunque Acannizaverit vaccam vel bovem, si bos vel vacca fecerit damnum casu fortuito, dum Acannizatur, cujus est amittat ipsum bovem vel vaccam, nisi Acannizetur causa nuptiarum;" and in Du Cange also: "Ut in anserem ludendo baculos torquere in usu fuit, ita et in bovem."

full of mead to drink. And this horn, moreover, besides serving as a cornucopia, becomes as a golden horn the war-trumpet of Odin (the Giallarhorn).

The Scandinavian hero then, it appears also, has his relationship with cows, though his life has far more of a warlike character than a pastoral one; he therefore accuses Loki, and in so doing fills him with shame, with having passed eight winters underground occupied in milking the cows like a woman. (It is known that the Hindoo word *duhitar*, whence Tochter, means she who milks). The Scandinavian hero, instead of milking cows, eats bulls. We find more than once in the *Eddas* the heroes occupied in roasting oxen. Atli, the husband of Gudrun, boasts of having killed some oxen and having eaten them with her. Gudrun, the Scandinavian Medea, gives Atli the hearts of his two sons to eat, assuring him that they are calves' hearts. The god Thor, disguised as the goddess Freya, drinks three barrels of mead, and eats a whole bull, when he sets out on the enterprise of recovering his marvellous hammer. The bull's or cow's horn, moreover, not only supplies mead to the hero, nor is it only used to call his friends to his aid and to throw down the enemy; it also forms the hero's bow, which therefore, in the *Vilkina Saga*,[1] also takes the name of Hornboge, and, as such, assists the greatest hero, Thidrek or Dîtrich, and is the parent of the celebrated hero Sigurd (Sîfrit, or Siegfried). And, in conclusion, the horns are considered such an important weapon of the cow and bull, that a proverb, which is at once Slavonic, German, and Italian, says, "To a wicked cow, God gives short horns" (that it may do no harm,

[1] *Die Deutsche Heldensage*, von Wilhelm Grimm, 2te Aus., No 102, 182.

or rather, because it wears them away by use); to cut off the cow's horns means, in a German proverb, to surmount a difficulty; and to take the bull or cow by the horns, is to disarm them.[1]

In the Greenland poem on Atli, in the *Edda* of Sömund, Högni says, that when many cattle are killed much blood is seen, and that when one dreams of eagles, oxen are not far distant. In the *Edda* of Snorri, whilst Odin, Loki, and Hönir are cooking an ox under a tree, an eagle on its summit prevents the meat from being cooked, till the heroes consent to give him part of it. The heroes consent, but the eagle carries off no less than the two thighs and the two shoulders of the ox. The eagle has in the *Edda* the same demoniacal and infernal character that is in other traditions ascribed to the crow, the funereal stork, and the vulture: it searches for oxen; and therefore to dream of eagles is an intimation that an ox is near, in the same way as they say the presence of a vulture is a sign of the proximity of a corpse.

A German legend, cited by Kuhn and Schwartz,[2] makes a battle begin "as soon as a red cow is led over a certain bridge." We remember the Russian story of the girl who, by means of the magical towel of her brother, makes a bridge arise over the river, over which the monster-serpent, in the form of a handsome young man, crosses to take her; how the brother is sacrificed in the battle which he is obliged to fight against the monster, who disarms him by fraud; and how the battle between the hero and the monster begins when the maiden, passing the bridge, abandons the hero, her brother, who falls and sheds his blood in the unequal struggle. I have

[1] Cfr. the chapter on the Goat and He-goat for more information on mythical horns.

[2] *Vide* p. 497.

already remarked that in the popular belief the bloody sun of evening forebodes war, and the red cow of German tradition represents no other than this sky. As to the bridge, an interesting note of Kuhn and Schwartz[1] seems to confirm the hypothesis which I have already hinted at in connection with the Slavonic story, *i.e.*, that it represents the milky way; from this note, too, in which a resemblance is noticed between the bridge of the red cow, which determines the beginning of a battle, and the Scandinavian celestial Bîfröst (as perhaps there is between it and even the Persian bridge Ćinvant itself), I gather that in Frisia the milky way is called Kau-pat (or Kuh-pfad, cow's-path). That is to say, it is supposed that the red cow of evening passes during the night along the milky way, scattering her milk over it; whence perhaps is derived the German proverb, "Even red cows yield white milk,"[2]—like that other which we have already seen current in India, and met with again in Turanian tradition, and which exists as a German, Slavonic, and Italian proverb, "Even the black cow yields white milk"—(the black night which produces the alba or white dawn of morning, and we might add, the silver moon and the milky way).

Since it seems to me, therefore, as I trust it also does to the reader, that the maiden who crosses the

[1] Diese Brücke wird keine andere sein, als die himmlische Bîfröst, deren er hütet, eine Vermuthung, die noch an Wahrscheinlichkeit gewinnt, wenn man den friesischen Namen der Milchstrasse Kaupat, der Kuhpfad, hinzunimmt; denn Milchstrasse und Regenbogen berühren einander sehr nahe. Dieser ist die Tagesbrücke zwischen Göttern und Menschen, jene die nächtliche.

[2] Rothe Kühe geben auch weisse Milch; Wander, *Deutsches Sprichwörter Lexicon*, Leipzig, Brockhaus, 1870.

[3] Auch eine schwarze Kuh gibt weisse Milch; Wander, *ibid.*

bridge in the Slavonic stories is, without doubt, the same as the red cow which does the like in German legend, and if I have not been mistaken in identifying the maiden who travels with her brother to the kingdom of the dead with the evening aurora and the dying sun, I shall here adduce a few other German proverbs, which may also be said to be universal in European tradition, relating to the cow, all pointing to a similar conclusion. They are as follows :—" Shutting the stable after the cow has been stolen." " He who has lost a cow, and recovers her tail, has not much, but he has more than nothing." " A cow's tail might reach heaven, if it were only a long one."[1] " A cow does not know what her tail is worth till she loses it." " To take the cow by her tail." " The black cow has crushed him, or has got upon him." " A cow cannot overtake a hare." " The cow has outrun the hare." " Not all who sound the horn hunt the hare." " When the cows laugh." " As a blind cow can find a pea." " He must be carried about in an old cow's hide." " If the cow-maid spins, there will be little yarn." " The cow will learn to spin first."[2]

Meditating upon all these German proverbs, it is, it

[1] This reminds us of the familiar English riddle, " How many cows' tails would it take to reach the moon? One, if it were long enough."

[2] Wenn die Kuh gestohlen ist, verwahrt man den Stall.—Wer eine Kuh verloren und den Schwanz zurück erhält, hat nicht viel, aber mehr als nichts.—Die Kuh könnte mit dem Schwanze bis an den Himmel reichen, wenn er nur lang genug wäre.—Une vache ne sceit que lui vault sa queue jusques elle l'a perdue.—Die Kuh beim Schwanz fassen.—Die schwarze Kuh hat ihn gedrückt.—Eine Kuh kann keinen Hasen erlaufen.—Die Kuh überläuft einen Hasen.—Nicht alle, die Hörner blasen, jagen Hasen.—Wenn die Kühe lachen.—Wie eine blinde Kuh eine Erbse findet.—Den sollt man in einer alten Kuhhaut herumfahren.—Soll die Kuhmagd spinnen, wird man wenig Garn gewinnen.—Man würde eher einer Kuh spinnen lehren ; Wander's *Lexicon of German Proverbs*, ii. 1666–1695.

appears to me, not difficult to recognise in them a reminiscence of ancient myths with which we are already acquainted. When we reflect that almost every proverb has passed into contradictory forms and varieties, and as in these varieties we may trace the elements of the history of a great number of strange proverbs, it does not seem rash to affirm that the said history generally had, in like manner, its origin in a myth. Not to wander from the subject in hand, that the same proverb is attributed to different animals, not only by different nations, but in the oral traditions of the same people, I must refer the reader to what I have remarked in the preface to this volume concerning the contradiction which exists between certain superstitious beliefs. The contradiction between many proverbs, as also between many superstitions, compared with each other, can only be reconciled by referring both back to the battle-field of mythology, where an inconceivable number of myths arise, and can only arise, out of contradictions; that is, out of contrasted aspects which celestial phenomena present, even to the same observer, still more so to different observers. The comparative history of mythical proverbs is yet to be written, and perhaps it is not yet possible to write it according to rigorous scientific method in all its completeness. A preliminary study of the details is necessary to understand a proverb as well as a popular custom, a superstitious belief, a legend, or a myth; and this study will demand some labour; for one proverb, completely illustrated, may involve the development of an entire epical history. I shall not presume here to solve the enigma of the above-quoted German proverbs, but only to indicate what seems to me to be the way of arriving at their most probable solution. In the study of a proverb, it is necessary to lay great stress upon its intonation. Upon the different tones in which an ancient proverb was originally pronounced, and afterwards repeated, passing from tongue to tongue, and from people to people, depends a great part of the alteration in the meaning even of the most interesting of the proverbs, which are a patrimony we owe in common to Aryan tradition. A proverb, for instance, began by being a simple affirmation, the simple expression of a natural mythical image; with the lapse of time the expression remained, and the myth was forgotten; the expression then appeared to refer to a strange thing, and was accompanied, when pronounced, with a doubtful mark of interrogation; it was now adopted in the denial of an impossible thing, and became an instrument for satire. Thus many proverbs which have become satirical, must have been originally nothing more than mythical affirmative phrases.

"To shut the stable after the cow has been stolen." In England, instead of the cow, we have in the proverb a girl: "When your daughter is stolen, shut Peppergate" (the name of a little gate of the city of Chester, which it is said the mayor ordered to be shut when his daughter had been carried off). The proverb is now used to stir up a laugh at the expense of those who are at pains to guard their property after it has been robbed; but it perhaps had not always the same meaning. We are already familiar in Hindoo tradition with the hero who delivers the beautiful maiden out of the enclosure, and have seen how she is scarcely free, when she is led away by iniquitous brothers or companions, after shutting up the legitimate proprietor of the cow or maiden in the cave whence the cow or girl came forth; how the ravishing brothers shut the door of the stable or cavern, after having carried off the maiden. The hero imprisoned in the stable, the hero shut up in the darkness of night, often assumed in mythology the form of a fool. Hence from the idea of shutting the gate of the stable upon the hero, by the ravishers of his cow, the transition seems natural, in my opinion, to the hero lost in the cavern, to the hero become foolish, to the peasant who shuts the door of the stable when the cow has been robbed, or to the mayor of Chester, who, being shut up in the town, shuts the Peppergate, through which the girl who had been carried off passed.

"He who has lost a cow and recovers its tail has not much, but he has more than nothing." This proverb also appears to me to have a mythical meaning. I have already remarked that the tail, the heel, the feet, that is to say, the lower or hinder extremities, betray the mythical animal; which we shall see more convincingly when we come to examine the legends which refer to the wolf, the fox, and the serpent. It is the footprint which, in all the European traditions, betrays the beautiful maiden in her flight; and when the brigand Cacus carried off the oxen of Hercules, the hero, to recover them, searches for their footprints. But in order that these may not be recognised, the cunning brigand, instead of leading the oxen by their heads, takes them by their tails,[1] and makes them walk backwards. Hence, to take by the tail, means to take hold of the wrong way, and it is applied to the ass as well as the cow. It is said in Germany that a cow once fell into a ditch from which none of the bystanders dared to extricate it. The peasant to whom the cow belonged came up, and,

[1] Livius i.: "Quia si, agendo, armentum in speluncam compulisset, ipsa vestigia quærentem dominum eo deductura erant, aversos boves eximium quemque pulchritudine caudis in speluncam traxit.

according to some, took it fearlessly by the horns, while, according to others, he dragged it out by its tail, whence can be explained the double proverb to take by the horns, *i.e.*, to take by the right side, and to take by the tail, or, as we have said, to take by the wrong. But the peasant could only take his cow out by the horns, or by the tail, according to the way in which it had fallen in; that is, if it had fallen down head foremost, it could only be dragged out by the tail, and if, on the contrary, it had fallen in tail foremost, he could only extricate it by laying hold of its horns. The cow-aurora is taken by surprise and devoured by the wolf, bear, wild-boar, or serpent of night, who takes her by the shoulders (it is on this account that, in the Russian story, we have seen the bull recommend the fugitive hero, accompanied by his sister, to keep his face turned in the direction whence the pursuing monster might be expected to come up). The monster (the shadow, or the cloud) clutches the cow by her tail and devours her, or drags her into his cave. The hero, in order to deliver his cow out of the cave, can take her by the horns only on condition that he penetrates into the cavern by the same way by which the cow entered, that is, by the monster's mouth; but, as the monster endeavours to surprise the hero from behind, so the hero often wounds the monster from behind, catches hold of him by the tail, and in this way drags him out of the cavern, ditch, or mud—his fallen cow. In a Hindoo fable in the second book of the *Pańćatantram*, we have the story of a jackal, who, to satisfy a desire of his wife, follows the bull for whole years together, in the hope that his two hanging testicles might fall some day or another. In a joke of Poggius, and in Lessing,[1] we find the same

[1] *Facetiæ*, Krakau, 1592, quoted by Benfey in his introduction to

subject spoken of, of which a variation is given in a German proverb, "Though the cow's tail moves, it does not fall."[1] In the hope of this it is that the wolf, or the fox, runs after the tail of the cow or bull. There is a Piedmontese story which I heard in my infancy, one comic feature of which lingers vividly in the memory: a boy who took the hogs to pasture, cut off their tails and stuck them in the mud, and then made off with the animals. The owner of the hogs, seeing their tails, is under the impression that they have sunk into the mud. He tugs at them, brings away their tails, but cannot fish up their bodies. In a Russian story given by *Afanassieff*,[2] we read that the cunning Little Thomas (Thomka, Fomka) cheats the priest of his horse (in some versions his ass) by cutting off its tail and planting it in the mud of a marsh. He makes the priest believe that his horse has fallen into the marsh; the priest, thinking to pull it out, gives one stiff tug, and falls down on his back with the tail in his hand; upon which Tom persuades him to believe that he has broken it off himself, and to be content with the recovery of so much of the lost animal. In the fifty-seventh Gaelic story of Campbell,[3] a priest endeavours to pull out of the water a drowning sheep,

the *Pańćatantram*, Leipzig, Brockhaus, p. 323: "Quia testiculi mei quadraginta annos pependerunt casuro similes et nunquam ceciderant."—And in Lessing, xi. 250, we read of Lachmann-Maltzahn: "De vulpe quadam asini testiculos manducandi cupido."—In Aldrovandi, *De Quadrupedibus Bisulcis*, i. Bologna, 1642, we read, "Membrum tauri in aceto maceratum et illitum, splendidam, teste secto, facit faciem; Rasis ait, genitale tauri rubri aridum tritum, et aurei pondere propinatum mulieri, fastidium coitus afferre; e contrario quidam recentiores, ut in viris Venerem excitent, tauri membrum cæteris hujus facultatibus admiscent."

[1] Wenn auch der Kuhschwanz wackelt, so fällt er doch nicht ab; in Wander, *Deutsches Sprichwörter Lexicon*. [2] v. 8.

[3] Referred to by Köhler in *Orient und Occident*.

but the tail comes away, and the story-teller adds, "If the tail had not come off, the story would have been longer." And so the owner of the cow, the robber of which has left the tail behind as a consolation, has in reality but little, but yet this little is something; for, just as the slipper left behind her by the fugitive girl, although it is of little value, enables the hero to identify her, so in the tail of his cow the owner has something in hand to set out on its search with, and to recover his lost property; either because the tail of an animal is like its shadow and serves to trace it, as the slipper does the maiden by showing the footstep; or else, because tailless cows are evidently stolen ones. (In the myth of Cacus, in which Hercules traces the stolen oxen by the foot-prints, and Cacus drags them by their tails, the mythical figure of the slipper and that of the lost tail are perhaps united. It is possible that the tails of the oxen came off in the hands of Cacus when dragging them into the cavern, and that, thrown away by the brigand, and found by Hercules, they may have served him as a guide to recover his oxen. It is also possible that Cacus, pursued by Hercules, had not time to drive the oxen in entirely, but that their tails still protruded and betrayed their whereabouts. Relative to the Latin legend of Cacus, these are simply hypotheses, and I have therefore enclosed them in a parenthesis; but inasmuch as in the above-quoted Russian story, we find the horse's tail cut off by the robber, and as in the chapter on the fox, we shall see the fox who betrays himself by not drawing in his tail, whence the proverb, "Cauda de vulpe testatur," the two hypotheses advanced above are, after all, not so visionary.) In *Pausanias*,[1] the hero Aristomenes, who has been thrown into a deep cistern, liberates himself in a

[1] iv. 15.

marvellous manner by means of an eagle, after a fox had opened a passage. The fox's tail has such a bewitching power of attraction, that according to popular tradition, when it is moved the cock falls down unable to resist the charm. According to popular belief, the tail (as well as the nose and mouth) is the most splendid part of the body of an animal. The great monkey Hanumant, with his tail on fire, burns Lanka (in the same way as the burning tails of the foxes of the biblical Samson burn the ripe harvests of the Philistines). The grey, or black, horse of mythology (having devoured the solar white, or red horse) emits fire from his mouth or tail. This black horse being the night, the horse's jaws and tail, which emit fire, represent the luminous heavens of evening and of morning; when, therefore, the tail of his horse (stolen by the robber in the same way as the bull and the cow[1]) remains in the mythical hero's hand, this light-streaming tail is enough to enable him to find the whole animal, *i.e.*, the solar hero comes out of his hiding-place (Hanumant comes out of the hinder parts of the marine monster, the dwarf comes out of the wolf's back[2]), the bull-sun finds his cow the aurora again; the prince sun, the princess aurora; the peasant recovers his ass or his cow; Hercules, his oxen; the white horse comes out of the tail of the black horse, who had eaten him, and then, by means of the tail, ascends to heaven;[3] the white

[1] Whence the proverb quoted above, relating to the stable that is shut when the cow is stolen, is also quoted as follows: "Shutting the stable when the horse has been stolen."

[2] Cfr. the chapter on the Wolf, where the dwarf enters the wolf by his mouth and comes out by his tail.

[3] In a Russian story, in *Afanassieff*, vi. 2, when the old peasant (the old sun) falls from the sky into a marsh (the sea of night), a duck (the moon or the aurora) comes to make its nest and lay an egg upon his head; the peasant clutches hold of its tail; the duck struggles

bull comes out of the black one; the white, or the red, cow comes out of the black cow; the tail comes out of the body; the hero comes out of the sack, or hide, in which he had been enclosed or sewed up. The sack plays a great part in the tradition of the hidden or persecuted hero; this sack is the night or the cloud, or the winter; the hero shut up in the sack, and thrown into the sea, is the sun. The hero enclosed in the sack and thrown into the sea, and the heroine shut up in a chest (covered, moreover, with a cow's hide, in the myth of Pasiphäe) or barrel, and abandoned to the water,[1] are equivalent to each other, and so are the heroes shut up in the well, in the cavern, in the stables, and even in the cow. Inasmuch as the sack in which, according to the proverb quoted above, the delinquent hero is to be sewed, is an old cow's-hide, or else the hide of an old cow, or a dark one (of the night), when this black cow sits on the eggs of the bird of evening, to hatch them, the eggs come to evil; whence I derive the German proverb, "When the cow sits upon the

and draws the peasant out of the marsh (the sun out of the night), and the peasant with the duck and its egg flies and returns to his house (the sky whence he had fallen).—In a variation of the same story in *Afanassieff* (the two stories together refer to that of Aristomenes) the old man falls from heaven into the mud. A fox places seven young foxes on his head. A wolf comes to eat the young foxes; the peasant catches hold of his tail; the wolf, by one pull, draws him out; by another, leaves his tail in the peasant's hand. The tail of the wolf of night is the morning aurora.—In the story of *Turn-Little-Pea*, *Afanassieff*, iii. 2, the young hero enters into the horse after having taken off his (black) hide, and after having taken him by the tail, *i.e.*, he becomes the luminous horse of the sun.

[1] In the Russian story of lazy and stupid Emilius, who makes his fortune, the hero is shut up in a barrel with the heroine, and thrown into the sea: the sun and the aurora, made prisoners, and shut up together, cross together the sea of night.

eggs, do not expect fowls."[1] And when the night was observed to overwhelm the sun and withdraw him from human sight, this other proverb took its origin, "The black cow has crushed him." The black cow does not only crush the hero, but, as the wolf does, shuts him up in her own hide,[2] in her own sack, *i.e.*, devours him—to fill the sack is the same as to fill the body, and to empty the sack as to empty the body. In the Piedmontese story of the dwarf child (the Norwegian Schmierbock), whom the wolf[3] encloses in the sack, the dwarf comes out of the sack while the wolf is emptying his body. Of two Russian stories given by *Afanassieff*, which we shall examine in the chapter on the wolf, one shows us the wolf who puts the peasant in a sack, and the other the wolf who puts the dwarf-hero in his body; and both peasant and dwarf save themselves. The two variations took their origin in the comparison drawn between the body and a sack, which, in mythical speech, are therefore the same thing. The hide of the black bull, black ox, black or grey horse, or black or grey wolf, and the sack which wraps up the hero or the devil,

[1] Wenn sich eine Kuh auf die Eier legt, so erwarte keine Hühner; Wander, the work quoted before.

[2] In the Russian story of *Afanassieff*, v. 36, the hero-workman kills the monster-serpent by gambling with him for the price of his own skin. Thinking that he may lose, he has provided himself beforehand with seven ox hides and with iron claws. He loses seven times; each time the monster thinks he has him in his power, but the workman as often imposes upon him with an ox's hide, inducing him to believe that it is his own. At last the serpent loses, and the workman, with his iron claws, really takes off his skin, upon which the serpent dies. To take the sack or hide from the monster, to burn the skin of the monster-serpent, goat, hog, frog, &c., to burn the enchanted mantle or hood in which the hero is wrapped up, is the same as to kill the monster.

[3] See the chapter on the Wolf.

play a great part in popular Indo-European tradition.[1] From the sack of the funeral stork (the night), in a Russian story,[2] come forth two young heroes (the Açvinâu), defeaters of their enemies, who spread out the tablecloth of abundance (the aurora), and a horse which drops gold (the sun). The hero shut up in the sack, or the cow's hide, and thrown into the water, escapes from shipwreck in the same way as those navigators of the Chinese sea described in his voyages by Benjamin of Tudela, who, he says, when shipwrecked, escaped being swallowed up by the waves by covering themselves with the whole hide of a cow or an ox; for the eagles, mistaking them for real, flew to the spot and pouncing upon them, drew them ashore. The ship with the buffalo's hide is found again in popular stories. This is evidently a reminiscence of mythical derivation (from which was, perhaps, afterwards derived the idea of torture, as in the famous bull of Phalaris, in which many see a symbol of the god of the waters, the bull's hide in which the tetrarch Acarnides, vanquished by Memnon, was sewed up,[3] in antiquity, and, in the Middle Ages, the ox's hide in which, according to the chronicles, the horrid Duke of Spalato Euroia orders Paulus Chuporus, prefect of the Emperor Sigismond, to be sewed, to revenge himself upon him, because he had, out of contempt, saluted him by bellowing like an ox). Thus with the Celtic hero Brian,[4] the pretended fool, who speculates upon the stupidity of those who are reputed wise. When one

[1] For the German one, cfr. Simrock, the work quoted before, p. 199.

[2] *Afanassieff*, ii. 17.

[3] Acarnides insutus pelle juvenci; Ovidius, *In Ibin.*

[4] Köhler, *Ueber T. F. Campbell's Sammlung gälischer Märchen*, in *Orient und Occident.*—Cfr. the 30th of the *Novelline di Santo Stefano di Calcinaia.*

of these so-called sages, deceived by him, proposes to throw him into the sea shut up in a sack, he makes another man take his place by means of a witty invention, as Goldoni's liar would say, whilst he himself comes back to the shore with a whole herd of cattle. In the other Celtic, Slavonic, German, and Italian variations of this story, the would-be fool begins his fortune-making, in one version, by putting a few coins into his dead cow's hide, and then selling it at a very high price as a purse which will give out money whenever shaken; and in another, by palming off his ass or horse, persuading the purchaser, by means of an easy deceit, to believe that it yields gold and silver, and thus obtaining a high price for it. With the cow are also connected the two horns, by blowing into which he causes his wife, who feigns death, to rise to life again, which horns he thus prevails on his brothers or companions to buy at a great ransom, who, thinking themselves cunning, and wishing by means of the horns to speculate upon corpses,[1] begin by killing people, and are ruined. I have said above, that the sack in which the hero is generally enclosed is the same as the chest in which the heroine is usually shut up on account of her beauty, that is to say, in which the beautiful heroine hides her splendour, or in which the red cow, the evening aurora with the sun, loses herself. The fourteenth Scottish story of Mr J. F. Campbell's contains the following narrative :—A king, whose first wife (the morning aurora) is dead, engages to marry the woman whom the dead queen's dresses will fit, and finds no one who can wear them except his own daughter (the evening aurora). She makes her father give her gold and silver dresses and shoes (that is, she takes from her father, the

[1] Köhler, the work quoted above.

sun, the splendour of the morning aurora); she shuts herself up with them in a chest, and lets herself be thrown into the sea. The chest drifts about on the waves, and comes at last to the shore; the beautiful maiden enters the service of a young king; she shows herself in church with her splendid robes; the young king, who does not recognise his servant-maid in this beautiful princess, becomes enamoured of her, and hastens to overtake her; she flees and loses her golden slipper; the king finds it, and to discover her, has it measured on every foot; many maidens cut off their toes to make the slipper go on, but a bird divulges the deceit; the young king marries the beautiful maiden who came out of the wooden chest. Here we have again, not only the heroine who escapes, but the walking heroine; this heroine is the aurora, and the aurora is often a cow. Another swift cow passes in the proverb before the hare (the leaping moon), in the fable of the ant and the grasshopper, of which the former represents the cloud or the night, or Indras or the aurora in the cloud of night, or the earth,[1] and the latter, the leaping one, the moon; the ant passes the grasshopper in the race, not because it walks faster, but because the two runners must necessarily meet, and therefore the one must pass the other. The English infantile rhyme, "Hey! diddle, diddle, the cat and the fiddle, the cow jumped over the moon," refers to the myth of the cow which jumps over the hare. The observation of celestial phenomena being afterwards neglected, and it being forgotten that the

[1] To this myth of the cow which goes over the moon, the observation of a lunar eclipse might have contributed materially, in which the cow earth (in Sanskṛit, *go* means earth as well as cow) really passes over the moon or hare. Or else, the cloud and the night, as a black cow, very frequently goes over the hare or moon.

running ant or cow meant the cloud, or the sun, or the aurora, or the earth, and the jumping hare or grasshopper the moon, only a regular and parallel race, on the terrestrial soil, between cow and hare, or ant and grasshopper, was seen ; and from the myth of the two animals which meet and pass each other in the sky, was derived, according to the different characters of nations or eras, a double proverb—one deriding the slow and rash animal which presumes to try and overtake the swift one in the race, the other serving as an example to prove the truth of the sentence, "Tarde sed tute," which, in Italian, is "Chi va piano va sano e va lontano" (he who goes slowly, goes well and far). The first proverb has for its parent the Greek one, "to hunt the hare with an ox," which, in Italian, is "pigliar la lepre col carro" (to take the hare with a car) ;[1] referring to cases where means disproportionate to the end are made use of. When the hare and the cow meet, if the cow is obliged to stop the hare, she crushes it, as we have seen above that she crushes the bird's eggs instead of hatching them. The idea, moreover, of the ox hunting the hare arose naturally out of the idea of the ox or cow overtaking and passing beyond the hare. To these proverbs can perhaps be joined the next German one :—"All who blow the horn do not hunt hares," which is now directed against those who think by an easy method, such as blowing a horn, to accomplish a difficult enterprise, such as hunting a hare ; in the same way as in Germany it is said, that all thunder-clouds do not give rain, and the cow must do more than low in

[1] In the Russian superstition, when a hare passes between the wheels of the vehicle which carries a newly-married couple, it bodes misfortune ; nor is this without reason : the hare is the moon ; the moon is the protectress of marriages ; if she throws obstacles in the way, the marriage cannot be happy ; consequently, marriages in India were celebrated at full moon.

order to have much milk, or the cow that lows most is not the one that yields most milk.[1] In fact, a cow which lows much is unwell, neither while it is lowing can it eat and make milk; so he who fatigues himself with blowing the horn is not able, at the same time, to run after the hare; as in the Italian proverb, "Il can che abbaia non morde" (the dog that barks does not bite), for the simple reason that whilst he opens his mouth to bark, he cannot shut it to bite. The hen that clucks, on the other hand, is the one that lays the egg, because the act of clucking with the mouth does not interfere with the operation of egg-laying; there is no incompatibility of offices.

The German proverb, "As a blind cow finds a pea," is now used to indicate an impossibility; and yet in the myth the blind cow (or the night) really finds the pea, kidney-bean, or bean (the moon), which are the same thing to all intents and purposes. The night is sacred to the dead; for the dead are as eaten vegetables—kidney-beans, vetches, peas, and cabbages—lunar symbols of resurrection and abundance. In the ninth story of the fourth book of *Afanassieff*, the daughter of the old man and woman eats beans; a bean falls upon the ground, and grows up to the sky; upon this bean the old man (the sun) climbs up to heaven and sees everything. In the numerous stories in which the young hero sells a cow or cow's hide, we almost always find a pipkin full of kidney-beans, which he induces people to think can cook themselves, the hero having first cooked them, and then placed them upon the fire covered with ashes (the darkness); the pipkin is also the moon. The stories of the pipkin belonging to the house-mother in the *Mahâbhâratam*,

[1] Die Kuh, die viel brüllt, gibt nicht die meiste Milch.

which the god Kṛishṇas, having been hospitably entertained by her, refills with beans, and of the lord who, in an unpublished Piedmontese legend, disguised as a poor old man, throws pebbles into the kettle of the pious widow, which, as soon as thrown in, become kidney-beans, involve the same myth. In the same way I think the kidney-bean is evidently intended by the fruit of fruits, which, according to the *Mahâbhâratam*, the merciful man receives in exchange for the little black cow (*kṛishṇadhenukâ*) given to the priest.[1] In the English fairy tale of "Jack and the Bean-stalk," Jack barters his cow for some beans; his mother (the blind cow) scatters the beans; one of them takes root, and grows up to the sky.[2] By means of the black cow, of the funereal or blind cow, of the cow-aurora, which becomes black or blind during the night, the hero finds the bean or the pea of abundance (the moon), by means of which he sees again in the morning and becomes rich.

We have seen a sack, instead of the hide of a black cow, used to signify the night; in like manner, after or instead of this same cow's hide (which the hero goes to sell), as well as the pea or bean, we have the pipkin—the poor hero finds the moon. The Slavonic story of the potter who becomes rich, and that of the brother believed to be stupid, who sells at a high price his pipkin, which

[1] Phalânâm phalam açnoti tadâ dattvâ; *Mahâbhâratam*, iii. 13, 423.

[2] In the German legend of King Volmar, in Simrock, the work quoted before, p. 451, we find the peas in the ashes. In the seventh of the *Contes Merveilleux* of Porchat, we have the pot in which the cabbages are boiled, from which come forth money and partridges. In the sixth of the same *Contes Merveilleux*, the young curioso sees a nest upon an elm-tree, and wishes to climb up; the ascent never comes to an end; the tree takes him up near to heaven. On the summit of the elm-tree there is a nest, from which comes forth a beautiful fair-haired maiden (the moon).

makes the beans boil without a fire, are varieties of the same subject. In a Russian story in *Afanassieff*,[1] the amphora takes the place of the pipkin that makes its owner rich. The poor brother draws it out of the water; from the broken amphora comes a duck, which lays one day golden eggs, and the next silver ones—the sun and the moon (at morning the aurora hatches the golden day, at evening the silver night).

We have still to explain the proverbs of the cow that laughs and the cow that spins. The laughing aurora (after having, during the night, acted the princess that never laughs) and the spinning aurora (in relation with the cow, the moon, that spins by means of its horns) are already known to us. The aurora laughs at morn in the sky, at the sight of her husband; thus the princess that never laughs, in a numerous series of Slavonic, German, and Italian stories, laughs when she sees her predestined husband.[2] The proverb of the cow that laughs is connected with that of the cow that speaks; it is perhaps on this account that bulls and cows (and other animals) which speak, and say and do complimentary things among themselves, in an entire cycle of Indo-European

---

[1] i. 53.

[2] In the story, vi. 58, of *Afanassieff*, the honest workman, when he wishes to fix his eyes upon the princess who never laughs, falls into a marsh; the fish, the beetle, and the mouse, in gratitude, clean him again; then the princess laughs for the first time, and marries the honest workman. In the 25th of the *Novelline di Santo Stefano*, an analogous detail is found, but this is not enough to make the princess laugh; it is the eagles which draw after themselves everything they touch that accomplish the miracle of making the queen's daughter laugh. In the third story of the *Pentameron*, the princess laughs upon seeing Pervonto carried by the faggot of wood, instead of carrying it. The Russian stories of the ducks which save the hero, in *Afanassieff*, vi. 17–19, and the faithless wife and her lover bound together, are variations of the eagles of the Tuscan story.

stories, which have been learnedly illustrated by Professor Benfey, in *Orient und Occident,* under the title of "Ein Märchen von der Thiersprachen," always make the man who understands, and indiscreetly listens to their language, laugh. But if the man reveals what the bulls or cows (or other animals) have said to each other, he prepares his own ruin : the language and the inner life of animals must not be divulged to all ; if published abroad, the augury is a sinister one. That which makes the princess of the Russian tale laugh, is seeing the courtesy which the animals, like men, show to the man taken out of the mud ; that which makes the man who understands the language of animals laugh, is seeing them speak and act to each other exactly as men do in similar private relations. To betray this mystery is to wish for one's death. No one must know what the bull said in secret to the cow, the sun to his mistress, what the king said in the queen's ear. The violator of the mysteries of Venus is guilty of sacrilege, and merits the punishment of death, or at least brings evil down upon his head. Woe to the heroine if the hero hidden in the skin of an animal, on account of some indiscretion, or because she has spoken to her sisters, shows himself naked in his human form ; she loses him, and their separation is inevitable.

We are already acquainted with the cloud-cow and the cloud-bull ; the cloud thunders, the bull bellows and speaks. The clouds, the Vedic *gnâ devapatnîs, gnâ devîs,*[1] that is, the goddesses, or divine and knowing wives, the fairy goddesses (women with their presentiments, the women that know more than the devil), are also prophetic cows ; these cows, in their character of fairies, speak with

[1] *Ṛigvedas,* v. 46, 8 ; v. 43, 6 ; i. 61, 8.

a human voice, and so do the cloud-bulls. Hence the Romans could take their auguries from an ox that spoke with a human voice. It has been said that this omen was a sinister one, but it is a mistake. According to Livy, under the consulate of Cn. Domitius and L. Quintius, an ox threw Rome into terror by the words, *Cave tibi, Roma.* These words seem to have a sinister meaning, but they are in reality nothing more than a friendly counsel or admonition, as much as to say, Look to your field occupations, O Rome; the thunder has been heard which announces the summer. Thus, when we read in the fifth book of Pliny's *Natural History* that whenever an ox was known to have spoken with a man's voice, the Roman Senate was accustomed to meet in the open air—*sub dio,* I only see in this allusion, and in ascribing this practice to the Senate, one way of saying that when thunder is heard (that is to say, when the ox speaks) it is a sign of summer, and we may go out into the country and sleep in the open air. And so, finally, when, according to Eusebius, an ox said, that for the death of Cæsar (which, as every one knows, took place on the Ides of March, that is to say, at the beginning of spring) there would be more blades of corn than men, I see a most evident announcement of the approach of summer, in which men or reapers are in fact never too many, and even rare when the harvest is a large one. The ox that with a man's voice heralds the near advent of summer corresponds to the cuckoo, the legend of which we shall reserve for a special chapter. Meanwhile, to confirm still more our identification, we shall cite here the almost proverbial verse of Theocritos: Women know everything, even how Zeus married Hêra (or that which the king said in the queen's ear). Zeus, transformed into a cuckoo, flew to the mountain, and alighted on the knees of Hêra, who, to protect him from the cold, covered him over with her robes. The cuckoo, or Zeus, disappears soon after having spoken, that is, announced the summer loves of the sun. After St John's Day the cuckoo, who appears in March, is no longer seen; so the ox, soon after it has spoken and betrayed the loves of Zeus, or soon after the cloud has thundered, revealing the secret loves of the sun within the sky covered with clouds, or the confidential speeches and secret caresses of the animals, pays for this indiscretion by his own death. As the aurora is represented in the Vedic hymns by a maiden who does not laugh, and smiles only when she sees her husband,[1] so the lightning that tears the cloud and comes before the thunder is compared to the laughing of an ox or a cow, or else of the man who has seen their loves. As long as the sky only lightens, or merely smiles,[2] there is little harm done. No one can know as yet why the ox or the cow, the hero or heroine, or the third person who is looking on, smiles before the spectator; but when the hero or the heroine speaks, betraying the thought or singular surprise which makes him or her smile, the penalty of the indiscretion is death; the thundering cloud is soon dissolved into rain. Nor will my identification

[1] In the *Nibelungen*, Krîmhilt, who has never saluted any one, (diu nie gruozte reeken), salutes for the first time the young Sîfrit, the victorious and predestined hero, and, whilst she is saluting him, turns the colour of flame (do erzunde sich sîn varwe).

[2] In a mediæval paper in Du Cange, s. v. *Abocellus*, we read: "De quodam cæco vaccarum custode," who, "quod colores et staturam vaccarum singularium specialiter discerneret," was believed to be demoniacal; hence the sacrament of confirmation was given him to deliver him from this diabolical faculty, and the paper narrates that he was immediately deprived of it. The blind hero who sees, who distinguishes his cows from each other, is the sun in the cloud. No sooner does he receive confirmation (which is a second baptism), than he ceases to see his cows, for the simple reason that the clouds are dissolved in rain, or that himself has recovered his vision.

of the cloud that lightens (making a distinction between the lightning and the thunderbolt) with the smiling cow, or ox, or man who, understanding the language of animals, as they speak in low tones, and seeing their most familiar habits, smiles, seem forced when we reflect that our language has preserved the figures of a ray of joy, of a flash of joy, to indicate a smile, of which we say that it shines, illumines, or lightens. Lightning is the cloud's smile. In the ninth story of the third book of *Afanassieff*, we meet with a fish which laughs in the face of the onlooker (the cloud that lightens, and also the moon that comes out of the ocean of night), and for which, on account of this singular property, the poor man (the sun in the cloud or in the night) obtains an extraordinary sum from a rich lord, even all his riches—*i.e.*, the poor man takes the place of the lord; the splendid sun takes the place of the sun hidden in the cloud or in the darkness. In a Hindoo story of *Somadevas* (i. 5), a fish laughs upon seeing men disguised as women in the king's apartment. In the *Tuti-Name* (ii. 21), the fishes laugh when they see the prudery of an adulteresss. With this is connected the fable of Lafontane, "Le Rieur et les Poissons" (viii. 8). In the legend of Merlin, the magician also laughs because the wife of Julius Cæsar lives with twelve heroes disguised as women, and because he himself allowed himself to be taken by Grisandole, a princess disguised as a cavalier.[1]

The fish is a phallic symbol (in the Neapolitan dialect, *pesce*, fish, is the phallos itself). The fish that laughs because it has been the spectator of adultery is the phallos itself *in gaudio Veneris*. The thunderbolt of Indras is

[1] Cfr. the papers relative to Merlin by Liebrecht and Benfey in *Orient und Occident*.

his phallos that breaks the cloud. In Ovid,[1] we have Jupiter, who, by means of riddles, teaches Numa the way of forming the thunderbolt.

> "Cœde caput, dixit, cui Rex, Parebimus, inquit;
> Cœdenda est hortis eruta cepa meis.
> Addidit hic, Hominis: Summos, ait ille, capillos.
> Postulat hic animam: cui Numa, Piscis, ait.
> Risit; et His, inquit, facito mea tela procures,
> O vir colloquio non abigende meo."

The joke of the April fish (le poisson d'Avril), with which so many of our ladies ingenuously amuse themselves, has a scandalously phallical signification.[2] The fishes of the Zodiac are twins, a male and a female bound together, born of Erôs (Amor) and Aphroditê (Venus). In the Adiparvam of the *Mahâbhâratam*, we read of a fish which devours a man's seed, and a girl who, having eaten it, brings forth a child. The same myth occurs again in the Western popular tales.

The cow that spins still remains to be explained. We have already seen that the cow spins with her horns for the maiden; this cow is, generally, the moon, which spins gold and silver during the night. The aurora is ordered by her step-mother, the night, both to pasture the cow (the moon) and spin. If the cow-maid is to take care of her cow and guard her well, she will be able to spin but little; whence the German proverb is right when it says that if the cow-maid must spin there will be little yarn. The good cow-maid prefers to keep her cow well, and pays every regard to it, in order that it may find good pasturage; then the grateful cow (the moon) puts gold and silver upon its horns to spin for the

[1] *Fasti*, iii. 339.

[2] Cfr. the chapter on the Fishes; where the custom of eating fish on Friday is also explained.

maiden.[1] In the morning the girl appears upon the mountain with the gold and silver yarn, with the gold and silver robes given her by the good fairy or by the good cow.[2] And when the old woman kills the cow, the girl who keeps its bones and sows them in the garden sees, instead of the cow, an apple-tree with gold and silver apples grow up, by offering one of which to a young prince the maiden obtains a husband, whilst perverse women are beaten by the apple-tree or find themselves opposed by horns. This apple-legend is a variation of the star which falls upon the good maiden's forehead on the mountain, and of the horns, or donkey's tail, which grow out of the forehead of the bad sister who has maltreated the cow or badly combed the Madonna's head. The story of the good maiden and the wicked one, of the beautiful and the ugly one, finishes with the attempt made by the ugly and wicked girl to take the place of the beautiful and good one in her husband's bed, in the same way as, in other stories, a black washerwoman tries to take the place of the beautiful princess; and this conclusion brings us to the interesting story of the spinning Berta, or Queen Bertha, as she is called.

In German mythology we have the luminous Berchta, who spins, in contrast with the dark and wild Holda at the fountain (the washerwoman of fairy tales). The former

[1] In the first of the stories of *Santo Stefano di Calcinaia*, the cow-maid says to her cow, "Cow, my cow, spin with your mouth and wind with your horns; I will make you a faggot of green boughs."

[2] The maiden spins for her step-mother; the fairy gives luminous robes to the maiden; the maiden weaves dresses for her husband; these are all details which confound themselves in one. In the *Nibelungen*, the virgins prepared dresses of gold and pearls for the young hero Sîfrit.

seems to be (besides the moon as a white woman, in her period of light, the silvery night) the aurora, the spring, or the luminous aspect of the heavens; the latter (besides the moon in her period of darkness, Proserpina or Persephonê in hell), the dark night, winter, the old witch.[1] The same name is given to the various phenomena of the gloomy sky, in the same way as a contrary name is given to the various phenomena of the luminous heavens. On this account lunar and solar myths, daily and annual myths, enter into the story of Berta or Berchta.

Berta, like the cow of the fairy tales, spins silver and gold. Therefore, when we say in Italy that the time when Berta spun is past,[2] this expression means, that the golden age, the age in which gold abounded is past. And instead of this expression we also use another in Italy to denote an incident which took place in a very ancient era, at a time very remote from the memory of men; we say, in the times of King Pipino (Pepin). Queen Berta having been the wife of Pepin, it was natural that the times of the husband should correspond to the fabled era of his wife, who was, tradition alleges, mother of Charlemagne, the hero so-named of the legends, of whom it is said, in Turpin's Chronicle, that he had long feet, and his *alter ego* Orlando (a new and splendid mediæval form of the twin heroes), rather than of the King Charlemagne of history.

Berta has a large foot, like the goddess Freya, the

---

[1] Holda, or Frau Holle, is burnt every year in Thuringia on the day of Epiphany, on which day (or, perhaps, better still, on the Berchtennacht, the preceding night, or Berta's night) the good fairy expels the wicked one. In England, too, the witch is burned on the day of Epiphany.—Cfr. Reinsberg von Düringsfeld, *Das festliche Jahr*, p. 19.

[2] In the *Pentameron* of Basil, i. 9, we read: "Passaie lo tiempo che Berta filava; mo hanno apierto l'huocchie li gattille."

German Venus, who has swan's feet. It is this large foot that distinguishes her from other women, and enables her husband to recognise her, in the same way as it is the foot, or footprint (the sun follows the path taken by the aurora), that betrays and discovers the fugitive maiden, who, we have said, is the aurora with the vast chariot (the vast chariot which, if it pass over the hare, may crush it. Frau Stempe, and Frau Trempe, and the large-footed Bertha, are the same person)—vast, because she occupies a large extent of the heavens when she appears. When standing on the chariot, she seems to have no feet, or a very small, an imperceptible foot; but the chariot on which she stands and which represents her foot is so much the larger; therefore when we leave the chariot out of account, and suppose, on the contrary, that she goes on foot, inasmuch as, when walking, she takes up much room, the swan's, or goose's, or duck's foot given to her in the myth of Freya and the legend of Berta is quite suited to her. And seeing, as we have said, that the foot (the myths almost always speak of one foot alone; even the devil is lame, or has only one foot) and the tail of an animal are often substituted for each other in mythology, we can understand how, in a Russian story,[1] the hero who has fallen into a marsh was able to deliver himself by clutching hold of the tail of a duck. This duck being the aurora, and having a wide spreading tail as well as a large foot, the solar hero, or the sun, can easily, by holding on to her, raise himself out of the swamp of night. There is a German story[2] in

[1] *Afanassieff*, vi. 2.

[2] Cfr. Simrock, the work quoted before, p. 409, and the ninth of the *Novelline di Santo Stefano di Calcinaia*, in which the luminous maiden disguised as an old woman is uncovered by the geese, when she puts down the dress of an old woman.

which the white woman, or the Berta, is transformed into a duck. In another German legend,[1] instead of the swan-footed Berta, we have the Virgin Mary (who, as a maiden, represents the virgin aurora, always pure, even after having given birth to the sun; like the Kuntî of the *Mahâbhâratam*, who gives birth to Karṇas, the child of the sun, and yet is still a virgin. On the other hand, when a good old woman, good woman or Madonna, she generally personifies, in the legends, the moon) who, in the shape of a swan, comes to deliver from the prison of the infidels (the Saracens or Turks, here the black demons, or the darkness of night), and carry off by land and by sea, the young hero whom she protects (the aurora delivers the sun from the night).[2] The same luminous Berta also assumes, in popular German tradition, the form of St Lucia, that is, the saint who, after having been made blind, became the protectress of eyesight. Of the blind or black cow of night is born the luminous cow of morning, the aurora that sees everything herself and makes us see everything. For the same reason that the cow or duck, Berta, is consecrated

[1] Simrock, the work quoted before, p. 410.

[2] Wuotan also saves him whom he protects upon a mantle;—this is the flying carpet or mantle, hood, or hat, which renders the wearer invisible, and for which the three brothers disputed, which is also represented as a tablecloth that lays itself. Thus the poor man who goes to sell his cow's hide finds the pot of abundance and riches. The dispute for the tablecloth is the same as the dispute for riches, for the beautiful princess who is afterwards divided, or else carried off by a third or fourth person who takes the lion's share. We must not forget the fable of the animals who wish to divide the stag among themselves, of which the lion takes all, because he is named lion. In the *Nibelungen*, Schilbung and Nibelung dispute with each other for the division of a treasure; they beg Sîfrit to divide it; Sîfrit solves the question by killing them both and taking to himself the treasure, and the hood that makes its wearer invisible (Tarnkappe).

to St Lucia, whose appearance she assumes, the bull (the sun) is sacred to St Luke, the festival of whom is on this account celebrated at Charlton, near London, with a horn-fair or exhibition of horns, generally ornamented and perfumed.

In the above-quoted Hindoo legend of the *Mahâbhâratam*, the queen will not sleep with the old blind man, but sends instead her servant-maid. In the *Reali di Francia*, King Pepin is advised by his barons to take a wife, when he is already "far advanced in years" (he is a form of St Joseph). The barons look for a wife, and find, in Hungary, Berta, the daughter of King Philip, "the most beautiful and skilful horsewoman," or Berta with the large foot upon a beautiful and stately horse, which goes along the road bounding, whilst she is always laughing. Berta has a maid called Elizabeth, who resembles her in every respect except her feet. King Pepin is married by proxy to Berta, sends for her, and comes to meet her. Berta when she sees that King Pepin is so ill-favoured, grieves "although forewarned of his old age." When evening comes she takes off her royal robes and gives them to Elizabeth, that she may take her place and sleep with the king.[1] Hence the

[1] The romance of Berta continues in the *Reali di Francia* in harmony with the popular stories of an analogous character; the false wife really causes King Pepin to marry her, and sends Berta into the forest to be killed; the hired murderers pity her, and grant her her life. Berta, whilst in the forest bound to a tree (like the Vedic cow), is found by a hunter; out of gratitude she works (she, no doubt, spins and weaves), in order that the hunter may sell her work at Paris for a high price. Meanwhile her father and mother dream that she is beset by bears and wolves who threaten to devour her, that thereupon, throwing herself into the water, a fisherman saves her (in the dream, the water has taken the place of the forest, and the fisherman that of the hunter). King Pepin goes into the forest, finds her, recognises

Italian proverbs, "Dar la Berta" (to give the Berta), and "Pigliar la Berta" (to take the Berta), meaning to deride and to be derided. But instead of to give the Berta, in Italy we also say, "Dar la madre d'Orlando" (to give the mother of Orlando). The *Reali di Francia* informs us that King Pepin had, by Elizabeth, two perverse bastards, Lanfroi and Olderigi, and by Berta, Charlemagne and another Berta, mother of Orlando; but the Italian proverb is perhaps nearer the mythical truth when it recognises the mother of Orlando as herself Pepin's wife, so that Charlemagne and Orlando are brothers; and, in fact, they accomplish several of the undertakings mentioned in the legend of the two brothers. In the so-called Chronicle of Turpin[1] when Orlando dies, Charlemagne says that Orlando was his right arm, and he has no longer anything to do in life without him; but he lives long enough to avenge the death of Orlando; and after this vengeance, the heroic life of Charlemagne comes at once to an end. In the *Chanson de Roland*, too, after the death of his hero, whom he avenges, Charlemagne feels the burden of life, weeps, tears his beard, unable to support this solitude; but in the *Chanson*, as well as in the *Reali di Francia*, Orlando explicitly appears as the nephew of Charlemagne, that is, as the son of his sister Berta. (As the Vedic aurora was now the mother, now the sister of the sun and of the

and marries her, whilst Elizabeth is burnt alive. The change of wives also occurs in a graceful form (with a variation of the episode of the beauty thrown into the fountain) in the twelfth of the *Contes Merveilleux* of Porchat, Paris, 1863.

[1] *Histoire de la Vie de Charlemagne et de Roland*, par Jean Turpin, traduction de Alex. de Saint-Albin, Paris, 1865, preceded by the Chanson de Roland, poème de Théroulde.—Cfr. the *Histoire Poétique de Charlemagne*, par Gaston Paris.

Açvinâu, thus Berta may, mythically, be mother or sister of Charlemagne, and yet be always the mother of Orlando).

It would be a never-ending work to collect together all the Germanic, Scandinavian, and Celtic legends which, in one way or another, are connected with the myth of the cow and of the bull. The literature relating to this subject is composed not of one or a hundred, but of thousands of volumes, of which some (such, for instance, as the poem of the *Nibelungen*, and the poems of the *Round Table*) individually contain, in the germ, almost the whole diverse world of fairy tales. I must therefore limit myself to the indication of the more general features, leaving to more diligent investigators the minuter comparisons; and esteeming myself, I repeat, too happy if my brief notices should be found clear enough to spare others the labour of preparing the warp upon which to weave comparisons.

From what we have said thus far, it seems to me that two essential particulars have been made clear:—1st, That the worship of the bull and the cow was widespread, even in northern nations; 2d, That the mythical bull and cow were easily transformed into a hero and heroine.

The sacred character ascribed to the cow and the bull is further evidenced by a Scandinavian song, in which, on the occasion of the nuptials of the animals (the crow and the crane), the calf (perhaps the bull) appears as a priest, and reads a beautiful text.[1] As a symbol of generation, the bull is the best adapted to propitiate the married couple; so the priest in the *Atharvavedas* teaches the inexperienced husband and wife, by formulas *ad hoc*,

[1] Uhland's *Schriften zur Geschichte der Dichtung und Sage*, iii. 77.

the mysteries of Venus. Thus the *jus primæ noctis* was conceded to the Brahman in mediæval India; and so in the ritual of mediæval France, we still find indications of the priest *pronubus*. The beautiful text that the calf, or bull, recites in the Scandinavian song must be the same which, according to the ceremonial recorded by Villemarqué, the priest recited, whilst sprinkling them with incense, to the married couple *sedentes vel jacentes in lectulo suo*.[1] Thus, when the wolf dies (in a German writing of the twelfth century), it is the ox that reads the gospel.[2] Besides marriages and funerals, the bull or ox also appears, finally, as in the Hindoo ceremonial, in pregnancy. Gargamelle, while she has Gargantua in her womb, eats an excessive quantity[3] of tripe of fattened

[1] "Seigneur, bénissez ce lit et ceux qui s'y trouvent; bénissez ces chers enfants, comme vous avez béni Tobie et Sara; daignez les bénir ainsi, Seigneur, afin qu'en votre nom ils vivent et vieillissent et multiplient, par le Christ notre Seigneur.—Ainsi soit-il." Villemarqué, *Barzaz Breiz, Chants Populaires de la Bretagne*, sixième édition, Paris, 1867, p. 423.

[2] Uhland, the work quoted above, p. 81.—In the French romance of *Renard*, on occasion of the apparent death of the fox, the gospel is read, on the contrary, by the horse. In the German customs the bull also appears as a funeral animal, and is fastened to the hearse. If, while he is drawing the hearse, he turns his head back, it is considered a sinister omen. According to a popular belief, the bulls and other stalled animals speak to each other on Christmas night. A tradition narrates, that a peasant wished on that night to hide himself and hear what the bulls were saying; he heard them say that they would soon have to draw him to the grave, and died of terror. This is the usual indiscretion and its punishment.—Cfr. Rochholz, *Deutsches Glaube und Brauch*, Berlin, 1867, i. 164, and Menzel, *Die Vorchristliche Unsterblichkeits-Lehre*, Leipzig, 1870.—We have the speaking oxen again in Phædrus's fable of the stag who takes refuge in the stable, ii. 8, where the master is called "ille qui oculos centum habet."

[3] Elle en mangea seze muiz, deux bussars et six tupins; Rabelais, *Gargantua*, i. 4.

oxen. When she feels the pains of child-birth, her husband comforts her with an agricultural proverb of Poitou, "Laissez faire aux quatre beufz de devant;" and she then gives birth to Gargantua, who comes out of her left ear, in the same way as in the Slavonic stories we find the heroes come out of the ears of the horse (or of the ass of night; the luminous solar hero comes out of the ears of the ass, or of the grey or black horse; the twin horsemen come out of the two ears). Rabelais, to explain this extraordinary birth, asks "Minerve ne naquit-elle pas du cerveau par l'aureille de Iupiter?" No sooner is Gargantua born, than he asks with loud cries for something to drink; to give him milk, 17,913 cows are brought, his mother's breasts not being enough, although each time she is milked she yields "quatorze cens deux pipes neuf potées de laict." This is the giant of popular tradition, whom the gigantic phantasy of Rabelais has coloured in order to make him the butt of an immense satire. It is an amplified and humorous rendering in a literary form of the popular Superlatif,[1] whose mythical character is revealed in the curse hurled against him by the old dwarf-fairy, whom he maltreated: "One sun, to accomplish his work, eats eleven entire moons; but this time every moon will eat the work of a sun." The ascending and descending life of the solar hero is thus indicated. Superlatif will become continually smaller, until it seems as though he were about to disappear altogether; but at that very instant the curse comes to an end, and from a dwarf, he grows into a giant again in the arms of his bride.[2] Thus the days

[1] Cfr. Porchat, *Contes Merveilleux*, Paris, 1863.

[2] In *Porchat*, Superlatif, while he is a dwarf, is shut up in a clothes-press; he is a male form of the wooden girl, of the wise puppet, of the sun hidden in the trunk of a tree, in the tree of night, in the

become continually shorter and shorter, till the winter solstice, till Christmas. At Christmas the sun is born again, the days lengthen, the dwarf grows tall; the sun, by a double but analogous conception of ideas, passes once each day and once each year from giant to dwarf, and from dwarf to giant.

And the dwarfs of tradition know and reveal the mythical how and why of their transformations, since, though they are dwarfs and hidden, they see all and learn all. It is from the knowing dwarf Allwis, his diminutive *alter ego*, that the mighty Thor, in the *Edda*, learns the names of the moon, the sun, the clouds, and the winds. The moon, according to Allwis, when it is in the kingdom of hell (in the kingdom of death, in the infernal world, when it is Proserpina), is called a wheel that is hurrying on; it then shines among the dwarfs (*i.e.*, in the luminous night, in which the sun hides itself; it becomes an invisible dwarf). The sun among the dwarfs (*i.e.*, when it is a dwarf) plays with Dwalin (the mythical stag, probably the horned moon); among the giants (*i.e.*, when in the aurora, it becomes a giant again), it is a burning brand; among the gods (the Ases), it is the light of the world. The cloud, the dwarf Allwis goes on to inform us, is the ship of the winds, the strength of the winds, the helmet (or hat, or hood) which makes its wearer invisible. The wind, again, is the wanderer, the noisy one, the weeper, the bellower, the whistler

nocturnal (or cloudy, or wintry) night, full of mysteries, which the little solar hero surprises from his hiding-place. The hero in hell, or who, educated by the devil, learns every kind of evil, is a variation of this multiform idea. The dwarf of *Porchat*, who comes out of the clothes-press, is in perfect accord with the popular belief which makes the man be born in the wood, on the stump of a tree, of which the Christmas-tree is a lively reminiscence.

(no one can resist the cries or the whistling of the hero of fairy tales ; the bellowing of the bull makes the lion tremble in his cave). In this learned lesson on Germanico-Scandinavian mythology, given us by the dwarf Allwis, we have a further justification of the transition which we here assume to have been made from the natural celestial phenomenon to its personification in an animal, and to the personification of the animal in a man : Allwis, who knew all things, has explained the mystery to us.

SECTION VI.

The Bull and the Cow in Greek and Latin Tradition.

SUMMARY.

Preparatory works.—Bos quoque formosa est.—Zeus as a bull.—Iô and Eurôpê as cows.—The cow sacred to Minerva, the calf to Mercury, and the bull to Zeus.—Demoniacal bulls.—Taurus draconem genuit et taurum draco.—White bulls sacrificed to Zeus, and black ones to Poseidôn.—Poseidôn as a bull.—The horn of abundance broken off the bull Acheloos.—The bulls of Aiêtas.—The bull who kills Ampelos.—Dionysos a bull.—The bull that comes out of the sea.—The eaters of bulls.—The sacrifice of the bull.—The intestines of the bull.—From the cow, the lamb.—The bull's entrails are wanting when the hero is about to die, that is, when the hero has no heart.—Even the bull goes into the forest. —The bull that flees is a good omen when taken and sacrificed.— The bull and the cow guide the lost hero.—Analogy between solar and lunar phenomena.—Hêraklês passes the sea now on the cow's neck, now in a golden cup.—Hêraklês shoots at the sun.—The moon, the bull of Hêraklês, becomes an apple-tree ; anecdote relating to this.—The moon as a golden apple.—The moon as a cake. —The funeral cake.—Instead of a cow of flesh, a cow made of paste, in Plutarch and Æsop.—Ashes and excrement of the cow. —L'eau de millefleurs.—The bulls of the sun.—Hêraklês stable-boy and cleaner of the herds.—The bull Phaethôn.—The myth of the bull and the lion.—The bull's horns.—The god a witty thief; the demon an infamous one.—The myth of Cacus again.—The worm or serpent that eats bulls.—The bellowing or thundering bull, celestial musician.—The bull and the lyre.—The voice of Zeus—Bull-god and cow-goddess.

In descending now from the North upon the Hellenic and Latin soils, to search for the mythical and legendary forms assumed there by the bull and the cow, the mass of available material in point which offers, instead of diminishing, has increased prodigiously. Not to speak of the rich literary traditions of mediæval Italy and Spain (as to those of France, they are often but an echo of the Celtic and Germanic), nor the significant traditions of the Latin historians and poets themselves, nor the beliefs, superstitious customs, and legends still existing on the half-Catholic, half-Pagan soil of Italy, all of which are notably fraught with the earliest mythical ideas, we here find ourselves face to face with the colossal and splendid edifice of Greek poetry or mythology itself; for that which constitutes the greatness and real originality of Greek poetry is its mythology, by means of which it is that a divinity breathes in every artistic work of Hellenic genius. The poet and the artist are almost always in direct correspondence with the deities, and therefore it is that they so often assume such a divine and inspired expression. It would, therefore, be a bold presumption on my part if I were to essay to extract and present, in a few pages, the soul, the contents of this endless mythology. I have, moreover, the good fortune of being able to plead relief from the obligation to venture on any such attempt, by referring the reader to the learned preparatory works published in England, in the same interest, by Max Müller and George Cox, upon the Hellenic myths in relation to the other mythologies. It is certainly possible to take exception to interpretations of particular myths proposed by these two eminent scholars, as, no doubt, might be the fate of many of mine, were I to enter into minute explanations, and were my lucubrations fortunate enough to obtain any measure of consideration. But as I flatter myself with the hope that, notwithstanding occasional diversions, in which I may have gone aside and lost myself for a few minutes, I am taking the royal road which alone leads to the solution of the great questions of comparative mythology, I recognise with gratitude the labours of Max Müller and Cox upon Greek mythology, the writings of Michael Bréal upon Roman mythology, the immortal work of Adalbert Kuhn upon the Indo-European myth of fire and water, and a few other helpful beacon-towers which send their light-shafts clear and steady athwart the waste, and serve as useful guides to the studious navigator of the *mare magnum* of the myths. And because that which there is yet to do is immense in proportion to the little that has been done well, I shall take for granted what has already been demonstrated by my learned predecessors (to one and all of whom I confidently and respectfully refer my readers), and go on with my own researches, restricting myself, however, entirely to the zoological field, in order not to increase, out of all proportion, the dimensions of this opening chapter, which already threatens to straiten the space I must leave for the rest of my undertaking.

"Bos quoque formosa est,"

says Ovid, in the first book of the *Metamorphoses*, when the daughter of Inachos is transformed into a luminous cow by Jupiter. The bull Zeus of Nonnos is also beautiful, as he swims on the sea, carrying the beautiful maiden Eurôpê. Her brothers wonder why oxen wish to marry women; but we shall not wonder when we remark that Iô and Eurôpê are duplicates of one and the same animal, or, at least, that Iô and Eurôpê both took the shape of a cow—one as the moon especially,[1] the other, the far-observing daughter of Telephaessa, the far-shining,[2] as the moon also, or the aurora. In the first case it is the heroine that becomes a cow; in the second, it is the hero who shows himself in the shape of a bull.[3] These forms are, however, only provisional and unnatural, in the same way as in the Vedic hymns the representation of the aurora, the moon, and the sun as cow and bull is only a passing one. The cow and the bull send their calf before them; the sun, the moon, and the aurora are preceded or followed by the twilight. Jupiter and Minerva have for their messenger the winged Mercurius; and hence also Ovid[4] was able to sing:—

> "Mactatur vacca Minervæ,
> Alipedi vitulus, taurus tibi, summe Deorum."[5]

---

[1] According to Eustatius, "Iô gar hê selênê katà tên tôn Argetôn dialekton."

[2] Cfr. Pott, *Studien zur griechischen Mythologie*, Leipzig, Teubner, 1859; and Cox, the work quoted before.

[3] *Dionysiakôn*, i. 45, and following; iii. 306, and following.

[4] *Metamorphoseôn*, iv. 754.

[5] In England, as I have already noticed, the bull or ox is sacred to St Luke; in Russia, to the saints Froh and Laver. In Sicily, the protector of oxen is San Cataldo, who was bishop of Taranto. (For the notices relating to Sicilian beliefs concerning animals, I am indebted to my good friend Giuseppe Pitrè.) In Tuscany, and in other parts of Italy, oxen and horses are recommended to the care of St Antony, the great protector of domestic animals. In the rural parts of Tuscany, it was the custom, on the 17th of February, to lead oxen and horses to the church-door, that they might be blessed. Now, to save trouble, only a basket of hay is carried to be blessed; which done, it is taken to the animals that they may eat it and be preserved from evil. On Palm Sunday, to drive away every evil, juniper is put into the stables in Tuscany.

The fruit of the nuptials of Iô and of Eurôpê with Zeus is of a monstrous nature, such as the evil-doing daughters of Danaos, who, on account of their crimes, are condemned in hell to fill the famous barrel (the cloud) that is ever emptying (the counterpart of the cup which, in the Scandinavian myth, is never emptied); such too as Minôs, he who ordered the labyrinth to be made, the infernal judge, the feeder of the Minôtauros (of which the monstrous bull of Marathon, first subdued by Hêraklês and afterwards killed by Theseus, is a later form), the son of his wife and the gloomy and watery black bull Poseidôn. Even Kadmos, the brother of Eurôpê, ends his life badly. He descends into the kingdom of the dead in the form of a serpent. Of good, evil is born, and of evil, good; of the beautiful, the hideous, and of the hideous, the beautiful; of light, darkness, and of darkness, light; of day, night, and of night, day; of heat, cold, and of cold, heat. Each day and each year the monotonous antithesis is renewed; the serpent's head always finds and bites its tail again. A Tarentine verse of Arnobius expresses very happily these celestial vicissitudes:

> "Taurus draconem genuit et taurum draco."

Thus, in the romance of Heliodoros (*Aithiopika*) we read that the queen of Ethiopia, being black, gave birth to a white son; that is to say, the black night gives birth to the white moon and to the white dawn of morning. To Zeus (Dyâus, the luminous,) are sacrificed white bulls; to his brother Poseidôn, black ones; indeed, entirely black[1] ones, according to the Homeric expression.

Poseidôn, in Hesiod (*Theog.* 453), is the eldest brother;

[1] Taúrous pammélanai, in the *Odyssey;* the commentator explains that the bulls are black because they resemble the colour of water.

in Homer (*Il.* xv. 187), he is, on the contrary, the youngest; and both are right; it is the question of the egg and the hen; which is born first, darkness or light? The son of Poseidôn, Polyphêmos the Cyclop, is blinded by Odysseus. Poseidôn, representing the watery, cloudy, or nocturnal sky, his one-eyed son seems to be that sky itself, with the solar star, the eye of the heavens, in the midst of the darkness or of the clouds (the mouth of the barrel). When Odysseus blinds his son, Poseidôn avenges him by condemning Odysseus to wander on the waters (that is, lost in the ocean or the clouds of night). Inasmuch, moreover, as Zeus, properly the luminous one, is often called and represented by Homer as black as the clouds and pluvial,[1] he is assimilated to Poseidôn, the *presbýtatos* or oldest; in fact, in the oldest Hellenic myths, Poseidôn is essentially the pluvial form of Zeus. When Poseidôn, in the form of a bull, seduces Pasiphaê, the daughter of the sun and wife of Minôs, he appears, indeed, of a white colour, but has between his horns a black spot.[2] This spot, however small, is enough to betray his tenebrous nature. Thus Acheloos, vanquished by Hêraklês in the shape of a serpent, rises again in that of a pugnacious bull, one of whose horns Hêraklês breaks,[3] which he gives to the Ætolians, who receive abundance from it (the waters of the Acheloos fertilise

[1] Kelainefès-nefelêgeréta Zeús; *Odyssey*, xiii. 147 and 153.

[2] Signatus tenui media inter cornua nigro
Una fuit labes; cœtera lactis erant.
Ovidius, *De Arte Amandi.*

[3] In *Diodoros*, Hammon loves the virgin Amalthea, who has a horn resembling that of an ox. The goat and the cow in the lunar and cloudy myth are the same; and on this account we find them both in connection with the apple-tree, a vegetable form, and with the cornucopia, since both are seers, and spies, and guides. The golden doe is a variation of the same lunar myth.

the country traversed by them; the dragon of the cloud kept back the waters; Hêraklês discomfits the dragon, *i.e.*, the darkness, and it then reappears in the form of a bull; when its horns are broken, abundance is the consequence). This monster reappears in the two perverse and terrible bulls of King Aiêtas, with copper feet (*taurô chalkópode*), which breathe dark-red flames and smoke, and advance against the hero Iêsôn in the cavern; in the same way as the king of the monkeys in the *Râmâyaṇam* vanquishes the demoniacal bull that fights with its horns, by taking hold of the horns themselves, and throwing it down; so Iêsôn does in Apollônios.[1] The same bull is repeated in that ridden by the youth Ampelos, dear to Diónysos (who has also the nature of a bull, *taurophüsês*, but of a luminous one). Ampelos, persuaded by the death-bringing Atê (*thanatêphóros Atê*), mounts on this bull, and is thrown by it upon a rock where his skull is broken, because he was full of pride against the horned moon, her who agitates the oxen, who, offended, sends a gadfly to the bull and maddens it. The bull Diónysos wishes to avenge the young Ampelos, by fixing his horns in the belly of the perverse and homicidal bull.[2] In this myth, the black bull of night and the bull-moon are confounded together in one sinister action.

From the ocean of night comes forth the head of the solar and lunar bull, and on this account, in Euripides[3] Okeanos is called the bull-headed (*taurókranos*); or else the head of the solar bull enters the nocturnal forest, or that of the lunar bull comes out of it. This phenomenon

[1] *Argonantikôn*, iii. 410, 1277.

[2] Nonnos, *Dionysiakôn*, xi. 113 and following.

[3] *Orestês*, 1380.

gave rise to several poetical images. The bull is devoured by the monsters of night; hence in the *Seven at Thebes* (xlii.) of Æschylos, the messenger accuses of impiety the seven eaters of bulls, who touch with their hands the blood of bulls; hence in the forty-third fable of Æsop, the dogs flee, horrified, from the peasant who, being of a gluttonous nature (like the old man of the Russian story who eats all his cows), after having devoured sheep and goats, prepares to eat the working oxen themselves.[1] The bull's head, or even the bull itself, or the milch-cow, which must not be eaten, can, however, be sacrificed; nay, he is lucky who offers them up (except when the deity is named Heliogabalus, who receives the *taurobolium* as a homage due to him, without giving anything in exchange to the devoted sacrificers).[2] According to Valerius Maximus,[3] the empire of the world would, by an oracle of the time of Servius Tullius, belong to the nation who should sacrifice to the Diana of the Aventine a certain wonderful cow belonging to a Sabine (the aurora or the moon, from the sacrifice of which the sun comes out at morning). The Sabine prepares to sacrifice it, but a Roman priest takes it from him by fraud, whilst the Sabine is sent to purify himself in the water near at hand. This is a zoological form of the epico-mythic rape of the Sabines, of the exchange of the wife or of the precious object, of the exchange effected in the sack.

---

[1] *Ergazomĕnous Bŏas.*—In the twelfth book of his *History of Animals,* Ælianos writes: "Among the Phrygians, if any one kills a working ox, he atones for it with his life." And Varro, *De Re Rusticâ:* "Bos socius hominum in rustico opere et Cereris minister. Ab hoc antiqui ita manus abstineri voluerunt ut capite sanxerint si quis occidisset."

[2] *Scriptores Historiæ Augustæ,* Lampridius, in the life of Heliogabalus.

[3] vii. 3.

In Ovid,[1] the same myth occurs again with a variation:

> "Matre satus Terra, monstrum mirabile, taurus
> Parte sui serpens posteriore fuit.
> Hunc triplici muro lucis incluserat atris
> Parcarum monitu Styx violenta trium.
> Viscera qui tauri flammis adolenda dedisset,
> Sors erat, æternos vincere posse Deos.
> Immolat hunc Briareus factu ex adamante securi;
> Et jam jam flammis exta daturus erat.
> Jupiter alitibus rapere imperat. Attulit illi
> Milvus; et meritis venit in astra suis."

We shall return to this myth in the following chapters. The monster is killed only when his heart, which he keeps shut up, is taken away. Sometimes he does not keep it shut up in his own body, but in a duck (the aurora), which comes out of a hare (the moon sacrificed in the morning).[2] When this duck is opened, a golden egg (the sun) is found. When the egg is thrown on the ground, or at the monster's head, the monster dies. The golden duck, whence the monster's heart, the sun, comes forth, is the same as the cow which gives birth to the lamb (the night gives birth to the aurora, and the aurora to the solar lamb). The historian Flavius cites, among the prodigies which preceded the destruction of the temple of Jerusalem, a miracle of this kind, which took place in the middle of the temple itself, in the case of a cow led thither to be sacrificed. It occurs still every morning in the mythical heavens, and was a phenomenon familiar to human observation in the remotest antiquity, when it became a proverb; but, as often happened, the proverb which affirmed an evident myth, when its sense was lost,

---

[1] *Fasti,* iii. 800.

[2] Cfr. the chapter on the Hare.

was adopted to indicate an impossibility; wherefore we read in the second satire (cxxii.) of Juvenal :—

> "Scilicet horreres maioraque monstra putares,
> Si mulier vitulum, vel si bos ederet agnum ?"

In Greek and Latin authors[1] we find frequent examples of the sacrifice of a bull a short time before the death of the hero by whom it was ordered, in which it was noticed as a very sinister omen that the entrails were missing, and particularly the heart or the liver. Having observed that the monster's heart is the solar hero, or the sun itself, we can easily understand how, in the sacrifice of a bull, this heart must be wanting when the hero approaches his end. In the mythical bull sacrificed at evening, the hero's heart is not to be found; the monster has eaten his intestines, of which, according to the legend, he is particularly greedy.

But the bull does not always let himself be sacrificed patiently; he often flees in order not to be killed. We have seen in the Russian stories how the bull, which his owner intends to sacrifice, flees into the forest, with the lamb (the bull and the lamb are two equivalent forms of the morning and evening solar hero) and the other domestic animals. The proverb of Theokritos, "Even the bull goes into the forest,"[2] can have no other origin than in the two analogous myths of the moon which wanders through the forest of night, and of the sun who hides himself in the same forest, when he sees the pre-

[1] Plutarch, in the Life of Marcellus, Arrianos and Appianos among the Greeks, Livy, Cicero (De Divinatione), Pliny the elder, Julius Capitolinus, Julius Obsequens among the Latins.

[2] *Éba kai táuros an hülan,* xiv. 43. In Theokritos, the proverb is used to intimate that he is gone to other and perfidious loves; he, too, is a traitor.

parations made for the sacrifice; the sun in the night becomes the moon.

I have said that the bull, when sacrificed, often, on account of his being devoid of intestines, forebodes unlucky occurrences to the hero; the solar bull of the evening is without strength, he has no heroic entrails. But after he has been to pasture freely in the forest, after having exercised his powers in battle with the wolves of night, after having, by his bellowing (in the darkness, in the thundering cloud), filled all the animals with terror, the bull is found again and led towards his dwelling of the morning, full of light, like a sacrificed hero; heroic entrails are found in him; from the black bull who is sacrificed towards morning, from the forest, from the bull of night, come forth the heart, the liver, the life and strength, the sun, the hero-sun; and the human hero, observing his sacrifice, considers it a good omen. We can thus understand the narrative of Ammianus Marcellinus · "Decimus (taurus) diffractis vinculis, lapsus ægre reductus est, et mactatus ominosa signa monstravit."[1] Whilst he is hidden in the forest, the solar bull is black, but often (*i.e.*, in all the nights illumined by the moon), giving up his place to the moon, he appears in the form of a white bull or cow, who guides the hero lost in the darkness. Thoas is called the king of the Tauroi (or bulls) in the *Iphigenia in Tauris* of Euripides, because he has wings on his feet. The cow Iô flees without stopping in the *Prometheus* of

[1] *Rerum gestarum*, xxii.—Cfr. the episode of the ox which lets itself fall into the marsh or swamp, in the various versions of the first book of the *Paňćatantram.*—The astrologers placed the brain under the protection of the moon, and the heart under that of the sun; Celoria, *La Luna*, Milano, 1871.

Æschylos. Euripides[1] says that she gave birth to the king of the Kadmœans. Here, therefore, we find once more the intimate relation between Iô and Eurôpê, the sister of Kadmos, which I noticed above. Kadmos, the brother of Eurôpê, unites himself with Iô. But Iô is a cow, and we find a cow, a travelling cow, marked with a white spot in the shape of a full moon (the moon itself, or Iô), in the legend of Kadmos in Bœotia, according to Pausanias,[2] and to Ovid,[3] who sings—

> "Bos tibi, Phœbus ait, solis occurret in arvis,[4]
> Nullum passa jugum, curvique immunis aratri.
> Hac duce carpe vias, et, qua requieverit herba,
> Mœnia fac condas : Bœotia illa vocato.
> Vix bene Castalio Cadmus descenderat antro :
> Incustoditam lente videt ire juvencam,
> Nullum servitii signum cervice gerentem.
> Subsequitur, pressoque legit vestigia gressu ;
> Auctoremque viæ Phœbum taciturnus adorat.
> Jam vada Cephisi, Panopesque evaserat arva ;
> Bos stetit ; et, tollens spatiosam cornibus altis
> Ad cœlum frontem, mugitibus impulit auras.
> Atque ita, respiciens comites sua terga sequentes,
> Procubuit, teneraque latus submisit in herba."

This is the good fairy, or good old man, who shows the way to the heroes in popular tales ; it is the cow which succours the maiden persecuted by her step-mother, the puppet which spins, sews, and weaves for the maiden aurora. For just as we have seen that the wooden girl is the aurora herself, which at morn comes out of, and at

---

[1] Kadmeiôn Basilêas egeinato ; *Phoinissai*, 835.
[2] *Boiotia.*
[3] *Metam.*, iii. 10.—Cfr. Nonnos, *Dionys.*, iv. 290, and following.
[4] Or, on the path of the sun in the sky.

even re-enters, the forest of night,[1] as is clearly shown by the myths of Urvaçî and of Daphne, so in like manner the moon comes out of and re-enters the nocturnal forest, transforming herself from a tree to a cow, and from a cow to a tree, wooden girl, or puppet. Some myths relating to the aurora are also applicable to the moon, on account of the resemblance of the phenomena (the lunar and solar bulls also are interchangeable), as they both come out of the nocturnal gloom, both drop dewy humours, and both run after the sun, of which the aurora is the deliverer in the morning, and the moon the protectress, guide, hostess, and good advising fairy, who teaches him the secret by which to avoid the ambuscades of the monster. Hêraklês passes the sea upon the neck of the cow-moon ; but instead of the cow, we also find in the mythical sky of Hêraklês the golden cup, which is the same thing. From the cow-moon comes forth the horn of abundance ; from the cornucopia to the cup the passage is easy. It is said that Hêraklês, approaching the oxen of Geryon, the West, felt himself burned by the sun's rays, and shot arrows at him (in the same way as Indras in the *Ṛigvedas* breaks a wheel of the car of Sûryas, the sun). The sun admires the courage and strength of the hero, and lends him his golden cup, upon which Hêraklês passes the sea. This being accomplished, Hêraklês restores the cup to the sun, and finds the oxen.

The bull which carries the hero and heroine, in the Russian story, arises again in another form, if its essential part (now the intestines, now the bones, now the ashes)

[1] In an unpublished Piedmotese story, which is very widely spread, the girl carried off by robbers escapes from their hands, and hides in the trunk of a tree.

is preserved. The cow which helps the maiden becomes, as we have already seen, an apple-tree, and helps her again in this form. We find the same myth transformed in Greece. In *Cœlius,* quoted by Aldrovandi,[1] we read, "Cum rustici quidam Herculi Alexicaco bovem essent immolaturi, isque rupto fune profugisset (the bull destined to the sacrifice repairs to the forest of night), nec esset quod sacrificaretur, malum arreptum suppositis quatuor ramis crurum vice, deinde additis alteris duobus ceu cornuum loco, bovem utcumque fuisse imitatos, idque ridiculum simulacrum pro victima sacrificasse Herculi." This account is confirmed by the facts recorded by Julius Pollux,[2] that the apple-tree was sacrificed to Hêraklês. The moon, on account of its circular form, assumed, besides the figure of a pea, a pumpkin and a cabbage, also that of a golden apple. As it contains honey, the sweet apple represents well the ambrosial moon. Moreover, in the same way as we have seen the pea which fell on the ground become a tree, and rise to heaven, so the apple became an apple-tree, the tree of golden apples found in the Western garden of the Hesperides.

The moon, besides the form of a horned cow, also assumed, in the popular Âryan belief, that of a tart, of a cake, either on account of its circular shape, or of the ambrosial honey supposed to be contained by the moon, because of the dew or rain which it spreads on the ground. The cake has in Slavonic tradition the same importance as the pea, kidney-bean, or cabbage. The bull or cow of the fool, bartered for a pea, is perhaps the same as the sun or aurora of evening, bartered during the night for the moon, or else meeting the moon. The funereal pea

---

[1] *De Quadrupedibus Bisulcis,* i.

[2] *De Vocabulis,* i., quoted by Aldrovandi.

or kidney-bean, the vegetable which serves as provision for the journey in the kingdom of the dead, and which brings the hero riches, is perhaps only the moon, which the solar hero finds on the way during the night, and which he receives in exchange for his cow's hide. When the hero possesses this pea, he is assured of every kind of good fortune, and can enter or ascend into the luminous sky, as well as come out of the gloomy hell, into which the monster has drawn him. A similar virtue is attributed to the cake, which we find in Indo-European funeral customs instead of the vegetable of the dead.

After this we can understand what Plutarch tells us in the Life of Lucullus concerning the Cyziceni, of whom he writes, that, pressed by siege, they offered up to Proserpine (the moon in hell) a cow of black paste, not being able to offer up one of flesh; and he adds, that the sacrifice was agreeable to the goddess. Thus, in the thirty-sixth fable of Æsop, we read of an invalid who promises to the gods that he will sacrifice a hundred oxen to them in the event of a cure; when cured, as he does not possess a hundred oxen of flesh, he makes a hundred of paste, and burns them upon the hearth. But, according to Æsop, the gods were not satisfied, and endeavoured to play off a joke upon him; an attempt, which, however, did not succeed, inasmuch as the cunning man used it to his own profit; for the solar hero in the night, not being really a fool, merely feigns to be one.

But, to return to the cow-moon: we must complete the explanation of another myth, that of the excrement of the cow considered as purifying. The moon, as the aurora, yields ambrosia; it is considered to be a cow; the urine of this cow is ambrosia or holy water; he who drinks this water purifies himself, as the ambrosia which rains from the lunar ray and the aurora cleans the paths of the sky, purifies and makes clear (*dîrghaya ćakshase*) the paths of the sky which the shadows of night darken and contaminate. The same virtue is attributed, moreover, to cow's dung, a conception also derived from the cow, and given to the moon as well as to the morning aurora. These two cows are conceived as making the earth fruitful by means of their ambrosial excrements; these excrements, being also luminous, both those of the moon and those of the aurora are considered as purifiers. The ashes of these cows (which their friend the heroine preserves) are not only ashes, but golden powder or golden flour (the golden cake occurs again in that flour or powder of gold which the witch demands from the hero in Russian stories), which, mixed with excrement, brings good fortune to the cunning and robber hero. The ashes of the sacrificed pregnant cow (*i.e.*, the cow which dies after having given birth to a calf) were religiously preserved by the Romans in the temple of Vesta, with bean-stalks (which are used to fatten the earth sown with corn), as a means of expiation. Ovid[1] mentions this rite:—

> "Nox abiit, oriturque Aurora. Palilia poscor,
> Non poscor frustra, si favet alma Pales.
> Alma Pales, faveas pastoria sacra canenti;
> Prosequor officio si tua festa pio.
> Certe ego de vitulo cinerem, stipulasque fabales,
> Sæpe tuli plena februa casta, manu."

The ashes of a cow are preserved both as a symbol of resurrection and as a means of purification. As to the excrements of the cow, they are still used to form the

[1] *Fasti*, iv. 721.

so-called *eau de millefleurs*, recommended by several pharmacopœias as a remedy for cachexy.[1]

I have noticed above the myth of Hêraklês, in which, having passed the sea upon the golden cup, he finds the oxen upon the shore. These oxen are thus described by Theokritos, in the myth of King Augeias, as the child of the sun. The sun, says Theokritos, granted to his son the honour of being richer than all other men in herds. All these herds are healthy, and multiply without limit, always becoming better. Among the bulls, three hundred have white legs (like the alba of morning), two hundred are red (like the sun's rays), with curved horns. These bulls are to be used for purposes of reproduction; besides them there are twelve sacred to the sun, which shine like swans. One of them is superior to all the rest in size, and is called a star, or Phaethôn (the luminous, an epithet given to Hêlios, the sun, in the *Odyssey*, the guider of the chariot of the sun, who, after finishing his diurnal course, is unable to rein in the horses, and is precipitated with the chariot into the water, in order that the burning horses may not set fire to the world. Instead of solar oxen, which draw the chariot, and fall, at evening, into the nocturnal marsh, we find in this myth the chariot drawn by horses overturned into the waves; but the Phaethôn, the very luminous and excellent ox, as represented by Theokritos, justifies our identification of the two mythical episodes of the ox and of the horse which falls into the water). The bull Phaethôn of Theokritos sees Hêraklês, and, taking him for a lion, rushes upon him and endeavours to wound him with his horns. The sun, as a golden-haired hero, is a very strong

[1] Cfr. Ott. Targioni Tozzetti, *Lezioni di Materia Medica*, Firenze, 1821.

lion (Hêraklês, Samson); as a golden-horned hero, he is a very strong bull; enclosed in the cloud, they roar and bellow. The two images of the sun-lion and of the sun-bull are now in harmony and now in discordance, and fight with one another. In the *Râmâyaṇam* we found the two brother-heroes Râmas and Lakshmaṇas, an epic form of the two Açvinâu, represented respectively as a bull and a lion. In the Hellenic fables we frequently find the lion and the bull together, and afterwards in discordance, as happens in the legend of the two brother-heroes. In Æsop and in Avianus, the bull (perhaps the moon) fleeing from the lion (*i.e.*, from the sun in its monstrous evening or autumnal form of a lion), enters the hiding-place of the goat (the moon in the grotto of night), and is insulted and provoked by it. In another Æsopian fable, on the contrary, it is the lion who fears the horns of the bull, and induces him to part with them, in order that the bull may become his prey.[1] In yet another Æsopian fable taken from Syntipa, the bull kills the lion, while asleep, with his horns. In Phædrus, the wild boar with his tusks, the bull with his horns, and the ass with kicks, put an end to the old and infirm lion. In Phædrus's fable of the ox and the ass drawing together, the ox falls inert upon the ground when he loses his horns. Aristoteles, in the third book on the Parts of Animals, censures the Momos of Æsop, who laughs at the bull because he has his horns on his forehead instead of on his arms, showing that if the bull had his horns on

[1] In an Æsopian fable taken from Syntipa, which corresponds to the first of Lokman, two bulls combine against the lion, and resist him; the lion excites them against each other, and tears them to pieces. In the sixth fable of Aphtonios, the bulls are three; in the eighteenth of Avianus, they are four. The lion already knew the motto of kings: "Divide et impera."

any other part of his body, they would be a useless weight, and would impede his other functions without aiding him in anything. The ox and the lion were also painted together in Christian churches.[1]

To continue the legend of the solar hero and the oxen, we find again in Hêraklês, as employed among the herds in the service of King Augeias, the sun, the usual hostler-hero; he is not only to guard the herds well, but in one day to cleanse them thoroughly, and make them shine. Defrauded of the price by Augeias, he kills him, and ravages all his country. In the same way, in Homer, Apollo guards, for a stipulated price, the herds of King Laomedon upon Mount Ida, and is cheated of his reward. In the same way, Hermes takes the herds of King Admetos to pasture; he leads them to browse near the herds of Apollo, from whom he steals a hundred bulls and twelve cows, preventing the dogs from barking (as Hêraklês does when he leads away Geryon's oxen). This Hermes, this god Mercury, god of merchants, this merchant and robber, is the same as the skilful and cunning thief of the stories who carries off horses, draught oxen, caskets, and ear-rings from the king; he is the hero-thief; but a shade distinguishes him from the monster brigand or Vedic demoniacal Paṇis; the hero who hides himself and the monster that hides things both do a furtive action. When Hermes leads away the herds stolen from the solar god, the sun, he also takes care to fasten branches of trees to their tails, which, by sweeping the road, shall destroy the track of the bulls and cows that have been led away. The shepherd Battos plays the spy, although, as the price of his silence, Hermes has promised him a white cow (the moon, and perhaps

[1] Durandus, *Rational.* i. 3, quoted by Du Cange.

Battos himself, the spy, is the moon). Hermes tests him, by disguising himself and promising him a bull and a cow if he speaks. Battos speaks, and Hermes punishes him by transforming him into a stone :—

"Vertit
In durum silicem, qui nunc quoque dicitur index."[1]

This god Mercury, who steals the bulls from Apollo (as Hêraklês leads away the oxen of Geryon), is the divine form of the thief. His demoniacal form, is—Cacus, the son of Vulcan (as the Vedic Vṛitras is the son of Tvashṭar), who vomits fire; a giant who envelops himself in darkness, in Virgil; three-headed (like the Vedic monster), in Propertius;[2] who inhabits in the Aventine forest a cavern full of human bones (like the monster of fairy tales); who thunders (flammas ore sonante vomit), who fights with rocks and trunks of trees, in Ovid[3] (like the heroes in the Hindoo, Slavonic, German, and Homeric tradition); who steals the cows from Hêraklês, and hides their footprints by dragging them backwards into the cavern, in Livy; who also tells us that the cows in the cavern low, wishing for the bulls from whom they are separated (as in the Vedic hymns). The hero, hearing them, finds the cavern, overturns with a great noise the rock which five pair of oxen yoked together could scarcely have moved (like the Marutas who break the rock, like Indras who splits the crag open), and with the three-knotted club (trinodis) kills the monster and frees the cows. The solar hero who at evening leads away oxen or cows, or who at morning steals them from the stable, is a skilful robber who has acted meritoriously,

---

[1] Ovidius, *Metam.*, ii. 706.

[2] Per tria partitos qui dabat ora sonos; *Ecl.* iv.

[3] *Fasti*, i. 550.

and marries, in reward, the princess aurora; the cloudy or gloomy monster who steals the solar cows to shut them up in the cavern, whence he then throws out smoke and flames, is an infamous criminal. The divine thief steals almost out of playfulness, either to show his craftiness or to prove his valour; the demoniacal thief steals because of his malevolent character, and instinct to devour what he steals, as does the fabled worm of the river Indus (the Vedic Sindhus, or heavenly ocean), who draws into the abyss and devours the thirsty oxen who go to drink.[1]

The monster of the clouds who whistles and thunders only terrifies; the god who whistles and thunders in the cloud, on the other hand, is *par excellence* a celestial musician; his musical instrument, the thunder, astonishes us by its marvels,[2] and makes stones and plants tremble, that is, makes stones and plants move, especially celestial ones (*i.e.*, cloud-mountains and cloud-trees); it draws after it the wild animals (of the heavenly forest), tames and subdues them. The bellowing bull terrifies the lion himself. We, therefore, also read in Nonnos,[3] that Dionysos gives a bull in reward to Æagros, who has won in the competition of song and of the lyre, whilst he reserves a hirsute he-goat for him who loses; on this account we find on the capitals of columns in old Milanese churches, calves and bulls represented as playing on the lyre.[4] It is a variation of the myth of the ass and the lyre, which has the same meaning. The bull and the ass, for the same reason, are found represented together, because they bellow and bray (like Christian

[1] Philê, *Stichoi peri zôôn idiotêtos*, lix.

[2] In Italian, *attonito* (or, properly speaking, struck by thunder) is the same as "who is much surprised").

[3] *Dionys.* xix. 58.

[4] Cfr. Martigny, *Dictionnaire des Antiquités Chrétiennes*, s. v. *veau.*

Corybantes) near the cradle of the new-born god, in order to hide, by their noise, his birth from the old king or deity who is to be dethroned.[1] The conch of Bhîmas, the elephant-horn of Orlando, the Greek war-bugle tauraia, by means of which armies were moved, derived their character and their name from the mythical bull, the thundering god. The voice of the bull is compared in Euripides to the voice of Zeus;[2] the music which pleases the heroes is certainly not the air of the *Casta diva;* it is the braying of the ass,[3] the roar of the lion, the bellowing of the bull, who occupies the first place in the heavens, and has occupied us so long, because the supreme god took his form, after having carried off Eurôpê. Zeus left on the earth his divine form, and the more generally preferred heroic form of a bull took him up to heaven :—

> "Litoribus tactis stabat sine cornibus ullis
> Juppiter, inque deum de bove versus erat.
> Taurus init cœlum."[4]

We thus, after a long pilgrimage in the fields of tradition, return to the Vedic bull Indras, from whom we started, and to his female form, which, having a human nature, became a cow, and being a cow, assumed a divine shape :—

> "Quæ bos ex homine, ex bove facta Dea."[5]

---

1 In *Phœdrus*, as we have already observed, the ox and the ass are yoked together.

2 *Ippolitos, Ôs fonê Diòs*, 1200–1229.

3 Cfr. the chapter relating to the Ass.

4 Ovidius, *Fasti*, v. 615.

5 *Ib.* v. 620.

CHAPTER II.

THE HORSE.

SUMMARY.

The horse, favourite animal of the solar hero.—Attributes of the Vedic solar hero.—Animals which draw the Vedic gods.—The Açvinâu sons of a mare.—The mule, the ass, and the horse in relation to each other.—The hero's horse, prior to being noble and handsome, is vile and ill-favoured; proofs.—The teeth of the horse.—The figs that make tails grow.—The excrement of the horse.—Three colours of the heroic horse.—Pluto's horses abhor the light.—Pêgasos an imperfect horse.—The black horse generally demoniacal.—The hippomanes.—The monster that makes horses perspire and grow lean; the fire in stables.—To dream of black horses.—The horse of the third brother is small, humpbacked, and lame.—The hero transforms himself into a horse.—The grey horse differs from the black one.—The red horse frees the hero.—The three steps, the three races, the three leaps, the three castles, the three days, the three brothers, and the three horses correspond to each other.—Two horsemen change the hero's bad horse into a heroic steed.—The horse's ears; the hero in the horse's ears.—The horse's head blesses the good maiden, and devours the wicked one.—The black horseman, the white horseman, and the red one.—The horse-monster that devastates the field surprised by the hero, and destroyed by fire, in the *Ṛigvedas*.—The Dioscuri washing the sweat off their horses.—Salt on the horse's back.—The hero-horse covered by the waters.—The Açvinâu and Agnis give a good horse to the hero who has a bad one.—The three steps of Vishṇus are made by the horses of Indras.—Vishṇus as horse.—Indras and the Açvinâu find the bride on horseback.—Râmas as horse.—Dadhyańć and his ambrosial horse's head, which discomfits the hostile monsters.—The bones of the horse.—The exchange of heads.—The two brother horses Pêgasos and Chrüsaor in opposition to one another.—Castor and Pollux.—Discussion upon the nature of the Açvinâu.—The two brothers at discord; Sundas and Upasundas.—Nakulas and Vasudevas.—Râmas and Lakshmaṇas.—The brothers who resemble each other; Bâlin and Sugrîvas; the brother betrays his brother and steals his wife.—Kereçâçpa and Urvâksha.—Piran and Pilsem.—The sky a mountain of stone; heroes, heroines, and horses of stone.—The brother seducer in the *Tuti Name.*—Sunlight and moonlight, two brothers.—The minister's son and the king's son.—Horse and cat.—The two brothers on a journey; one becomes a king, the other spits gold; the candle of one of the two brothers lights of its own accord, and he therefore obtains the kingdom; the other brother's treasure.—Digression concerning the interpretation of the myth.—Agamêdês and Trophonios; Piedmontese story of the skilful thief.—The two brothers who resemble each other; mistaken one for the other by the wife of one of them; the brother sleeps with his sister-in-law without touching her; the legend of the pilgrim who comes from Rome; the head fastened on again.—The horse led away out of hell.—The solar horse destined for sacrifice carried off by Kapilas; that is, the solar horse escapes, like the solar bull, from the sacrifice.—The stallion destined for the sacrifice touched, and the horse's fat smelted by Kâuçalyâ as an augury of fruitfulness.—The horse's head as the mouth of hell.—The robber of the horse and of the treasure.—The horns of the stag, the horns or mane of the horse, and the hair of the hero, which catch and fasten themselves to the trees of the forest.—The thief now protects thieves, and now protects men from thieves.—The Miles gloriosus; hero, horse, and tree, united together, discomfit the enemies.—The heroic horse.—The tail of Indras's horse, and the Hindoo war-horse.—The war-horses of Rustem, of Alexander, of Bellerophon, and of Cæsar; the winged horse.—The horse goes through water and fire.—The horse and the apple.—The chains of the heroic horse, and the difficulty of riding him.—The horse that speaks; the horse-spy.—The chariot that speaks.—The solar horse bound that it may not come back again.—The hero who flees in the shape of a horse, and the horse sold with the bridle; transformations of the horse.—The sun without a horse and without a bridle.—The horses of the sun, arrested or wounded, precipitate the solar hero into the waters.—The eternal hunter.—Etaças, Phaethôn, Hippolytos.—The horse that delivers the hero.—The neighing of Indras's horse; the horse of Darius which neighs at the sight of the sun on account of the smell of a mare.—Number of the solar horses.—The hero born of a mare.—The mare's egg.—The hare born of a mare devours the mare.—Spanish mares made pregnant by the wind.—Horses sons of the wind.—The hero Açvatthâman neighs immediately after birth.—The horses that weep; mythical signification of these tears.—Vedic riddle and play of words upon the letter *r*, and the root *varsh* relative to the horse.—The foam from the horse's mouth destroys enemies and cures the cough.—The Açvinâu, the Dioscuri, Asklêpios and his two sons as physicians.—Caballus.—Ambrosia from the hoof of the Vedic horse.—Hippokrênê; the horse's hoof in relation with water.—Exchanges between moon and sun and between bull and horse.—Horses sacred to the gods and to saints.—Holy horsemen who help the heroes *mercede pacta.*

THE myth of the horse is perhaps not so rich in legends as that of the bull and the cow, but certainly no less interesting. As the horseman is the finest type of the hero, so the horse which carries him is in mythology the noblest of animals.

We have already observed that the best of the three brothers, the third, the victorious one, the morning sun, is, in tradition, distinguished from the other brothers by his swiftness; and that the morning dawn or aurora, which is the third sister, the good one, the best of the three sisters, is she who wins the race. It is, therefore, natural that the favourite animal of the hero should be his horse. The two Hindoo Dioscuri, that is, the Açvinâu, the two horsemen, derive their name from the açvas or horse, as being the swift one;[1] and they are very probably identical with the two fair-haired, amiable, splendid, and ardent coursers of Indras, of Savitar (the sun), and proper and worthy to bear heroes,[2] who yoke them-

[1] The word *atyas* has the same meaning.

[2] Yuṅgantv asya kâmyâ harî vipakshasâ rathe çonâ dhṛishṇû nṛivâhasâ; *Ṛigv.* i. 6, 2.

selves at a word,[1] are maned, adapted to make fruitful, full of life,[2] having eyes like the sun,[3] made by the Ṛibhavas,[4] who, as they made the cow out of a cow, also made a horse out of the horse,[5] black, with white feet, drawing the chariot with the golden yoke, revealing the beings;[6] the two rapid ones; the two most rapid ones;[7] plunging into the inebriating drink before Indras yokes them;[8] beautiful, by means of which the chariot of the Açvinâu is as swift as thought;[9] who carry Indras, as every day they carry the sun;[10] are the two rays of the sun;[11] who neigh, dropping ambrosia;[12] the very pure horses of the bull Indras, inebriated, who illumine the sky,[13] with manes the colour of a peacock,[14] bridled sixty times (properly six times twice five);[15] beneficent, winged, indefatigable, resolute destroyers (of the enemies).[16] The *Âitareya Brâhmanam*, when giving the characteristics of the race of each god, whilst it tells us that Agnis, at the

[1] Vaćoyuǵâu; *Ṛigv.* i. 7, 2.

[2] Yukshvâ hi keçinâ harî vṛishaṇâ kakshyaprâ; *Ṛigv.* i. 10, 3.

[3] Sûraćakshasaḥ; *Ṛigv.* i. 16, 1.

[4] Indrâya vaćoyuǵâ tatakshur manasâ harî; *Ṛigv.* i. 20, 2.

[5] Saudhanvanâ açvâd açvam atakshata; *Ṛigv.* i. 161, 7.

[6] Vi ǵanâń ćhyâvaḥ çitipâdo akhyan ratham̆ hiraṇyaprâugam̆ vahantaḥ; *Ṛigv.* i. 33, 5.

[7] Indro vañkû vañkutarâdhi tishṭhati; *Ṛigv.* i. 5, 11.

[8] Yukshvâ madaćyutâ harî; *Ṛigv.* i. 81, 3.

[9] Vâm açvinâ manaso ǵaviyân rathaḥ svaçvaḥ; *Ṛigv.* i. 117, 2.

[10] Â tvâ yaćhantu harito na sûryam ahâ viçveva sûryam; *Ṛigv.* i. 130, 2.

[11] Harî sûryasya ketû; *Ṛigv.* ii. 11, 6.

[12] Ghṛitaçćutam̆ svâram asvârshṭâm; *Ṛigv.* ii. 11, 7.

[13] Pra ye dvitâ diva ṛińǵanty âtâḥ susam̆mṛishṭâso vṛishabhasya mûraḥ; *Ṛigv.* iii. 43, 6.

[14] Indra haribhir yâhi mayûraromabhiḥ; *Ṛigv.* iii. 45. 1.

[15] Shoḷhâ yuktâh pańća-pańćâ vahanti; *Ṛigv.* iii. 55, 18.

[16] Patatribhir açramâir avyatibhir dam̆sanâbhiḥ; *Ṛigv.* vii. 69, 7. The Açvinâu also are called dravatpânî (swift-hoofed); *Ṛigv.* i. 3, 1.

marriage of Somas and Sûryâ, is drawn by mules, and the aurora by red cows (or bulls), teaches us that Indras is drawn by horses, and the Açvinâu by asses; the Açvinâu carried off the prize.[1] In the *Mahâbhâratam*,[2] we find another important circumstance, *i.e.*, the Açvinâu represented as sons of a mare, or of Tvashtrî, wife of the sun Savitar, who took the form of a mare. Therefore we have here the sons of the mare, who may be horses or mules, according as the mare united herself with a horse or with an ass. Here, then, we have already an evident proof of the identification of the heroes Açvinâu with the animals, horses or asses, which draw them. The *Ṛigvedas* does not as yet know the word *açvatara*, or mule, but in representing the Açvinâu drawn now by horses and now by asses, it shows us the intermediate character of the real animal that draws the Açvinâu, a grey beast, dark-coloured, and white only in its fore parts. Night is the mule that carries the Açvinâu or twilights, in the same way as, in the above-quoted *Âitareya*, it carries or awakens Agnis, fire or light. In the *Iliad*,[3] mules are sung of as being better adapted than oxen to draw the plough.

The hero's horse, like the hero himself, begins by being ugly, deformed, and inept, and ends by becoming beautiful, luminous, heroic, and victorious.

---

[1] Açvatarî—rathenâgnir âǵimadhâvattâsâṁ prâgamâno yonimakû-layattásmâttâ na vigâyaṅte. Gobhirarunâirushâ âǵimadhâvattasmâ-dushasyagatâyâmaruṇamivaeva prabhâtyushasorûpamaçvarathenendra âǵimadhâvattasmâtsa uććâirghosha upabdimânkshatrasya rûpamâindro hi sa gadarbharathenâçvinâ udaǵayatâmaçvinâvâçnuvâtâm; *Ait. Br.* iv. 2, 9.

[2] Tvâshtrî tu savitur bhâryâ vadavârupadhâriṇî asûyata mahâbhâgâ sâ 'ntarîkshe 'çvinâvubhâu; *Mbh.* i. 2599.

[3] *Il.* x. 352.

The mythical horse of the Hungarians, the horse Tátos, or Tátos lo, when born, is of an ugly aspect, defective and lean; it is therefore said in Hungarian, that "the Tátos comes out of a defective horse." It is, however, always born with teeth,[1] although its chin is sometimes wanting; its bursts out of a black pentagonal egg on an Ash Wednesday, after the hero has carried it for seven summers and seven winters under his arm. In the *Mahâbhâratam*,[2] the first created horse Uććâiḥçravas, the king of the horses (and therefore the horse of Indras), which is as swift as thought, follows the path of the sun, and is luminous and white, has, however, a black tail, made so by the magic of the serpents, who have covered it with black hairs. This is probably the black ass's or horse's tail which remains upon the ugly or wicked sister's forehead, in the popular European story of the two sisters.[3] It must also be remarked that, as the word

---

[1] In the Monferrato, according to the information kindly given me, concerning the beliefs relative to animals current in this country, by Dr Giuseppe Ferraro, the young collector of the popular songs and stories of the Monferrato, it is believed that the horse's teeth hung upon the necks of infants at the breast cause them to cut their teeth, and that the two incisors of the horse, when worn, are a spell to charm away every evil.

[2] *Mbh.* i. 1093–1237.

[3] Cfr. the first of the Tuscan stories of *Santo Stefano di Calcinaia.*—In the preceding chapter, we have seen how the apples of a certain apple-tree cause horns to grow on whoever eats them. In an unpublished Italian story, instead of the apple-tree, we have the fig-tree, and instead of horns, the tail. It is narrated by an old man of Osimo, in the Marches:—Three poor brothers, having but little inclination for work, go in search of fortune round the world. Overtaken in the country by night, they fall asleep in the open air. A fairy, under the aspect of a hideous old woman, comes up and wakens them, offering herself as their wife. The three brothers excuse themselves, and declare that they wish for nothing except a little money with which to make merry. The fairy answers, "Tell me what you

Uććâiḥçravas means, properly, him of the high ears, it indicates the ass better than the horse.

---

wish for, and you shall have it." The first asks for a purse, which shall always be full of money; the second for a whistle, by blowing into which a whole army of brave combatants would be summoned to his side; the third a mantle, which would make its wearer invisible. The fairy satisfies them, and then disappears in flames, like the devil. The eldest brother, Stephen, goes with his purse into Portugal, where he plays and loses, but still remains rich. This comes to the queen-dowager's ears, who wishes to see the stranger, hoping to possess herself of his secret; she feigns to love him, and the wedding-day is fixed; but before it comes she has already gained his confidence, and taking the purse from him, she orders him to be flogged. Stephen returns to his brothers, relates his grievance, and proposing to revenge himself upon the queen, induces them to lend him the whistle, which calls armies into existence. The queen softens towards him, protesting that she expected to the last that he would have appeared on the day appointed for the wedding, and that he had been flogged without her knowledge. Stephen gives way, and the whistle passes out of his hands into those of the queen. He is flogged again, but twice as severely as before. Again he has recourse to his brothers; he implores, supplicates, and promises to get everything back by the miraculous mantle; but having obtained it, he allows himself to be deceived once more by the queen. Deprived of everything, he wanders about in despair, reduced to beggary. In the middle of January, he sees a tree covered with beautiful figs; desirous of them, he eats with avidity; but for every fig that he swallows, a span of tail as thick as a boa grows on to him. He goes on his way, still more desperate, till he finds more figs, of a smaller size; he eats them, and the tail disappears. Contented with this discovery, he fills a basket with the first figs, and disguised as a countryman, comes to the palace of the Queen of Portugal. Every one marvels on seeing such fine figs in January. The queen buys the basket, and every one eats; but tails immediately grow on their backs. Stephen then dresses himself as a doctor, and with the little figs, cures many persons. The queen has him called; he obliges her to confess to him first, and in the confession makes her say where the three marvellous gifts of the fairy are kept. Having recovered them, he leaves the queen with ten spans of tail, and returns rich and happy to his brothers. In this story there must be some parts wanting; it is probable that the fairy warned the brothers not

In the same way, therefore, as the hero of popular tales before becoming a wise man is generally an ass, the animal ridden by the solar hero, prior to being a real and noble horse, is usually a worthless jade, or a dark-coloured ass. The sun, in the beginning of the night, rides a black horse, and afterwards a grey one, or else an ass or a mule, but in the morning, on the contrary, a white and luminous horse, which has a black tail; or else the dark horse of night has a white head, or white legs, or anterior parts of the body, with golden ears, and the nape of the neck formed of pearls.[1] The monstrous Trojan horse, too, of Epeios, a figure which represents the horse of mythology, in Tryphiodôros the Egyptian,[2] has a golden mane, red eyes, and silver teeth.

In the Turkish stories of Siberia,[3] it is upon an iron-coloured horse that the third brother, hated by his father and his two elder brothers, advances against the demon Ker Iutpa. The hero becomes the excrement of a horse, and the horse a crow; the former glues the monster's lower lip to the earth, the latter suspends his upper lip to the sky. In order better to understand this strange myth, we must remember that the name of one of the Valkiries is "Mist," a word which means excrement and fog. The fog, or frost, or rain, or dew, falls to the ground;

to discover their secret to any one. The last enterprise, moreover, is more likely to have been undertaken by the third brother, who always assumes in fairy tales the part of the cunning one, than by the first-born, who in this story represents the part of the fool.—Polydorus speaks of the horse's tail as a chastisement for an insult to Thomas Archbishop of Canterbury, in the thirteenth book of his *Hist. Angl.*:—"Irridentes Archiepiscopum, caudam equi cui insidebat, amputarunt. At postea nutu Dei ita accidit, ut omnes ex eo hominum genere qui id facinus fecissent, nati sunt instar brutorum caudati."

[1] Hiraṇyakarṇam maṇigrîvam arṇas; *Ṛigv.* i. 122, 14.

[2] *Ilíou Halôsis*, 65–72.

[3] In the before-quoted collection of Radloff, *Täktäbäi Märgän.*

the solar horse, or the sun, rises in the sky; the monster of night or of clouds is dispersed.

In the thirteenth Esthonian story of *Kreutzwald*, the third brother comes three times to deliver the princess from the mountain of glass (or ice), where she sleeps. The first time he is dressed the colour of bronze, upon a bronze-coloured horse; the second time dressed in silver, upon a horse the colour of silver; and the third time upon a gold-coloured horse, dressed in gold.

In an unpublished Piedmontese story, the young prince, whose beloved princess has been ravished beyond seas, is borne over the waves by an eagle, which he feeds with his own flesh. Arrived beyond the sea, he hears that the princess is destined to be the wife of the hero who wins the race three times; the first time he appears dressed in black, upon a black horse; the second time dressed in white, upon a white horse; and the third time dressed in red, upon a red horse. Each time he wins the race, and thereafter receives the beautiful princess in marriage.

Thus we see the first horse of the hero is always dark-coloured, like the devil's horse, like the horses of Pluto, which, accustomed to darkness, are terrified by light;[1] it then becomes the grey horse of the giantess, the grey horse which smells the dead hero Sigurd in the *Edda*. Pêgasos himself, the *hieros hippos* of Aratos, is born semi-perfect (êmitelês),[2] an expression which reminds me of the *equus dimidius* of an Alsatian paper of 1336, in Du Cange, by which the mule is meant. The Hindoo

[1] Longa solitos caligine pasci
Terruit orbis equos; pressis hæsere lupatis
Attoniti meliore polo; rursusque verendum
In chaos obliquo pugnant temone reverti.
Claudianus, *De Raptu Proserpinæ*, ii. 193.

[2] *Phainomena*, 215.

Aruṇas, charioteer of the sun (or even the brother of the sun himself, inasmuch as he is the brother of Garuḍas, the solar bird), is said to be born with an imperfect body;[1] he can be luminous and divine only in part. The black horse, on the contrary, has generally an evil and demoniacal nature; the black horse corresponds to the black devil; the colour black itself is, according to popular superstition, the product of bad humours.[2] Every horse, when born, has, according to Maestro Agostino, a piece of black flesh upon its lips, called hippomanes by the Greeks: "La quale carne dici lo vulgo essere molto sospettosa a li maleficii." Maestro Agostino adds, moreover, that the mother refuses to give suck to the colt as long as it carries this piece of flesh upon its lips, and some say that the mother herself eats it. In an idyll of Theokritos, we read that the Hippomanes is born among the Arcadians, and maddens colts and swift mares.[3] In the first chapter we mentioned the Russian *damavoi*, the demon who, during the night, rides upon cows, oxen, and horses, and makes them perspire. This superstition was already combated in Italy in the sixteenth century by Maestro Agostino;[4] and to it can probably be traced the

---

[1] *Mbh.* i. 1470, 1471.

[2] Quelli cavalli che sono de pilo morello se fanno de humore colerico impero che e più caldo humore et sicco che non e lo sangue et per questo produce ad nigredine el pelo. *I tre Libri della Natura Dei Cavalli et del Modo di medicar le Loro Infermità*, composti da Maestro Agostino Columbre; *Prologo.* 6, Vinegia, 1547.

[3] Hippomanes phüton esti par Arkasi tôi d'epi pasai
Kai pôloi mainontai an ôrea, kai thoai hippoi; ii. 48.

[4] Devennosi corrigere et emendare quelli li quali se posseno dire heretici, impero che voleno dire che quelle tal bestie che portano li crini advolte et atrezate; et con loro poco cognoscimento dicono che sono le streghe che li cavalcano et chiamanli cavalli stregari;" *Prologo.* 10, the work quoted before.—Cfr. on the Damavoi, Ralston, *The Songs of the Russian People*, p. 120, 139.

custom, still observed by many grooms, of leaving a lamp lighted in the stable during the night. The devil, as is well known, is afraid of the light (Agnis is called rakshohan, or monster-killer), and his black horse likewise. It is therefore a sinister omen, according to two verses in *Suidas*,[1] to dream of black horses, whilst, on the contrary, it is a good omen to dream of white ones. In the Norman legend of the priest Walchelm, a black horse presents itself to him in the first days of January of the year 1091, and tempts him to mount upon its back; scarcely has Walchelm done so, than the black horse sets off for hell.[2] The dead, too, according to the popular belief, often ride upon black or demoniacal horses.[3]

A well-known Russian story in verse, the *Kaniok Garbunok*, or *Little Hump-backed Horse*, of Jershoff, commences thus:—An old man has three sons, the youngest of which is the usual Ivan Durák, or Ivan the fool. The old man finds his corn-field devastated every morning; he wishes to find out who the devastator is, and sends his first-born son to watch the first night. The first-born has drunk too much, and falls asleep, and so does the second son, and from the same cause, on the second night. On the third night it is Ivan's turn to

---

[1] Hippous melaínas ou kalon pantôs blepein
Hippôn de leukôn opsis, aggelôn phasis.

In Tuscany, flying horses, when seen in dreams, announce news; no doubt, this flying horse seen in dreams can only refer to the nocturnal voyage of the solar horse.

[2] Cfr. Menzel, *Die Vorchristliche Unsterblichkeits-Lehre*, Leipzig, 1870.

[3] The Hungarians call the bier of the dead St Michael's horse; Neo-Greek popular songs represent the ferryman of the dead, Charon, on horseback; in Switzerland, the sight of a horse is a harbinger of approaching death for a person seriously ill.—Cfr. Rochholtz, *Deutscher Glaube und Brauch*, i. 163, 164.

watch; he does not fall asleep. At midnight he sees a mare which breathes flames coming. Ivan ties her by a rope, leaps upon her, seizes her by the mane, torments and subdues her, until the mare, to be let free, promises to give Ivan one of her young ones, and carries him to the stable where her three young ones are. She gives Ivan a little hump-backed horse with long ears (the Hindoo Uććâiḥsravas), that flies. By means of this little hump-backed horse, Ivan will make his fortune; when he leads it away, the mare and the two other colts follow it. Ivan's two brothers steal the mare and two colts, and go to sell them to the Sultan. Ivan rejoins them, and the three brothers stay in the Sultan's service as grooms; sometime afterwards, Ivan saves himself from drowning by means of his horse.

In the third of *Erlenwein's* Russian stories, a stallion is born to the Tzar's mare, that had drunk the water in which a certain fish (a pike, in the nineteenth story) had been washed, at the same time as the Tzar's daughter and her maid give birth to two heroes, Ivan Tzarević and Ivan Diević—*i.e.*, John of the Tzar and John of the girl, a form representing the Açvinâu. Ivan Tzarević rides upon the stallion. In the nineteenth story, the son of the mare is called Demetrius of the Tzar (Dmitri Tzarević); hero and horse being identified. In the fifth story of *Erlenwein*, a Cossack goes into the forest, where he is betrayed into the enemy's hands, who gives orders that he be cut in pieces, put into a sack, and attached to his horse. The horse starts, and carries him to the house of silver and gold, where he is resuscitated. During the following night, an old man and woman, whose guest the Cossack is, drag him, in order to waken him, by the cross which hangs on his neck, and he is thus transformed into a horse of gold and silver. Towards evening, the horse, by the

Tzar's order, is killed, and (like the bull and the cow) becomes an apple-tree of silver and gold. The apple-tree is cut down, and becomes a golden duck. The golden duck is the same as the golden horse, or as the hero resuscitated, *i.e.*, the morning sun. The sack and the horse which carry the hero cut in pieces represent the voyage of the sun in the gloom of night, or the voyage of the grey horse, the imperfect horse, the bastard mule, or the ass.

In the Russian tales, moreover, a distinction is made between the grey and the black horse; the grey horse helps the hero in the night very effectively, and the black one, on the contrary, is the herald of death. When, in the ninth story of *Erlenwein*, the horse of Ivan the merchant's son goes to search for the horses of the princess from beyond the sea, Ivan waits for him upon the shore. If he see grey horses come forth, it is to be a sign that his own steed is alive; but if, on the other hand, black horses appear, he is to conclude that his own horse is dead. Grey is the colour of sadness, black is the colour of death.

In *Afanassieff*, we find new interesting data. Ivan the fool watches during the night to surprise the horse which devastates his father's crops, and succeeds in binding it with rods from a linden-tree, after it has smelt the odour of tobacco. Then, by the help of the sister of the hero Nikanore, it acquires the faculty, when running after cows and horses, of turning their tails into gold, as well as their horns or manes, and their flanks into stars. What better image could there be of the starry sky of night, the golden tail of which is the red evening, and the front parts, also of gold, the morning aurora?[1]

In another story,[2] we have Ivan the son of the bitch

[1] *Afanassieff*, v. 37.

[2] *Ib.* v. 54.

occupying the place and playing the part of Ivan the son of the mare. Ivan of the bitch, after having delivered the three princesses from the deep cistern, is himself thrown into it. The black horse comes to deliver him, and cannot; the grey horse comes, and cannot either; the red horse comes, and succeeds in dragging the hero out. The black horse represents the dark night, the grey horse the night beginning to clear, and the red horse the roseate morning, which delivers the sun or solar hero.

The third brother Ivan, mounted on a marvellous horse, comes first to the bronze castle, then to the silver one, and lastly to that of gold.[1] This is a variety of the same myth, and represents similarly the solar voyage from evening to morning. The next mythical legend, however, probably alludes rather to the three days of the winter solstice, which the sun takes to return. The hero, Theodore, finds a horse that has been just brought forth, which the wolves have driven towards him; he makes it pasture upon the dew for three dawns (like the Hungarian Tátos, who feeds upon the golden oats in a silver field, that is to say, who, during the silvery night, or else during the white dawn, or the snowy winter, absorbs the dewy humours of the spring, or the morning aurora). The first day, the young horse becomes as high as half a tree; the second, higher than the tree; the third day it is as high as the heavens, and bears the hero Theodore and his wife Anastasia on its back.

Ivan Durák watches three nights at his father's tomb.[2] His father tells him that if at any time of need he calls with a hero's whistle, a wonderful grey horse will appear to help him, whose eyes shoot flames, and from whose nostrils issues smoke. Ivan does so, and is answered; he

---

[1] *Afanassieff*, i. 6.

[2] *Ib.* ii. 25.—Cfr. iii. 5, iv. 27.

gets into his right ear, and comes out of the left. By means of this horse, Ivan succeeds in taking down the portrait of the Tzar's daughter three times, though hung high up on the wall of the palace, and thus obtains the beautiful princess to wife.

According to another variety of this story,[1] Ivan, the third and foolish brother, goes with the most worthless jade in the stable into the open air, and calls up the grey horse with a loud shout; he enters into him by one ear, and comes out at the other. Two young horsemen (the Açvinâu) appear to him, and make a horse with golden mane and tail come forth; upon this horse Ivan succeeds in three times kissing, through twelve glasses (the glass mountain of the Esthonian story), the daughter of the Tzar, who therefore becomes his wife. Here, therefore, we find the ugly horse which is made beautiful by the two horsemen, represented by the two ears of the grey horse out of which they come. These two horsemen give the hero a better steed. Be it understood that their own heroic steed (that is, the sun's horse), from being ugly or asinine during the night, became beautiful and noble; in the Küllaros of the Dioscuri, too, we ought probably to recognise a courser that has been transformed from an ass to a heroic horse.

Sometimes, instead of the horse, we have only its head. The step-mother persecutes the old man's daughter;[2] the

---

[1] *Afanassieff*, ii. 28.

[2] *Ib.* iv. 41.—In the twenty-first story of *Erlenwein*, the poor brother obtains wealth by means of a mare's head, while the rich brother, on the other hand, becomes poor.—In *Af.* v. 21, the dwarf-boy, who possesses great strength, enters into the ear of one of the two horses when in the act of ploughing; upon which they plough of their own accord, and the old father of the dwarf is at liberty to rest.—In the sixth Calmuck story, the head of the dead horse, when

persecuted maiden finds a mare's head, which beseeches her to relieve and cover it; at last it invites her to enter the right ear and come out of the left one. The persecuted girl comes out in the form of an exceedingly beautiful maiden. The step-mother sends her own daughter to try the same means of becoming beautiful; but she maltreats the mare's head, and the mare's head devours her.

There is also a singularly clear allusion to the Açvinâu in the forty-fourth story of the fifth book of *Afanassieff*, which seems to me to be a full confirmation of these interpretations. When Basiliça, the girl persecuted by her step-mother, approaches the house of the old witch (the baba-jegá), she sees galloping towards the great door of it a black horseman, dressed all in black, upon a black horse, who disappears underground, upon which night begins.[1] When the day begins to appear, Basiliça sees before her a white horseman, dressed all in white, upon a white horse, caparisoned in white. The maiden goes on; when the sun begins to rise, she sees a red horseman, dressed in red, upon a red horse.[2] The myth does not require comment; but it happens to be given to us in the story itself by the witch, who, to appease the curiosity of the girl Basiliça, reveals to her that the black

fallen from the tree, brings riches and good luck to him who lets it fall, who finds under it a golden cup: this is a form of the ambrosia which comes out of the horse's head, which we shall find farther on.

[1] The Russian text seems to me of too much importance, in the history of myths, not to deserve to be recorded here: "Iediet apiát vsadnik: sam ćornoi, adiet va vsiem ćornom; na ćornom kanié; padskakál k varótam babijaghí i is-ćesz, kak skvosz szemliń pravalílsia; nastála noć."

[2] Idiót aná i draszít. Vdrúg skaćet mimo iejá vsadnik sam bieloi, adiet v bielom, kon pod nim bieloi, i sbruja na kanié biélaja; na dvarié stalo raszvietát. Idiót aná dalshe, kak skaćet drugoi vsadnik; sam krasnoi, adiét v krasnom i na krasnom kanie; stalo vshódit solntze.

horseman represents the dark night (noć tiómnaja), the white horseman the clear day (dien jasnoi), and the red horseman the little red sun (solnishko krasnoje).

Returning from Slavonic to Asiatic tradition, we meet with the same myths.

Let us begin with the demoniacal horse, or demon of horses. The *Ṛigvedas* already knows it; the yâtudhanas, or monster, feeds now upon human flesh (like the Bucephalus of the legend of Alexander), now upon horse flesh, and now milk from cows. We have said it seems probable that the custom of keeping a lamp lighted in the stables is a form of exorcism against the demon; the *Ṛigvedas*, indeed, tells us that Agnis (that is, Fire, with his flame) cuts off the heads of such monsters.[1] But this is not enough; the *Ṛigvedas* offers us in the same hymn the proof of another identification. We have seen in the last chapter how Rebhas, the invoker, is the third brother, whom his envious and perfidious brothers threw into the well; and we have seen above how Ivan, who is also the third brother, invokes with a sonorous voice the grey horse which is to help him, and how the same Ivan is the one that discovers the monstrous horse which ravages the seed or the crops in his father's field. In the same Vedic hymn where the flame of Agnis beats down the heads of the monster that torments horses, Agnis (that is, fire) is invoked in order that the hero Rebhas may see the monster which devastates with its claws.[2] Rebhas and Bhuǵyus are two names of the hero

[1] Yaḥ pâurusheyeṇa kravishâ samañkte yo açvyena paçunâ yâtudhânaḥ yo aghnyâyâ bharati kshîram agne teshâin çîrshâṇi harasâpi vṛiçća; *Ṛigv.* x. 87, 16.—Cfr. the dragon that torments the horses in the *Tuti-Name* of Rosen, ii. 300.

[2] Tad agne ćakshuḥ prati dhehi rebhe çaphâruǵam yena paçyasi yâtudhânam; *Ṛigv.* x. 87, 12.—The demon Háyagrîvas killed by

who falls into the cistern in the *Ṛigvedas.* We have seen, not long ago, in the Russian story, that Ivan, the third brother, who is thrown down into the cistern, is delivered by the red horse. The Açvinâu, in the *Ṛigvedas,* deliver Bhuǵyus out of the sea by means of red-winged horses.[1] Here the grey and imperfect horse of night is become a red horse. In the same Vedic hymn, Rebhas, overwhelmed in the waters, is identified with his own horse (Ivan is son of the bitch, or the cow, or the mare), he being compared to a horse hidden by wicked ones.[2]

Vishṇus, which is the same as horse's neck, and Hayaçiras, or horse's head, another monster giant in the *Râmâyaṇam,* iv. 43, 44, always refer to the Vedic açva-yâtudhânas. We are already acquainted with the demon who, during the night, makes the horses sweat and grow lean, *i.e.*, who makes them ugly. In the Latin tradition, after having assisted the Romans in the battle of the Lake Regillus, Castor and Pollux were seen, near the ambrosial lacus Iuturnæ (Ovidius, *Fasti,* i.), to wash the sweat off their horses with the water of this lake, which was near the temple of Vesta. To this Macaulay alludes in his verses—

"And washed their horses in the well
That springs by Vesta's fane."
—*Battle of the Lake Regillus,* xxxix.

The salutary water of the Dioscuri, or sons of the luminous one, would here occupy the place of the fire lighted by night in stables, and of the Vedic Agnis who kills the monster of horses. My friend Giuseppe Pitrè writes me, that in Sicily, when an ass, a mule, or a horse is to enter a new stable, salt is put upon its back (a form of Christian baptism), in order that the fairies may not lame it.—The Küllaros, the heroic horse of the Dioscuri, is perhaps not unrelated to the word *küllos,* which means lame and bent; the solar horse, before being heroic, is hump-backed, lame, lean, and ugly; the lame hero, the lame horse (ass or mule), the lame devil, seem to me to be three *penumbræ* of the solar hero, or of the sun in the darkness.

[1] Vibhir ûhathur ṛigrebhir açvâiḥ; *Ṛigv.* i. 117, 14.—Cfr. vii. 69, 7.

[2] Açvain na gûḷham açvinâ durevâir ṛishiṁ narâ vṛishaṇâ rebham apsu; *Ṛigv.* i. 117, 4.—The Açvinâu pass the sea upon a chariot, which resembles a ship; this chariot is said to have the sun for a covering—rathena sûryatvaćâ; *Ṛigv.* i. 47, 9.

We saw above, in the Russian story, how the two horsemen who come out of the grey horse's ear give to the foolish Ivan, who has an ugly and worthless horse, a handsome hero's palfrey, by means of which he accomplishes the arduous undertakings which entitle him to the hand of the king's daughter. It is remarkable how completely the Vedic myth agrees with this European legend. The Açvinâu have given, for his eternal happiness, a luminous horse to him who has a bad one.[1] In another hymn, the god Agnis gives to his worshipper a pious, truthful, invincible, and very glorious son, who vanquishes heroes, and a swift, victorious, and unconquered horse.[2]

We have seen, moreover, how Ivan, the most popular type of the Russian hero, has always to make three essays before he accomplishes his undertaking upon the wonderful horse which he has obtained from the two horsemen. The *Ṛigvedas*, which celebrates the famous mythical enterprise of the three steps of Vishṇus, of the great body (bṛihaććharîraḥ),[3] of the very vast step (urukramishṭaḥ),[4] who, in three steps, measured or traversed the whole span of the heavens,[5] betrays in another hymn the secret of Vishṇus's success in this divine enterprise, since it says that when, with the strength of Indras, he made his three steps, he was drawn by the two fair-haired horses

1 Yam açvinâ dadathuḥ çvetam açvam aghâçvâya çaçvad it svasti; *Ṛigv.* i. 116, 6.

2 Agnis tuviçravastamain tuvibrahmâṇam uttamam atûrtaṁ çrâvayatpatim putram dadâti dâçushe—Agnir dadâti satpatiṁ sâsâha yo yudhâ nṛibhiḥ agnir atyaṁ raghushyadaṁ ǵetâram aparâǵitam; *Ṛigv.* v. 25, 5, 6.

3 *Ṛigv.* i. 155, 6.

4 i. 154, 4.

5 Vishṇor nu kaṁ vîryaṇi pra voćam yaḥ pârthivâni vimame raǵâṅsi yo askabhâyad uttaraṁ sadhasthaṁ vićakramâṇas tredhorugâyah; *Ṛigv.* i. 154, 1.

of Indras[1] (that is, the two Açvinâu lent him the swift and strong horse which was to bear him on to victory). The three steps of Vishṇus correspond, therefore, to the three stations of Ivan, to the three races of the young hero to win the beautiful princess. Vishṇus also appears in the *Râmâyaṇam*,[2] in the midst of the sea of liquified butter, attractive to all beings, in the form of a horse's head. Hero and the solar or lunar horse are identified.

Indras is requested to yoke his right and his left (horses), to approach, inebriated, his dear wife.[3] By means of the horse obtained from the two horsemen, the Russian Ivan acquires his wife; in the *Ṛigvedas*, the two Açvinâu themselves, by means of their rapid chariot, became husbands of the daughter of the sun.[4] The horses of the sun are so fully identified with the chariot drawn by them, that they are said to be dependent on it, united with it, and almost born of it.[5] The Açvinâu, therefore, by means of the horse now enable the wife to be found by the solar hero, by the old Ćyavanas made young again (Tithôn),[6] now by the sun, and now find her themselves (perhaps drawing the chariot like horses). Râmas, too, who is represented in the *Râmâyaṇam*[7] as the deliverer of Sîtâ, is compared to the solar horse, to the sun born upon the mountain.

---

1 Yadâ te vishṇur ośasâ trîṇi padâ vićakram âd it te haryatâ harî vavakshatuḥ ; *Ṛigv.* viii. 12, 27,

2 *Râmây.* iv. 40.

3 Yuktas te astu dakshiṇa uta savyaḥ çatakrato tena ǵâyâm upa priyâm mandâno yâhy andhaso yoǵâ ; *Ṛigv.* i. 82, 5.

4 Tad û shu vâm aǵiraṁ ćeti yânain yena patî bhavathaḥ sûryâyâh ; *Ṛigv.* iv. 43, 6.—In the following hymn, strophe 1st, the aurora is called now daughter of the sun, now cow: Tam vâṁ rathaṁ vayam adyâ huvema pṛithuǵrayam açvinâ saṁgatiṁ goḥ—Taḥ sûryâṁ vahati.

5 Rathasya naptyaḥ ; *Ṛigv.* i. 50. 9.

6 *Ṛigv.* i. 116, 10.

7 vi. 9.

We have seen in the Russian stories how the horse's head possesses the same magic power as the marvellous horse which the two horsemen give to the hero Ivan. Thus, in the Vedic myth, and in the corresponding brâhmanic tradition, the horse's head Dadhyańć stands in direct relation with the myth of the Açvinâu. The wise Dadhyańć shows himself pious towards the Açvinâu, to whom, although he knows that he will pay with his head for the revelation he makes, he communicates what he knows concerning the ambrosia or the Madhuvidyâ. For this, accordingly, Dadhyańć forfeits his head; but the Açvinâu present him with a horse's head (his own), which heroically achieves wonders. With the bones of Dadhyańć, or with the head of the horse Dadhyańć (he who walks in butter or ambrosia), fished up in the ambrosial lake Çaryaṇâvat (the head of the horse Vishṇus in the sea of butter),[1] Indras discomfits the ninety-nine hostile monsters (as Samson the Philistines with the jawbone of an ass).[2] This exchange of heads seems to be common to the traditions which are founded upon the myth of the Açvinâu, that is, to the legends of the two brother or companion heroes. In the *Tuti-Name*,[3] the heads of the prince and of the Brâhman, who are exceedingly like each other, are cut off and then fastened on

[1] The lake of Brâhman, visited by Hanumant in the *Râmâyaṇam*, vi. 53, has the form of a horse's snout (hayânanam).

[2] Indro dadhîćo asthabhir vṛitrâṇy apratishkutaḥ ǵaghâna navatîr nava; *Ṛigv.* i. 84, 13, 14, i. 117, 22, and the corresponding commentary of Sâyaṇas.—The bones of the heroic horse possess strength equal to that of the horse itself; thus in the last chapter we have seen how, when the bones of the sacrificed bull or cow are kept, it springs up again with renewed strength.—Cfr. concerning this subject the interesting and copious details relating to European beliefs to be found in Rochholtz, *Deutscher Glaube und Brauch*, i. 219–253.

[3] ii. 24.

again; but, by some mistake, the head of the one is attached to the body of the other, so that the prince's wife is embarrassed between them. This exchange of the husband (which corresponds to the exchange of the wife in the legend of Berta, referred to in the first chapter) is very frequent in the legend of the two brothers, and often ends in the rupture of the perfect concord reigning between them. The two brothers or companions who dispute about the wife, is a variety of the legend of the three brothers who, having delivered the beautiful princess, wish to divide her between them.

The *Ṛigvedas* does not seem as yet explicitly to exhibit the two Açvinâu at discord—they generally are united in doing good; but as we already know the Vedic blind man and lame man who are cured by the grace of Indras, or of the Açvinâu themselves; as we know that the Açvinâu, in the *Ṛigvedas,* make Dadhyańć, who has a horse's head, conduct them to the ambrosia, or indicate where it is, probably in order that they may procure health and strength for themselves; as in the ninth strophe of the 117th hymn of the first book of the *Ṛigvedas,* the marvellous horse of the Açvinâu, which kills the monster-serpent (ahihan), is but one; as we know that the Açvinâu run to gain the bride for themselves; and as we cannot ignore the fact that in the story of the blind and lame man, when a woman comes upon the scene, they endeavour to do harm to each other; as we know that of the two Hellenic brothers, the Dioscuri, one alone had from the gods the gift of immortality; as, finally, it is known to us that of the two brothers, he alone is the true hero who, by means of his horse, gains the victory over the monster,—it is clear that if we have not as yet in the *Ṛigvedas* the myth of the two brothers at discord, we have, at least, in the ambrosia, and in the bride won by them the origin of the myth already indicated; and from the idea of the privileged brother that of the envious one would naturally arise.

In Hesiod's *Theogony* we have the two brothers Chrysäor and Pêgasos, that come out of the Medusa (the evening aurora), who is made pregnant by Poseidôn, after Perseus has cut off her head. Pêgasos, the younger brother, becomes the heroic horse. In Hesiod himself, and in the *Metamorphoses* of Ovid, he carries the thunder and the thunderbolts for Zeus. The hero Bellerophontes rides him, and vanquishes, by his help, the Chimaira and the Amazons; he becomes the horse of the aurora, the horse of the Muses, the ambrosial steed. The monstrous Chimaira appears, in the *Theogony* of Hesiod, as the daughter of Typhaon and the Echidna, the monstrous daughter of Chrysäor. Therefore in the conflict which Bellerophontes maintains against the Chimaira, we have a form of the battle which goes on between the twin horses Pêgasos and Chrysäor, the one divine, the other demoniacal.

In the analogous myth of the Hellenic Dioscuri (the sons of the luminous one, *i.e.*, of Zeus, just as the Vedic Açvinâu are the sons of the luminous sky;[1] Zeus is united with the Dioscuri, as Indras is with the Açvinâu), we again find the twins who fight to recover a woman who had been carried off from them, *i.e.*, their own sister Helen. One of the two brothers is mortal, and the other immortal; he who is immortal passes the night in hell with his mortal brother. The double aspect of the sun, which at evening enters and loses itself in the night, now black, now illumined by the moon, and which, in the morning, comes forth in a luminous form, has enriched

[1] Divo napâtâ; *Ṛigv.* i. 182, 1.

the story of the two brothers of mythology. One of the two brothers, the red horseman, is in especial relation with the morning sun; the other, in intimate connection with the silvery moon, the white horseman, and when the latter is amissing, with the infernal gloom.

Several mythologists have interpreted the Açvinâu as only the two twilights; but it seems more exact, inasmuch as they are often found together, whilst the two twilights are always apart, to recognise in them two crepuscular lights, the lunar of evening and autumn, and the solar of morning and spring.[1] Of the twin-brothers, one is always imperfect; the lunar crepuscular light offers us a similar imperfection, with respect to the sun. Inasmuch as the Açvinâu are affiliated both to the sun and the moon, when they come out of the two ears of the horse of night, we should understand, it would appear, that on one side the moon goes down, while on the other the sun is born, or that the solar horse arises, upon which the young hero lost in the night mounts and wins the princess aurora. In the Russian stories referred to in the preceding chapter, we have seen how the maiden abandons her hero-husband, or brother, to give herself into the monster's hands; the evening aurora forsakes the sun to throw herself into the night, and the evening twilight stays for a long time with the evening aurora

[1] As to the Vedic passage, v. 76, 3, where it would seem that the Açvinâu are invoked in the morning, at midday, and in the evening, there seems to me to be room for discussion. The text says: Utâ yâtam sañgave prâtar ahno (that is, in the early dawn, when the cows are gathered together), madhyandine (which, in my mind, is the middle term which separates the gloomy hours from the luminous ones), uditâ sûryasya (which, meaning the rising of the sun, cannot express evening, but precisely the rising of the morning sun). We too would have thus expressed the three moments in the morning in which it was opportune to invoke the Açvinâu.

(the reddish sky of evening), when the sun is already gone. In the morning the two lovers, the twilight, or sun and moon, and the aurora, meet once more; when the sun, or solar hero, arrives, he surprises them *in flagrante delicto,* and punishes them. Sometimes, on the contrary, the twilight and the aurora stay together, preserving their chastity; in this case the brother twilight figures as the good and honest guardian of the rights of his brother the sun. This appears to me to have been the most ancient, as it is the most subtle, interpretation of the myth; afterwards, it is possible, and even probable, that in the two Açvinâu only the two gods of morning and of evening were seen, with their respective twilights, considered as two brothers, so like that they were easily mistaken for each other. But from the data of the Russian story, which gives us the lunar twilight as a white horseman and the rising sun as a red one, the aurora being found exactly between the white and the red horsemen, between the moon or the white dawn (alba) and the sunrise, and seeing that the *Ṛigvedas,* which makes the aurora mount upon the chariot of the Açvinâu, considers them in the celebrated nuptial hymn as the *paranymphoi* of Sûryâ, the daughter of the sun or of the aurora herself, I venture to insist upon my interpretation as the most obvious, and perhaps the most logical one. The two brothers may very naturally be conceived of as contending for the possession of the bride when they have her between them, since the Açvinâu, considered as lunar light and sun, really take the aurora between them. The Vedic hymn cited above shows us how both the Açvinâu, arriving on the swift-running chariot, became the husbands of Sûryâ, the daughter of the sun. But this very Sûryâ, in the Vedic nuptial hymn, must be satisfied with one husband, who is called Somas, so that the Açvinâu can only occupy the place of paranymphs. The Açvinâu, therefore, would appear to be excluded from the wedding of Sûryâ as principal personages; they would seem to be nothing more than assistants, and, in fact, they often assume this part in the Vedic hymns, by enabling now the bride to find a husband, now the husband to recover his bride. We know already that by means of them Ćyavanas, the old sun (a Vedic Tithôn), became young again, and was able to espouse the aurora. We know that they gave sight to Vandanas (properly, the Face), that they made the blind see,[1] the lame walk, and performed sundry other works of charity, which would, however, have been much more glorious if these acts did not, in fact, always issue in benefit to themselves, as blind, lame, or drowned. It is hence very probable that when they give a bride to the hero, they, being now lunar, now solar heroes, do only appropriate her to themselves. When, therefore, we read that the Açvinâu assist as paranymphs at the nuptials of Sûryâ and Somas, we are much inclined to think that under Somas in this case one of the Açvinâu is hidden. In Indras and Somas, often sung of together in the *Ṛigvedas*, it seems to me that we have just another form of the Açvinâu, the more so because I also find them both, like the Açvinâu, personified in one and the same horse, whose back is covered with honey, and who is terrible and swift,[2] and because they are invoked together against the yâtudhânas, which, by the grace of the Açvinâu, the hero Rebhas succeeds in discovering and then chasing away.[3] The *Tâittiriya*

[1] Sushupvâṅsaṁ na nirṛiter upasthe sûryaṁ na dasrâ tamasi kshiyantam çubhe rukmaṁ na darçataṁ nikhâtam ud ûpathur açvinâ vandanâya; *Ṛigv.* i. 117, 5.

[2] Madhupṛishṭhaṁ ghoram ayâsam açvam; *Ṛigv.* ix. 89, 4.

[3] *Ṛigv.* viii. 104, 15–25.

Brâhmaṇam[1] represents to us the daughter of the sun (Sâvitrî) by the name of Sîtâ, as enamoured of Somas, who, on the contrary, loves another woman, the Çraddhâ (*i.e.*, Faith), almost as if the daughter of the sun, the aurora, were, for him at least, a symbol of infidelity. Probably this embryo of a myth refers to the passage of the aurora, in the morning, from her amours with the white horseman (the white twilight), which, as we have said, was supposed to be in particular relation with the moon (Somas), to her amours with the red horseman (the sun), or, *vice versa*, to the aurora who, in the evening, abandons the red horseman, the sun (now her father, now her husband), to throw herself into the arms of the white horseman, the white twilight, the king Somas, or silver god Lunus. Moreover, Yâskas, in the *Niruktam*,[2] already notices that the Açvinâu were identified now with the day and the night,[3] now with the sun and the moon.

When, therefore, we read that the Açvinâu obtained for their wife the daughter of the sun, and when we learn that she chose both for husbands,[4] we must interpret the passage with discrimination, and conclude that one of

[1] Quoted in Muir's *Sanskṛit Texts*, v. 264.—Somas united with Agnis in the *Ṛigvedas*, Somas united with Rudras, seem, in my opinion, to be the same as Somas united with Indras.—Cfr. Muir, v. 269, 270.

[2] xii. 1, quoted by Muir in his *Sanskṛit Texts*, v. 224.

[3] In the *Edda* we find the Açvinâu under the forms of night and day. Odin took Natt and Dag her son, gave them two horses and two drays, and placed them in the heavens to go round the earth in twenty-four hours. Natt was the first to advance with Hrimfaxe, her horse; he scatters every morning the foam from his bit upon the earth; it is the dew. The horse of Dag is named Skenfaxe; the air and the earth are illumined by his mane.

[4] Â vâm patitvaṁ sakhyâya ǵagmushî yoshâvṛiṇîta ǵenyâ yuvâm patî; *Ṛigv.* i. 119, 5.

them was sometimes preferred, inasmuch as the Vedic nuptial hymn speaks of only one husband of Sûryâ, with the name of Somas, with whom, as we have said, Yâskas identifies one of the Açvinâu. We read in *Pausanias* that, among the Greek usages, when the bride was conducted to the bridegroom's house, she was accustomed to mount a chariot and sit down in the middle, having the bridegroom on one side, and on the other her nearest relation as paranymphos. The preference given to one of the two brothers over the other is naturally suggestive of a contention between them; however, as I say, the *Ṛigvedas,* which offers us already the myth of the third brother abandoned in the well by his relations, does not record any example of an open strife between the two brothers (*i.e.,* the Açvinâu, the lunar and the solar light).

An evidently Hindoo variation of this myth is contained in the well-known episode of the *Mahâbhâratam,* which relates the adventures of Sundas and Upasundas, two inseparable brothers, who lived together in love and concord, each being ruled by the will of the other, and who had never all their lives either said or done anything to displease each other. The gods become envious of their virtue, and wish to prove it, and send to seduce them a nymph of enchanting beauty. The two brothers, on seeing her, desire each the exclusive possession of the divine maiden, and strive between themselves to carry her off. They fight so long and so desperately that they both die (the moon and the sun see the aurora in the morning, and dispute for her; they see her again in the evening, and fight so long that they both perish miserably, and die in the night). The gods who are envious of the virtue of the two brothers Sundas and Upasundas, are the same as those who, envying the good which the Açvinâu do to mankind, treat them as celestial Çudrâs, under the pretext that they pollute themselves by their contact with men, and refuse to admit them, being impure, to the sacrifices.[1]

In the twin brothers, Nakulas and Saladevas, sons of the Açvinâu, the Açvinâu themselves revive again, are made better, according to the expression of the first book of the *Mahâbhâratam.* The first-born, Nakulas, too, is perhaps the real Açvin who kills the monster. Nakulas is the name given to the *viverra ichneumon,* the mortal enemy of the serpents, which refers us back to the horse Ahihan (or killer of the serpent), as the horse of the Açvinâu, or perhaps rather of one of the Açvinâu, is called, in the *Ṛigvedas.* Of the two Dioscuri, moreover, one alone is especially the horseman; the other is the valiant in combat.[2] The mortal brother, he who has to remain in hell, and who has to fight the monsters of night, is Castor the horseman. Pollux, the strong-armed, is, on the contrary, the immortal one, the daily sun, he who profits from the victory obtained by his brother who has fought in the night, during which the Gandharvâs (the horses in the perfumes, they who walk in perfume) also ride upon war-horses, heroic, invulnerable, divine, exceedingly swift, who change colour at will—the Gandharvâs, whose strength increases during the night, as one of them informs Arǵunas in the *Mahâhâratam,* when communicating to him Gandharvic knowledge.[3]

In the *Râmâyaṇam,* the two brothers Râmas and

[1] Cfr. the legends relating to Ćyavanas cured by the Açvinâu in the *Çatapatha Brâhmaṇam* and in the *Mahâbhâratam,* referred to by Muir in the above-quoted fifth volume of the *Sanskṛit Texts,* p. 250, and those following.

[2] In the *Ṛigv.* i. 8, 2, also, the invokers of Indras desire to fight the enemies, the monsters Mushṭihatyayâ and Arvatâ, by fist and by horses.

[3] *Mbh.* i. 6484–6504.

Lakshmaṇas are compared to the Açvinâu, to the sun and moon, as similar the one to the other; and their reciprocal love reminds us of that of the Açvinâu.[1] Râmas and Lakshmaṇas are always at peace with each other; there is, however, a passage which may serve as a link to connect the myth of the two friendly brothers and that of the two hostile ones. When Râmas combats alone in the forest thousands of monsters, Lakshmaṇas stays with Sîtâ, hidden in a cavern.

But the *Râmâyaṇam* itself shows us the two brothers in open strife in the legend of the two brothers Bâlin and Sugrîvas, children of the sun, beauteous as the two Açvinâu, so perfectly like one another that it is impossible to distinguish one from the other; and so that when Râmas, to please Sugrîvas, wishes to kill Bâlin, he does not know which to strike, until Sugrîvas puts a garland on his head as a sign of recognition.[2] Once Bâlin and Sugrîvas were intimate friends, but, on account of a woman, they became mortal enemies. Sugrîvas complains that Bâlin, his elder brother, has deprived him of his wife Rumâ;[3] but it is not certain that Sugrîvas did not rather steal Bâlin's wife. Bâlin seems especially to represent the evening sun; the *Râmâyaṇam*[4] says of him that, while the sun is not risen (*i.e.*, in the night), he is unweariedly passing from the western to the eastern ocean; by this is described the supposed voyage of the sun in the ocean of night, in the grotto or the darkness. When Bâlin is in the grotto, he is betrayed by his brother Sugrîvas. The two brothers, Bâlin and Sugrîvas, while still friends, set out together to follow the monster Mâyâvin (the brother of Dundubhis, who, in the *Râmâyaṇam* itself,[5] fights in

[1] *Râmây.* i. 49, ii. 7.
[2] iv. 12.
[3] iv. 7, 17.
[4] iv. 8.
[5] iv. 10.

the shape of a demoniacal buffalo against Bâlin, near the entrance of the cave). The moon rises to show them the way. The monster escapes into the cavern, upon which Bâlin enters and follows him, whilst Sugrîvas remains without, awaiting his return. After waiting a long time, Sugrîvas sees blood flow out of the cave (in analogous legends, instead of blood, it is a treasure, or else a princess or a beautiful maiden comes out in shining garments). This is the blood of the monster, killed by Bâlin; but Sugrîvas believes it to be that of his brother Bâlin. He returns home, and showing his sorrow in public, declares that Bâlin is dead, and allows himself to be consecrated king in his stead (probably also enjoying with the crown the wife of his brother). Meanwhile Bâlin, after having killed the monster Mâyâvin, endeavours to come out of the cavern, but he finds the entrance closed. Attributing at once this wicked action to the brother Sugrîvas, he succeeds, after great efforts, in effecting an opening; he comes out, returns to the palace, and expels Sugrîvas from it, whom he persecutes ever after.[1] Even Añgadas, Bâlin's son, irritated one day with Sugrîvas, accuses him of having once shut up his brother Bâlin in the cave, in order to possess himself of the latter's wife.

In the *Avesta*, the name and the myth of Kereçâçpa seems to me to be of special interest. To the Zend word *kereçâçpa* corresponds the Sanskrit *kṛiçâçvas* (the name of a warlike ṛishis and hero), that is, he of the lean horse. The hero Kereçâçpa has, in the *Avesta*, a brother called Urvâksha (a word which is perhaps the same as *urvâçpa*, and, if this equivalence is admitted, *urvâksha* would mean him of the fat or great horse, of the heroic

[1] *Râmây.* iv. 8.

horse.[1] We have already noticed that the Vedic and Slavonic hero begins his fortune with an ugly and bad horse; the hero Kereçâçpa, too, of the two brothers of the Zend myth, is the good, the heroic, and truly glorious one. His brother, Urvâksha, according to a Parsee tradition,[2] was banished to hell because he had struck the fire which did not obey his commands (the evening sun which descends into the infernal night); Kereçâçpa avenges him. This is evidently a Persian form of the myth of the Dioscuri, who, as it seems to me, reappear once more in the two Zend brothers, Gustâçp and Açpâyaodha (he who fights with the horse).

In the epic poem of Firdusi, the two brothers Piran and Pilsem, who fight together against the Turanians, and of whom the former and elder delivers the latter and younger from the dangers that he is exposed to among the enemies, seem to me re-embodiments of the same myth.

We find the cloudy or tenebrous sky of night represented in the *Ṛigvedas* and in the *Avesta* as açman, or mountain of stone. When the evening sun falls upon the mountain, it turns to stone, and the whole sky assumes the colour of this mountain. When the hero of the popular story follows the monster, the latter hides under a rock; the hero lifts up the rock and descends into the grotto, that is, hides himself in the mountain of stone, or is turned to stone, and if he has a horse, it undergoes the same transformation.

[1] The Persian hero often takes his name from his horse or his horses; hence Kereçâçpa, Vîstâçpa, Argâçp, Gustâçp, Yapâçp, Pûrushâçpa, Açpâyaodha, &c.

[2] Cfr. Spiegel's *Avesta*, ii. 72.—In the Servian stories of Wuck, one of two brothers sleeps, transformed into stone with all his people, until the other comes to free and resuscitate him.

In the story of Merhuma, who is stoned (the aurora lost in the mountain of stone), in the *Tuti-Name*,[1] we have the brother possessed by a demon, who seduces the wife of his brother, who is travelling abroad. In that of Mansûr, in the same *Tuti-Name*,[2] the monstrous Fari assumes the very shape of the absent husband, and succeeds in seducing his wife. In another story in the *Tuti-Name*,[3] two brothers, finding themselves deceived in their expectations, set out together, each, for love of the other, wandering about the world in search of a better fate. These are three forms of the myth of the Açvinâu. With them is connected the story of the maiden who comes out of the wood, of whom as many men, when she appears, become enamoured.[4]

The fifth Calmuck story (of Hindoo origin) is unmistakably a reproduction of the myth of the Açvinâu, even to the very mythical names themselves. The king, Kun-snang (he who illumines all, like the Vedic Viçvavedas and the Slavonic Vsievedas, the all-seer), has by two different mothers two sons—Sunlight (born in the year of the tiger; perhaps in the sol-leo, in July, in summer, under the solar influence) and Moonlight. The second wife does not love her step-son Sunlight, and persecutes him, but the two brothers are devoted to each other, and when Sunlight goes into exile (like Râmas), Moonlight follows him (as Lakshmaṇas follows Râmas, as the white lunar twilight follows the sun in the forest of night). On the way, Moonlight is thirsty; Sunlight goes to find water for him, but in the meantime Moon-

---

[1] i. 91, and following, Rosen's version.

[2] ii. 20, and following.

[3] ii. 157.

[4] *Tuti-Name*, i, 151.

light dies.[1] Sunlight returns, and is in despair at the sight of his dead brother; however, a hermit has pity upon him, and, having resuscitated Moonlight, adopts the two brothers as his own sons. Near his abode there is a kingdom where the dragons keep back the waters, unless they are given a young man born in the year of the tiger. It oozes out that Sunlight is such a young man, and he is led away to the king of that country. The daughter of the king falls in love with him, and begs Sunlight not to be given to the dragons. The king is furious against his daughter, and has her thrown with Sunlight into the swamp where the dragons are.[2] The young couple break out into such piteous lamentations, that the dragons are touched, and let Sunlight and the young princess go free. When free, they find Moonlight, who also becomes the husband of the beautiful princess, the two brothers being inseparable, like the Vedic Açvinâu. The three personages (white twilight, or white moonlight, aurora, and sun) return together into the kingdom of their birth, where, upon seeing them arrive, Sunlight's step-mother (Night) dies of terror. Here the legend has all its mythical splendour.

In the sixteenth Mongol story, on the contrary, the friendship of the two companions cannot last, because of the perfidy of one of them; while they are travelling in the forest, the minister's son kills the king's son.

In the history of *Ardshi-Bordshi*, the two men born

[1] Cfr. a zoological variety of this myth in the chapter on the Cock and the Hen.

[2] This is a variety of the legend of the Tzar's daughter enamoured of Emilius, the foolish and idle, though fortunate, youth, whom the indignant Tzar orders to be shut up in a cask and thrown with her lover into the sea, as we have seen in the first chapter.

in the palace are so like each other in everything, in shape, complexion, dress, and horses, that they cannot be distinguished one from the other; hence they dispute between themselves for the possession of everything, of wife and sons. One is made like the other by witchcraft; he is the son of a demon; and it is the marvellous king of the children who discovers the secret.[1]

This exchange of husbands, or heroes, by means of demoniacal craft, often occurs in European fairy-tales, like the exchange of wives. The demon is now a water-carrier, now a washerman, now a woodcutter, now a charcoal-burner, now a gipsy, now a Saracen, and now the devil *in propria persona.*

The Russian fairy-tales show us the two forms of the two brothers or companions, *i.e.*, the two that remain friends *usque ad mortem*, and the friend betrayed by his perfidious companion.

We find a zoological form of the legend of the two friends in one of Afanassieff's stories. The horse delivers the child of one of his masters from the bear, upon which his grateful masters feed him better, whereas before they had almost let him die of starvation. The horse (the sun) remembers in prosperity his companion in misfortune, the cat (the moon), who is also allowed to starve, and gives it a part of what he receives from his masters. The latter perceive this, and again ill-treat the horse, who then forms the resolution of killing himself, in order that the cat may eat him; but the cat refuses to eat his friend the horse,[2] and is also determined to die.

The two brothers who, because they have eaten one the head and the other the heart of a duck, are pre-

---

[1] iv. 24.

[2] We shall shortly find the hare (the moon) who devours the mare.

destined, in *Afanassieff*,[1] one to be king and the other to spit gold, flee from their perfidious mother (probably step-mother), who persecutes them in their father's absence. They meet with a cowherd taking his cows to the pasturage, and are hospitably entertained by him. Then, continuing their journey, they come to a place where two roads meet, where, upon a pillar, this is written, "He who goes to the right (to the east) will become a king; he who goes to the left (to the west, into the kingdom of Kuveras, the western sun, the god of riches; when the sun rises in the east the moon goes down in the west) will become rich." One goes to the right; when it is morning, he rises, washes, and dresses himself. He learns that the old king is dead (the old sun), and that funeral honours are being paid to him in church. A decree says that he whose candle lights of itself will be the new Tzar.[2] The Vedic god also has the distinctive attribute of this wonderful candle, that of being lighted by himself, of shining of himself, *i.e.*, he is svabhânus. The candle, therefore, of our youth predestined to be king lights of its own accord, and he is immediately proclaimed the new king. The daughter of the old king (the aurora) marries him, recognising in him her predestined husband, and makes with her golden ring (the solar disc) a mark upon his forehead (as Râmas does with Sîtâ). The young man (the sun), after having remained some time with his bride (the aurora), wishes to go towards the part where his brother went (that is, to the left, to the west). He traverses for a long time different countries (*i.e.*, the sun describes the whole arc of heaven which arches over the earth), and finds at last (in the western

[1] i. 53.

[2] U kavó preszde sviećâ sama saboi zagaritsia, tot tzar budiet.

sky, towards the setting sun) his brother, who lives in great wealth. In his rooms whole mountains of gold arise; when he spits, all is gold; there is no place to put it,[1] (the evening sky is one mass of gold). The two brothers then set out together to find their poor old father (the sun during the night). The younger brother goes to find for himself a bride (probably the silvery moon), and the wicked mother (the step-mother, night) is forsaken. Here, too, the legend is entirely of a mythical character. In the two brothers we see now twilight and sun, now the two twilights, now the spring and autumnal lights, now the sun and the moon, but always the Açvinâu, always two deities, two heavenly beings closely connected with the phenomena of the lunar and solar light.

And here allow me to say that I deem it enough for me to collect in one body legends which betray a common origin; as to explaining all mythology in the legends, this is beyond my power, and therefore outside my pretensions. I only point out, as I proceed, interpretations which I think come near the truth; but the objects embodied in mythology are so mobile and multiform, that, if grasped too tightly, they easily evaporate and disappear. Their richness consists in their very mobility and uncertainty. If the sun and moon were always seen in the same place, there would be no myths. The myths which originated the greatest number of legends are those which are founded upon the most fleeting phenomena of the sky.[2] The myth of the

[1] Tzelijá kući zolotá v anbarah nasipani; ćto ni pluniet on, to vsié zólotom; dievat niekudá!

[2] It will, I hope, be deemed not inappropriate to quote here the words with which Professor Roth begins his essay upon the legend of Çunaḥçepas in the first volume of the *Indische Studien:* "Die Deutung

Açvinâu cannot be solved by mathematical demonstrations, precisely on account of the uncertainty presented by the crepuscular light which probably gave rise to it. This continuous succession of shadows, penumbræ, chiaroscuri, and shades of light, from the black darkness to the silver moon, from the silver moon to the grey twilight of morning, which gradually melts into, and confounds itself with the dawn, from the dawn to the aurora, from the aurora to the sun; the same variations recurring, but inversely, in the evening, from the dying sun to the reddish and blood-coloured sky or evening aurora, from the evening aurora to the grey twilight, from the grey twilight to the silver moon, from the silver moon to the gloomy night,—this continual change of colours, which meet, unite with, and pass into each other, originated the idea of celestial companions, friends, or relations, who are now in unison and now separate, who now approach to love each other, to move together and affectionately follow each other, now rush upon each other to fight, despoil, betray, and destroy each other turn by turn, who now attract and are now attracted, are now seduced and now seducers, now cheated and now deceivers, now victims, now sacrificers. Where there

der indischen Sagengeschichte sucht noch die Regeln, nach welchen die das überlieferte verworrene Material behanden soll. Eine und dieselbe Sage wird vielleicht in zehn verschiedenen Büchern in zehnfacher Form erzählt. Glaubt man einen festen Punkt gefunden zu haben, auf welchen nach einem Berichte die Spitze der Erzählung zusammenläuft, so streben andere Berichte wieder nach ganz anderem Ziele und treiben denjenigen, der einen festen Kern der Sage fassen will, rathlos im Kreise herum. Die Widersprüche, mit welchen ein Sammler und Ordner griechischer Heldensagen zu kämpfen hat, sind lauter Einklang und Klarheit im Vergleiche zu dem wirren Knäuel, in welchen die Willkühr indischer Poeten die reichen Ueberlieferungen ihrer Vorzeit zusammengeballt hat."

is a family, there is love, hence come exemplary brothers, husbands, wives, sons, daughters, fathers, and mothers, full of tenderness; that is the obverse of the medal: where there are relations, there are disputes, hence contentions between brothers, out of jealousy in love, or envy of riches; perverse mothers-in-law, step-mothers, and sisters-in-law, tyrannous fathers, perfidious wives; that is the reverse. This contradiction of feelings is difficult to explain psychologically even in man; how much more, therefore, is it so when it has to be analysed in a mythical image, which assumes an animal form in one rapid flash of imagination, and then disappears? On this account, in the case of some myths, we must content ourselves with a general demonstration, at least until new and positive data appear, on which it may be possible to base, in a solid foundation, the real nature of the details of mythology. In the absence of these data, we can only offer probabilities, and not rules to the reader. As to the Vedic Açvinâu, this much is certain: they are found in unison with their wife, the aurora, after having passed through the dangers of night, or after having enabled the heroes protected by them—that is to say, their own heroic forms—to pass through them; they are two splendid brother-horsemen; and they are especially invoked in the first hours of morning. The myth in this Vedic form would not appear to be of dubious interpretation. The white moon and the sun take the aurora between them, that is, marry her; or else they present her in marriage to Somas (with whom one of the Açvinâu, the white light or twilight, is in particular relation), in the quality of paranymphs. The aurora, in the morning, as well as in the evening, taken between the sun and the moon, disappears. One would think that the twilight and the sun present her together at the same time to the king or god Somas, or Lunus, for whom the daughter of the sun has affection. One would also think that she was especially united with the twilight, which is in especial relation with Somas, observing how in the morning the aurora immediately succeeds the twilight, and disappears when the sun shows himself, that is, rejoins the twilight and forsakes the sun; and how in the evening, when the sun hides himself, or when her husband is absent, she again unites herself with the twilight, with whom she again flees and disappears, to reappear once more with him in the morning. To continue; the absence of the sun during the night tormented the popular phantasy in several ways. As much as the aspect of the sky was negative with regard to the mythical hero—that is to say, as much as the hero or god hides himself from the view—just so much the more does popular imagination invest him with positive qualities and exalt his greatness. The greatest of all deities is that which is seen the least;—would that Roman Catholic priests understood this mythological truth! Indras and Zeus are great when within the thundering and lightning cloud. The sun becomes a hero when he loses himself in the darkness of night and in the cloud. But it is just at this very point that the demonstration of mythical particulars becomes more difficult, because the myths are now founded, not merely upon an external appearance or image, but often upon a simple subjective hypothesis; and while the ancient image, possessing an objectivity irrespective of the subject, can always be reconciled with the observation of the new celestial phenomena which reproduce it, the subjective hypothesis, being an individual phantasy, is lost. The demonstration is therefore possible only in the essential parts. When the sun was seen to disappear in the nocturnal sky, this sky appeared in the various aspects of an ocean, a mountain, a forest, a cavern, or a voracious monster which devoured the hero. But has the sun lost himself by accident, or has he been precipitated into the night by the aurora and her crepuscular lover, perfidiously united together, in order that they may have more freedom in their loves? This is a dilemma of which the two solutions originate a double series of legends,—the brother betrayed by the brother, and the hero who goes to succour his unfortunate brother fallen into the power of the monsters. The hour of day which the French indicate by the expressive phrase *entre chien et loup*, is the great epical hour of the fox, which partakes of the nature of the domestic dog and the savage wolf. It is the hour of betrayals, of perfidies, of doubts, and mythical uncertainties. Who can tell whether the aurora is a widow by an accident which happens to her husband the sun, or whether she herself has betrayed him?—whether she has been a chaste and faithful Geneviève, or a perfidious and luxurious Helen? It is these very mythical doubts which have made the fortune and the charm of tradition, as they are the despair of mythologists. When, moreover, the sun is within the night, what can he do? According to the different aspect assumed by the night, the acts of the solar hero lost in it are modified, and these modifications can be explained without too great an effort of imagination; but, sometimes, the relations between the hero and his companions or brothers in the world of the dead, can only be conceived by means of poetical dreams. When the sun is seen to enter the obscure night in the evening, and to come out of it safe and sound in the morning, after having dispersed the darkness, it is natural to think that throughout the night he is singly intent upon killing the monster. The action of the principal hero is well defined, and therefore evident; and the reference is equally clear when the aurora is represented as experiencing the same fate as the sun, her husband or brother. They descend together into the night, which makes them invisible, and together emerge from it happily.

The myth becomes richer when the aurora throws herself into the arms of a rival of her husband, because the character of this rival is various. Now he is a handsome youth who resembles the legitimate husband, either as the twilight or as Lunus; now he is a real demoniacal monster, the demon himself, the black night. In proportion to the variety of aspects and relations which the hero's rival assumes, does the myth become more complicated, and its interpretation more difficult; hence the story-tellers are often in the habit of interrupting their narrative by saying, "Now, let us leave this or that hero, and return to such or such another." These interruptions of the stories have their mythological reason. We can understand, for instance, how the aurora, or daughter of the sun, should be conceived of as, in a moment of feminine weakness, falling in love with the moon, which she sees on the other side of the heavens, and desirous of being conducted to him as his bride. We can understand how Lunus, reciprocating the love-glance of the aurora at the other extremity of the sky, should appear to be drawing her to himself, and wishing to seduce her. We can also understand how now the moon, now the sun, appears to seduce the aurora and carry her off from her legitimate husband. In these cases the infidelity of the hero or the heroine is evident; but woe to him who attempts to carry the demonstration or the proof of this interpretation too far, for when the seducer and seduced, be the seducer male or female, are thought of as enjoying together the fruits of their perfidy, the myth must come to an end, as no one can conceive the possibility of the moon and the aurora living or doing anything together; no one can tell what the aurora and the twilight, phenomena appertaining exclusively to the morning and evening, and which only appear when the sun rises from the mountain, do together in the night. The phenomenon ceases, the mythical personages vanish too, and the story-teller breaks off his narrative, because he possesses no data upon which to continue it. And so with all the myths; they can only be explained on the condition that we do not insist upon explaining too much. We must therefore be contented to see the girl aurora carried off in the evening and the hero sun recover her in the morning, or to conceive of the aurora and the sun fleeing away together into the night, but we must not be too inquisitive as to the manner in which they do so. The moon, or good fairy, sometimes teaches them the way; but their nocturnal actions are but little seen into; those which are spoken of as performed by them at night refer either to the moment in which night begins, or to that in which it comes to an end. During the night they wander about until they see a light (the guiding moon or delivering light of day); they remain in the chest or cask thrown into the water until it is carried to the other shore beyond the sea, or on the eastern coast. In their nocturnal journey the moon plays the part now of the good old man, or the good fairy; now of the good cow, or the bull; now of the grey horse, the steed of night, who, in three stations, bears them to their goal; now of the bird who, nourished upon their flesh, carries them to their destination; and now we have, on the contrary, the monster itself, or the step-mother who threatens, tortures, and persecutes them. The hero shows his greatest strength when hidden, but it is used now to send out the cows, now to recover the ravished bride, now to unchain the rivers kept back by the dragons, now to make the water of health gush forth, and now to destroy the monster and deliver himself. The hero displays his greatest powers when contending with the monster; but it is in order to his own deliverance. In the earliest epochs of the legend he is foolish, ill, drunken, unhappy, and stony; one can only speak of him by what is seen of him externally. The cloud-barrel moves; it is the barrel full of water which moves of its own accord in order to please the hero: the cloud-barrel drops rain upon the earth; it is the foolish one who lets the wine run out of the cask: the cloud-forest moves; it is the trunk of a tree which attaches itself to the horse ridden by the hero, and massacres his enemies—*i.e.*, the cloud or darkness disappears, and the hero comes out victorious. The part performed by the solar hero in the night or in the cloud seems to me, therefore, almost always of a nearly certain interpretation, but only so long as he is alone, or with but one companion; when the one hero is transformed into three, or five, or six, who accompany each other, or when he meets other mythical personages of a nature akin to his own, and when he speaks and acts in unison with them, the legend confuses the myth, in order to explain which, we are often obliged to stretch the sense of the adverb *together* to the signification, now of a whole night, and now of an entire year. When we find, for instance, in tradition, the twelve months of the year associated with twelve old men round the fire, we know that the fire is the sun, round which the twelve months turn in the sky in the space of a year. Here *together* is amplified to denote, therefore, the period of a year and the entire width of the sky.

I have been led into this long, but, I trust, not idle digression, in order to explain the Russian story of the two brothers, of whom it is said that they go together, one to the right and the other to the left. In whatever way the Açvinâu are to be understood, whether as twilight and sun, as spring and autumn, or as sun and moon, it is impossible to comprehend how they can travel in the same direction; the ways they take must therefore be separate. The sun and the evening twilight do not advance in opposite directions; the morning sun and that of evening occupy opposite positions, but not at the same time; the sun and moon advance at the same time in the sky, but not conjointly and upon the same path, like two travelling companions. It is therefore necessary to suppose that the journey of the two brothers either happens at different periods, although it may be in the same night or the same day, or else takes its start from different places, although always in the sky; in the evening the moon is seen advancing from east to west, whilst the hidden sun travels from west to east; when the sun has arrived in the east, the moon goes down in the west. The eastern sun is bent, in the daytime, upon following and finding his brother who has gone to the west; and when he arrives there he sees, besides his brother, his brother's immense treasures also. With this is connected the other version of the myth of the Açvinâu, the poor brother and the rich one. This is probably the weary, thirsty, and hungry sun, who, having during the day given all his wealth away, demands hospitality from, and offers his services to, his rich brother; the latter drives him away, and the poor brother wanders alone, poorer and sadder than before, into the forest, where he makes his fortune by digging up a treasure which enriches him, whilst his rich brother in the west becomes poor. The story of the treasure, in connection with the two brothers and the skilful thief, was familiar to the Greeks in the vicissitudes of Agamêdês and Trophonios (in *Pausanias*[1]), who stole King Hürieus's treasure, on which account one of the two brothers was to lose his head.

Were I to follow the story of the two brothers in its Western versions, I could compose an entire volume on the subject, which is indeed of such interest that a student, by connecting it with that of the three brothers, might profitably address himself to the work. But to resume the account of the horse. I must here limit myself to recording only one other interesting variety of this legend, offered us in the seventh story of Basile's *Pentamarone.*[2]

[1] ix. 37, 3.—I observe that the same craft as that used by the two brothers to steal the treasure, in an as yet unpublished fairy tale of the Canavese in Piedmont, was employed by the inexperienced robber, who becomes at length very skilful to rob the loaves from the baker's oven. The Piedmontese thief makes an opening from without, and thus carries the bread off. The same thief then steals the king's horse. At first, he learns his profession from the chief of the robbers. The chief sends him the first time to waylay some travellers, and bids him leap upon them; the young thief obeys these directions to the letter; he makes the travellers lie down and then jumps upon them, but does not rob them. The second time the chief tells him to take the travellers' quattrini (the name of a very small coin, by which money in general is also expressed). The young thief takes the quattrini alone, and lets the travellers keep their dollars and napoleons. At last, however, he becomes an accomplished thief.

[2] Cfr. in the same *Pentamerone*, the ninth story of the first book; the eighteenth of the *Novelline di Santo Stefano di Calcinaia;* the thirty-ninth of the Sicilian stories of the *Gonzenbach;* the sixtieth and the eighty-fifth story of Grimm's collection, *Kinder und Hausmärchen;* the tenth of Kuhn and Schwartz's *Märchen;* the twenty-second of the Greek stories of Hahn, *Griechische und Albanesische Märchen;* the fourth of Campbell's in *Orient und Occident;* the first book of the *Pańćatantram,* and the twelfth story of the fifth book of the same; and Cox, the work quoted before, i. 141, 142, 161, 281, 393, &c.

There were once two brothers, named respectively Cienzo and Meo (Vincenzo and Meo). When they were born two enchanted horses and two enchanted dogs also came into the world. Cienzo goes about the world in search of fortune; he comes to a place where there is a dragon with seven heads, from whom a beautiful princess must be delivered. As long as he does not cut all the heads off, the dragon goes and rubs itself against a herb which possesses the virtue of fastening on to the body again the head which had been cut off. Cienzo cuts off all the dragon's heads, "pe gratia de lo sole Lione" (by the grace of the Lion sun, *i.e.*, when the sun is in the sign of Leo, which corresponds to the tiger of the Indo-Turanian story recorded above, or when the solar hero possesses all his strength; the lion and the tiger are equivalent in Hindoo symbolism as heroic types, and are therefore all the same in the zodiac). Cienzo marries the beautiful princess delivered by him; but a beautiful fairy who lives in the opposite house fascinates him by her beauty, attracts him, and binds him with her hair. Meanwhile Meo, who by signs settled upon beforehand learns that his brother Cienzo is in danger, comes to the house where the latter's wife lives, accompanied by his enchanted horse and dog. The wife believes him to be Cienzo (the story of the Menechmi, of the two brothers who resemble each other in everything, was no doubt taken by the Greek poet, and afterwards by Plautus, from popular tradition), fêtes him on his arrival, and receives him into her bed; but the faithful brother, in order not to touch her, divides the sheets between them so that they have one each, and refuses to touch his sister-in-law. Thus Sifrît, as well as his Scandinavian *alter ego* Sigurd, places a sword between himself and Brünhilt, the destined bride of the king, in order not to touch her when she lies beside him;

and when Brünhilt throws herself upon the funeral pyre, she also places a sword between herself and Sigurd's corpse.[1] In the royal or heroic weddings by proxy of the Middle Ages a similar custom was observed. In the popular Piedmontese, Bergamasc, and Venetian song[2] of the pilgrim who comes from Rome, the pilgrim is separated from the woman only by a wisp of straw. Towards morning Meo also sees the beautiful fairy in the house over the way; he guesses that Cienzo has been drawn into her snare, and goes to deliver him. He makes his enchanted dog devour her, and frees his brother, awakening him out of his sleep. Cienzo learning that Meo had slept with his wife, cuts off his head; but when he learns from his wife how Meo had divided the sheets when he lay beside her, he bewails his rashness, has recourse to the herb with which the dragon rubbed itself when one of its heads had been cut off, and by this means fastens Meo's head on to his body again.

The principal auxiliary, however, to one in particular of the two brothers, as of the third in the legend of the three brothers, is his horse.

When the hero devotes himself to the trade of thieving, his most glorious achievement is robbing the king's horse.

When the young hero has been educated by the devil, it is in the shape of a horse that he succeeds in escaping from him.

When the solar hero fights, his greatest strength is in his horse.

---

[1] In the *Pentamerone*, i. 9, the queen's son does the same with the wife of his twin-brother; "Mese la spata arrancata comme staccione 'miego ad isso ed a Fenizia."

[2] In the corresponding collections of Ferraro, Bolza, and Wolf.—Cfr. the end of the twenty-eighth of the *Novelline di Santo Stefano di Calcinaia.*

When the hero dies, his horse, too, is sacrificed.

Let us now illustrate, by some examples, these four circumstances relative to the myth of the horse.

In the *Mahâbhâratam*,[1] the god Indras appears in the form now of a horseman, now of a horse. It is, moreover, upon such a heroic horse that the young Utañkas flees from the king of the serpents, after having recovered from him the queen's earrings, which the king of the serpents had stolen. In this legend reference is made to several myths; to that of the hero in the infernal regions, to that of the hero-thief, and to the legend of the horse which saves the fugitive hero, the same as the hero who leads away the horse.

In the *Vishṇu P.*,[2] we have Kapilas, a form of Vishṇus, or of the solar hero (inasmuch as he is of a reddish colour, or else of the evening sun), who carries off the horse destined for the açvamedhas, that is to be sacrificed. (In other words, the solar horse, the horse which was meant for the sacrifice, escapes from it, in the same way as, in the preceding chapter, we have seen the bull escape into the forests.) In the *Râmâyaṇam*,[3] the horse destined for the sacrifice is, on the contrary, carried off by a serpent (*i.e.*, the monster of night ravishes the evening sun, whilst, in the western sky, the fire is being prepared for his immolation). The sons of Sagaras (the clouds of the heavenly ocean, the word *sagaras* meaning sea), make a noise like thunder, searching for the horse that had been carried off from them. They find it near the god Vishṇus or Kapilas (here the sun himself, the solar horse itself, carried off into the cloudy ocean of night); believing him to be the ravisher, they assail him; Kapilas (or the solar horse), full of indignation, burns them to

[1] i. 807 and following. [2] iv. 4. [3] i. 41-43.

ashes. Their nephew, Añsumant (he who is furnished with rays, the radiant sun of morning), on the contrary, delivers the horse out of the forest. In the evening he is reconducted back to the place of sacrifice, on the golden pavement, after having made the journey round the world.[1] In the same way as we have seen, in the preceding chapter, that the bull or the cow is touched or struck as an augury of fruitfulness and abundance, in the *Râmâyaṇam*,[2] Kâuçalyâ touches the horse (a stallion) in order to be fruitful, as he desires to have sons (*putrakâmyayâ*), and the king and queen smell the odour of the burnt marrow or fat of the horse, as a talisman which may work for them the gratification of a like wish.[3] Of course we must always refer the legend to the myth of the solar horse, which, even when sacrificed, makes itself fruitful, so that it may rise again in the morning in a new and young form. And we can easily prove that the horse of the açvamedhas was a mythical horse, since the açvamedhas was originally a celestial ceremony, seeing we read in the *Ṛigvedas* how the swift heroic horse destined to be sacrificed was born of the gods, and how the Vasavas had adorned it with the colours of the sun.[4] We saw a short time ago

---

1 *Râmây.* i. 13. 2 i. 13.

3 In the Western stories, instead of the horse's fat or marrow, it is generally the fish eaten by the queen and her servant-maid which gives life to the two brothers, who become three when the water in which the fish was washed is given to be drunk by the mare or the bitch, whence the son of the mare or bitch is born. I have already attempted to prove the identity of the fish with the phallos; the fish eaten by the queen, the maid, the mare, or the bitch, which renders them pregnant, seems to me a symbol of coition. The horse's fat or marrow smelled by the queen seems to have the same meaning.

4 Vâgino devagâtasya sapteḥ pravakshyâmo vidathe vîryâṇi; *Ṛigv.* i. 162, 1.—Sûrâd açvaṁ vasavo nir atashṭa; *Ṛigv.* i. 163, 2.

how in the *Ṛigvedas* itself it is now the Açvinâu, and now Agnis who give the heroic steed to the predestined youth. Agnis, moreover, who gives a horse to the hero, is himself now a handsome red horse, and now an excellent ghṛidhnus,[1] a word which means the ravisher, as well as the vulture (as a bird of prey). The thief plays a principal part, even in the Vedic myths. In the war between the demons and the gods, described at length in the first book of the *Mahâbhâratam*, there is a continual strife between the two sides as to who will show himself the most skilful in stealing the cup which contains the ambrosia. And the horse's head which, according to Hindoo cosmogomy, is born in the very production of the ambrosia with the mythical gem, the horse's heads of Dadhyańć and of Vishṇus, which are found in the ambrosia [through the mouth of which (Vaḍavamukhas) it is necessary to pass in order to enter hell, where one hears the cries and howls of the tormented, who inhabit the water[2]], shows us how already in the myth the legend of the theft of the earrings (the Açvinâu), or of the queen's gem (the sun), or of the treasure, must be united with the theft of the horse (the sun itself), as it seems to be united in the legend of Utañkas, before quoted, in which Utañkas flees upon the divine horse as he carries away from hell the earrings of the queen, which another skilful thief, the king of the serpents, had, in his turn, stolen from him. (Herodotos already knew the story of the skilful thief who robs the king's treasure and obtains

[1] Sâdhur na gṛidhnuḥ; *Ṛigv.* i. 70, 11.

[2] Vikroçatâm nâdo bhûtânâm salilâukasâm çrûyate bhṛiçâmârttânâṁ viçatâm vaḍavâmukham; *Râmây.* iv. 40.—Aurvas, who, in the shape of a horse's head, swallows the water of the sea and vomits flames, is a variety of the same solar myth; *Mbh.* i. 6802, and following verses.

the king's daughter to wife; he applies it to the king of Egypt, Rampsinitos.)

When the stag, in the fable, flees in the forest, his high horns betray him; when the bull flees, he fears that his horns may betray the fugitives; even the mane of the solar hero takes the name of horns. The Vedic hymn describing the horse destined for the sacrifice, represents it as having golden horns, and feet as rapid as thought (like the stag), whose horns (or whose mane, like the hair of the biblical Absalom, who revives again in the legendary tradition of Mediæval Europe under an analogous form), stretching here and there, are caught in the trees of the forest.[1] Here, therefore, we have the swift-footed animal, whose mane and horns are entangled to the trees. Another Vedic hymn presents to us the hero Tugras lost in the sea, who embraces a tree, and is saved by means of it.[2] In popular stories, the hero is often saved upon a tree, either because the thieves or the bear cannot see him, or because he is thus able to see the horizon; the tree brings good luck to him, now because by letting something drop or making a noise, he terrifies the thieves, now because he cheats the cowherds, whose cattle he wishes to possess himself of, by appearing now

[1] Hiraṇyaçriñgo yo asya pâdâ manoǵavâ; *Ṛigv.* i. 163, 9.—Tava çriñgâṇi vishṭhitâ purutr âraṇyeshu ǵarbhurâṇâ ćaranti. 11.—We find the stag in relation with the horse, as his stronger rival until man mounts upon the horse's back, in the well-known apologue of Horace, *Epist.* i. 10.

> "Cervus equum pugna melior communibus herbis
> Pellebat, donec minor in certamine longo
> Imploravit opes hominis, frenumque recepit;
> Sed postquam victor discessit ab hoste,
> Non equitem dorso, non frenum depulit ore."

[2] Vṛiksho nishṭhito madhye arṇaso yaṁ tâugryo nâdhitaḥ paryashasvaǵat; *Ṛigv.* i. 182, 7.

upon one tree, and now upon another; whereupon the cowherds begin to dispute about his identity, one affirming that it is the same person, another that it cannot be; they therefore hastily go back to inspect the first tree, and leave the cattle unguarded, upon which the hero-thief descends from the tree, and drives them away before him (this occurs in *Afanassieff;* the enemy of robbers is generally himself an exceedingly skilful thief; Kereçâçpa was no less a cunning thief than Mercury, the god of robbers, who discovers the deceit of others, because he is himself so expert a deceiver). In the nineteenth Mongol story, which is of Hindoo origin, the young hero, after having discharged his pious filial duties at the tomb of his father, mounts a fiery horse, while he seizes the the branch of a tree. The tree is uprooted, and with it the horse and the hero massacre the army of the king, whose daughter the hero wishes to marry. In the Russian story[1] which narrates the adventures of Little Thomas Berennikoff, blind of an eye, the *miles gloriosus,* Little Tom, after killing an army of flies, begins to boast of the heroism he had shown in overthrowing, by himself, a whole army of light cavalry. He meets with two real heroes, Elias of Murom and Alexin Papović (son of the priest), who, on hearing him narrate his achievements, immediately own and honour him as their elder brother. The valour of the three is soon put to the proof; Elias and Alexin show themselves to be true heroes; at last it comes to Little Tom's turn to make proof of his valour; he kills a hostile hero whilst his eyes are shut, and then endeavours to ride his horse, but cannot. It is a hero's horse, and can be ridden only by a hero. At length he fastens the horse to an oak-tree, and climbs up the tree

[1] *Afanassieff,* v. 11.

in order to leap from it upon the horse's back. The horse feels the man on his back, and plunges so much that he roots up the whole tree, and drags it after him, carrying Tom away into the heart of the Chinese army. The Chinese are struck down by the oak-tree and trodden under foot by the furious charger, and those who are not killed are put to flight. (The mythical wooden horse which proved so fatal to the Trojans appears to be a mythical variety of this horse with the tree so fatal to the Chinese.) The Emperor of China declares that he will never make war again with a hero of Little Tom's strength. Then the King of Prussia, an enemy of the Chinese, gives, in gratitude to Tom, and as a reward for his valour, his own daughter to wife. It is remarkable that, in the course of the story, Alexin once observes to Elias that the horse which Little Tom had brought from his house showed none of the characteristic qualities of a hero's horse. Alexin, as the priest's son, is the wise hero; Elias, the strong one, who had conceived a high opinion of his new colleague, Little Tom, seriously answers that a hero's strength consists in himself, and not in his horse. However, the development of the story shows that Alexin was right; without the fiery horse of the dead hero, Tom would not have dispersed the Chinese.

Thus, in a Vedic hymn,[1] we read that Indras, when he removes himself from his two horses, becomes like to a weak and wearied mortal; when he yokes them, he becomes strong. The enemies in the battles cannot resist the charge of the two fair-coloured horses of the god Indras;[2] and not only this, but one part alone of the

[1] Apa yor indraḥ pâpaǵa â marto na çaçramâṇo bibhîvân çubhe yad yuyuǵe tavishîvân; *Ṛigv.* x. 105, 3.

[2] Iasya saṁsthe na vṛiṇvate harî samatsu çatravaḥ; *Ṛigv.* i. 5, 4.

divine horse is sometimes sufficient to give assurance of victory to the hero-god. Another hymn[1] sings, "A horse's tail wert thou then, O Indras;" that is, when Indras vanquished the monster serpent. It is with the head of the horse Dadhyańć that Indras discomfits his enemies.[2] The horse of the Açvinâu, which kills the monster serpent, has already been referred to in these pages. The solar horse Dadhikrâ, the same as Dadhyańć, in another hymn of the *Ṛigvedas*,[3] is celebrated as a swift falcon, luminous, impetuous, who destroys his enemies like a hero-prince, who runs like the wind. His enemies tremble, terrified by him, as by the thundering sky; he fights against a thousand enemies—invincible, formidable, and resplendent. Finally, the horses of the god Agnis are said to vanquish the enemies with their fore-feet.[4]

When Añgadas wishes to fight with the monster Narântakas, in the *Râmâyaṇam*,[5] he strikes with his fist the head of his great and swift-footed horse, and then with another blow he smites the monster in the chest, and kills him.

In the seven adventures of Rustem, related by Firdusi,

[1] Açvyo vâro abhavas tad indra; *Ṛigv.* i. 32, 12; and the Hindoo commentator notes that Indras chased the enemy as the tail of a horse shakes off the insects that place themselves upon it, which it is much more natural to believe of the tail of Indras's horse, which is covered with milk, butter, honey, and ambrosia.

[2] *Ṛigv.*, the hymn quoted before, i. 84, 13, 14; Agnis, too, is honoured as a tailed horse (vâravantam açvam), *Ṛigv.* i. 27, 1.

[3] Ṛiǵipyaṁ çyenam prushitapsum âçum ćarkṛityam aryo nṛipatiṁ na çûram—vâtam iva dhraǵantam—uta smâsya tanyator iva dyor ṛighâyato abhiyuǵo bhayante yadâ sahasram abhi shîm ayodhîd durvartuḥ smâ bhavati bhîma ṛińgan; *Ṛigv.* iv. 38, 2, 3, 8.

[4] Avakrâmantaḥ prapadâir amitrân; *Ṛigv.* vi. 75, 7.

[5] vi. 49.

the hero's horse fights against the monster, and drives him away, while the hero sleeps.

It is said of Bucephalus, the horse which Alexander the Great alone was able to tame—so called because he had, it would seem, on his head protuberances similar to the horns of a bull (we saw not long since how the mane of the solar horse is spoken of as horns in the Vedic hymns)—that he several times saved Alexander in battle, and that, though mortally wounded, in an engagement in India, in the flank and head, he still summoned up strength enough to flee away with extraordinary swiftness and save his master, and then died. Pliny, quoting Philarcus, says that when Antiochus was slain, the warrior who had killed him endeavoured to ride his horse, but that the latter threw him on the ground, and he expired.

Of Pêgasos, the winged horse which bore the hero Bellerophon over the waters, and by means of whom that hero won his glorious victories, we know that the warrior-goddess Pallas wore the effigy upon her helmet.

Suetonius writes of the horse of Julius Cæsar that it had almost human feet, with toes ("pedibus prope humanis, et in modum digitorum ungulis fissis"), from which the aruspices prognosticated to Cæsar the empire of the world; this horse, like Bucephalus, and every heroic courser, would bear no other rider than its master—the great conqueror.

The horse Baiardo, in *Ariosto*, fights the enemies with its feet. The hippogriff of Ariosto has, moreover, the privilege of being winged like Pêgasos, and of walking on air, like the Tatos of the Hungarians. The name of Falke, given to the horse of the Germanic and Scandinavian hero Dietrich or Thidrek (Theodoricus), induces us to believe that it too had the same winged nature.

In the *Edda,* Skirner receives from Frey a horse which carried its rider through fogs (waters) and flames, and the sword which strikes of itself when the wearer of it happens to be a hero. The horse of Sigurd or Sîfrit exhibits the same bravery in bearing the hero intact through the flames. This happens in the morning, when the sun emerges safe and sound from the flames of the aurora; in the evening, on the contrary, when the sun loses itself in the flames of the aurora, or when the solar hero dies, his horse, too, like the horse of Balder in the *Edda,* is burned upon the pyre or sacrificed; the resurrection of the dead horse and that of the dead hero happen at the same time. The horse's head which protrudes out of the window, represented in ancient Hellenic tombs, and preserved in Germanic customs,[1] is, for man, a symbol of resurrection. The head of Vishṇus, that of Uććâiḥçravas, and that of Dadhyańć, in Hindoo tradition, have the same meaning. He who enters into this head finds death and hell; he who comes out of it rises again to new life. The pious Christian belief in the resurrection that is to come, and the numerous mediæval legends of Europe concerning dead heroes or maidens who are resuscitated, had their origin and ground in the contemplation of the annual and daily resurrection of the sun.

In the thirty-eighth story of the fifth book of *Afanassieff,* the young prince receives from an enchanted bird the present of a war-charger, and of an apple the colour of the sun. (The youth gives the golden apple to a beautiful princess for the pleasure of passing the night with her; remark here, again, the relation of the horse and the apple, and probably of the horse and the bull, the sun and moon).

[1] Cfr. Simrock, *Handbuch der Deutschen Mythologie,* p. 375, and Rochholtz, the work quoted before.

In other Russian stories, the horse of the hero, Ivan Tzarević, is at first bound underground by twelve iron chains; when Ivan rides him, he breaks them all.[1] The horse which Ivan the thief is told to carry off from his master[2] is shut up within three gates made fast by six bolts; if he steals it, he is to receive a reward of 200 roubles; and if he does not, 200 bastinadoes will be his punishment. Ivan takes his master's clothes, disguises himself as a gentleman, and, imitating his voice, orders the grooms to bring him his favourite horse. The grooms are deceived, and obey, and thus Ivan carries the horse off. Finally, in a third Russian story,[3] Ivan Tzarević must ride a hero's horse on the occasion of his nuptials with the beautiful but wicked Anna. He has recourse to his preceptor Katoma, surnamed Hat of Oak (here we find again the hero in relation with the tree and the horse), who orders the blacksmith to prepare a hero's horse; twelve young blacksmiths (the twelve hours of the night, or else the twelve months of the year) draw twelve bolts, open twelve doors, and lead out an enchanted horse, bound with twelve iron chains. Scarcely has the preceptor mounted on its back when it flies higher than the forest which stays still, and lower than the cloud which moves.[4] The preceptor subdues it by taking hold of its mane with one hand, and striking it with the other between the ears with four pieces, one after another, of an enchanted iron pillar. The horse then begs, with a man's voice, for its life, the power of speech being a distinctive attribute of the hero's horse (a power of which it often makes use, as Rustem's horse does, for instance, to warn the hero of the dangers which surround him, and to give him good

[1] *Afanassieff*, ii. 24. [2] *Ib.* v. 6. [3] *Ib.* v. 35.

[4] Povíshe liessú stajáćavo, ponísze ablaká hadiáćavo.

advice; sometimes, on the contrary, when it is in the monster's power, it plays the part of a spy upon the hero's actions, and reports them to the monster);[1] it promises also to do the will of the preceptor. Katoma, calling the horse dog's flesh, orders it to stay still the next day, which is the day fixed for the wedding, and, when the bridegroom Ivan is to ride it, to seem as though it were oppressed by a great weight.

In the seventh Esthonian story, the young hero steals the horse from the master (the devil, or the black monster of night) in whose service he had engaged himself. When he comes to the place where the sun sets, he bethinks himself of binding the horse with iron chains (the rope of Yamas, or Varuṇas, the nocturnal coverer or binder, which binds the Vedic hero Çunaḥçepas, the sun, he of the golden rod), in order that it may not escape and go back again. This particular is very interesting, as rendering the meaning of the myth more manifest. Seeing that the sun, in the evening, does not return, it was supposed that the solar horse had been bound by the hero himself, who had stolen it.

In the European popular tales we sometimes have, instead of the hero who carries off his master's horse, the hero himself, who escapes from his master in the form of a horse, helped in his flight by the daughter of his master, by the magician's or demon's daughter or black maiden

[1] For instance, in the *Pentamerone*, iii. 7, where the king of Scotland sends Corvetto to steal the horse of the ogre who lives ten miles distant from Scotland: "Haveva st' Huorco no bellissimo cavallo, che pareva fatto co lo penniello, e tra le autre bellizze no le mancava manco la parola." When Corvetto carries off the horse, it cries out, "A l'erta ca Corvetto me ne porta."—Cfr. also the *Pentamerone*, iii. 1. —Not only has the horse the gift of speech, but the chariot too: in the seventh book of the *Râmâyaṇam*, 44, the chariot Pushpakam speaks to Râmas, and says to him that he alone is worthy of driving it.

(who afterwards becomes beautiful and luminous). In the Hungarian belief, the youngest of the witch's daughters (the aurora) often assumes the form of the heroic horse of the Tatos. She becomes Tatos when the hero, meeting her, strikes her on the forehead with the bridle; then she carries him, in the shape of a horse, into the air. In the Russian story,[1] the son of a merchant goes to be instructed by a wise magician, who teaches him every kind of knowledge, and, among the rest, what sheep say when they bleat, birds when they sing, and horses when they neigh. At last the young man, having learned every species of mischief, returns home and transforms himself into a horse, in order that his father may sell him at the market and make money; but he warns his father not to give up the bridle, that he may not fall again into the hands of the magician. The father forgets, and sells horse and bridle together. The magician attaches the horse by a ring to an oak-tree; the black maiden (dievki ćernavke), the sister of the devil, gives the horse millet and hydromel; the horse thus gains strength enough to break the chain which binds him to the tree, and escapes. The devil follows him; the horse becomes a fish, and from a fish a ring; the king's daughter buys the ring and puts it on her finger; during the day it is a ring (the solar disc), and during the night a handsome youth, who lies in the bed of the queen's daughter (the hidden sun, or the moon, in the darkness of night). One day the princess lets the ring fall on the ground, and it breaks into a thousand pieces (the evening sun which falls upon the mountain); then the devil becomes a cock, to pick up the pieces of the broken ring; but a little piece falls

---

[1] *Afanassieff*, vi. 46.—Cfr. also v. 22, and the 26th of the *Novelline di Santo Stefano di Calcinaia.*

under the princess's foot; this piece is transformed into a falcon, which strangles and devours the cock.

In the bridle which binds this hero who becomes a horse, I think I can recognise the lasso with which Varuṇas keeps Çunaḥçepas bound in the *Âitareya Br.* In the *Ṛigvedas,*[1] we have Sûryas, the sun, as Sâuvaçvyas, or son of Svaçvyas, that is, of him who has fine horses; but as, besides Svaçvyas, we find Svaçvas, he who has a fine horse, the sun itself would seem to be this horse. The legend narrates that Svaçvas, having no children, requested the sun to give him some, and that the sun, to please him, was himself born of him. Svaçvas, he who has a fine horse and has no sons, is perhaps the same as the old man who has lost his son by selling the horse; when the sun returns his son also comes back again. In the Vedic expressions, *without a horse, born without a bridle, the sun* (as a courser[2]), the hero would seem to be indicated who has not as yet that horse or that bridle, without which he is powerless; for the idea of the hero is rarely unaccompanied by that of the horseman.

For the horseman hero his horse is his all, and sometimes it even takes the bit in its mouth, then the hero punishes it. We have already noticed the well-known Hellenic myth of Phaethôn, who is, with both the chariot and the horses, precipitated into the waters, because the horses threatened to set the earth on fire. This happens every day towards evening, when the sun sets; the whole sky goes down, then the sun is thrown down into the ocean of night; the course of the solar steeds is interrupted, and the wheels of the chariot no longer turn. A similar catastrophe is repeated on St John's Day, at the

[1] i. 61, 15.
[2] Anaçvo ǵâto anabhîçur arvâ; *Ṛigv.* i. 152, 5.

summer solstice, in which the sun stops and begins to retire, for which reason the light of day, from this time to Christmas, grows less and less.

It is a custom on St John's Day, in Germany,[1] for hunters to fire at the sun, believing that they will thereby become infallible hunters. According to another popular German belief, he who, on St John's Day, fires towards the sun is condemned ever after to hunt for ever, like Odin, the eternal hunter; and both superstitions have their reason. In the night, as well as in the period during which the splendour of the sun diminishes, and especially in autumn, the gloomy forest of heaven is filled with every kind of ferocious animal; the sun enters this forest, becomes moon, and hunts the wild beasts in it during the whole of the night, or of the year, that is, until he is born again. In the *Ṛigvedas,* where we have seven sister-mares yoked to the sun-chariot,[2] Indras, to please his favourite, Etaças, after having drunk the ambrosia, pushes the clouds that had fallen behind before the flying steeds of the sun,[3] that is to say, he prevents the solar hero, drawn by horses, either by the cloud in a tempest, or by the darkness of night, from going on; and he even strikes the wheels themselves of the solar chariot to arrest its incendiary course. From these Vedic data it is easy to pass to the Hellenic Phaethôn, who is precipitated into the waters on account of the horses. The hero killed on account of his horses is a frequent subject of mythology, and the Greek name Hippolytos refers to this

---

1 Cfr. Menzel, *Die Vorchristliche Unsterblichkeits-Lehre.*

2 Sapta svasârah̤ suvitâya sûryaṁ vahanti harito rathe; *Ṛigv.* vii. 66, 15.

3 Adha kratvâ maghavan tubhyaṁ devâ anu viçve adaduh̤ somapeyam yat sûryasya haritah̤ patantîh̤ purah satîr uparâ etaçe kah̤; *Ṛigv.* v. 29, 5.

kind of death. Hippolytos, the son of Theseus, fleeing from his father, who supposes him guilty of incest with his step-mother Phedra, is thrown from the chariot broken to pieces, when the horses that draw it approach the sea and are terrified by marine monsters. This is a variation of the legend of the young hero, persecuted by his step-mother, who is thrown into the sea, with the novel and remarkable accompaniment that it is his horses themselves which are the cause of his death. The Christian legend of St Hippolytos has appropriated this particular trait, representing the holy martyr, who was prefect under the emperors Decius and Valerian, as dying, having been condemned to be torn in pieces by horses. The poet Prudentius comments upon the story in these two curious distichs, on the occasion of the Roman judge pronouncing capital punishment against St Hippolytos—

> "Ille supinata residens cervice, quis inquit
> Dicitur? affirmant dicier Hippolytum.
> Ergo sit Hippolytus; quatiat turbetque jugales
> Intereatque feris dilaceratus equis."

But the horses which draw the hero into the water are the same as those that save him by carrying him over the deep, drawing the chariot or ship on the sea towards the shore. The Açvinâu do the same in the *Ṛigvedas*, where they save from the waves both themselves and other heroes upon their chariot, which is compared to a ship.[1] Hero and horse always have the same fate.

When the hero approaches, or when some fortunate incident is about to happen to the hero, his horse neighs for joy.

[1] Â no nâvâ matînâṁ yâtam parâya gantave, yuṅgâthâm açvinâ ratham; *Ṛigv.* i. 46, 7.

In the *Ṛigvedas*,[1] on the arrival of the god Indras, the horse neighs, the cow lows, like a messenger between heaven and earth. The neighing of this horse, and the lowing of this cow, are the thundering of the sun in the cloud. By this neighing or lowing, man is informed that the hero-god Indras is beginning his battles in heaven. Another hymn, which calls the two horses of Indras two rays of the sun (sûryasya ketû), celebrates them as neighing and pouring out ambrosia,[2] *i.e.*, the sun makes rain fall from the clouds; when he shows himself in the east at morn, his horse neighs and drops the dew on the ground.

Herodotus, and, after him, Oppianos and Valerius Maximus, relate the mythical story of Darius Hystaspes, who unexpectedly succeeded to the empire from having persuaded his colleagues to decree that he should obtain the crown whose horse happened first to neigh at the sight of the sun. It is narrated that when he came to the place, Darius, in order to assure himself of success, made his horse smell the odour of a mare.[3] Neighing is the laughter of the horse. We have seen, in the preceding chapter, how the bull speaks and the fish laughs at sight of coition; and so we have here, in the story of Darius, the horse who neighs on account of the mare.—To return to the horse of mythology; the solar horse neighs

[1] Krandad açvo nayamâno ruvad gâur antar dûto na rodasî ćarad vâk; *Ṛigv.* i. 173, 3.

[2] Ghṛitaçćutaṁ svâram asvârshṭâm; *Ṛigv.* ii. 11, 7.

[3] . . . in equæ genitalem partem demissam manum, cum ad eum locum ventum esset, naribus equi admovit, quo odore irritatus ante omnes hinnitum edidit, auditoque eo sex reliqui summæ potestatis continuo equis dilapsi candidati, ut mos est Persarum, humi prostratis corporibus Darium regem salutarunt; Valerius Maximus, *Mem.* vii.; *Herodotus*, iii. 87. Herodotus also refers to another variation of the same anecdote, where he adds, that at the first dawn of day it lightned and thundered.

within the thundering-cloud which, as a cow, the bull makes pregnant, and as a mare, the stallion, and neighs at the approach of the aurora, who appears now as the driver of a hundred chariots [1] (a round number, like the hundred thousand horses which, in another hymn,[2] the god Indras drives ; a favourite number, like seven, which is applied to the same solar horses, solar rays and Añgirasas[3])—on which account it can be compared with the Hellenic Aphroditê Hippodameia—now even as a real mare. The sun is now a driver of horses, and now himself a horse ; in the same way, the aurora is now an Amazon horsewoman, now a driver of chariots, now açvâvatî, and now a mare. When the sun approaches the aurora, or when the horse approaches the mare, the horse neighs. We know how the Açvinâu considered themselves sons of the wife of the sun, Saraṇyû, daughter of Tvashṭar, who united herself to the sun in the form of a mare. Whether this Saraṇyû be the cloud or the aurora, we have in her, anyhow, a mare with which the sun, solar hero, or solar horse, unites himself to produce the twin heroes, who are, for this reason, also called the two sons of the mare.[4] We have already seen, in the preceding chapter, a hero and a heroine who are hatched from eggs ; of the Dioscuri, we know that they were born of the egg of Leda ; and the mare's egg is the subject of a story in the *Ukermark.*[5] Greek writers have handed down several

---

[1] Devî ĝîrâ rathânâm ; *Ṛigv.* i. 48, 3.—Çataṁ rathebhiḥ subhagoshâ iyaṁ vi yâty abhi mânushân ; i. 48, 7.

[2] Upa tmani dadhâno dhury âçûnt sahasrâṇi çatâni vaĝrabâhuḥ ; *Ṛigv.* iv. 29, 4.

[3] Cfr. *Ṛigv.* iv. 3, 11 ; iv. 13, 3.

[4] Cfr. Böhtling u. Roth, *Sansksṛit Wörterbuch,* s. v. *açvin.*

[5] Kuhn u. Schwartz, p. 330.—The English proverbial expression, "a mare's nest," now used to denote an impossibility, probably originally referred to a real myth.

cases of coition between men and mares, and between horses and women, with corresponding births of monstrous conformation. Now, unnatural as such births must appear to us, they are, in mythology, in strict accordance with nature. In the preceding chapter we saw the cow which leaps over the hare, and explained this phenomenon by the cloud or darkness covering the moon, and also by the earth covering the moon in eclipses. In Herodotus and Valerius Maximus, a mare, in the time of Xerxes, gives birth to a hare; and we must here understand the hare to be the moon, coming out of the darkness or clouds; and when we read that the hare suffocated the mare, we must understand it to mean the moon as dispersing the darkness or clouds (perhaps also the sun or evening aurora). We must have recourse in this way to the myth to comprehend the examples of parturition without coition found in some Hindoo legends, and applied to heroes, as well as the curious discussions and information which we find in the ancients, from Aristotle, Varro, Pliny, Columella, Solinus, and St Augustin, to Albertus Magnus and Aldrovandi, concerning mares, and especially Spanish and Portuguese mares, made pregnant by the wind (called by Oppianos[1] of the windy feet), and which are also spoken of in the *Pentamerone*,[2] with less

[1] *Künêgetikôn*, i. 284.

[2] ii. 3.—"Allecordatose d'haver 'ntiso na vota da certe stodiante, che le cavalle de Spagna se'mpreñano co lo viento;" and the story goes on to speak of the ogre's surprise, who, seeing a beautiful maiden in his garden, "penzaie che lo shiavro de lo pideto, havesse 'ngravedato quarche arvolo, e ne fosse sciuta sta penta criatura; perzo abbracciatala co gran'ammore, decette, figlia mia, parte de sto cuorpo, shiato de lo spireto mio, e chi me l' havesse ditto mai, che co na ventosetate, havesse dato forma a ssa bella facce?" Varro seriously wrote: "In fætura res incredibilis est in Hispania, sed est vera, quod in Lusitania ad Oceanum in ea regione, ubi est oppidum Olyssipo monte Tagro,

decency, in reference to the myth of the maiden born of the tree.

The horse of Ariosto, too, has a similar nature—

> "Questo è il destrier che fu dell' Argalia
> Che di fiamma e di vento era concetto
> E senza fieno e biada si nutria
> De l' aria pura e Rabican fu detto."

The horse of Ciolle, in a Tuscan proverb, also feeds upon wind alone.

The horse of Dardanos, son of Zeus, was also said to be born of the wind, which brings us back to the Vedic Marutas, whose chariots have horses for wings, and to the *volucer currus* of the Diespiter of Horace.[1] In the Sanskṛit tongue, the expression *vâtâçvas*, or wind-horse, is very common, to indicate a very swift-footed horse.

No sooner is the horse Uććâiḥçravas born than he neighs; and like him, in the *Mahâbhâratam*, the hero Açvatthâman laughs, the son of Droṇas, properly he who has strength in his horse, which is the same as the hero-horse.

Moreover, as the horse exults by neighing over the good fortune of the hero who rides him, so he not only becomes sad, but sheds real tears when his rider is about to meet with misfortune.

When Râvaṇas, in the *Râmâyaṇam*, comes forth in his chariot, to join in final combat with Râmas, his

quædam e vento concipiunt equæ, ut hic gallinæ solent, quarum ova hypanemia appellant, sed ex his equis qui nati pulli, non plus triennium vivunt."

[1] Rathebhir açvaparṇâiḥ; *Ṛigv.* i. 88, 1.—In Horace, *Carm.* i. 14—

> "Namque Diespiter,
> Igni corusco nubila dividens,
> Plerumque per purum tonantes
> Egit equos, volucremque currum."

coursers shed tears,[1] as a sinister omen, Râvanas is the monster of darkness and clouds; when the cloud begins to disperse, drops of rain fall, that is, the horses of the monster weep. The treacherous sister who is confederate with the monster against her brother, in Russian stories, is condemned by her brother, who kills the monster, to fill a whole basin with her tears.[2] These tears are also a legendary symbol of the rain which falls when the solar hero has torn the cloud in two.

Suetonius, in the Life of Cæsar, writes that the horses consecrated by Cæsar to Mars, and then set at liberty after the passage of the Rubicon, refused to eat, and wept abundantly.[3] Note that this legend of the horses that weep is connected with the passage of water, of the Rubicon (a river which no geographer has been able to identify with certainty, probably because the legend of Cæsar relating to it is a fable of mythical origin. We know how mythical beliefs incline to assume a human form, and are especially prone to group themselves round the great personages of history—Cyrus, Alexander, Romulus, Cæsar, Augustus, Vespasian, Attila, Theodoric, and Charlemagne are proofs of this; and perhaps a day will come in which Napoleon I. or Garibaldi will offer a new *mannequin* to some popular tradition, which is now uncertain and wandering). Thus it is said that Cæsar's horse itself shed tears for three days before the hero's death. In the *Iliad*,[4] the horses of Achilleus

[1] Açrûṇi ćâsya mumucurvâǵinaḥ; *Râmây.* vi. 75.

[2] In the corresponding Italian stories, the hero or heroine, punished for some indiscretion, must, before being pardoned, wear out seven pairs of iron shoes, and fill seven flasks with their tears.

[3] Proximus diebus equorum greges, quos in trajiciendo Rubicon Marti consacraverat, ac sine custodibus vagos dimiserat, comperit pabulo pertinacissime abstinere, ubertimque flere.

[4] xvii. 426.

weep for the death of Patroklos, whom Hektor has thrown from his chariot into the dust; in the *Paraleipomenoi* of Quintus Smyrneus,[1] the horses of Achilleus weep bitterly for the death of their hero. This is a variety of the legend of the horses which throw the solar hero down into the waters, the ocean of night or the clouds, and of that of the horses of Poseidôn. The mists which after sunset in the evening impregnate the air, and the diurnal or nocturnal rains, as well as the autumnal ones, cause tears to fall upon the ground, or weep over the (apparent) death of the solar hero.

The dew of the morning, on the contrary, which comes from the mouth of the solar horse like foam, or from its hoof as ambrosia and salutary water, is fraught with every species of healthful influence.

The horse and the bull of mythology are pourers out *par excellence.* In a Vedic strophe—which seems in my eyes to be one of those riddles which are recited in order to loosen the thread of the tongue—relative to the two outpouring or fertilising horses of Indras, there is a continual play kept up upon the root *varsh* or *vṛish,* which means at once to pour out and to make fruitful,[2] and upon the letter *r* which enters into almost every word of the verse. Not only do the horses of Indras pour out and make fruitful; the same virtue is attributed to the chariot which they draw.[3] We have seen already that

---

[1] iii. 740.

[2] Vṛishâ tvâ vṛishaṇaṁ vardhatu dyâur vṛishâ vṛishabhyâm vahase haribhyâm sa no vṛisha vṛisharathaḥ suçipra vṛishakrato vṛishâ vagrin bhare dhâh; *Ṛigv.* v. 36, 5.—In Piedmont there exists a game of conversation, consisting in the description of the presents which one intends making to one's bride, in which description the letter *r* must never enter; he who introduces it loses the game.

[3] Vṛishâyam indra te ratha uto te vṛishaṇâ harî; *Ṛigv.* viii. 13, 31.

the horse of the Açvinâu is the killer of the monster serpent, and that the horse's head Dadhyańć, he who goes in the milk or in the liquefied butter, and who is found in a sea of milk, discomfits the enemies of Indras. A Vedic hymn sings that, with the foam of the waters, Indras beats down the head of the monster serpent.[1] In Tuscany, the whooping-cough is called the horse-cough or asinine-cough,[2] and it is thought that the cough is cured by giving the children to drink the foam from the horse's mouth, or causing them to drink in the water where a horse has been drinking. This is a remedy founded upon the principle *similia similibus,* the foam being used against the convulsive cough, which, like all convulsions in general, brings much saliva or foam to the mouth. The credit, however, of this marvellous medicine is slightly compromised when we read that the same foam is also very efficacious for ear-ache. Pliny, Sextus Empiricus, and Marcellus, quoted by Aldrovandi,[3] also recommend the saliva of a horse as a cure for cough, particularly in the case of consumptive patients, adding that the sick person is cured in three days, but that the horse dies; a superstition which must have had its origin in the mythical horse who feeds on ambrosia, and who loses his strength, and expires when his saliva, foam, ambrosia, or dew is taken from him. It is well known that the Açvinâu, besides being luminous horsemen, were, as friends of men, also exceedingly skilful physicians; nor could they be otherwise, having in their power the head of Dadhyańć which is in

[1] Apâm phenena namućeḥ çira indrod avartayaḥ; *Ṛigv.* viii. 14, 13.

[2] It is also called the canine cough, and it is believed on this account that it is cured when the children are made to drink where a dog has been drinking.

[3] *De Quadrupedibus* i.

the ambrosia, that is, whose foam is ambrosia. The Dioscuri also frequently appear, in European legends, as unexpected and miraculous deliverers. With this mythical belief of the horse that produces ambrosia, is also connected the transformation, described by Ovid in the second book of the *Metamorphoses*, of Ocyroe into a mare, because she had predicted that Æsculapius would save men from death by the medical art. It is a well-known fact that Æsculapius was revered near fountains whose waters were supposed to have salutary effects, and that he was protected by the sun-god Apollo; and the two physicians, sons of Asklêpios or Æsculapius, seem to be nothing more than a specific form of the Dioscuri.

But the solar horse does not produce ambrosia with his mouth alone.

He has great strength in his hoofs (whence Isidorus and other mediæval etymologists derived the name *caballus*, thus, "Quod ungula terram cavet"[1]), and makes use of them in the myth, and in the legend, not only to combat the enemies, but also to break open the earth, and cause ambrosial fountains to spring out of it. Sometimes ambrosia pours out of the hoof of the horse itself. In the *Ṛigvedas*,[2] the horses of Agnis are said to have hands (*i.e.*, hoofs of the fore-feet) that pour out; and the horse given by the Açvinâu to the hero protected by them (that is, to the solar horse, to the morning sun), with his strong hoof fills a hundred jars with inebriating liquor.[3] It is not necessary for me to instance here the famous fountain of the horse, or

[1] Du Cange, *Gloss. Mediæ et Infimæ Latinitatis*, s. v. *caballus*.

[2] Vṛshapâṇayo 'çvâḥ; *Ṛigv.* vi. 75, 7.

[3] Kârotarâć ćhaphâd açvasya vṛishṇaḥ çataṁ kumbhâṅ asińćataṁ surâyaḥ; *Ṛigv.* i. 116, 7.

Hippokrênê, which Bellerophon's horse Pêgasos caused to spring out of the earth by breaking the soil with his hoof (called also for this reason *Pêgasía krênê*). In Latin tradition, the horse's hoof was worshipped on a spot near Lake Regillus, where it is said that the Dioscuri had appeared.[1] In a Russian story,[2] when Johnny (Ivanushka) sees a horse's hoof, he is sorely tempted to drink out of it, but is dissuaded by his sister. He experiences the same temptation upon seeing a bull's hoof, and afterwards that of a kid. At last he gives way, drinks from the kid's hoof, and is himself transformed into a kid. In the footprint of a horse's hoof, in other stories, the ant is in danger of being drowned; saved by a man, it is ever afterwards grateful to him.[3]

Several myths which we have already noticed in the preceding chapter as applied to the bull, occur again in connection with the horse; as, for instance, the birds which come out of the horse; the hero who takes the horse's skin off, seizing it by the tail in order to make a sack of it; the swift horse of Adrastus, which runs after the tortoise (a Greek proverb);[4] the lunar horse, and

[1] "One spot on the margin of Lake Regillus was for many ages regarded with superstitious awe. A mark, resembling in shape a horse's hoof, was discernible in the volcanic rock; and this mark was believed to have been made by one of the celestial chargers."—Macaulay, Preface to the *Battle of the Lake Regillus.*

[2] *Afanassieff*, iv. 45.

[3] The milk of white mares, which, according to Olaus Magnus (i. 24) was poured into the ground by the king of the Goths every year, on the 28th of August, in honour of the gods, who received it with great avidity, would seem to be an announcement of the imminent rains of autumn; the horse loses his ambrosial humour, and his end is at hand.

[4] The Græco-Latin proverb, "Equus me portat, alit rex," would seem also to have a mythical origin, and to refer to the mythical legend

the solar one. These exchanges between moon and sun, and between bull and horse, are happily indicated by the Latin poet, Fulgentius :—

> "Jam Phœbus disjungit equos, jam Cynthia jungit,
> Quasque soror liquit, frater pede temperat undas :
> Tum nox stellato cœlum circumlita peplo
> Cœrula rorigenis pigrescere jusserat alis
> Astrigeroque nitens diademate luna bicornis
> Bullarum bijugis conscenderat æquora tauris."

The gods had often a liking to transform themselves into horses ; so much so, that the sacrifice of the god, that is, the god's death, is represented by the death of the horse. Every one knows that gods and heroes delighted in showing themselves good horsemen, or, at least, good charioteers. On this account, it would be difficult to say to which god in particular the horse is sacred. The Vedic Açvinâu, the Vedic aurora, who wins the race in her chariot, Agnis, Savitar, Indras, victorious and splendid by means of their steeds, the hippios Poseidôn, the hippeia Athênê, the hippodameia Aphroditê, the horsemen Dioscuri, Mars, Apollo, Zeus, Pluto, and the German Wuotan (like his *alter ego*, St Zacchæus), never show themselves otherwise than on horseback ; hence the horse was naturally sacred to all of them. In the Christian faith, the innumerable gods of the ancients having become innumerable saints (when they were not so unfortunate as to degenerate into devils), the horse is now recommended in its stable to the protection of several saints, from the obscure Sicilian St Aloi to the no less modest Russians St Froh and St

---

of the betrayed blind man, who carries the cunning hunchback or lame man ; who sometimes only feigns lameness, in order to play off his practical jokes upon his companion.

Laver, who take the horse, as well as the mule and the ass, under their especial protection, not to speak of the glorious horsemen St George, St Michael, St James, St Maurice, St Stephen, St Vladimir, and St Martin, especially revered by warriors, and in whose honour the principal orders of knighthood in Europe were founded. But religions being, from one point of view, the caricature of mythologies, there is now some difference between the mythical old deities and the legendary new ones, inasmuch as the former would at times ingenuously accept the homage of the animal in effigy, as we have observed in the preceding chapter; while the latter, and they who purvey to them upon earth, not being quite so simple, never leave their devotee in peace until they have received, at sight and without discount, the full value of their favours. In the Life of San Gallo, we read that, in the times of King Pepin (we already know what these times mean), a certain Willimar, being ill, promised, if cured, to offer a horse to the Church of San Gallo. Having recovered his health, he forgot his promise; but passing one day before the church of the saint, his horse stopped before the gate, and by no possibility could it be induced to move on, until Willimar had at last declared his intention of fulfilling his vow. In the Life of St Martin, there is a rather gayer variation of the same anecdote. King Clodoveus, after having become a Christian, when fighting against the Visigoths, promises his own horse to St Martin, if he grants the victory to him. Having obtained it, Clodoveus regrets being obliged to deprive himself of his good charger, and beseeches St Martin to be kind enough to take money instead, offering him a hundred pieces of gold. St Martin thinks the sum insufficient, and asks for double, which Clodoveus gives; but, inasmuch as a little heretic blood still runs in his veins, he cannot refrain from aiming a pointed witticism at him: "Martinus, quantum video, auxiliator est facilis, sed mercator difficilis!"[1]

[1] The fable in *Phædrus*, iv. 24, of the poet Simonides saved by the Dioscuri, is well known; but the gods punish the miser who refuses to give the reward that he had promised, not on their own account, but on account of the wrong done to the poet, whom they love. It is remarkable that, as the Latin legend shows us the horses of the Dioscuri perspiring, so Phædrus represents the Dioscuri themselves as—

"Sparsi pulvere
Sudore multo diffluentes corpore."

This sweat must be the crepuscular mists, in the same way as the poet Simonides, who alone escapes, being delivered by the Dioscuri, the ceiling of whose banqueting-hall he had ruined, seems to conceal an image of the sun saved from the night.

CHAPTER III.

THE ASS.

SUMMARY.

Glory has been pernicious to the ass.—The purely stupid ass not an ancient belief in India.—Eastern and Western asses; the ass of an inferior quality pays the penalty of the reputation acquired in the East by his superior congener.—Christianity, instead of improving the condition of the ass, has aggravated it.—The mediæval hymn in honour of the ass is a satire.—The ass in the sacred ceremonies of the Church.—Physical and moral decadence of the ass.—Indian names of the ass; equivoques in language form myths.—Gardabhas and gandharbas.—Identification of the mythical ass with the gandharvas; both are in connection with salutary waters, with perfumes or unguents, and with women.—The ass which carries mysteries.—The flight into Egypt; the ass laden; the old man, the boy, and the ass.—Peau d'âne.—The onokentauros.—Urvaçî and Purûravas in connection with the gandharvas; Cupid and Psyche in connection with the ass.—The mythical ass and the kentauros correspond, as well as the ass and the gandharvas.—The Hindoo onocentaur and satyr; monkey and gandharvas as warriors.—Kentauros, gandharvas, and ass in the capacity of musicians and dancers.—Kṛiçâçvas dancing-master.—Kṛiçânus and Kereçâni.—Hybrid nature of the mythical ass and of the gandharvas.—The Açvinâu ride asses, and give youth to Ćyavanas; the youthfulness of the ass.—The Vedic ass as a warrior.—The Vedic ass flies.—The decadence of the ass dates as far back as the Vedâs; its explanation.—The phallic ass and the punishment of the ass for adulterers.—The braying of the ass in heaven; Indras kills the ass.—The funereal and demoniacal ass of the Hindoos; the ass piçâćas; the faces of parrots; equivoque originated by the words *haris* and *harit*.—The golden ass.—The ass in love.—The ass in the tiger's skin.—

The ass who betrays himself by singing.—The Zend lame ass who brays in the water.—Rustem, devourer of asses.—The ass's kick.—The fool and the ass, the trumpet and the drum, the trumpet of Malacoda.—The king Midas in the Mongol story; the hero forced to speak, in order not to burst.—The ass among the monkeys.—Midas, king of Phrygia, in connection with the ass, with Silenos, Dionysos, the roses, gold, blades of corn, and waters.—The centaurs among the flowers.—The ass awakens Vesta whilst she is being seduced.—Priapos and the ass of Silenos.—The ass as a musical umpire between the cuckoo and the nightingale.—Midas judges between Pan and Apollo.—The ears of King Midas; his secret revealed by the young man who combs his hair.—The Phrygian ass held up to derision by the Greeks.—The Greek spirit of nationality still more pernicious to the ass.—The ass of Vicenza impaled.—Pan and the ass.—Gandharvâs and satyrs.—Pan and the nymphs.—Syrinx and the reed or cane; the leaf of the cane, and the ass.—Pan chases away fear; the ass's skin gives courage.—The ass in hell; golden excrements.—The heroic ass and Pan.—Perseus who eats asses.—The ass and the water of the Styx; the horned ass.—The cornucopia.—Ass and goat.—The asses save the hero out of the water.—The asses in heaven.—The ass carries the water of youth.—Ass's milk has a cosmetic virtue.—Youth and beauty of the ass.—The deaths of the ass.—The ass carries wine and drinks water.—The ass wet by the rain, the ass's ears predict rainy weather.—The shadow of the ass; the ass's wool; lana caprina; to shear the ass; the gold on the ass's head.—Asini prospectus.—The ass and the gardener.—The ass chases the winds away.—The third braying or flatus of the ass kills the fool.—The prophetic ass; the kick of the ass kills the lion; the ass a good listener, who hears everything; the hero Oidin Oidon; the ears of Lucifer.

THE ass, in Europe at least, has had the misfortune to have been born under an evil star, a circumstance which must be reckoned to the account of the Greeks and Romans, whose humour it was to treat it as a sort of Don Quixote of animals. Its liability to be flogged has always increased with its celebrity, which, no one can deny, is great and indefeasible. The poor ass has paid very dear, and continues to pay still dearer, upon earth for the flight which the fantasy of primeval men made it take in the mythical heavens. May this chapter—if it produce no other effect—have at least that of sparing the poor calumniated animal some few of the many blows which, given in fun, it is accustomed to receive, as if to afford a vent for the satirical humour of our race, and *ad exhilarandam caveam.*

The germ of the reputation the ass has of being both a stupid and a petulant animal, acquired in Greece and in Italy, spreading thence into all the other parts of Europe, may already be found in the ancient myths of the Hindoos. Professor Weber,[1] however, has proved, in answer to Herr Wagener, that the idea of a stupid and presumptuous ass, such as we always find it represented in the fables of the *Pańćatantram,* was diffused in India by the Greeks, and is not indigenous to Hindoo faith and literature.

In India, the ass was not a particular object of ridicule; and this was perhaps for the simple reason that the Eastern varieties of the asinine family are far handsomer and nobler than the Western ones. The ass in the East is generally ardent, lively, and swift-footed, as in the West it is generally slow and lazy, having no real energy except of a sensual nature. For if even the West (and especially the south of Europe) possesses a distinct species of ass, which reminds us of the *multinummus* ass of Varro (in the same way as the East also, though exceptionally, has inferior varieties), the asinine multitude in Europe is composed of animals of a low type and a down-trodden appearance, and it is against them that our jests and our floggings are especially directed. This is the proverbial ass's kick against the fallen; the poor outcast of the West

[1] *Ueber den Zusammenhang indischer Fabeln mit griechischen,* eine kritische Abhandlung von A. Weber, Berlin, 1855.

dearly pays the penalty of the honours conceded to his illustrious mythical ancestors of the East. We think that the ass of which we hear heroic achievements related is the same as that which now humbly carries the pack; and since we no longer regard him as capable of a magnanimous action, we suppose that he (unfortunate animal!) appropriates to himself all these ancient glories out of vain presumption, for which reason there is no affront which we do not feel entitled to offer to him. Nor did Christianity succeed in delivering him from persecution,—Christianity, which, as it represents the Sun of nations, the Redeemer of the world, as born between the two musical animals, the ox and the ass (who were to prevent His cries from being heard), and introduces the ass as the saviour of the Divine Child persecuted during the night, and as the animal ridden by Christ, in his last entry into Jerusalem, invested him with more than one sacred title which ought from its devotees to have procured for him a little more regard. Unfortunately, the same famous mediæval ecclesiastical hymn which was sung in France on the 14th of January in honour of the ass, richly caparisoned near the altar, to celebrate the flight into Egypt, was turned into a satire. It must have been not without some gay levity that priest and people exclaimed "Hinham!" three times after the conclusion of the mass, on the day of the festival of the ass.[1] Nor

[1] Here is the hymn as given by Du Cange in his *Gloss. M. et I. L.*:—

"Orientis partibus
Adventavit Asinus,
Pulcher et fortissimus,
Sarcinis aptissimus.
Hez, Sire Asnes, car chantez,
Belle bouche rechignez,
Vous aurez du fom assez
Et de l'avoine à plantez.

"Lentus erat pedibus
Nisi foret baculus
Et eum in clunibus
Pungeret aculeus.
Hez, Sire Asnes, &c.

"Hic in collibus Sichem,
Jam nutritus sub Ruben,

did the inhabitants of Empoli show him more reverence, when, on the eighth day after the festival of the *Corpus Domini*—that is, near the summer solstice—they made him fly in the air, amid the jeers of the crowd; nor the Germans, who, in Westphalia, made the ass a symbol of the dull St Thomas, who was the last of the apostles to believe in the resurrection. The Westphalians were accustomed to call by the name of "the ass Thomas" (as in Holland he is called "luilak") the boy who on St Thomas's Day was the last to enter school.[1] On Christmas Day, in the Carnival, on Palm-Sunday, and in the processions which follow the festival of *Corpus Domini*,[2]

Transiit per Jordanem,
Saliit in Bethleem.
Hez, Sire Asnes, &c.

"Ecce magnis auribus
Subjugalis filius
Asinus egregius
Asinorum dominus.
Hez, Sire Asnes, &c.

"Saltu vincit hinnulos,
Damas et capreolos,
Super dromedarios
Velox Madianeos.
Hez, Sire Asnes, &c.

"Aurum de Arabia,
Thus et myrrhum de Saba
Tulit in ecclesia
Virtus Asinaria.
Hez, Sire Asnes, &c.

"Dum trahit vehicula
Multa cum sarcinula,
Illius mandibula,
Dura terit pabula,
Hez, Sire Asnes, &c.

"Cum aristis hordeum
Comedit et carduum;
Triticum a palea
Segregat in area.
Hez, Sire Asnes, &c.

"Amen, dicas, Asine,
(*Hic genuflectabatur.*)
Jam satur de gramine:
Amen, amen itera
Aspernare vetera.
Hez va! hez va! hez va! hez!
Bialz, Sire Asne, car allez;
Belle bouche car chantez."

[1] Cfr. Reinsberg von Düringsfeld, *Das festliche Jahr*.

[2] Sometimes the place of the ass is taken by the mule. At Turin, for instance, it is narrated that the church dedicated to the *Corpus Domini* was erected several centuries ago on account of the miracle of a mule which carried some sacred goods stolen by an impious thief. Having arrived in the little square where the Church of the *Corpus*

the Church often introduced the ass into her ceremonies, but more in order to exhilarate the minds of her devotees than to edify them by any suggestion of the virtues it represents in the Gospels; so that, notwithstanding the great services rendered by the ass to the Founder of the new religion, he not only received no benefit in return from Christianity, but became instead the unfortunate object of new attentions, which rather depressed than heightened his already sufficiently degraded social condition.

And so the Greeks and Romans first, and the Catholic priests afterwards, combined, by their treatment of him, to make the ass more indifferent than he would otherwise have been to the passion and spirited struggle for life shown in all the other animals. He was perhaps intended for a higher fate, if man had not come upon earth, and interfered too persistently to thwart his vocation. And probably his race gradually deteriorated, just because, having become ridiculous, few cared to preserve or increase his nobleness. As the proverb said that it was useless to wash the ass's head, so it seemed useless for man to endeavour to ameliorate or civilise his form: the physical

Domini now stands, the mule refused to go any farther; and out of a cup, which was among the sacred objects stolen, a wafer containing the body of our Saviour rose into the air. Nor would it come down again until the bishop came forth, and, holding the cup high in the air, besought the wafer to come back into it; which having been miraculously accomplished, the Church of the *Corpus Domini* was erected on the spot, from which starts and to which returns the solemn procession which takes place annually at Turin on the festival of *Corpus Domini*, and in which, about twenty years ago, the princes and great dignitaries of the state, with the professors of the university, used to take part in all the pomp of mediæval ceremony and costume.—In Persia the festival of asses is celebrated at the approach of spring; the ass personifying here the end of the winter season.

decadence of the ass was contemporary and parallel with his decline morally.

But although it was in Greece and Rome that the poor ass was thrown completely down from his rank in the animal kingdom, the first decree of his fall was pronounced in his ancient Asiatic abode. Let us prove this.

In the *Ṛigvedas*, the ass already appears under two differents aspects—one divine and the other demoniacal—to which may perhaps be added a third intermediate or gandharvic aspect.

In the *Ṛigvedas*, the ass has the names of *gardabhas* and *râsabhas;* in Sanskṛit, also those of *kharas, ćakrîvant, ćiramehin,* and *bâleyas.*

It is important to notice how each of these designations tends to lapse into ambiguity; and ambiguity in words plays a considerable part in the formation of myths and popular beliefs.

Let us begin with the most modern designations.

Bâleyas may mean the childish one (from *bâlas* = child, and stupid[1]), as well as the demoniacal (from *balis;* and indeed, besides being a name given to the ass, *bâleyas* is also a name for a demon).

Ćiramehin is the ass as *longe mingens* (a quality which can apply to the ass, but still more so to the rainy cloud).

Ćakrîvant means he who is furnished with wheels, with round objects or testicles (an epithet equally applicable to the ass and his phallos).

Kharas signifies he who cries out, as well as the ardent one (and *kharus,* which ought to have the same meaning, signifies, according to the Petropolitan Dictionary, foolish, and horse; perhaps ass too).

[1] The same analogy presents itself in the Sanskṛit word *arbhakas,* which means little and foolish.

Râsabhas is derived from the double root *ras,* whence *rasa* = humour, juice, water, savour, sperm, and *râsa* = din, tumultuous noise.

Gardabhas comes from the root *gard,*[1] to resound, to bellow; but I think I can recognise in the word *gardabhas* the same meaning as *gandharbas* or *gandharvas,* and *vice versa.* The *gardabhas* explains to me how the *gandharvas* was conceived to be a musician; and the *gandharvas* (a word which, I repeat, seems to me composed of *gandha* + *arvas,* developed out of a hypothetic *rivas,*[2] that is, he who walks in the unguent, or he who goes in the perfume) helps me to understand the proverb, "Asinus in unguento," and the corresponding legends. The equivocal word *râsabhas,* in its two meanings, seems to unite together the sonorous *gardabhas* with the *gandharbas* who likes perfumes, or the *gandharvo apsu* (*gandharvas* in the waters) of the *Ṛigvedas,*[3] the guardian of the ambrosial plant.[4] The mythical ass and the Vedic *gandharvas* have the same qualities and the same instincts. The gandharvâs, for instance, are represented in the *Âitareya Br.* as lovers of women,[5] so much so that for a woman's sake they allow themselves to be deprived of the ambrosia (or somas); and it is also known from the story of Urvaçî how jealous they are of their nymphs, the *apsarâs,* or them who flow by on the waters (the clouds), and from the story of Hanumant, in the *Râmâyaṇam,* how greedy they are of their salutary herbs

[1] Cfr. the root *gad,* from which we might perhaps deduce an imaginary intermediate form, gadarbhas, besides the known gardabhas and gandharbas or gandharvas.

[2] Cfr. *arvan* with the roots *arv, arb, arp, ṛiph, riph, riv, ṛinv.*

[3] x. 10, 5.

[4] Gandharva itthâ padam asya rakshati; *Ṛigv.* ix. 83, 4.

[5] Strîkâmâḥ vâi gandharvâḥ; i. 27.

and waters.[1] The mythical and legendary ass also has a foible for beautiful maidens; it is unnecessary to give the reason of this belief.[2] When Circe wishes to give, by means of an unguent, an ass's head to Odysseus, we find an allusion to the loves of the ass and the beautiful woman. When the Lucius of Apuleius, while endeavouring to change himself into a bird (another of the names by which the phallos is indicated), becomes instead, by means of the woman's unguent, an ass, the ass is another name for the phallical bird. And as the Vedic ass delights in the *rasas*, or humour, water or sperm (the two words *râsas* and *rasas*, derived from a common root, being easily interchangeable); as the mythical ass, when it finds the ambrosia of the roseate morning aurora, once more becomes the splendid young sun; so the ass of Apuleius, too, becomes Lucius again, or the luminous and handsome youth that he was before, as soon as he has an opportunity of feeding upon roses: he becomes an ass for love of a woman, and regains his splendour in the rosy aurora. During the night, being subject to the enchantment of a beautiful fairy, the hero remains an ass; and in the form of an ass, and under an ass's skin,

[1] Professor Kuhn (*Die Herabkunft*, d. f. &c.) has already compared to this the Zend Gandhrawa, who, in the Lake Vôuru-Kasha, keeps guard over the tree *hom* (the Vedic Somas). Kuhn and Weber, moreover, have identified the Vedic gandharvas, Kṛiçânus, who wounds the ravisher of the Somas, with the Zend Kereçâni, who endeavours to destroy riches; here the gandharvas would appear to be a monstrous and demoniacal being.

[2] . . . ut omittam eos, quos libidinis ac fœdæ voluptatis causa, coluisse nomen illud atque imposuisse suis, a scriptoribus notatur, qualis olim Onos ille Commodi; qualis exsecrandus Marci Verotrasinus, qualis et alterius Onobelos, quales, quos matronis in deliciis fuisse scimus. Unde illud atque alium bipedem sibi quærit asellum, ejus nempe membri causa, quod, in asino, clava, a Nicandro dicitur; *Laus Asini*, Lugd. Batavorum, ex officina Elzeviriana, p. 194.

he carries the priapœan mysteries, whence the expression of Aristophanes in the *Frogs*, "The ass which carries mysteries" (onos agôn müstêria), the same mysteries as the Phallagia or Perifallia of Rome. In the Christian myth, this mystery is the flight of the new-born Divine Child into Egypt;[1] in the story of Perrault, it is the beautiful maiden, the evening aurora, the girl persecuted by her father and would-be seducer, who disguises herself during the night with an ass's skin;[2] the beautiful girl evidently transfers her erotic sympathies to the ass that loves her. Of loves such as these,—of an ass with a maiden, or of the young hero and an ass,—are born the monstrous onokentaurs and Empusa, now a beautiful maiden, and now the terrifier of children, who is represented with ass's feet, because her mother was an ass, and her father, Aristoxenes, enamoured of an ass. It is now the evening aurora, now the dying sun, and now both, who, under the cloud of night, or in winter, are represented as covered with an ass's skin. Professor Kuhn has already proved the close affinity, amounting to identity, between the gandharvâs and the Hellenic kentauroi, both of which come before us in connection with the inebriating drink; but the kentauros is essentially a hippokentauros,

[1] To this flight into Egypt upon the ass can be referred the Piedmontese custom among children in the middle of Lent—that is, near the festival of St Joseph—of attaching to their companions now a saw, now a devil's head, now an ass's head, pronouncing the words, "L'asu cariá che gnün lu sa" (the ass burdened, and no one knows it). Moreover, it seems to me that to the Christian tradition of Joseph, and of the child Jesus carried upon the ass, can be referred the well-known European fable of the old man, the boy, and the ass, of which numerous varieties may be read in the article upon the *asinus vulgi* in the *Orient und Occident* of Benfey.

[2] Professor Benfey, in his learned Einleitung to the *Pańćatantram*, p. 268, says that the disguise by means of the skin of an ass is found in a Latin poem of the fifteenth century.

or, still better, an onokentauros,[1] or centaur ass. The fable of Cupid and Psyche in Apuleius, in its relation

[1] "Addo ex Conrado Lycosthene in libro de ostentis et prodigiis hanc iconem quam hippokentauri esse credebam, ipse vero (nescio ex quo) Apothami vocat, Apothami (inquit) in aqua morantes, qui una parte hominem, alia vero caballum sive equum referunt. Sic etiam memoriæ tradiderunt mulieres esse capite plano sine crinibus, promissas autem barbas habentes. Atqui ea descriptio plane ad Onocentauros pertinere videtur, quos Aelianus et Philes sic fere delineant. Quæ vero de Onocentauro fama accepi, hæc sunt: Eum homini ore et promissa barba similem esse, simul et collum et pectus, humanam speciem gerere; mammas distantes tamquam mulieris ex pectore pendere; humeros, brachia, digitos, humanam figuram habere; dorsum, ventrem, latera, posteriores pedes, asino persimiles et quemadmodum asinum sic cinereo colore esse; imum ventrem leviter exalbescere: duplicem usum ei manus præstare; nam celeritate ubi sit opus eæ manus præcurrunt ante posteriores pedes; ex quo fit, ut non cæterorum quadrupedum cursu superetur. Ac ubi rursus habet necesse vel cibum capere vel aliud quidpiam tollere, qui ante pedes erant manus efficiuntur, tumque non graditur, sed in sessione quiescit: Animal est gravi animi acerbitate; nam si capiatur, non ferens servitutem, libertatis desiderio ab omni cibo abhorret, et fame sibi mortem consciscit, licet pullus adhuc fuerit. Hæc de Onocentauro Pythagoram narrare testatur Crates, ex Mysio Pergamo profectus;" Aldrovandi, *De Quadrupedibus*, i.—In the Indian satyrs described by Pliny, in the seventh book of his *Natural History*, we find represented an analogous animal: "Sunt et satyri subsolanis Indorum montibus (Cartadulonum dicitur regio) pernicissimum animal, tum quadrupes, tum recte currens, humana effigie, propter velocitatem nisi senes aut ægri, aut capiuntur." Evidently this refers to some kind of monkey (probably the orang-outang); but as the myth of the monkey does not differ much from that of the ass, as we shall see, even the Hindoo gandharvas is represented as a monkey.—"In *A. V.* iv. 37, 11, the gandharvas, a class of gods, who are described as hairy, like dogs and monkeys, but as assuming a handsome appearance to seduce the affections of earthly females, are implored to desist from this unbecoming practice, and not to interfere with mortals, as they had wives of their own, the Apsarases;" Muir's *Sanskṛit Texts*, v. 309.—We have the monkey-gandharvas and the warrior-gandharvas in the Vedic hymns, the warrior-monkey in the *Râmâyaṇam*, and the warrior-kentauros and warrior-ass in Hellenic myths.

with the story of the ass, perfectly agrees with the analogous Hindoo fable of the loves of Purûravas and Urvaçî, united with the story of the Gandharvâs. Peau d'âne, Psyche, and Urvaçî are therefore mythical sisters.

Professor Kuhn's proof of the identity of the gandharvas and the kentauros being admitted, the identity of the gardabhas with the gandharbas, and of the ass with the gandharvas, seems to follow as a natural consequence. The myth of the kentauros, either hippokentauros or onokentauros, no less than the myth of the gandharvas, corresponds entirely with that of the ass. The kentauros loves wine and women; he plays the lyre upon the car of Dionysos in conjunction with satyrs, nymphs, and bacchantes; he teaches on Mount Pelion music,[1] the science of health, and the prophetic art to the Dioscuri, which are all subjects that occur again with slight modifications in the Hindoo legends concerning the gandharvâs, and in the fable of the ass, as we shall prove hereafter.—But to return to the Hindoo myth; in the same way as the gandharvâs has a hybrid nature, and shows himself at one time in the aspect of a demi-god, at another in that of a semi-demon, so the mythical ass of

[1] We also read of the ass that dances, which reminds us of the gandharvas in their capacity of heavenly musicians and dancers, who teach the gods how to dance. Nor is it perhaps without reason that the author of precepts for dancers and mimics is named *Kṛiçâçvas:* kṛiçâçvas means, as we already know, he who possesses a lean horse, or simply the lean horse. Between the lean horse, the mule, and the ass, the distance is short; nor can we overlook the fact that in the gandharvas Kṛiçânus is recognised as he who causes to become lean, which calls us back to the monster who makes horses grow lean, to the monster of horses, the ugly horse, the horse-monster, who destroys the golden ears of the fields, making them dry up, like the monster Çushṇas, or the destroyer of riches, like the Zend Kereçâni.—In the before-quoted book, *Laus Asini,* the author says in jest, "Fortassis Pegasum fuisse asinum;" and in this jest a great truth is contained.

India has now a divine nature, and now a human. The gandharvas is the guardian of riches and waters: inasmuch as he defends them from the demoniacal robbers, preserves them from mortals, and distributes them among the pious, he appears under a beneficent and divine aspect; inasmuch, on the other hand, as he carries them off and keeps them shut up like a miser, he resembles the monster that is fabled to guard fountains and treasures, the demon who keeps the waters shut up, the thieves who gather treasures together, and the devil, the master of all riches. For the same reason we already find in Hindoo tradition the beneficent ass and his evil-doing congener. The sun (sometimes the moon also) in the cloud and the darkness of night is the same as the treasure in the cavern, the treasure in hell, and the hero or heroine in the gloomy forest; and this cavern and hell sometimes assume the form of an ass's skin, or of an ass simply. That which comes out of the cloud, and of the gloom, also comes out of the ass; the soul of the ass is the sun, or the hero or heroine, or the riches which he conceals. The Açvinâu are often found in connection with the worthless horse, which afterwards becomes handsome by means of the ambrosia itself that the horse produces; the gandharvâs, a more nocturnal and cloudy form, if I may use the expression, of the solar or lunar hero, are in near relation with the ass, their *alter ego*, who enjoys the blessing of eternal youth. The Açvinâu themselves, the two horsemen who have given youth to the old Ćyavanas, rode upon asses before they rode upon horses. The myth of the gandharvâs and that of the Açvinâu, the myth of the horse and that of the ass, are intimately connected: from the gandharvâs the açvin comes forth; from the mythical ass the horse comes out. This is unnatural in zoology, but it is very natural in mythology: the sun comes, now out of the grey shades of night, and now out of the grey cloud.

The Vedic hymns already present us with several interesting myths concerning the ass.

The ass of the Açvinâu is swift; the devotees ask the Açvinâu when they are to yoke it, that they may be carried by it to the sacrifice.[1] In another hymn, as the Açvinâu are two, so are their asses two (râsabhâv açvinoḥ). Finally, the second strophe of the 116th hymn offers us a twofold significant particularity, viz., the ass, that vanquishes a thousand in the rich battlefield of Yamas (or in the nocturnal battle, in the struggle in hell, in which the ass appears as a real warrior, joined with riches, and fighting for riches), and is helped by strong and rapid wings (in which it shows us the ass that flies).[2]

The *Ṛigvedas* also represents the ass of Indras as swift-footed.[3] But in the same hymn we already see the reverse of the medal, that is to say, the swift ones who deride him who is not swift, the horses that are urged before the ass.[4] The solar hero, towards morning, substitutes the horse for the ass, or appears with horses, leaving the ass or asses behind. We have learned in the preceding chapter how, in the heavenly race of the Vedic gods, the asses gained the palm of victory; but it was an effort superior to their powers. The *Âitareya Br.*

[1] Kadâ yogo vâǵino râsabhasya yena yaǵńaṁ nâsatyopayâthaḥ; *Ṛigv.* i. 34, 9.

[2] Viḷupatmabhir âçuhemabhir vâ devânâṁ vâ ǵûtibhiḥ çâçadânâ tad râsabho nâsatyâ sahasram âǵâ yamasya pradhane ǵigâya.

[3] Yatrâ rathasya bṛihato nidhânaṁ vimoćanaṁ vâǵino râsabhasya; *Ṛigv.* iii. 53, 5.

[4] Nâvâǵinaṁ vâǵinâ hâsayanti na gardabhaṁ puro açvân nayanti; *Ṛigv.* iii. 53, 23.

informs us that by this effort they lost their swiftness and became draught animals, deprived of honey, but yet preserving great vigour in their sperm, so that the male ass can generate offspring in two ways, that is, mules by union with a mare, and asses by union with an ass.[1] Here, therefore, the ass is already considered an animal of an essentially phallical nature, which notion is confirmed by the precept of Kâtyâyanas, recorded by Professor Weber,[2] which enjoins the sacrificing of an ass to expiate violated chastity. To chastise the ass, to sacrifice the ass, must mean the same as to chastise and to mortify the body,[3] and especially the phallos; and the Eastern and Western punishment of leading adulterers about upon an ass has the same meaning; the real martyr, however, in this punishment being the ass, who is exposed to every kind of derision and ill-treatment. In the same way, the henpecked husband who allowed himself to be beaten by his wife, used, in several villages of Piedmont, only a few years ago, to be led about ignominiously upon an ass: a husband who lets his wife impose upon him, and cannot subdue her, deserves to be chastised by means of an ass; he is not a man, and his ass, the emblem of his manly strength, must on this account suffer the punish-

[1] Gardabharathenâçvinâ udağayatâmaçvinâvâçnuvâtâṁ yadaçvinâ udağayatâmaçvinâvâçnuvâtâṁ tasmâtsasṛitağavo dugdhadohaḥ sarveshâmetarhi vâhanânâmanâçishṭo retasastvasya vîryaṁ nâharatâm tasmâtsa dviretâ vâğî; *Âit. Br.* iv. 2, 9.

[2] *Ueber den Zusammenhang indischer Fabeln mit griechischen*, Berlin, 1855.

[3] St Jerome, in the Life of Saint Hilarion: "Ego, inquit, Aselle, faciam ut non calcitres necte hordeo alam, sed paleis; fame te conficiam et sitis gravi onerabo pondere; per æstus indagabo et frigore, ut cibum potius quam lasciviam cogites."—St Paulinus wrote, "Sit fortis anima mortificans asinum suum."—In Italian, too, there is a low term by which we say, *il mio asino*, instead of *il mio corpo*.

ment, because he has not shown himself able to assert his marital rights. The adulterer upon the ass, and the silly husband upon the ass, are punishments for phallic offences in, and in connection with, the person of that which represents the phallos: one is chastised for having wished, in this regard, to do too much, and the other for not having been able to do enough. On this account the condemned person was forced, in similar cases, to ride upon an ass with his face turned towards the animal's tail, another image which is yet more manifestly phallical; whence the very name of the punishment, "asini caudam in manu tenere."[1] As to the other proverb which says, "He to whom the ass belongs, holds him by the tail," it is explained by the narrative of a peasant who drew his ass out of a swamp, taking it by the tail; but this story too seems to have a phallic signification.

---

[1] A. c. i. m. t.,—pœna seu mulcta, quæ reis irrogari solebat, ut colligitur ex decreto Nepesini populi ann. 1134.—Iis et maxime maritis, qui a suis vapulabant mulieribus; quod eo usque insaniæ deventum erat, ut si maritus aufugisset, proximior vicinus eam ipse pœnam luere teneretur; quem morem non omnino periisse audivi. Du Cange, whose words these are, gives several examples of a similar chastisement.—In the *Tuti-Name*, ii. 20, a certain man complains to a sage that he has lost his ass, and begs the wise man to find it again for him; the latter points out a man who grew old without having known love; he who does not love is a fool.—It is a remarkable fact that the ass, generally considered a very lustful animal, is sometimes despised as unadapted to make fruitful, and the reason of this is given by Aldrovandi (*De Quadrupedibus*, i.)—Quamvis modo libidine maxime pruriat, ob verendi tamen enormitatem, qua supra modum præditus est, ad generandum admodum segnem esse compertum est, sicuti et homines qui simili genitalis productione conspicui sunt, quod in emissione per eam longitudinem semen transmeans hebetetur et frigidius fiat. Testaturque Ælianus inter causas cur Ægyptii asinos odere, et hanc quoque accedere putari, quod eum populi prædicti omnes fœcundos animantes colant, asinus minime fœcundans nullus in honore sit.

The ass, therefore, is already deposed from his noble place as a swift-footed courser in the *Ṛigvedas* itself. And in the *Ṛigvedas*, too, where we have observed the ass described as a warrior who fights for the gods, we find him in the demoniacal form of a disagreeable singer who terrifies the worshippers of the god Indras; the latter is therefore requested by the poet to kill the ass who sings with a horrible voice.[1] Here the ass already appears as a real monster, worthy even of the steel of the prince of the celestial heroes himself, who prepares to combat him. The ass, therefore, is already sacred to the monsters in the white Yaǵurvedas.[2]

In the *Râmâyaṇam*,[3] the slowness of the ass has already become proverbial. The modest Bharatas excuses himself from not being able to equal his brother Râmas in the science of government, just as the ass, he says, cannot run like the horse, or other birds cannot fly like the vulture. The mythical ass, moreover, appears in this epic poem[4] in a demoniacal and infernal aspect:

---

1 Sam, indra, gardabham mṛiṇa nuvantam pâpayâmuyâ; *Ṛigv.* i. 29, 5.

2 Quoted by Weber, *Ueber den Zusammenhang indischer Fabeln mit griechischen*, where the braying ass would also appear to be born of the omniform monster: "Entsteht, nach Ç. xii. 7, 1, 5, nebst Ross und Maulthier, aus dem Ruhm (yaças, which, however, may perhaps here also simply mean splendour), welcher dem Ohr des getödteten Viçvarûpa Tvâshṭra entfloss, worin der Bezug auf sein lautes Geschrei wohl nicht zu verkennen ist."—We have already seen, in the Russian stories quoted in the preceding chapter, how the two horsemen who protect the hero come out of the ears of the grey horse, and how the hero himself, entering by one ear, and coming out of the other, finds a heroic horse. Here we can, perhaps, detect an allusion to the long-eared ass, in the same way as in the appellation of âçrutkarṇas, or the ear which listens, given to Indras (*Ṛigv.* i. 10, 9), the long-eared Indras may possibly be a form representing the long-eared Midas, or the ass with long ears.

3 Gatiṁ khara ivâçvasya suparṇasyeva pakshiṇaḥ anâgantuṁ na çakto 'smi râǵyam tava mahîpate.

4 *Râmây.* ii. 71.

Bharatas, in fact, dreams of seeing his dead father Daçarathas, in blood-coloured clothes, borne to the southern funereal region on a car drawn by asses; and we are told that when a man is seen upon a car drawn by asses, it is a sign of his departure for the abode of Yamas. Kharas, a word which, as we already know, means ass, is also the name of a younger brother of the great monster Râvaṇas. Râvaṇas himself is drawn by asses upon a chariot adorned with gold and gems. These asses have the faces of the monster Piçâćâs,[2] that is, faces of parrots, as Hanumant afterwards informs us when he speaks of the monsters which he has seen in Lañkâ, which he also says are as swift as thought.[3] We know that the coursers of Râvaṇas were asses, and therefore the asses with the faces of the Piçâćâs, and the horses of the monsters with the faces of parrots, are the same. The monster Piçâćas, therefore, has the face of a parrot. How is it that the parrot is reared in India as a sacred bird? It appears to me that equivocation in language had something to do with the formation of this singular mythological image. The word *piçâćas* is derived, like *piçañgas*, which means golden and red, from the root *piç*, to adorn; whence also the Vedic feminine *piç*, ornament, and the Vedic neuter, *peças*, coloured tissue. The ass piçâćas, who draw the chariot full of gold, are therefore themselves, at least in their face, in their foremost part, golden asses, or red like the colour of gold, red like the colour of the sun; in fact, we find kharas (the ardent) as the proper name of an attendant on the sun, and kharâṇçus or khararaçmiḥ, he of the burning ray, as Sanskṛit names of the sun. Kharaketus, he who has a burning ray, is also the name of one of the monsters in the *Râmâyaṇam*.[3] We there-

---

1 *Râmây*. iii. 38, 48. 2 *Ib*. v 12. 3 vi. 74.

fore already see here the golden ass and the infernal monster identified with the sun; and hence we are very near the monster with the parrot's face. In the preceding chapter we observed how the solar horse appears in the morning luminous at first in its foremost parts,—now in its legs, now in its face, now in its mane, which is called golden; it is only the head of the horse which is found in the butter; of Dadhyańć we perceive only his head in connection with the ambrosia. Thus of the nocturnal ass, of the demoniacal ass, of the demon himself, the piçâćas (the piçâćâs are called carnivorous[1]), only the face is seen, in the same way as of the piçâćâs, and of the horses belonging to the monsters, only the head is that of a parrot. But what connection can there be between the gold colour of the ass piçâćas and the green colour of the parrot? The equivoque lies probably in the words *hari* and *harit*, both of which, in the Hindoo tongue mean yellow, as well as green. Haris and hari signify the sun, and the moon, as being yellow; harayas and haritas are the horses of the sun; harî are the two horses of Indras and of the Açvinâu, of whom we also know that they more usually rode upon asses. We thus arrive at the light-coloured asses, at the asses that are golden, at least in their foremost parts, that is, in the morning twilight, when after his nocturnal course, the solar horseman is on the point of arriving at his golden eastern destination, whence the head of the ass which carries the divine horseman is illumined by him. But *haris,* besides signifying the solar hero as being yellow, also signifies the parrot as green; on this account the ass or demon with a golden head was exchanged with the ass or monster with the green head, or with the parrot's head. We

[1] Kravyâdaḥ piçâćâḥ, in the *Atharvavedas*, viii. 2, 12.

shall see in the chapters concerning birds how the bird was often substituted for the horse in the office of carrying the deity or the hero.

To conclude the subject of the Hindoo mythical ass, it is certain that it existed in the heavens; it is certain that it flies in the sky, that it fights in the sky like a valiant warrior, that it terrifies its enemies in the sky with its terrible voice; that, in a word, it was a real and legitimate heroic animal. It is certain, moreover, that, considered under another aspect, it not only throws down the heroes, but carries them to hell, serves the infernal monsters, and is found in connection with the treasures of hell. Moreover, admitting, as I hope the reader will, my identification of the mythical ass with the gandharvas, we have the ass as dancer, the ass as musician, the ass who loves women, and the ass in the odorous ointment and in the inebriating drink, the somas which occupies the place of the wine of the Dionysian mysteries, in which the Hellenic ass took a solemn part.

In the fables of the *Pańćatantram*, the ass is partly modelled on the Hellenic type and partly preserves its primitive character. The fourth book shows us the ass twice attracted towards the lion by the jackal, who induces him to believe that a beautiful female ass is awaiting him. The ass is distrustful and shows his fear, but the argument of the female ass, upon which the artful jackal insists, overcomes his timidity. He is, however, cunning enough to send the jackal before him; and at the sight of the lion he perceives the jackal's treachery and turns, fleeing away with such rapidity that the lion cannot overtake him. The jackal returns to the assault, and convinces the ass that he did wrong to abandon the beautiful female ass when he was on the point of receiving her favours; and thus touching the tender chord of his heart, he goes on to assure him that the female ass will throw herself into the fire or the water if she does not see him return. "Omnia vincit amor;" the ass returns, and this time the lion surprises and tears him to pieces; upon which the lion, before partaking of his meal, goes to perform his ablutions and devotions. Meanwhile the jackal eats the ass's heart and ears, and makes the lion, on his return, believe that the stupid animal had neither the one nor the other, because if he had had them, he would not have returned to the dangerous spot after having once escaped. The lion declares himself to be perfectly satisfied with this explanation. Here we have a mixture in the ass of swift-footedness, lust, and stupidity, his stupidity being caused by his lustfulness. Now, it is possible that his acquaintance with the Hellenic ass may have induced the author of the *Pańćatantram* to embody in the ass a quality which is generally attributed in fables of Hindoo origin to the monkey; but this is not absolutely necessary in order to explain the narrative of which we have now given the epitome.

On the other hand, in the fourth book of the *Pańćatantram*, the fable of the ass in the tiger's skin—an insignificant variety of the ass in the lion's skin—was, as Professor Weber has already proved, taken from the Æsopian fable. Another fable, in the fifth book, which tells us of the ass who, being passionately fond of music,[1] insisted upon singing, and was thus discovered and made a slave of, also seems to be of Hellenic origin. But, although the editing of these two Hindoo fables in a literary form had its origin in the knowledge of Hellenic

[1] Cfr. also the *Tuti-Name* of Rosen, ii. 218, for the musical ass; and the same, ii. 149, for the ass in a lion's skin.

literature, the original myth of the ass-lion (haris, which is the horse of Indras, also means the lion), and that of the ass-musician (as gandharvas and gardabhas), can be traced as far back as the Vedic scriptures.

In the Zendic *Yaçna*,[1] I find a new proof, which appears to me a very satisfactory one, of the identification which I have proposed of the ass with the gandharvas. I have already mentioned the gandharvas who guards over the somas in the midst of the waters, and I observed how the gandharvas kṛiçânus of the Vedâs, and the Zend kereçâni who guards over the *hom* in the *Vôuru-Kasha*, have been identified. But the same office is fulfilled in the *Yaçna* by a three-legged ass, that is, a lame ass (or the solar horse who has become lame during the night, in the same way as the solar hero becomes lame, or a lame devil), who, by braying, terrifies the monsters and prevents them from contaminating the water.

In the first of the seven adventures of Rustem, in the *Shah-Name* of Firdusi, the starving Rustem goes with his brave heroic horse to chase wild asses. The asses flee, but the hero's horse is swifter than they, and overtakes them; Rustem takes one by means of a lasso, and has it cooked, throwing away the bones. He then goes to sleep (*then* sometimes expresses in the myths the interval of a whole day or of a whole year.—The hero does almost the same in his second adventure and in the book of *Sohrab*). While Rustem sleeps, a monstrous lion makes its appearance to surprise the hero; Rustem's heroic horse throws the lion down and tears it to pieces

[1] xli. 28.—Cfr. the *Khorda Avesta*, Spiegel's *Einleitung*, p. 54: "Dort ist der dreibeinige Esel der in der Mitte des Sees steht und mit seinem Geschrei die bösen Wesen vertreibt und alles Wasser, das mit unreinen Wesen und Dingen in Berührung kommt, sogleich reinigt."

with its hoofs and teeth. This battle between the horse of the sleeping hero and the monster lion is an epic form of the fable which represents the animals as being terrified in the forest by the braying of the ass, and of that of the lion itself killed by the ass's kick. Probably the bones of the dead ass, when preserved, gave heroic strength to Rustem's horse.

In the Mongol stories, of which we have on a previous occasion indicated the Hindoo origin, we find two other legends relating to the ass. In the eighteenth Mongol story, a foolish man goes with his ass to hang up some rice; he hides his ass in a cave; some merchants pass by with their goods, and the fool sends forth, by means of a trumpet, such a sonorous shout, that the merchants, thinking brigands are hidden in the cavern, escape, leaving their goods in the ass's possession. Here the fool and the ass are already identified. The trumpet and the blowing made by the fool correspond to the braying of the ass, of whom we shall soon see other miracles related. The sense of the myth is this: the solar hero in the night or in the cloud grows stupid; he becomes an ass during the night or in the cloud; the cloud thunders, and the thunder of the cloud gives rise to the idea now of the braying and now of the flatus of the ass (or the fool), now of a trumpet,[1] and now of a drum. We must not forget that the word *dundubhis* which properly means kettledrum or drum, is also the name of a monster, and that Dundubhî is the proper name of the wife of a gandharvas, or of a gandharvî. The skin of the drum being made of an ass's hide is one

1 Readers of Dante are acquainted with the trumpet of the devil Malacoda, which is used in the same way as the fool uses his in the Mongol story.

more reason why the thundering cloud, being very naturally likened to a drum, the thunder should be also considered now as a *flatus oris,* now as a *flatus ventris* of the celestial ass, or of the foolish hero who accompanies him.

In the twenty-second Mongol story we have a variety, though partly a less complete and partly a richer one, of the fable of the Phrygian king Midas. A king who has golden ass ears, has his head combed every night with golden combs by young men, who are immediately after put to death (to comb the ass's head is about the same as to wash it; but however much it is combed, the ears can never be abolished). One day a young man predestined to the highest honours, before going to comb the king's head, receives from his mother a cake made of her own milk and flour. The young man offers the cake to the king, who likes it, and spares the youth's life on condition that he tells no one, not even his mother, the great secret, *viz.*, that the king has golden ears. The youth promises to preserve silence, and makes a very great effort indeed to keep his promise, but this effort makes him seriously ill, so much so that he feels he will burst if he does not tell the secret. His mother then advises him to go and relieve his mind by whispering it into a fissure of the earth or of a tree. The young man does so; he goes into the open country, finds a squirrel's hole, and breathes gently down it, "Our king has ass's ears;" but animals have understanding and can speak, and there are men who understand their language. The secret is conveyed from one to another, till the king hears that the young man has divulged it. He threatens to take his life; but relents when he hears from him how it happened, and not only pardons him, but makes him his prime minister. The fortunate youth's first act is to invent a cap of the shape of the ears of an ass, in order that the king may be able to conceal the deformity; and when the people see the king with a cap of this shape, it pleases them so much that they all adopt it; and so the king, by means of his young minister, is no longer obliged to live secluded, and in the constant tormenting dread of discovery, but lives at his ease and happily ever afterwards.

Having thus examined under its principal aspects the most popular Asiatic tradition relative to the ass, let us now go on to epitomise the European tradition, and, if possible, more briefly; all the more that the reader, having, as I hope, now the key of the myth, will be of himself able to refer to it many analogous particulars of Græco-Latin tradition. I say Græco-Latin alone, because the myth of the ass among Slavonic and Germanic nations, where the ass is little, if at all, known, had no especial and independent development. In Slavonic countries, the part of the ass is generally sustained by Ivan the fool or Emilius the lazy one, as also by the bear or wolf, as in India it is often sustained by the monkey;[1] ass, bear, wolf, and monkey, as mythical animals, represent almost identical phenomena.

Let us take the story of Midas again at its commencement.

Midas appears in *Herodotus*, not only as a king of Phrygia, but as a progenitor of the Phrygians. In the Tusculans of Cicero, the drunken satyr Silenos (originally

[1] In Menander, quoted by Aulus Gellius, a husband complains of the injuries done him by his wife, using the proverb, "The ass amongst the monkeys." Monkeys are well known for their impudent lasciviousness; the ass, who represents the phallos, among this lascivious fraternity finds himself often in the condition of an impotent and weak husband.

another form of the same Midas, the satyrs having ass's ears), the master of Dionysos, loses himself in the rose-garden belonging to Midas, before whom he is conducted, and by whom he is benevolently received and entertained, and then sent back with honour to the god, who, in gratitude, concedes to Midas the gift of turning to gold everything that he touches, to such an extent as to affect the food that he wishes to eat and the water in which he bathes. This myth is probably of a complex nature. Midas ought, like the ass, to turn to gold what he has eaten, that is, to turn his food and drink into excrements of gold, to fructify the golden ears of corn, *i.e.*, in heaven, the solar rays. Cicero himself leads us to suppose that the myth of Midas is in relation with the ears of corn, when, in his first book *De Divinatione*, he says that the ants carried grains of wheat into the mouth of Midas when a child; these being symbols of abundance and of fecundity which are quite applicable to the mythical ass. For although the common ass is not a privileged fœcundator, the mythical ass, in its capacity of a rain-giving cloud or ćiramehin, is the best fertiliser of the fields. The sun, or gold, or treasure, comes out of the ass-darkness or ass-cloud. The ass Lucius, after having eaten the roses of morning or the east, again becomes Lucius the luminous one (the sun). On this account the ass Midas, too, who also delights in roses, turns to gold whatever he eats, as well as the dew or ambrosial fountain in which he bathes; the rosy becomes the golden; the sun comes out of the contact of the ass of night with the aurora.

Servius, in his commentary on the sixth book of the *Æneid*, also tells us the centauri "in floribus stabulant," as the Hindoo gandharvas in the perfumes. These perfumes are rain and dew. The ass crowned with loaves of bread[1] and flowers, in the Latin worship of Vesta, who remembered the service rendered to her one day by the braying of the ass, which aroused her from her sleep when some one was attempting to violate her, is another variety of the myth of the aurora who awakes out of the night, golden, that is, rich in golden oats and in golden wheat. The ass itself is sacrificed, because, perhaps, it was the ass itself that had made an attempt to deprive Vesta of her chastity; but having betrayed itself, as it often happens in fables, by its braying, it arouses Vesta, who punishes it by offering it in sacrifice. In a variation of the same story in the first book of Ovid's *Fasti*, where instead of Vesta we have the nymph Lothis asleep, the red Priapos, who wishes to violate her, also loses his opportunity, because the ass of Silenos—

> "Intempestivos edidit ore sonos,"

on which account it is killed by Priapos:

> "Morte dedit pœnas auctor clamoris, et hæc est
> Hellespontiaco victima sacra Deo."

The apologue is well known of the long-eared ass, who, when called upon to judge between the nightingale and the cuckoo as to who has the sweetest voice, decides in favour of the cuckoo. The nightingale then appeals to man with the sweet song that we are all acquainted with.[2] In the myth of Midas, the Phrygian hero is

---

[1] Lampsacus huic soli solita est mactare Priapo.
Apta asini flammis indicis exta damus.
Quem tu diva memor de pane monilibus ornas;
Cessat opus; vacuæ conticuere molæ.
—Ovidius, *Fasti*, vi.

[2] From the myth of the ass, as a musician and judge of music, is derived the Tuscan game of the ass, which is thus described by Signor Fanfani in his *Vocabolario dell 'Uso Tuscano*, Firenze, 1863:—"Each member of the party chooses an animal whose voice or song he must

given ass's ears as a chastisement by Apollo, because, having been called upon to judge between the cithern or lyre of Apollo (whence the proverb "Asinus ad lyram") and the pastoral pipe (calamus agrestis) of Pan (who is represented as a horned and bearded satyr, with a tail and long ears), he pronounced that the pan-pipes were the most harmonious instrument. Midas hides his ears in a red cap, but his comber lets out the secret, as in the Mongol story, and in a manner almost identical—

> "Ille quidem celat, turpique onerata pudore
> Tempora purpureis tentat velare tiaris:
> Sed, solitus longos ferro resecare capillos,
> Viderat hoc famulus: qui, cum nec prodere visum
> Dedecus auderet, cupiens efferre sub auras,
> Nec posset reticere tamen, secedit; humumque
> Effodit, et domini quales aspexerit aures,
> Voce refert parva: terræque immurmurat haustæ.
> Indiciumque suæ vocis tellure regesta
> Obruit, et scrobibus tacitus discedit opertis.
> Creber arundinibus tremulis ibi surgere lucus
> Cœpit; et, ut primum pleno maturuit anno,
> Prodidit agricolam: leni jam motus ab Austro
> Obruta verba refert; dominique coarguit aures." [1]

The same Greeks who held the ass up to derision, made the Phrygian king Midas, of the ass's ears, the object of their satire. This is a particular form of the mythico-heroic struggle between Greeks and Phrygians or Trojans. Apollo is the enemy of the Trojans, as he is the enemy of the Phrygian king Midas. The Trojans

imitate. The head player represents the ass, and is the king of the other animals. When the head player, sitting in the middle, calls one of the animals who encircle him, the dog, for instance, this animal must bark; when he calls the cock, it must cry chicchiricù; when he calls the ox, he who represents it must bellow, and so on. When the ass brays, then all the animals emit their respective cries. Whoever laughs, or omits to give forth the voice or song of the animal which he represents, pays a forfeit."

[1] Ovidius, *Metam.* xi. 180.

and Troy are represented by the ass, and the Greeks, who vanquish and take by assault the Trojan fortress, by the horse; the sun disperses the night; the hero kills the centaur; the horse defeats the ass, the Greek the Trojan; and every one can see how the fact that the Greeks personified in the ass their enemies in Asia Minor, must have damaged the reputation of the poor long-eared animal. The most bitter and cutting satire is always that which is directed towards one's own enemies; and the ass, unfortunately, had at one time the honour of representing the Phrygian, the traditional enemy of the Greek. The ass bore the load of this heroic war, in the same way as in the Middle Ages he was publicly impaled by the Paduans for having had the misfortune of being the sacred animal on the arms of the city of Vicenza, with which the Paduans lived in rivalry.[1]

In the same eleventh book of Ovid where the transformation of the human ears of Midas into ass's ears is described, it is very remarkable that the new ears are called whitish, as in the Mongol story they are said to be golden. This confirms still more the interpretation of the myth, to the effect that the ass is the solar steed during the night. The head and the tail of the night, conceived as an animal, are now the two whitish or grey twilights, and now the two golden auroras of morning and evening.

> "Nec Delius aures
> Humanam stolidas patitur retinere figuram,
> Sed trahit in spatium villisque albentibus implet
> Instabilesque illas facit et dat posse moveri."

The changeableness of the twilights must have served very well to express the mobility of the ears of an ass.

---

[1] According to the *Annals of Padova*, cited by Berrardino Scardeone, in Aldrovandi. *De Quadrupedibus*, i.

In the story of the ass, Midas, the musical critic, the predestined ass, pronounces in favour of Pan; and he does so not only on account of the consanguinity between himself and the god, but also from a patriotic feeling. Pan was born in a forest of Arcadia, of Zeus and the nymph Kallisto; and it is well known that antiquity celebrated the asses of Arcadia above those of every other country. The ass as a musician, the ass as a musical critic, Pan the musician, and Pan preferred by the ass, are the same person. Arcadia, the country of pastoral music, of whistling shepherds, which made the Italy of the seventeenth and eighteenth centuries bleat out so many useless verses, the country of Pan the satyr, *par excellence*, is the country of the ass. Arcadia is the most mountainous and wooded part of Greece,[1] and therefore, when the Olympians came down from heaven, celestial nymphs and satyrs came to people the forests and fountains of Arcadia. The divine guardian of the ambrosia in the heavenly cloud takes, in the Arcadian forest, the form of Pan, god of shepherds, who keeps guard over the honey. The gandharvâs, who danced and sung in the Hindoo Olympus with the apsarasas, has descended into Arcadia in the shape of Pan, to dance and sing with the nymphs.[2] Pan who goes alone into the gloomy forest, Pan who chases fear away, connected as he is

[1] The German proverb, "Wald hat Ohren, Feld hat Gesicht," is well known. Cfr. the varieties of this proverb upon the ears of the forest, in the third vol. pp. 120 and 173, of Uhland's *Schriften zur Geschichte der Dichtung und Sage*, Stüttgart, 1866.

[2] The reader is acquainted with the myth of the nymph Syrinx, beloved of Pan, who was changed into a cane or reed, from which Pan made a flute. We find the leaf of the cane in connection with the ass in Hungarian tradition. A singular indentation can be observed upon the leaves of the cane, which has a great resemblance to the mark of three teeth. To explain this strange mark the Hungarian people

with the story of the ass, reminds us on the one hand of the superstition recorded by Pliny, to the effect that an ass's skin put upon children chases fear from them[1] (in the same way as in the province of Girgenti, in Sicily, it is believed that shoes made of a wolf's skin, put on children's feet, make them daring and lucky in battle), and, on the other hand, of the unpublished Piedmontese story of the fearless Giovannino, who, in reward for his courage in going alone to hell, brings away with him an ass which throws gold from its tail.[2] In

narrate, that the ass of the Redeemer once bit the leaf of a cane, but as Christ was in a hurry, the ass was unable to eat the leaf, and so it happened that its three teeth only left the mark of the bite upon the cane. From that time forward every leaf of a cane bears record to this. The two lines which stretch down the two flanks of the ass are said in Hungary to be caused by the blood of our Redeemer. The popular belief in Ireland is that these lines remain as a memorial of Christ having once struck the ass.—Cfr. the chapter on the Peacock and that on the Eel, where we shall find the hero and the heroine again transformed into canes.

[1] The loss of heart or courage is expressed in Italian by the low term "Quí mi casca l'asino" (here my ass falls). This expression, however, may perhaps be of Hellenic origin; the equivoque between the two equisonant expressions, "ap' onou" and "apo nou" is well-known; whence to fall off the ass and to fall from one's mind became synonymous.

[2] There is an unpublished story which I heard narrated at Antignano, near Leghorn, of a mother who has a silly son named Pipetta. The latter asks his mother for a quattrino (a small coin) to buy a vetch, and afterwards a bean, because it grows higher; he sows it, and it attains a marvellous height. Climbing up the bean-stalk he comes to the gates of paradise, which are opened to him, but St Peter sends him back; he then finds the entrance to hell, which he wishes to visit. The devil shows him all the sights; the two then play at cards, and Pipetta wins a sackful of souls. The devil fears that Pipetta will empty hell, so he allows him to depart with the sack, and an ass which throws gold from its tail; he mounts up to heaven, and consigns the sack of souls to St Peter. The story ends with the usual exchange of asses at the inn where Pipetta sleeps upon his descent from the beanstalk.

Tzetzas[1] I find again the curious notion that Midas sold his own *stercus* out of avarice, that is, that he changed it into gold, as Vespasian used to do by selling the excrement of his horse.

The Æsopian ass, when he goes to battle, terrifies by his braying all the animals of the forest; so Pan defeats his enemies by means of his terrible voice; and according to Herodotus,[2] in the heroic battle of Marathon, the Athenians were helped by the powerful voice of the god Pan. Finally, as we have seen Apollo to be the rival of Pan and the enemy of the Phrygian Midas, the predestined ass, as well as of the Trojans, so, in the eleventh of the Pythic odes of Pindar, we find the hero Perseus, among the Hyperboreans,[3] eating asses.[4] The morning sun devours the ass of night, as we have seen the solar hero Rustem do in the *Shah-Name,* where he eats the wild asses.

But we must look for more mythical personages in connection with the ass Midas in Arcadia, as the region of Pan and of asses. The ass Midas is considered as a rich progenitor of races, and is supposed to have been the first Phrygian. Windischmann has already observed

1 *Biblion Istorikon,* i. 116.—It is added, that when Titus remonstrated with his father on his avarice, Vespasian made him smell the gold for which the horse's dung had been sold, asking him whether it smelt bad.—In the Mongol story we saw the fool who goes out with his ass and hides it in a cavern afterwards despoiling a merchant's caravan.—*Tzetzas,* i. 128, records the existence in Phrygia of a village called "Ass's-ears" (ê klêsis onou ôta), inhabited by robbers, and belonging to Midas; he thinks, moreover, that Midas was surnamed the large-eared on account of this village of his.

2 vi. 105.

3 Kleitas onôn hekatombas, xi. 51.

4 In *Anton. Liberalis* we find a long narrative from which we gather that Apollo would only suffer the ass to be sacrificed to him among the Hyperboreans.

(with the examples of Yamas, Yima, Manus, Minos, and Radamanthüs) the connection between the rich progenitor of races and the rich king or judge of hell. To Midas the progenitor and to Midas the judge, corresponds the ass whose excrements are of gold, the ass judge and prophet, the Arcadian and prophetic Pan. The Arcadians considered themselves not only autocthonoi, but proselênoi, or anterior to the moon. But they are also considered in the light of inhabitants of an infernal region. In Arcadia was situated the lake Stümphalos, the demoniacal birds of which were slain by Hêraklês in Arcadia; in a chasm formed of wild rocks was the source of the Styx, the principal infernal river, that by which the Hellenic infernal beings were accustomed to swear. Greek and Latin writers used to narrate of the ass (and the mule) that it had an especial aversion to the water of the Styx, as being poisonous. This superstition, when referred to the myth, appears to mean that, when the solar hero drinks this water—the water of the dark or cloudy ocean—he becomes a dark ass. (We find in Russian stories the hero who is transformed into a bull, a horse, or a he-goat, when he drinks water of which a demoniacal bull, horse, or he-goat has previously drunk.) Ælianos, in his tenth book relative to animals, speaking of the horned asses of Scythia, writes that they held in their horns the water of the Styx. A similar narrative is given by Philostratos in the third book of his romantic Life of Apollonios, concerning the fabulous horned ass of India. "It is said," he writes, "that in the marshy ground near the Indian river Hyphasis many wild asses are to be found; and that these wild beasts have on their heads a horn with which they fight bravely like bulls" (this seems to be a reminiscence of the Indian rhinoceros); "and that the Indians form out of these horns drinking-cups, affirming that those who drink out of these cups are delivered from every illness for all that day; when wounded they feel no pain, they pass safely through flames, nor, when they have drunk out of it, can they be hurt by any poison. They say that these cups belong to kings alone, nor is it permitted to any other than a king to hunt the animal. It is narrated that Apollonios (the hero of the romance) had seen this animal and observed its nature with wonder. Moreover, to Damis, who asked him whether he had faith in what was commonly said concerning the virtue of this cup, he answered 'I will believe it when I shall have learned that in this country the king is immortal.'" And no doubt Apollonios would have believed had it been impossible for him to divine that the king who makes use of this marvellous cup is the immortal sun, to whom alone it is reserved to kill the ass of the nocturnal forest, the ass whose hairy ears are like horns,[1] whose ears are of gold.

The horn of the Scythian ass full of Stygian water, the horn of the ass which, when used as a cup, gives health and happiness to him who drinks out of it, remind us (not to speak of Samson's jaw-bone of an ass, which makes water flow) especially of the myth of the cornucopia and that of the goat, with which the satyrs and fauns, having goat's feet, stand in particular connection. It is also for this reason that the ass is found in relation with Pan; wherefore it is too that Silenos rides upon an ass, and appears, as we have already seen, in the story of Midas, in his garden of roses; indeed the

[1] I read on this subject in the curious volume *Laus Asini*, printed at Leyden by Elzevir, the following notice: "Si quis graviter a scorpione ictus, id in aurem insusurret asino, ex tempore curetur."

mythical centaurs or onocentaurs, satyr, faun, ass, and goat are equivalent expressions. We have seen, a few pages back, the Zendic three-legged ass; in the following chapter we shall find the lame goat.

As the ass was ridden by Silenos,[1] so was he the animal dedicated to Bacchus and to Priapos, whose mysteries were celebrated in the Dionysian feasts. It is said that when Bacchus had to traverse a marsh, he met with two young asses, and was conveyed by one of them, who was endowed with human speech, to the other side without touching the water. (The 116th hymn of the first book of the *Ṛigvedas* merits being especially compared with this. In it, immediately after having represented the Açvinâu as drawn by winged asses, the poet celebrates the Açvinâu as delivering the hero Bhugyus out of the waters upon a vessel that moved of itself in the air.)[2] On this account it is said that Bacchus, in gratitude, placed the two young asses among the stars.[3] This is another confirmation of the fact that the mythical ass really had the virtue of flying; and the proverb "Asinus si volat habet alas"[4] alludes to this myth. The fable of the ass who wishes to fly, and the flight of the ass, are derisive allusions, applied to the earthly ass.

---

[1] "Te senior turpi sequitur Silenus asello
Turgida pampineis redimitus tempora sertis
Condita lascivi deducunt orgya mystæ."
—Seneca, *Œdipus.*

[2] Tam ûhathur nâubhir âtmanvatîbhir antarikshaprudbhir apodakâbhiḥ; strophe 3.—Cfr. strophe 4th and 5th of the same hymn.

[3] Another reason is also assigned for the honour given to the ass in heaven: the ass and Priapos contend together as to who is superior; Priapos defeats the ass, and Dionysos takes pity upon the vanquished, and places it in heaven among the stars.

[4] *Laus Asini,* Ludg. Batavorum, ex officina Elzeviriana.

The celestial myth lingers in the memory, but is no longer understood.

In the myth of Prometheus, in *Ælianos* (vi. 5), we have the ass who carries the talisman which makes young again, which Zeus intended for him who should discover the robber of the divine fire (Prometheus). The ass, being thirsty, approaches a fountain, and is about to drink, when a snake who guards the fountain prevents him from doing so. The ass offers the snake the charm which he is carrying, upon which the serpent strips off its old age, and the ass, drinking at the fountain, acquires the power of becoming young again. The ass of night, when he drinks the dew of the dawn, grows young and handsome again every day. It is on this account, I repeat, that youth is celebrated as a peculiar virtue of the ass; it is on this account that the Romans attributed a great cosmetic virtue to ass's milk[1] (the white dawn, or moon).

The mythical ass seems to die every day, whereas, on the contrary it is born anew every day, and becomes young again; whence the Greek proverb does not celebrate the death in the singular, but the deaths of the ass ("Onou thanatous").

The Italian proverb of the ass that carries wine and drinks water, probably alludes to the ass that carries the water of youth, and then, being thirsty, drinks at the fountain in the legend of Prometheus. The wine of the

---

[1] "Conferre aliquid et candori in mulierum cute existimatur. Poppaea certe Domitii Neronis conjux quingentas secum per omnia trahens fætas balnearum etiam solio totum corpus illo lacte macerabat, extendi quoque cutem credens;" *Aldrov.* To which custom Juvenal alludes in his 6th satire:

> "Atque illo lacte fovetur
> Propter quod secum comites educit asellas
> Exul hyperboreum si dimittetur ad axim."

Hellenic and Latin myth corresponds to the inebriating drink or somas in which Indras delights so much in the *Ṛigvedas.* The ass bears the drunken Silenos on its back.

The sun, who in the cloud is covered with the skin of an ass, carries the rain; whence the Greek proverb the ass is wetted by the rain ("Onos hüetai"), and the popular belief that when the ears of the ass or of a satyr (that is to say, of the ass itself) move, it is an indication of rainy weather (or dew). When the sun comes out of the shadows of night, he drinks the milk or white humour of the early morning sky, the same white foaming humour which caused the birth of Aphroditê, the same humour out of which, by the loves of Dionysos (or of Pan, of a satyr, or of the ass itself) and Aphroditê, the satyr was procreated—Priapos, whose phallic loves are discovered by the ass. The satyr serves as a link between the myth of the ass and that of the goat. On this account (that is, on account of the close relation between the mythical ass and the mythical goat) two ancient Greek and Latin proverbs—*i.e.*, to dispute about the shadow of the ass ("Peri onou skias") and to dispute, "De lana caprina"—have the same meaning, a dispute concerning a bagatelle (but which is no trifle in the myth, where the skin of the goat or of the ass is sometimes changed into a golden fleece), which seems so much the more probable, as the Greeks have also handed down to us another proverb in which the man who expects to reap where he has not sown is laughed at as one who looks for the wool of the ass ("Onou pokas zêteis"), or who shears the ass ("Ton onon keireis"). We have seen, in the myth of Midas, the king, whose ears, when combed, betray his asinine nature. The Piedmontese story of the maiden on whose forehead a horn or an ass's tail grows, because she has badly combed the good fairy's head, is connected with this story of the combing of the long-eared Midas. The combed ass and the sheared ass correspond with one another; the combed ass has golden ears, in the same way as gold and gems fall from the head of the good fairy combed by the good girl in the fairy tale. To this mythical belief, I think, may be traced the origin of the mediæval custom in the Roman Church, which lasted till the time of Gregory VII., in which public ovations were offered to the Pope, and an ass bearing money upon its head was brought before him.[1]

The shadow of the ass[2] betrays him, no less than his ears, his nose, and his braying. The shadow of the ass and his nose are found in connection with each other in the legend of the Golden Ass of Apuleius, which, after narrating how the ass, by putting his head out of the window, had betrayed his master the greengrocer or gardener (the friend of perfumes, "Gandharvas, asinus, in unguento, onos en müro"), concludes thus: "The miserable gardener having been found again, and taken before the magistrates to pay the fine, they lead him to a public prison, and with great laughter cease not, says the ass Lucius, to "make merry with my face;" whence also was derived the popular proverb concerning the face and shadow of the ass ('De prospectu et umbra asini')." The ass who betrays his master the greengrocer or gardener by his face is a variety of the ass who, dressed in the forest

[1] "Finitis laudibus, surgit quidam archipresbyter, retro se ascendit asinum preparatum a curia; quidam cubicularius tenet in capite asini bacilem cum xx. solidis denariorum," &c.; in Du Cange, the work quoted before, *s. v. cornomannia.*—We also find in Du Cange that a soldier was called in the middle ages "caput asini, pro magnitudine capitis et congerie capillorum."

[2] In the *Pentamerone*, iii. 8, the night is called "l'aseno de l'ombre."

in the lion's skin[1] (like Hêraklês who goes into hell dressed in a lion's skin), betrays himself by his braying, and of the ass who discovers by his braying Priapos, who delights in gardens (the vulva), Priapos the gardener, like the ogre[2] of the *Pentamerone*, who finds before him in his garden a beautiful maiden.

The ass can restrain neither his voice nor his flatus; we have already seen something similar in the story of Midas, where the comber of the ass feels he will burst if he is not permitted to relieve himself of the secret of the ass. Diogenês of Laertes narrates that the fields of Agrigentum being devastated by malignant winds which destroyed the crops, the philosopher Empedocles instructed them to take asses' skins, and having made sacks of them, carry them to the summits of the hills and mountains, to chase the winds away. Ælianos, confounding one noise with another, suggests, to prevent the ass from braying, the advantage of appending a

[1] In the *Pentamerone*, ii. 1, we have a variation of the other Æsopian fable of the lion who is afraid of the ass. The old witch, in order to deliver herself from the lion which Petrosinella has caused to rise, flays an ass and dresses herself in its skin; the lion, believing it to be really an ass, runs off.—In the thirteenth of the Sicilian stories collected by Signora Laura Gonzenbach, and published at Leipzig by Brockhaus, the ass and the lion dispute the spoil; the young hero divides it, giving to the ass the hay that the lion has in its mouth, and to the lion the bones in the ass's mouth. But probably the lion here represents the dog, according to the Greek proverb, "Küni didôs achüra, onôi ta ostea," to express a thing done the wrong way.

[2] In the *Pentamerone* again, in the island of the ogres, an old ogress feeds a number of asses, who afterwards jump on to the bank of a river and kick the swans; here the ass is demoniacal, as it is in the *Râmâyaṇam;* the swans, as we shall see, are a form of the luminous Açvinâu.—In obscene literature, the *mentula* as a gardener, and the *vulva* as a garden, are two frequent images; cfr., among others, the Italian poem, *La Menta.*

stone to its tail. This ancient Greek fable is to this day very popular in Italy, and the narrator is accustomed to furbish it up with a character of actuality, as if it had happened yesterday, and among his acquaintances.

In the Italian stories,[1] when the ass brays upon the mountain, a tail grows on the forehead of the stepmother's ugly daughter; the third crowing of the cock is the signal for the monster's death; the third braying or flatus of the ass announces the death of the fool. With the end of the night the ass disappears, and the fool also disappears or dies. The braying of the ass cannot mount up into heaven; after the ass has brayed, after the cloud has thundered, the ass comes down upon the earth, is dissolved into rain, is dispersed and dies; the dark ass cannot remain in the luminous sky, it can only inhabit the cloudy, watery, or gloomy sky of hell. The way in which the fool of the story tries to elude death resembles that which was used, according to Ælianos, to prevent the ass from braying. In a story of Armagnac,[2] Joan lou Pec runs after a man whom he believes to be a sage, and asks him when he will die; the man answers, "Joan lou Péc, mouriras au troisièmo pet de toun ase." The ass does so twice; the fool endeavours to prevent the third: "Cop sec s'en angonc

[1] Cfr. the first of the *Novelline di Santo Stefano di Calcinaia*, in which we also find the third brother, believed to be stupid, who makes his ass throw gold from its tail; the foolish Pimpi, who kills his ass whilst cutting wood; the son of the poor man, who amuses himself by sending the ass before him tied to a string, and then making it return; the peasant who drags up the ass which had fallen into the marsh, and who then marries the daughter of the king of Russia (the wintry, the gloomy, the nocturnal one), who never laughed and whom he causes to laugh; and the ass who dies after eating a poisoned loaf.

[2] *Contes et Proverbes Populaires recueillis en Armagnac*, par J. F. Bladé, Paris, Franck.

cerca un pau (a stake) bien pounchut et l'enfouncéc das un martet dens lou cu de l'ase. Mes l'ase s'enflec tant, e hasconc tant gran effort, que lou pau sourtisconc coumo no balo e tuèc lou praube Joan lou Péc."

In *Herodotus*, the Scythians are defeated when the asses bray, and the dogs bark among Darius's tents. The braying of the ass, the thunder of the cloud, is an oracle; the ass that brays is a judge and a prophet. In hell everything is known; the devil knows every art, every species of malice, every secret; the ass in hell participates in this knowledge. The ass Nicon, in *Plutarch*, in the Life of Antony, predicts to Augustus his victory at the battle of Actium; on the contrary, in the Life of Alexander, by the same author, an ass who kills with a kick a great-lion belonging to the Macedonian, appears to the great conqueror in the light of an evil omen. The dying sun of evening, the old lion, is killed in the evening by the ass of night; in the morning, on the contrary, the ass of night announces his fortune to the solar hero, who again becomes luminous and wise. The ass can predict all things, because it knows all things; it knows everything, because it hears everything, and it hears everything by means of its exceedingly long ears; the ass of Apuleius says of itself: "Recreabar quod auribus præditus cuncta longule etiam dissita sentiebam." And this ass which listens from a distance reminds us again of the third brother, now a fool, and now only supposed to be a fool; to the Andalusian Oidin-Oidon, hijo del buen oidor (a relation of the already cited Vedic Indras âçrutkarṇas), of the second cuento of Caballero,[1] who hears everything that is done in the deepest parts of

[1] *Cuentos y Poesias Populares Andaluces*, collecionados por Fernan Caballero, Leipzig, Brockhaus, 1866.

hell, where Lucifer sits, horned and large-eared. The hero who combats with Lucifer only thinks of cutting off his ear; the ass without ears is no longer an ass; the ears of the mythical ass are its vital and characteristic organs. Instead of ears, give horns to the mythical ass, and we have the mythical goat; take the horns away and we have now the mythical abject sheep, now the hog; this is what we shall see in the two next chapters.

CHAPTER IV.

The Sheep, the Ram, and the Goat.

SUMMARY.

The sun-shepherd, and the sun-lamb, ram, or goat.—The dark-coloured he-goat.—The goat-moon.—Agas ; explanation given by Professor Bréal ; the Finnic aija.—Meshas ; she-goat, ram, skin, sack.—The ram Indras.—The goats Açvinâu.—The he-goat Veretraghna.—The lamb and the goat in the forest opposed to the wolf.—The apple-tree and the she-goat ; the cloud and the apple-tree.—The goat, the nut-tree and the hazel-nuts.—The wolf assumes the goat's voice ; the wolf in the fire.—The witch takes the voice of the little hero's mother ; the child born of a tree.—The hero among the sheep, or in the spoils of the sheep, escapes from the witch.—Pûshan agâçvas and his sister.—The brother who becomes a kid while drinking ; the sister in the sea.—The husband-goat ; the goat's skin burned ; the monster appears once more a handsome youth ; the funereal mantle of the young hero ; when it is burned, the hero lives again handsome and splendid.—The children changed into kids.—The cunning Schmier-bock in the sack.—Agamukhî.—Ilvalas and Wâtâpis.—Indras meshâṇḍas, sahasradhâras and sahasradâras.—The rams of the wolf eaten.—The goat of expiation, the goat and the stupidity of the hero disappear at the same time.—The devil-ram ; the putrid sheep that throws gold behind it.—The goat which deprives men of sight.—The young prince, riding on the goat, solves the riddle.—The spy of heaven ; the eye of God.—The constellation of the she-goat and two kids.—The lame goat.—The heroine and the goat her guide and nurse.—The milky way and the she-goat.—The goat's blood, manus Dei ; the stone bezoar.—The cunning goat.—The goat deceives the wolf ; the goat eats the leaf.—The she-goat possessed of a devil.—The ram-vessel.—Ram and he-goat fœcundators.—The he-goat and the horned husband.—Zeus he-goat and the satyr Pan ;

Hêraklês the rival of a goat; the old powerless man called a he-goat.—Hellenic forms of the myth of the goat.—Phrixos and Helle; Jupiter Ammon; the altar of Apollo; the fleece of the Iberians; the golden ram of Atreus; Aigüsthos; Diana and the white sheep; Neptune a ram; satyrs and fauns; Hermês krioforos; the sheep of Epimenis; lambs, rams, and he-goats sacrificed; aixourania and the cornucopia.—The mythical goat; its threefold form; black, white, and light-coloured lambs.—Pecus and pecunia.

WHEN the girl aurora leads out of the stable in the morning her radiant flock, among them there are found to be white lambs, white kids, and luminous sheep; in the evening the same aurora leads the lambs, the kids, and the sheep back to the fold. In the early dawn all this flock is white, by and by their fleeces are golden fleeces; the white, and afterwards the golden heavens of the east (or the west) constituting this white and golden flock, and the sun's rays their fleeces. Then the sun himself, who steps forth from this flock, is now its young shepherd-king, and now the lamb, the ram, or he-goat. When the sun enters into the region of night, the he-goat or lamb goes back to the fold and becomes dark-coloured; the sun veiled by the night or the cloud is a dark-coloured ram, he-goat, or she-goat. In the night, says the proverb, all cows are black; and the same might be said of goats, except in the case of the goat, luminous and all-seeing, coming out of the nocturnal darkness in the form of the moon. We must, therefore, consider the sheep or goat under a triple aspect; the principal and most interesting aspect being that of the sun veiled by the gloom, or by the cloud, which wears often a demoniacal form, such as that of the ass or of the hero in hell; the second being that of the grey-white, and afterwards golden sky of morning, or of the golden and thereafter grey-white sky of evening which, as a luminous, is therefore generally a divine form of the goat; and the third aspect being that of the moon.

The richest myths refer to the sun enclosed in the cloud or the shades of night, or to the cloud or darkness of night closing round the sun. The shifting shadow and the moving cloud on the one side, the damp night and the rainy cloud on the other, easily came to be represented as a goat and as a ram. In the Indian tongue, or even the Vedic, *aǵas* is a word which means, properly speaking, pushing, drawing, moving (agens), and afterwards he-goat; the he-goat butts with its horns; the sun in the cloud butts with its rays until it opens the stable and its horns come out.[1] The ram is called *meshas*, or *mehas*, that is, the pourer or spreader, mingens (like the ass ćiramehin), which corresponds with the *meghas*, or cloud mingens. Moreover, as in Greek from *aix*,[2] a goat, we have *aigis*, a skin (Ægis), so in

[1] The Petropolitan Dictionary sees in the he-goat aǵas, the movable one (agilis). To illustrate the same analogies in the case of the Greek myth, it will be useful to repeat the words of Professor Bréal: "Le verbe grec *aïssô*, qui signifie s'élancer, a fait d'une part le substantif *aix*, chèvre (à cause de la nature bondissante de l'animal), et de l'autre les mots *kataïx*, *kataigis*, *tempête* (as it seems to me, that which shakes, which causes to move or tremble, inasmuch as I maintain that *aǵas* does not mean the movable, or him that rushes, so much as him that pushes, that butts, or causes to move). De là une nouvelle série d'images et de fables où la chèvre joue le rôle principal. L'égide, avant d'être un bouclier fait en peau de chèvre, était le ciel au moment de l'orage; Jupiter aigiochos était le dieu qui envoie la tempête; plus tard, on traduisit le dieu qui porte l'égide. Homère semble se souvenir de la première signification, quand il nous montre, au seul mouvement du bouclier le tonnerre qui éclate, l'Ida qui se couvre de nuages et les hommes frappés de terreur." Mr Ralston compares very well the Russian *ablakagragonniki* (cloud-compellers) to the Zeus *nephelêgeretes*. In the *Ṛigv.* i. 10, 8, it is said similarly to Indras: ǵeshaḥ svarvatîr apaḥ saṁ gâ asmabhyaṁ dhûnuhi.

[2] Let Finnish philologists observe whether it is not possible to refer

Sanskṛit from *aǵas*, a goat, we have *aǵinas*, a skin; and from *meshas*, a ram, *meshas*, a fleece, a skin, and that which is formed from it; whence the Petropolitan Dictionary compares with it the Russian *mieh* (Lithuanian, *maiszas*) skin and sack.

Let us now first of all see how these simple images developed themselves in the Hindoo myth.

Indras, the pluvial and thundering god, is represented in the first strophe of a Vedic hymn as a very celebrated heroic ram;[1] in the second strophe, as the one who pours out ambrosial honey (madaćyutam); in the third strophe, as opening the stable or precinct of the cows to the Añgirasas;[2] in the fourth strophe, as killing the serpent that covers or keeps back; in the fifth strophe, as expelling the enchanters with enchantments, and breaking the strong cities of the monster Piprus;[3] and in the sixth strophe, as crushing under his foot the giant-like monster Arbudas[4] or monster serpent. Thus far we have two aspects of the myth, the ram which pours out ambrosial honey, and the ram which opens the gate and crushes with its foot. In another hymn the Açvinâu are compared to two he-goats (aǵeva), to two horns (çṛiñgeva), and to two swift dogs.[5] A third hymn informs us

to this their Aija, an equivalent of Ukko, their Indras, called hattarojen hallitsia, the master of the cloud-lambs.—Cfr. Castren's *Kleinere Schriften*, St Petersburg, 1862, p. 230.

[1] Mesham puruhûtam; *Ṛigv.* i. 51, 1.—Tad indro arthaṁ ćetati yûthena vṛishṇir eǵati; *Ṛigv.* i. 10, 2.

[2] Tvaṁ gotram añgirobhyo 'vṛiṇor; *Ṛigv.* i. 51, 3.

[3] Tvaṁ mâyâbhir apa mâyino 'dhamaḥ—tvam pipror nṛimaṇaḥ prâruǵaḥ puraḥ; *Ṛigv.* i. 51, 5.

[4] Mahantaṁ ćid arbudaṁ ni kramîḥ padâ; *Ṛigv.* i. 51, 6.—Arbudas is also in Sanskṛit the proper name of a mountain and of a hell; the cloud-mountain and the hell in the cloudy and nocturnal sky have already been noticed in this volume.

[5] Çaphâv iva ǵarbhurâṇâ tarobhiḥ; *Ṛigv* ii. 39, 3.

that Indras by means of a ram killed a leonine monster.[1]

Here we evidently have a heroic he-goat or ram.

Let us compare it with other traditions. In the *Khorda Avesta*[2] we find Veretraghna (the Zend form of Indras, as Vṛitrahan) "with the body of a warrior he-goat, handsome, and with sharpened horns."

In the Russian tale given by *Afanassieff*,[3] the lamb, companion of the bull in the wood, kills the wolf by butting against its sides, while the bull also wounds the ferocious beast with its horns. In another variation of the same story,[4] the cat is confederate with the lamb against the wolf; the lamb butts hard at the wolf, while the cat scratches it till blood flows. In yet another version, besides the lamb, the he-goat also appears; the cat twists some of the bark of the birch-tree round the horns of the he-goat, and bids the lamb rub against it to produce fire; sparks come from it, the cat fetches hay, and the three companions warm themselves. The wolves come up, and the cat makes them run, presenting them the goat as a scarecrow, and frightening them further by ominous hints as to the strength contained in its beard. Finally, we have in the Russian stories two singular variations of the fable of the goat, the kids, and the wolf.[5]

---

[1] Siṅhyaṁ ćit petvenâ ǵaghâna; *Ṛigv.* vii. 18, 17.—In Firdusi we find, in the adventures of Isfendiar, two horned wolves that catch lions; these seem to be demoniacal forms of the ram of Indras which kills the lion.

[2] xxx. 9.—Here the horns are the sun's rays or the thunderbolts, which come again in the Italian superstition on the *iettatura;* the horns of the goat, it is said, and the red coral horns excel the devil and his magic.

[3] iv. 21.

[4] iii. 18.—In the story, i. 20, we are told that the lamb fled away into the forest with the he-goat, because its master took the skin off one of its sides (that is, the wool). The lambs appear in the morning and in the evening with luminous wool; they are sheared during the night.

[5] *Afanassieff*, ii. 4; iv. 17.

The goat is about to give birth to her young ones under an apple-tree. (We have seen in Chapter I. the apple-tree, the fruit of which, when eaten, causes horns to sprout. It is well-known that in Greek, *mêlon* means a goat and an apple-tree, as the Hindoo masculine noun *petvas*, which means a ram, is in the neuter *petvam* = ambrosia. The mythical apple-tree is ambrosial, like the cornucopia of the goat of mythology; and it seems to me that here, too, I can find an analogy in the Slavonic field itself between the Russian words *ŏblaka*, clouds, in the plural *ablaká*, the clouds, and *iablony*, apple-tree, plural *jăblogna*, the apple-trees, *jablok*, the apple.) The apple-tree advises the goat to betake itself to some other place, as the apples might fall upon its new-born kids and kill them. The goat then goes to give birth to her young ones under an equally shady walnut-tree; the walnut-tree also advises her to go away, as the nuts might fall and do serious harm to her little ones;[1] upon which the goat goes to a deserted tent in the forest, another form of the cloud of night. When the kids are brought forth, the goat issues

[1] The walnut-tree is also found in relation with the goat in a fable of *Afanassieff*, ii. 1, that of the accused who exculpate themselves by inculpating others. The cock and the hen gather nuts together; the cock throws one which strikes the hen on the ear; the hen weeps; a boiard asks the reason; the hen accuses the cock, the cock accuses the walnut-tree, the walnut-tree accuses the goat, the goat accuses the shepherd, the shepherd accuses the housewife, the housewife accuses the hog, the hog accuses the wolf, the wolf accuses God, but beyond God it is impossible to go.—In another jest in verse, intended to exercise the memory and loosen the tongue, and given by *Afanassieff*, iv. 16, we find the goat in connection with hazel-nuts. The he-goat begins to complain that the she-goat does not come back with the hazel-nuts (níet kaszi s ariehami); the song goes on to say, that the he-goat will send the wolf to find the she-goat, the bear after the wolf, the men after the bear, the oak-tree after the men, the axe after the oak-tree, the grindstone after the axe, the fire after the grindstone, the

forth out of the tent to procure food, and cautions her children not to open to any one (the fable is well known in the West, but the Slavonic variations are particularly interesting). The wolf comes and pronounces the same password as the goat to induce the kids to open, but they perceive by the rough voice of the wolf that it is not their mother, and refuse to admit him. The wolf then goes to the blacksmith, and has a voice made for him resembling that of the goat; the deceived kids open, and the wolf devours them all except the smallest, who hides under the stove (the favourite place where the little Slavonic hero, the third brother, the ill-favoured fool, who afterwards becomes handsome and wise, is accustomed to squat). The goat returns, and learns from the kid which has escaped the massacre of its brothers. She thinks how to avenge herself, and invites her friend and gossip the fox with the wolf to dinner; the unsuspecting wolf arrives along with the fox. After dinner, the goat, to divert her guests, invites them to amuse themselves by leaping over an opening made in the floor; the goat leaps first, then the fox leaps, and then the wolf, but falls down on the burning ashes and is burnt to death, like the witch in some other stories, as the night is burned by the morning aurora; and the goat chaunts a marvellous *Te Deum* (ćudesnoi pamin) in the wolf's honour. The other Russian version adds some new and curious details. The goat goes to find food, and leaves

water after the fire, and the hurricane after the water; then the hurricane sends the water, the water the fire, the fire burns the grindstone, the stone grinds the axe, the axe cuts down the oak-tree, the oak-tree made into a stick (as we have already seen in Chapters I. and II.) beats the men, the men shoot against the bear, the bear fights with the wolves, the wolves hunt the she-goat, and here the she-goat comes back with the hazel-nuts (vot kasza s ariehami).

the kids alone; they shut the door after her. She returns and says, "Open, my sons, my little fathers; your mother is come; she has brought some milk, half a side full of milk, half a horn full of fresh cheese, half a little horn full of clear water (the cornucopia)."[1] The kids open immediately. The second day the goat goes out again; the wolf, who had heard the song, tries to sing it to the kids; but the latter perceive that it is not their mother's voice, and do not open. Next day the wolf again imitates the mother's voice; the kids open the door, and are all devoured except one which hides itself in the stove, and afterwards narrates to the mother-goat all that has happened. The goat avenges herself as follows: She goes into the forest with the wolf, and comes to a ditch where some workmen had cooked some gruel, and left the fire still burning. The goat challenges the wolf to leap the ditch; the wolf tries and falls into it, where the fire makes his belly split open, from which the kids, still alive, skip out and run to their mother.

Another story, however,[2] affords us still more aid in the interpretation of the myth; that is, in leading us to see in the goat and her kids the sun horned or furnished with rays, as it issues radiant out of the cloud, or darkness, or ocean of night, and in the wolf, or in the wolf's skin, split open or burned, out of which the kids come,

[1] Ah vi, dietuski,
Moi batiuski
Ataprìtessia
Atamknítessia;
Vasha mat prishlá
Malaká prinieslá
Polni baká malaká,
Polni ragá tvaragá
Polni kopitzi vaditzi.

[2] *Afanassieff*, vi. 17.

the dark, cloudy, watery nocturnal sky. Instead of the wolf we have a witch, instead of the goat a woman, and instead of the kids the young Vaniushka (Little John); the witch has a voice made by the blacksmith like that of Vaniushka's or Tereshićko's mother, and thus attracts him to her. Tereshićha says that he was originally the stump of a tree, which his father and mother, being childless, had picked up in the forest, and wrapped up and rocked in a cradle till he was born.

The monster wolf, or the witch, having the faculty of simulating the voice of the goat,[1] and an especial predilection for both sheep and goats,—so much so that the witch Liho (properly Evil) keeps some in her house, and those which come out (of the dark sky) in the morning, and which re-enter (the dark sky) in the evening, are considered her peculiar property,[2]—often transforms the hero (the evening sun) into a kid (into the darkness or cloud of night). Of course, as the dark and cloudy monster is often represented as a wolf, it is easy to understand his wish that everything should be trans-

[1] In the story, ii. 32 of *Afanassieff*, a similar voice has the same effect as that of the ass; it terrifies all the other animals. However, here, a goat that has been shorn is alone spoken of,—that is, the goat which has lost its hair or luminous wool, the thundering goat-cloud.—In the twenty-fifth story of the first book of the *Narodnija iusznoruskija Skazki* (*Popular Stories of South Russia*), edited by Rudcenko, Kiev, 1869, the goat terrifies by its voice the first fox and then the wolf, until she herself is terrified by the voice of the cock. (The morning sun, personified in the cock, destroys the she-goat of night.)

[2] *Afanassieff*, iii. 15.—She sends them to the pasturage; a young blacksmith, who is in her power, adopts the follow mode of deliverance: He puts his pelisse on outside-in, feigns himself a sheep, and passes out with the other sheep, escaping thus from the witch: the young sun comes out at morn like a shepherd-hero among the sheep. Thus Odysseus delivers himself from the grotto of Polyphemos with his companions, by hiding himself among the flock which comes out of it.

formed into a lamb in order to eat it. But the mythical lamb or kid, the young solar hero, generally escapes out of the jaws of the wolf, out of the hands of the witch, or out of the darkness, the waters, or the cloud of night.

A Vedic hymn celebrates the strong Pûshan, who has a he-goat for his horse (or who is a goat-horse), and is called the lover of his sister. Perhaps these words contain the germ of the Russian story of Little John, brother of Little Helen, who is changed by witchcraft into a kid. I have already observed in Chapter I. how Helen, who at the commencement of the story shows affection for her brother John, ends by betraying him. The Vedic hymn would appear to contain the notion of the brother Pûshan transformed into a he-goat (the sun which enters into the cloud or darkness of night), because he has loved his sister. In another Vedic hymn we have the sister Yamî, who seduces her brother Yamas. In European fairy tales, the sister loves her brother, who is metamorphosed by the art of a witch, now into a young hog, and now into a kid. In the forty-fifth story of the fourth book of *Afanassieff*, Ivanushka (Little John) becomes a kid after drinking out of a goat's hoof. In the twenty-ninth story of the second book of *Afanassieff*, Ivanushka and Little Helen, the children of a Tzar, wander alone about the world. Ivanushka wishes to drink where cows, horses, sheep, and hogs feed and drink; his sister Little Helen advises him not to do so, lest he should turn into a calf, a colt, a lamb, or a young pig; but at last John is overcome by thirst, and, against the advice of his sister, he drinks where goats drink, and becomes a kid. A young Tzar marries the sister, and gives every honour to the kid, but a witch throws the young queen into the sea (Phrixos and Helle; in other European stories, into a cistern), and usurps her place, inducing the people to believe that she is Helen, and commanding the kid to be put to death. The kid runs to the shore and invokes his sister, who answers from the bottom of the sea that she can do nothing. The young Tzar, to whom the affair is referred, hastens to deliver Helen out of the sea; the kid can again skip about in safety, and everything is green again, and flourishes as much as it withered before; the witch is burnt alive.[1]

According to the fiftieth story of the sixth book of *Afanassieff*, a merchant has three daughters. He builds a new house, and sends his three daughters by turns to pass the night there, in order to see what they dream about. (The belief that the man dreamed of by a maiden during the night of St John's Day, Christmas Day, or the Epiphany, is her predestined husband, still exists in the popular superstitions of Europe.) The eldest daughter dreams that she marries a merchant's son, the second a noble, and the third a he-goat. The father commands his youngest daughter never to go out of the house; she disobeys; a he-goat appears and carries her off upon his horns towards a rocky place. Saliva and mucous matter fall from the goat's mouth and nostrils; the good maiden is not disgusted, but patiently wipes the goat's mouth. This pleases the animal, who tells her that if she had shown horror towards him, she would have had the same fate as his former wives, whose heads were impaled on a stake. The geese bring to the girl news of her father and sisters; they announce that the eldest sister is about to be married; she wishes to be present at the wedding, and is permitted by the goat to go, who orders for her

[1] Cfr. the eleventh of the *Novelline di Santo Stefano di Calcinaia*, where we have the lamb instead of the kid.

use three horses as black as a crow, who arrive at their destination in three leaps (the three steps of Vishṇus), whilst he himself sits upon a flying carpet, and is transported to the wedding in the form of a handsome and young stranger. The same happens on the occasion of the second sister's marriage, when the third sister guesses that this handsome youth is her own husband. She departs before the rest, comes home, finds the skin of the goat and burns it; then her husband always preserves the form of a handsome youth, inasmuch as the enchantment of the witch has come to an end.[1]

The lamb, the he-goat, and the sheep are favourite

[1] A very interesting variation of this is contained in another unpublished story which I heard from a certain Marianna Nesti of Fucecchio in Tuscany.

There was once a queen that had a son, who, at the age of seven years, was enchanted, so that he lay constantly in bed like one deprived of life. Only at midnight he went out of the house, returning at one o'clock, covered with blood, and throwing himself as if dead into the bed. A woman had to remain regularly on the watch for the purpose of opening the door for him at midnight and at one o'clock; but no girl had, from very fright, been able to continue in the service more than one night. Near the city lived an old woman with three daughters; the two eldest tried to discharge the prescribed duty, but were overcome with fear; the youngest, more courageous, remained. The first night, at twelve o'clock, the dead man lifts up one arm; she runs to him and lifts the other; he tries to raise himself; she helps him to get out of bed. At one o'clock he returns covered with blood, and the girl asks him who has reduced him to this condition, but he answers nothing, and throws himself on the bed as if a corpse. The second night she follows him, and sees him enter a subterranean cavern; he comes to the foot of a flight of stairs, puts down his mantle and remains as naked as when he was born, a handsome youth of eighteen years of age. At the summit of the stairs two great witches cry, "Here he is! come, pretty one!" He ascends and is beaten by the witches for an hour till blood flows, he crying out the while for mercy. At one o'clock he is allowed to go, comes back to the foot of the stairs, takes his mantle and returns home dead. The forms of the witch. In the European story, when the beautiful princess, in the absence of the prince, her husband, gives birth to two beautiful sons, the witch induces the absent prince to believe that, instead of real sons, his young wife has given birth to pups. In the seventh story of the third book of *Afanassieff*, the young queen gives birth, during the king's absence, to two sons, of whom one has the moon on his forehead, and the other a star on the nape of his neck (the Açvinâu). The wicked sister of the young queen buries the children. Where they were buried a golden sprout and a silver one spring up. A sheep feeds upon these plants, and gives birth to two lambs, having, the one the moon on its head, the other a star on its neck. The wicked sister, who has meanwhile been married to the king, orders them to be torn in pieces, and their intestines to be thrown out into the road. The good lawful queen has them cooked, eats them, and again gives birth to her two sons, who grow up hardy and strong, and who, when interrogated by the king, narrate to him the story of their origin; their mother is recognised, and becomes once more the king's wife; the wicked sister is put to death.[1]

The witch is sometimes herself (as a wolf-cloud or

third night his attendant again follows him, and when he puts down his mantle at the foot of the stairs and goes up, she takes the mantle and presses it tightly; the witches scream. The young man comes to the summit; but when they try to beat him they cannot lift the stick. Perceiving this, the girl presses and bites the mantle; when she does so, the witches feel themselves bitten; then the girl runs to the palace, orders a great fire to be lighted, and throws the mantle into it; upon its being burnt, the two witches expire, their enchantment is destroyed, and the prince marries his deliverer.

[1] In the eighth story of the first book of the *Pentamerone*, the ungrateful young woman, Renzolla, is condemned by her own protecting fairy to have the face of a horned goat until she shows her repentance.

wolf-darkness) a devourer of young luminous kids or lambs, such as the Schmierbock in the Norwegian story. The witch carries Schmierbock three times away in a sack; the first and second time Schmierbock escapes by making a hole in the sack; but the third time the witch succeeds in carrying him to her house, where she prepares to eat him. The cunning Schmierbock, however, smuggles the witch's own daughter into his place, and, climbing up, conceals himself in the chimney (a variation of the stove, the place where the young Russian hero usually hides himself, in the same way as in the Tuscan story the foolish Pimpi conceals himself in the oven). From this post of security he laughs at the witch, who endeavours to recapture him; he throws a stone down the chimney and kills her, upon which he descends, rifles her treasure-stores, and carries off all her gold. Here the young hero is called a he-goat; in the chapter on the wolf, we shall find the witch of the Norwegian story actually bears the name of wolf. These two data complete the myth; the wolf which wishes to devour the little hero, and the witch who endeavours to eat the little lamb, are completed by the fable which represents the wolf as, at the rivulet, eating the lamb, which, in the mythical heavens, means the cloudy and gloomy monster which devours the sun.

We have seen above the witch who imitates the voice of the mother of the little hero, in order to be able to eat him, and the wolf who mimics the voice of the goat and eats the kids; but the wolf does more than assume the goat's voice; he sometimes even takes her form.

In the *Râmâyaṇam*,[1] Aǵamukhî, or goat's face, is called a witch, who wishes Sîtâ to be torn to pieces. In

[1] v. 25.

the legend of Ilvalas and Vâtâpis,[1] the two wizard brothers who conspire to harm the Brâhmaṇâs, Vâtâpis transforms himself into a wether, and lets himself be sacrificed in the funeral rites by the Brâhmaṇâs. The unsuspecting Brâhmaṇâs eat its flesh; then Ilvalas cries out to his brother, "Come forth, O Vâtâpis!" and his brother, Vâtâpis, comes out of the bodies of the Brâhmaṇas, lacerating them, until the ṛishis Agastyas eats of himself the whole of Vâtâpis, and burns Ilvalas to ashes. The *Râmâyaṇam* itself explains to us why, in these sacrifices, a wether, and not a ram, is spoken of,[2] when it narrates the legend of Ahalyâ. It is said in this passage that the god Indras was one day condemned to lose his testicles by the malediction of the ṛishis Gâutamas, with whose wife, Ahalyâ, he had committed adultery. The gods, moved to pity, took the testicles of a ram and gave them to Indras, who was therefore called Meshâṇḍas; on this account, says the *Râmâyaṇam*, the Pitaras feed on wethers, and not on rams, in funeral oblations. This legend is evidently of brâhmanic origin. The Brâhmaṇâs, being interested in discrediting the god of the warriors, Indras, and finding him called in the Vedâs by the name of Meshas or ram, invented the story of the ram's testicles, in the same way as, finding Indras in the Vedâs called by the name of Sahasrâkshas (*i.e.*, he of the thousand eyes), they malignantly connected this appellation with the same scandalous story of the seduction of Ahalyâ, and degraded the honourable epithet into an infamous one, he of the thousand wombs, probably by the confusion arising out of the equivoque between the words *sahasradhâras*, the sun (as carrying, now a thousand stars, now a thousand rays), or *sahasr-*

[1] iii. 16.

[2] i. 50; vii. 38.

âṅçus, and *sahasradâras*, which has a very different meaning.

In the important 116th hymn of the first book of the *Ṛigvedas*, Ṛiǵrâçvas (*i.e.*, the red horse, or the hero of the red horse) eats a hundred rams belonging to the she-wolf (in the following hymn, a hundred and one); his father blinds him on this account; the two marvellous physicians, the Açvinâu, give him back his two eyes.[1] Evidently the father of the solar hero is here the gloomy monster of night himself; the sun, at evening, becomes the devourer of the rams who come out of the she-wolf, or who belong to the she-wolf; it is for this reason that the monster wolf blinds him when evening comes. The red horse Ṛiǵrâçvas, or the hero of the red horse, who eats the rams of the she-wolf, affords a further key to enable us to understand the expiatory goat, which in the *Ṛigvedas* itself is sacrificed instead of the horse. We are told in a hymn, that in the sacrifice of the horse the omniform he-goat (aǵo viçvarûpaḥ) has preceded the horse;[2] and the *Âitareya Br.*, commenting on this exchange of animals, also speaks of the he-goat as the last animal destined for the sacrifice. In the Russian stories, too, the goat has to pay the price of the follies or rogueries done by the man, and is sacrificed.[3] This sacrificed he-goat appears to be the same as the ass which undergoes punishment for all the animals in the

---

1 Çatam meshân vṛikye ćakshadânam ṛiǵrâçvam tam pitândhaṁ ćakâra tasma akshî nâsatyâ vićaksha âdhattam dasrâ bhishaǵâv anarvan; *Ṛigv.* i. 116, 16.—Cfr. 117, 18.

2 Esha ćhâgaḥ puro açvena vâǵinâ; *Ṛigv.* i. 162, 3.

3 Cfr. *Afanassieff*, v. 7, where the rogue passes the she-goat off as his sister, and lets her be killed, in order to oblige the murderer, by threats of exposure, to give him a large sum of money in compensation; and v. 52, where the head of a goat is cut off to conceal the murder of a sacristan, committed by the foolish third brother.—Cfr. *Erlenwein*, 17.

celebrated fable of Lafontaine (which becomes a bull in the hands of the Russian fabulist Kriloff, who could not introduce the ass, an animal almost unknown in Russia); and we already know that the ass represents the sun in the cloud or the sun in the darkness; and we have also said that the ass and the fool die together in the legend. The she-goat dies in the Russian story to deliver the fool, who, after her death, is a fool no longer, his folly having died with her.[1] The popular story offers us another proof of the identity of the mythical ass and the mythical goat. We have also seen above, in the Norwegian story, how the witch possesses a treasure which is carried off by the Schmierbock, who kills her; the magician, or the devil, is always rich. The ass which the devil gives to Little Johnny throws gold from its tail; the ass personifies the devil. But the devil, as we have observed, also has a predilection to embody himself in a ram, a lamb, or a he-goat. I remember the puppets who every day improvised popular representations in the little wooden theatre on the Piazza Castello, at Turin, when I was a boy; the final doom of the personage who represented the tyrant was generally to die under the bastinadoes of Arlecchino, or to be carried to hell by the devil in the form of a bleating lamb, which came

[1] The she-goat is also sacrificed, in the eighth of the Sicilian stories collected by Laura Gonzenbach, to test the virtue of a truthful peasant. The wife of a minister who is jealous of the peasant Verità (Truth), who has the custody of a goat, a lamb, a ram, and a wether belonging to the king, persuades him to believe that her life is forfeit, and can be ransomed only by the sacrifice of the wether. The peasant, overcome partly by love and partly by compassion, gives way and consents to the sacrifice. The minister hopes that the peasant will conceal his fault, but is disappointed in his expectation, inasmuch as, on the contrary, he ingenuously confesses everything; and he becomes, in consequence, yet dearer to the king.

upon the scene expressly to carry him away with him, this disappearance being accompanied by much throbbing of the spectators' hearts, to whom the manager preached a salutary sermon.[1] In the twenty-first of the Tuscan stories published by me, it is not the devil, but the little old man, Gesù, who gives to the third brother, instead of the usual ass, a putrid sheep, which, however, has the virtue of throwing louis-d'or behind it. This putrid, or wet, or damp sheep represents still better the damp night.

Ṛiǵrâçvas, as we have said, eats the ram and becomes blind, his father having blinded him to avenge the she-wolf to whom the rams belonged; but the mother of the rams being the sheep, it is probable that the she-wolf who possessed the rams had assumed the form of a putrid sheep, in the same way as we have seen her above transformed into a she-goat; the father of Ṛiǵrâçvas, who avenges the she-wolf on account of the hundred rams, may perhaps himself have been a horned wolf transformed into a he-goat, and have blinded Ṛiǵrâçvas with his horns. In the popular story, the she-goat, when she is in the forest, takes a special pleasure in wounding people's eyes with her horns; hence is probably derived the name of the reptile aǵakâvas, conjured with in the *Ṛigvedas*,[2] as durdṛiçikas, or making to see badly, damaging the eyesight, and the name of aǵakâ, given to an illness in

---

[1] The devil also presents himself to do his evil deeds in the *Bélier de Rochefort*, in Bonnafoux, *Légendes et Croyances Superstitieuses Conservées dans le Départment de la Creuse*, Gueret, 1867, p. 17.—In a legend of Baden, too, recorded by Simrock (work quoted before, p. 260; cfr., in the same work, p. 501), the devil appears with the feet of a he-goat.

[2] vii. 50, 1.—In the *Classical Dictionary of Natural History of Audouin, Bourdon*, &c., first Italian translation, Venice, Tasso, 1831, we read: "Goat, species of ophidian reptiles, indigenous in Congo, and also in Bengal; as yet unclassified by zoologists, and which, it is said, throw from afar a kind of saliva causing blindness."

the eyes by the Hindoo physician Suçrutas. However, we must not forget the connection between the idea of skin and that of goat, by which the aǵakâ might mean simply the thin membrane that sometimes harms the pupil of the eye, and produces blindness. This thin membrane, stretched over the eye of the solar hero, blinds him. We shall see in the chapter on the frog and the toad, which very often represent, in the myths, the cloud and the damp night, that the toad[1] causes blindness only by means of the venom which it is fabled to exude, like the reptile aǵakâvas.

But, as the hero in hell learns and sees everything, the goat, which deprives others of sight, has itself the property of seeing everything; this is the case, because the goat, being the sun enclosed in the cloud or gloomy night, sees the secrets of hell, and also because, being the horned moon or starry sky, it is the spy of the heavens. We have already observed in the first chapter how the marvellous girl of seven years of age, to answer the acted riddle proposed by the Tzar, arrives upon a hare, which, in mythology, represents the moon. In a variation of the same story given by *Afanassieff*,[2] instead of riding upon a hare, the royal boy comes upon a goat, and is recognised by his father; the goat, in its capacity of steed of the lost hero, seems here to represent the moon, as the hare does.

We have already spoken of Indras sahasrâkshas, *i.e.*, of the thousand eyes; Hindoo painters represent him with these thousand eyes, that is, as an azure sky bespangled with stars. Indras as the nocturnal sun hides himself, transformed, in the starry heavens; the stars are his eyes. The hundred-eyed or all-seeing (panoptês) Argos placed as a spy over the actions of the cow beloved

---

[1] Cfr. the lacerta cornuta of the *Pentamerone*. [2] vi. 42.

of Zeus, is the Hellenic equivalent of this form of Indras. In Chapter I. we also saw the witch's daughter of the Russian fairy tale who has three eyes, and with her third eye plays the spy over the cow, which protects the good maiden. In the second story of the sixth book of *Afanassieff*, when the peasant ascends into heaven upon the pea-plant, and enters into a room where geese, hogs, and pastry are being cooked, he sees a goat on guard; he only discovers six eyes, as the goat has its seventh eye in its back; the peasant puts the six eyes to sleep, but the goat, by means of its seventh eye, sees that the peasant eats and drinks as much as he likes, and informs the lord of the sky of the fact. In another variation of the story, given by *Afanassieff*,[1] the old man finds in heaven a little house guarded in turns by twelve goats, of which one has one eye, another two, a third three, and so on up to twelve. The old man says to one after the other, "One eye, two eyes, three eyes, &c., sleep." On the twelfth day, instead of saying "twelve eyes," he makes a mistake and says "eleven;" the goat with twelve eyes then sees and secures him. The eye of God which sees everything, in the popular faith, is a variation of Argos Panoptês, the Vedic Viçvavedas, and the Slavonic Vsievedas, the eye of the goat which sees what is being done in heaven. When the moon shines in the sky, the stars grow pale, the eyes of the witch of heaven fall asleep, but some few eyes still stay open, some few stars continue to shine to observe the movements of the cow-moon, the fairy-moon, the Madonna-moon, who protects the young hero and the beautiful solar maiden lost in the darkness of night.

This spying goat's eye is perhaps connected with the

[1] iv. 7.

constellation of the goat and two kids. Columella writes that the kids appear in the sky towards the end of September, when the west, and sometimes the south, wind blows and brings rain. According to Servius, the goat united with the two kids in the constellation of Aquarius is the same goat which was the nurse of Zeus; he says that it appears in October, with the sign of Scorpio. Ovid, in *De Arte Amandi*, and in the first book *Tristium*, and Virgil in the ninth book of the *Æneid*,[1] also celebrate the goat and the kids of heaven as bringers of rain. Horace, in the seventh ode, elegantly calls the goat's stars insane:—

"Ille nothis actus ad Oricum
Post insana capræ sidera, frigidas
Noctes non sine multis
Insomnis lachrymis agit."

We have already seen Indras as a ram or pluvial cloud; and the goat with only one foot (ekapâd aǵaḥ), or he who has but one goat's foot, who supports the heavens, who lightens and thunders,[2] is a form of the same pluvial Indras who supports the heavens in the rainy season. We have seen the Açvinâu compared to two goats, two horns, two hoofs; each, therefore, would seem to have

---

[1] Differ opus, tunc tristis hiems, tunc pleiades instant
Tunc et in æquorea mergitur hædus aqua.
Sæpe ego nimbosis dubius jactabar ab hædis.
Nascitur Oleneæ signum pluviale capellæ.
—*Ovid.*

Quantus ab occasu veniens pluvialibus hædis
Verberat imber humum.
—*Virgil.*

[2] Pâvîravî tanyatur ekapâd aǵo divo dhartâ; *Ṛigv.* x. 65, 13.—Cfr. the aǵa ekapâd invoked after Ahirbudhnya and before Tritas, in the *Ṛigv.* ii. 31, 6, and the aǵâikapâd, a name given to Vishṇus, in the *Hariv*; the reader remembers also *the goat-footed races* of Herodotus.

but one horn, but one goat's foot (which might perhaps explain the ekapâd aǵaḥ); hence on one side the cornucopia, and on the other the lame goat.[1] The nymph Galathea (the milky one), who loves a faun (or one who has goat's feet), seems to be a Hellenic form of the loves of Esmeralda and the goat with Quasimodo. The goat loves him who has goat's feet; the solar hero (or heroine) in the night has goat's feet; he is a satyr, a faun, a he-goat, an ass; he is deformed and foolish, but he interests the good fairy, who, in the form of a she-goat (as the moon and as the milky way), guides him in the night, and, as the dawn (white aurora) in the morning, saves him and makes him happy. In the German legend, the poor princess who, with her son, is persecuted in the forest, is assisted now by a she-goat, now by a doe, which gives milk to the child; by means of this animal, which serves as his guide, the prince finds his lost bride. This guiding she-goat, or doe, the nurse of the child-hero, which Servius recognised in the constellation of the goat (with respect to Zeus, who is essentially pluvial, as the Vedic Indras has the clouds himself for his nurses), must have generally represented the moon. But even the milky way of the sky (the bridge of souls) is the milk spilt by the she-goat of heaven; the white morning sky is also the milk of this same she-goat. The horned moon,[2] the milky way, and the white dawn are represented in the form of a beneficent she-goat which assists the hero and

[1] We also find the lame goat, or he-goat, in the legend of Thor. The god kills his he-goats, takes off their skins, and keeps their bones, to be able to resuscitate them at pleasure. His son, Thialfi, steals the thigh-bone of one of the goats, in order to go and sell it; then one of the he-goats of Thor, being resuscitated, is lame.—Cfr. for the analogous traditions the notices given by Simrock, work quoted before, p. 260.

[2] In a Russian song we read: "Moon! moon! golden horns!"

the heroine in the forest, in the darkness ; whilst, on the contrary, the sun enclosed in the cloud, the darkness, or the starry sky of night (with the insana capræ sidera), is now a good and wise he-goat or ram, full of good advice, like the ram who advises the king of India in the *Tuti-Name,*[1] and now a malignant monster, a demoniacal being. Inasmuch as the goat gives light and milk, it is divine; inasmuch as it conceals the beauty of the young hero or heroine and opposes them, it may be considered demoniacal.

The connection between the she-goat and the milky way can also be proved from the name St James's Way, given by the common people to the galaxy, or galathea, or way of milk;[2] and it is interesting to learn from Baron Reinsberg,[3] how, in several parts of Bohemia, it is the custom on St James's Day to throw a he-goat out of the window, and to preserve its blood, which is said to be of potent avail against several diseases, such, for instance, as the spitting of blood. In the *Lezioni di Materia Medica* of Professor Targioni-Tozzetti,[4] we also read that the he-goat's blood was known by no less a name than *manus Dei*, and believed to be especially useful against contusions of the back, pleurisy, and the stone. But the disease of the stone was supposed to be cured by the stone called *capra* (goat), which was said to be found in the bodies of some Indian goats. Targioni-Tozzetti himself seriously describes the goat-stones as follows :—" These stones are usually clear on their surface, and dark-coloured; they have an odour of musk when rubbed and heated by the hands. In them (the

[1] ii. 240.

[2] Cfr. Du Cange, *s. v.* galaxia.

[3] *Das festliche Jahr*, zweite Ausg., p. 216.

[4] Florence, Piatti, 1821.

stone Bezoar[1]) analeptic and alexipharmic virtues were supposed to exist, which were able to resist the evil effects of poison and contagious diseases, the plague not excepted, and to save the patient by causing an abundant and healthy perspiration to break out on his skin. For this reason these stones were sold very dear. The same virtues are attributed to those found in the West, but in a much less degree." When the heavenly goat dissolves in rain or in dew, when moisture comes from the goat-cloud, the mountain-cloud, or the stone-cloud, these humours are salutary. When St James, who is joined with the goat and the rain, pours out his bottle, as the Piedmontese people say, the vapour which falls from the sky on these days is considered by the peasants, as in fact it is for the country, and especially for the vines, a real blessing. In the fable of *Babrios,* the vine, whose leaves are eaten by the he-goat, threatens it, saying that it will nevertheless produce wine, and that when the wine is made (*i.e.*, at the Dionysian mysteries), the goat will be sacrificed to the gods. In the spring, on the other hand, or on the Easter of the resurrection, it was the custom to sacrifice in effigy the *Agnus Dei,* in the belief that it would serve to defend the fields and vineyards against demoniacal wiles, thunderbolts and thunder, facilitate parturition, and deliver from shipwreck, fire, and sudden death.[2] In the Witches' Sabbath in Germany, it was

---

[1] Concerning this stone, cfr. a whole chapter in Aldrovandi, *De Quadrupedibus bisulcis,* i.

[2] Cfr. Du Cange, *s. v. Agnus Dei,* where we even find the verses with which Urban V. accompanied the gift of an *Agnus Dei* to John Paleologus.—In the month of October, the Thuringians celebrate the festival of the race after the ram, which, when overtaken, is led to a large rock and there killed. For the race after the ram, cfr. also Villemarqué, *Chants Populaires de la Bretagne.*—In a popular song,

said that the witches burned a he-goat, and divided its ashes among themselves.[1]

The cunning she-goat is an intermediate form between the good wise fairy and the witch who is an expert in every kind of malice. In the same way as the hero, at first foolish, learns malice from the devil, to use it afterwards against the devil himself, it may be presumed that the hero, in his form of a goat, has learned from the monsters all that cunning by which he afterwards distinguishes himself. The Vedic ram, Indras, also uses magic against the monster magicians.

In the second of the Esthonian stories, we read that the king of the serpents has a golden cup containing the milk of a heavenly goat; if bread is dipped into this milk, and put into the mouth, one can discover every secret thing that has happened in the night, without any one perceiving how.

In the French mediæval poem of *Ysengrin*,[2] the she-goat deceives the wolf in a way similar to that in which, in the first number of *Afanassieff's* stories, the peasant cheats the bear, and in the Italian stories the same peasant defrauds the devil. The she-goat shows a fox-like cunning, keeping for itself the leaf of the corn, and leaving the root for the wolf. Hence, in my eyes, the origin of the Piedmontese proverbial expression, "La crava a l'à mangià la föja" (the goat ate the leaf), and

---

in which *England* is transformed into *Engelland* (or country of the angels), Mary, the nurse of God, appears with the white lamb :—

"Die Himmelsthür wird aufgehen ;
Maria Gottes Amme
Kommt mit dem weissen Lamme."

[1] Menzel, the work quoted before.

[2] Professor Emilio Teza has published a mediæval Italian version of this poem with notes.

even the simple one of "Mangé la föja" (to eat the leaf), meaning to understand cunning.[1] I heard from a certain Uliva Selvi, at Antignano (near Leghorn), the narrative of a witch who sent a boy every day to take the she-goat to the pasturage, ordering him to pay attention that it should eat well, but leave the corn alone. When the goat returned, the witch asked it—

"Capra, mia capra Mergolla,
Come se' ben satolla?"
(Goat, my goat Mergolla,
Are you quite satiated?)

To which the goat answered—

"Son satolla e cavalcata,
Tutto il giorno digiunata."
(I am satiated, and have been ridden;
I have fasted all day.)

Then the boy was put to death by the witch. It happened thus to twelve boys, until the thirteenth, more cunning, caressed the goat and gave it the corn to eat; then the goat answered to the witch's question—

"Son ben satolla e governata,
Tutto il giorno m' ha pasturata."
(I am quite satiated, and have been well kept;
He has given me to eat all day.)

And the boy, too, was well treated.

The devil's pupil always outwits his master; the she-goat beguiles the wolf to its destruction. We have seen this in the Russian story, and it is confirmed in the legend of *Ysengrin*. The peasants of Piedmont and ot

[1] Cfr. the before-quoted fable of *Babrios*, in which the vine complains of the he-goat which eats its leaves.—In the Italian proverb, "Salvar la capra e i cavoli," the she-goat is again indicated as an eater of leaves.—The leaves of the sorb-apple, according to the Norwegian belief, cure sick goats, by which the god Thor is drawn.—Cfr. Kuhn, *Die H. d. F. u. d. G.*

Sicily have, for this reason, so much respect for the goat, that they consider it brings a blessing to the house near which it is maintained; and if, by chance, they show a perverse nature, this perversity is attributed to the devil himself, who, they believe, has maliciously taken possession of them. A few years ago, a goatherd of the Val di Formazza, in the Ossola in Piedmont, had two goats which he believed to be possessed by some evil spirit, for which reason they always wandered about, in order, as he thought, that the demon might at last be able to throw them down some abyss. One day the two goats were lost; the goatherd searched for them for a short time, but finding his search bootless, he resolved to go and make a vow to the Madonna of Einsiedlen. Chance so arranged it, that at the very moment in which he was returning from his pious pilgrimage, his two goats also approached the door of his house; therefore, of course, this was declared to be a miracle in Formazza, and as such it is still believed in that district.[1]

In the preceding chapter we saw the ass represented in two aspects, as regards its generative capabilities; that is, it is now represented as an ardent, insatiable, and competent fœcundator, and now as a ridiculous imbecile, and powerless to generate. We also saw the ass closely connected with the satyrs with goat's or he-goat's feet. The he-goats and rams, too, have a double and self-contradictory reputation. We know, for instance, that the god Thor, the god of the Scandinavians, who thunders in the cloud, is drawn by he-goats (the vessel of Thor and Hymir, the cloud, is called in the *Edda* a navigating ram or he-goat, in the same way as

[1] From a narrative made to me by my friend Valentino Carrera, an intrepid Alp-climber and popular dramatist.

the Vedic Indràs is represented as a god-ram); he is, moreover, the protector of marriages. Scandinavian mythology, therefore, appears to regard the goat as essentially the one that makes fruitful, as a pluvial cloud. In the Hindoo mythology of the brâhmanic period, the god Indras loses, on the contrary, his divine power, becomes stupid and obscure, and is lost in his form of a ram. In one of his *Passeggiate nel Canavese,* Signor A. Bertolotti recently observed, at Muraglio, a curious custom which is observed by the young men of the country when a projected wedding falls through; they run up to the bride's house and obstreperously demand her to give her sheep up to them, upon which they go to the bridegroom's house and cry out, "Vente a sarrar quist motogn" (come and shut up these rams). Here the ram represents the husband, and the sheep the wife. In Du Cange the name of goat (caper) is given to the "in pueris insuavis odor cum ad virilitatem accedunt."[1] In *Apuleius,* unmeasured lasciviousness is called "cohircinatio." According to Ælianos, the he-goat, at the age of seven days (of seven months according to Columella), already yearns for coition.

But in the same way as the ass is the stupid patient animal, the ram is the stupid quiet one. The he-goat is said to be an indifferent husband, who allows his she-goats to be covered by other goats without showing a sign of jealousy; hence our expressions, "horned goat," and simply "horned," to indicate the husband of an unfaithful woman, that is, of a woman who makes him

[1] Referred to by Martial's epigram :—

> "Tam male Thais olet, quam non fullonis avari
> Tecta vetus media, sed modo fracta via.
> Non ab amore recens hircus," &c.

wear horns, like the goat, and the Italian proverb, "E meglio esser geloso che becco" (it is better to be jealous than a he-goat). This reputation, however, as assigned to the he-goat, is contrary to all that has been said and written, and that is known concerning the lust of the he-goat. On the contrary, Aristotle says explicitly that two he-goats, which have always lived together in concord at the pasturage, fall out and fight with violence in the time of coition. Moreover, the verse of Pindaros is well known, in which he makes he-goats unite even with women. It is also said that Hermês, or Zeus, assuming the form of a he-goat, united himself with Penelope, whence was born the great goat-footed satyr, Pan; that Hêraklês (as an ass, in his lion's skin) competed with a he-goat in phallical powers (in Athenaios he joins himself with fifty virgins in the space of seven nights); that, in Ælianos, a jealous he-goat punished with death the goat-herd Crathis, who had incestuously joined himself with one of his she-goats. Nevertheless, the Greeks already called by the name of *aix,* as we Italians by that of *capra,* a woman of an immoral life, or an adulteress. Columella gives us the key of the enigma, observing that the he-goat, by abuse of the Venus, which he uses too soon (like the ass), becomes powerless before the age of six years, so that it is not out of indifference that he is simply a spectator of his she-goat's infidelity, but only because he cannot do otherwise. Hence the application of *hircosus,* which Plautus gives to an old man.

It is the Hellenic tradition which, more than any other, developed to a greater extent the myth of the goat and the sheep, under all their aspects—demoniacal, divine, and hybrid.

The golden fleece, or the fleece of the sheep or ram which had been transported into Colchis by Phrixos, the son of Nephêlê (the cloud) and of Helle;[1] Jupiter Ammon (in the fifth book of Ovid's *Metamorphoses*), who, afraid of the giants (as, in the last book of the *Râmâyaṇam*, the gods, terrified by the monsters, transform themselves into different animals), hides himself in Lybia in the shape of a horned ram; the altar of Apollo in the isle of Delos, constructed with innumerable horns; the woolly skins in which, according to Strabo,[2] the Iberians gathered up gold, whence the Greek geographer believed the fable of the golden fleece to have arisen; the golden lamb kept by Atreüs, which was to bring Thyestes to the throne, and the name of Aigüsthos, born of the incestuous loves of Thyestes with his own daughter; Pan (with goat's feet, the son of the he-goat Zeus or Hermes), who, in the fifth book of the *Saturnalians* of Macrobius, loves the moon and obtains its favours by means of sheep with white but rough and coarse wool; Endymion, who, according to the commentator Servius, induces the moon to love him by means of exceedingly

---

[1] With this myth of the brother Phrixos and of the sister Helle, who pass the sea or fly through the air with the sheep, is connected the Russian story recorded above of Ivan and Helena; Ivan is changed into a little kid or lamb. In the Italian variety of the same story, the sister is thrown into the sea by the witch. Whilst the brother and sister pass the Hellespont upon the golden ram, Helle falls into the sea. We learn from Apôllonios, in the second book of the *Argon.*, that the fleece of the sheep became gold only when, on its arrival in Colchis, it was sacrificed and suspended upon an oak-tree. The cloud-ram becomes golden only in the morning and evening sky.—The luminous fleece can perhaps be recognised in the bride of the *Ṛigvedas*, who, leaning towards the relations of Kakshîvant, says: "Every day I shall be (properly speaking, I am) like the little woolly sheep of the gandhâri (sarvâham asmi romaçâ gandhârîṇâm ivâvikâ);" *Ṛigv.* i. 126. As there is an etymological analogy, so there may be a mythical analogy between the gandhâri and the gandharvâs.

[2] Book x.

white sheep; Neptune, who, in the form of a ram, in the sixth book of the *Metamorphoses* of Ovid, seduces the beautiful virgin Bisaltis; the satyrs, the fauns with goat's feet, into which the gods transform themselves in order to seduce nymphs or maidens of the earth, as, for instance, Jove again, in the same book of Ovid—

> "Satyri celatus imagine pulchram
> Jupiter implevit gemino Nycteida fœtu;"

Hermês, called Krioforos, or carrier of a ram (that is, of a ram which delivers the land from the plague, a form of St James); the two predestined sheep which Epimenides sacrifices to make the Athenian plague cease, in the twenty-seventh Olympiad, in Diogenes Laertês; the bleating goats that King Priam (in the fragments of Ennius) sacrifices to dissipate the evil threatened by sinister dreams; the black sheep sacrificed to Pluto, Proserpine, the Furies, and all the infernal deities; the lamb, the ram, and the he-goat sacrificed to the genital Fates in the Sybilline verses translated by Angelo Poliziano—

> "Cum nox atra premit terram, tectusque latet Sol;"

the white lamb sacrificed to Hercules, to Mars, to Jove, to Neptune, to Bacchus, to Pan (the goat being sacrificed to Diana), to Apollo (*i.e.*, when the sun shines), to Ceres (the goddess of the light-coloured ears of corn), to Venus, to the gods and goddesses; to his divine forms (similia similibus); and several other mythical notions (not to speak of the very popular legend relating to the goat Amalthea, who nourished Zeus with her milk, and was by Zeus translated for this service to the stars, under the name of Aixourania, or heavenly goat, after he had taken off one of its horns, to give, in gratitude to the two nymphs who had protected him, the faculty of pouring out everything that was wished for);[1] all these account, in an eloquent manner, for the wide-spread worship that the goat and the sheep received, even in Græco-Latin antiquity, enriching with many episodes the mythical and legendary traditions of these nations, now as the type of a god, now of a demon, and now of an intermediate being, such as the satyr, for instance.

In the same way as the mythical horse has, from evening to morning, three conspicuous moments of action—black, grey, and white or red—and as the mythical ass throws gold from behind and has golden ears, so the mythical goat and sheep, which are dark-coloured in the night or in the cloud, throw gold from behind and have golden horns which pour out ambrosia, or else have even the cornucopia itself. It is always the same myth of the cloudy and aqueous, of the nocturnal and tenebrous sky, with its two glowing twilights or auroras, or else of the luminous heavenly hero who traverses the night or the cloud (or the wintry season), disguised in the shapes of various animals, now by his own will, now by a divine malediction or by diabolical witchcraft.

In the third book of Aristotle's *History of Animals*, we read of the river Psikros in Thrace, that white sheep, when they drink of its waters, bring forth black lambs;

---

[1] Ovid calls the goat "hædorum mater formosa duorum," and sings that the goat herself broke one of her horns against a tree, which horn the nymph Amalthea wrapped—

> "decentibus herbis
> Et plenum pomis ad Jovis ora tulit;"

and Jupiter, when lord of heaven, in reward—

> "Sidera nutricem, nutricis fertile cornu
> Fecit, quod dominæ nunc quoque nomen habet."

that in Antandria there are two rivers, of which one makes the sheep black, and the other white, and that the river Xanthos or Skamandros makes the sheep fair (or golden). This belief involves in itself the three transformations of the celestial hero into the three he-goats or rams of different natures, of which we have spoken. The last transformation calls our attention to the sheep with golden wool, the golden lamb, and the *Agnus Dei*, the symbol of happiness, power and riches. Wealth in sheep, even more than wealth in cows, became the symbol of universal riches. The horn poured out every kind of treasure upon the earth, and upon the earth itself the *pecus* became *pecunia*.

END OF VOL. I.

WITHDRAWN